Contributors

Rob Carter
Steven Heller
Roy McKelvey
Bill Meggs
Elizabeth Meggs
Libby Meggs
Alston W. Purvis
R. Roger Remington

Editors

Rob Carter
Libby Meggs
Sandra Wheeler

Meggs:
Making Graphic Design History

Beautifully designed and written, *Meggs: Making Graphic Design History* captures the life and work of Philip Baxter Meggs, the graphic designer, educator, historian, and author of the seminal *A History of Graphic Design.* Before Phil Meggs wrote his ground-breaking book, graphic design was left largely unchronicled. *A History of Graphic Design* offered designers and students of design a foundation on which to build, a starting point from which to move forward, and a context in which to establish graphic design's place in history. This book is at once a retrospective of Phil Meggs' achievements as a historian, educator, and artist in his own right, a deserved tribute to his lasting influence on the graphic arts, and a loving memorial written by family, friends, and colleagues who were lucky enough to have known him.

This book is printed on acid-free paper. ♾

Published by John Wiley & Sons, Inc., Hoboken, New Jersey
Published simultaneously in Canada

For general information about our other products and services, please contact our Customer Care Department within the United States at (800) 762-2974, outside the United States at (317) 572-3993 or fax (317) 572-4002.

Wiley also publishes its books in a variety of electronic formats. Some content that appears in print may not be available in electronic books. For more information about Wiley products, visit our web site at www.wiley.com.

Library of Congress Cataloging-in-Publication Data:

Meggs : making graphic design history / [introduction by] Rob Carter.
p. cm.
Includes bibliographical references.
ISBN 978-0-470-00839-3 (cloth)
1. Meggs, Philip B.
2. Typographers – United States – Biography.
3. Book designers – United States – Biography.
4. Graphic design (Typography) – History.
I. Meggs, Philip B.
II. Carter, Rob.
Z246.M427 2007
686.2'2092--dc22
[B]

2007017038

Printed in Mexico

10 9 8 7 6 5 4 3 2 1

"Of all the things I've been involved in, I am most proud of my children and my students."

This book is dedicated to Andrew and Elizabeth Meggs and all of Phil's students – past, present, and future.

writing
rewriting
thinking
rethinking

writing
rewriting
thinking
rethinking

MEGGS

Contents

8 Foreword
From *A History of Graphic Design*
First Edition
12 Introduction by Rob Carter

17 Contributing Essays

18 Growing Up with Phil by Bill Meggs
25 The Collaboration by Libby Meggs
34 Life by Design: From Ephemeral to Historical by Elizabeth Meggs
36 Philip B. Meggs, A Memoir by Alston Purvis
41 America's First Graphic Design Historian by Steven Heller
48 Fond Personal Memories and Warm Professional Recollections by R. Roger Remington
51 Philip B. Meggs: A Personal Remembrance by Roy McKelvey

59 Selected Writings and Lectures

62 Marshall McLuhan Lecture Notes
65 Novum Education: Virginia Commonwealth University, Richmond
65 George Tscherny
67 The Demilitarization of Graphic Design
68 Graphic Design History: Discipline or Anarchy?
73 Design Education: Pedagogy vs. the Real World
77 The Swiss Influence: The Old New Wave
81 Toulouse-Lautrec: Superb But Not Alone
82 High Style, Low Style, Vile Style
84 An Oracle of the 21st-Century Book
88 What is American about American Graphic Design?
90 Government Style: Design Consciousness and the Feds
93 ITC Bashing
98 Test Your Typographic IQ
100 Louis Prang: The Man Who Brought Out the Artist in Children
104 A Pantheon of Design Eccentricity
105 Farewell to the Opulent Eighties
106 Future Issues in Graphic Design Education
108 The Women Who Saved New York
116 The Obscene Typography Machine
120 The 1940s: Rise of the Modernists
130 Excerpts from *Type & Image*
132 Saul Bass on Corporate Identity
137 The Design Education Quandary
139 The Vitality of Risk
146 The Designer, Paper, and the Environment
149 Landmarks of Book Design, Second of a Series: *For the Voice*
157 The Last Word on the Walker Show
162 Women's Place: Two at the Top
167 Peter Behrens: Design's Man of the Century?
174 Tibor the Pit Bull
179 Landmarks of Book Design, Fourth of a Series: *The Elements of Euclid*
183 I Am Type! Revisited
186 Introduction to *Typographic Specimens: The Great Typefaces*
189 Yin/Yang and the Art of Graphic Design
194 Landmarks of Book Design, Seventh of a Series: *American Typefounders Specimen Book and Catalogue, 1923*
202 Tribute to an Unrepentant Modernist
205 Landmarks of Book Design, Eighth of a Series: *The Bald Soprano*
211 Required Reading for the Millennium
219 Methods and Philosophy in Design History Research
227 Back Talk: Philip B. Meggs, Design Historian
230 Landmarks of Book Design, Tenth of a Series: *Before Rosebud was a Sled*
235 Excerpt from *Fotografiks*
237 Letters to *Print:* Critical Mass
238 Letters to *Print:* Departed Icons
239 Foreword to *Revival of the Fittest*
242 Introduction to *The Allure of Postage Stamps*
244 Introduction to the Fiftieth Anniversary Edition of *The Mechanical Bride* by Marshall McLuhan

249 Epilogue from *A History of Graphic Design,* First Edition
250 Chronology
251 The Complete Published Writings
254 Biographies of Editors and Contributors
255 Biography of Philip B. Meggs
256 Acknowledgements
256 Colophon

From *A History of Graphic Design*
First Edition (1983)

There is a German word, *Zeitgeist,* that does not have an English equivalent. It means the spirit of the time and refers to the cultural trends and tastes that are characteristic of a given era. The immediacy and the ephemeral nature of graphic design, combined with its link with the social, political, and economic life of its culture, enable it to more closely express the zeitgeist of an epoch than many other forms of human expression. Ivan Chermayeff, a noted designer, has said: the design of history is the history of design.

Since prehistoric times, people have searched for ways to give visual form to ideas and concepts, to store knowledge in graphic form, and to bring order and clarity to information. Over the course of history, these needs have been filled by various people, including scribes, printers, and artists. It was not until 1922, when the outstanding book designer William Addison Dwiggins coined the term *graphic designer* to describe his activities as an individual who brought structural order and visual form to printed communications, that an emerging profession received an appropriate name. However, the contemporary graphic designer is the heir to a distinguished ancestry. Sumerian scribes who invented writing, Egyptian artisans who combined words and images on papyrus manuscripts, Chinese block printers, medieval illuminators, and fifteenth-century printers and compositors who designed early European printed books all become part of the rich heritage and history of graphic design. By and large, this is an anonymous tradition, for the social value and aesthetic accomplishments of graphic designers, many of whom have been creative artists of extraordinary intelligence and vision, have not been sufficiently recognized.

History is in large measure a myth, because the historian looks back over the great sprawling network of human struggle and attempts to construct a web of meaning. Oversimplification, ignorance of causes and their effects, and the lack of an objective vantage point are grave risks for the historian. When we attempt to record the accomplishments of the past, we do so from the vantage point of our own time. History becomes a reflection of the needs, sensibilities, and attitudes of the chronicler's time as surely as it represents the accomplishments of bygone eras. As much as one might strive for objectivity, the limitations of individual knowledge and insights ultimately intrude.

The concept of art for art's sake, a beautiful object that exists solely for its aesthetic values, did not develop until the nineteenth century. Before the Industrial Revolution, the beauty of the forms and images that people made were linked to their function in human society. The aesthetic qualities of Greek pottery, Egyptian hieroglyphics, and medieval manuscripts were totally integrated with useful values; art and life were unified into a cohesive whole. The din and thunder of the Industrial Revolution turned the world upside down in a process of upheaval and technological progress that continues to accelerate at an ever-quickening pace. By jolting the arts and crafts from their social and economic roles, the machine age created a gulf between people's material life and their sensory and spiritual needs. Just as voices call for a restoration of humanity's unity with the natural environment, there is a growing awareness of the need to restore human and aesthetic values to the man-made environment and mass communications. The design arts — architectural, product, fashion, interior, and graphic design — offer one means for this restoration. Once more a society's shelter, artifacts, and communications might bind a people together. The endangered aesthetic and spiritual values might be restored. A wholeness of need and spirit, reunited through the process of design, can contribute in great measure to the quality and raison d'être of life in urban societies.

This chronicle of graphic design was written in the belief that if we understand the past, we will be better able to continue a cultural legacy of beautiful form and effective communication. If we ignore this legacy, we run the risk of becoming buried in the mindless morass of a commercialism whose molelike vision ignores human values and needs as it burrows forward into darkness.

Introduction

Rob Carter

Phil Meggs threw little or nothing away. In the wake of his remarkable achievements stand mountains of boxes containing file folders of correspondence, notes for research, notes from interviews, note cards for talks, and drafts of articles, essays, and book manuscripts. Other boxes in an array of sizes and shapes hold short stories written in longhand on yellow legal pads, sketches, graphic notations, and photographs. Flat files sag with samples of his professional design work.

A few months after Phil's death, I approached his wife, Libby Meggs, with the idea of compiling a book that would celebrate Phil's achievements and contributions to graphic design. She agreed and then immediately began the systematic task of organizing and archiving Phil's treasures. He readily saved everything he deemed important, but was not manic about its organization. Although he deposited the elements of his creative processes into labeled manila folders, stray and unrelated documents often found their way into them. Phil was too busy focusing on current projects or planning future projects; once something fell into a folder, it remained there.

Compiling material for this collection grew into a collaborative process. Libby, Sandy Wheeler, and I sifted through the layered archives, thoughtfully and methodically extracting a selection of material that would form a balanced cross-section of Phil's greater body of work. Our sifting simply confirmed what we already knew: Phil's vast interests and passions varied immensely. He possessed a curiosity about almost everything under the sun, fluidly writing or drawing his ideas and observations on scraps of paper or in his notebooks, which we had the distinct pleasure of discovering.

This book presents an anthology of Phil's writings, including articles from major publications, chapters from books, and manuscripts for lectures. Only a fraction of the visual examples included in original articles appears in this collection. Original sources are cited for readers wishing to visit them for further examination. The creative work accompanying Phil's writings – notations, sketchbooks, drawings, paintings, and graphic design – reveals Phil's processes and methods and provides a glimpse into his broad experience and productive life as a writer, artist, and designer.

Any attempt to package Phil's texts into tidy themes would prove an exercise in superficiality. Rather, the works unfold chronologically, providing readers with the sense that Phil is telling his own story. The features begin with "Marshall McLuhan Lecture Notes," written in 1972, and conclude with the 2001 introduction to the fiftieth anniversary edition of Marshall McLuhan's *The Mechanical Bride,* written in 2001. Phil, a scholar and admirer of McLuhan, considered it a great honor to have been asked by the publisher to write this introduction. While lying in his hospital bed just days before his passing, Libby read aloud the introduction from the book, which had just arrived in the mail. She recalls his smiling at her and saying, "That's the best thing I've ever written."

Meeting Phil

My relationship with Phil began in 1976. As Department Chair of the Communication Arts and Design Department at Virginia Commonwealth University, he had invited me to interview for a teaching position. I first became aware of VCU by reading a piece Phil had written for the Novum Education section of *Novum Gebrauchsgraphik.* Simply entitled "Virginia Commonwealth University," his description of the program and the collection of student work shown on the magazine's pages impressed me. I had never before heard about the school, or Philip B. Meggs for that matter, but the article piqued my interest, so I decided to apply for a job teaching graphic design at VCU.

Shortly after arriving in Richmond, I stood at the door of a two-story colonial house on Palmyra Avenue, where arching high above me towered two mighty magnolia trees dotted with large white blooms. The trees affirmed that I was in the heart of Dixie. I rang the doorbell and was cordially greeted by Phil and Libby. I shook their outstretched hands, as warm and gentle as their lilting voices, and we spent the rest of the evening discussing design education, books, children, cats, and Reaganomics. Little did I know then how significantly Phil would influence my life and career. And little did I know I was standing in

Libby Meggs in front of the Meggs house on Palmyra Avenue. Photograph: Philip Meggs (August 1975)

the presence of the person who would shape much of graphic-design history. Thus began a friendship and collaboration that endured twenty-six years, until his untimely death in 2002.

Leading the Department

Phil chaired the Communication Arts and Design Department for thirteen years, 1974 to 1987. During this time he led a movement catapulting the department into a major design program. He clearly envisioned our mission, and he intelligently negotiated the political minefield of academia like a seasoned soldier. Upper-level administrators, faculty, and students respected him for his valiant determination, fairness, and unwavering commitment to quality. I watched Phil continually tinker with the bureaucratic machine to reduce class sizes, hire top-notch faculty, and lead the program to international distinction.

Once while chairing the Sophomore Curriculum Committee, I received a memorandum from Phil, underscoring his determination to keep the department on task by responding to sociological and technological change. He wrote, "It should be apparent to all parties by now that the computer revolution is over; those who have resisted, desisted, and denied this catastrophic revolution in human affairs have capitulated. All areas of visual communications are irrevocably changed." He finished by saying, "This proposal suggests a fundamental shift in direction: all students should become visual communications generalists; then they can opt for specialized courses in the later semesters of their brief time in the department." Always looking forward, Phil never let the department rest on its laurels.

As department chair, Phil generously gave time and advice. I always thought of him as the father of the department – not because he was older than me, but because he was so wise. He mentored his faculty and encouraged them to excel in the area of their expertise. But he was also tough. If others did not carry their own weight, they were warned; if they continued down an unproductive path, they were fired.

He demanded and fought for quality education. He did not tolerate sloppy teaching, nor did he accept administrative attempts to crowd too many students into a classroom. During a particularly bloody period when severe budget cuts threatened the department's life, the former dean told Phil he would have to accommodate two hundred new students. Well aware that the department was already stressed at the seams, Phil vehemently rejected this proposal. He argued, "We will destroy this program by forcing it to grow this fast without additional faculty, space, furniture, and equipment." The dean yielded. Phil never told him that he came to school that day with a letter of resignation in his pocket.

How he cared about the department! I poignantly remember one faculty meeting during which Phil delivered an emotional report to the dean about several issues threatening the department's well-being. The tears welling up in Phil's eyes demonstrated his lifelong commitment to the department – as well as his sensitivity and strength.

On November 12, 2002, twelve days before he died, Phil emailed the department faculty from his hospital bed. This small correspondence attests to not only his sense of irony, but also his steadfast commitment to a design department he loved, with which he was affiliated for thirty-eight years: "I'd invite all of you to have faculty meeting here in mcv north hospital room 10-016 where I'm holding out – it's much cleaner than the pollak building and the air conditioning/heating systems actually work – but unfortunately they will only let me have three visitors at a time. Phil."

In the years just before his death, Phil became disillusioned with the university's expanding bureaucracy and corporate mindset. I'm sure if he were still with us, he would be severely disappointed, though not surprised, to see that the battles he once fought in defense of quality education are still being waged. I'm also sure he would continue leading the battles.

Teaching

Inside or outside the classroom, Phil played the teacher. (But he also played the student, eager to learn new things and explore new subjects in a different light.) In the classroom, he balanced criticism with strong doses of praise. He did not subscribe to teaching design through intimidation, a hard-nosed technique experienced at one time or another by all emergent design students. Instead of taking the low and easy road of generally destroying a weak effort, he took the more exhausting high road, artfully mixing criticism with praise. Phil treated his students and colleagues with dignity and humanity.

I have never seen anyone more skilled than Phil at thinking on his feet. I always admired his clear-headedness, his ability to make a point with minimal words, and his skill at creating simplicity from impossible complexity. Phil exuded confidence on or off stage. On stage, puffing up his chest, his tie slightly askew, he captivated his audiences with his own special brand of delivery. His slow and deliberate speech, shaded with an alluring Southern drawl and melodically punctuated by occasional shifts in tempo and volume, transfixed the audience into a world of wonder and discovery. Audiences loved him.

Phil's earliest audiences were his students of graphic-design history. Beginning in 1974, Phil taught two history courses each year: The Origins of Visual Communication and Twentieth-Century Visual Communication. During this time, he began researching and compiling his seminal work: *A History of Graphic Design.* From the beginning of his pursuits as a graphic-design historian, there existed an inseparable connection between his research and teaching. The moment lights dimmed and the humming carousel projector advanced slides, the marvels and secrets of graphic-design history unfolded.

Behind Phil's soft-spoken demeanor, a probing intellect methodically analyzed scattered relics and wrote on the subject of visual communication, establishing connections between them, redefining their contexts, and assembling them into new historical models. Lynne Cannoy Knecht, a student in one of Phil's earliest graphic-design history courses, recalls, "Phil Meggs' enthusiastic, expansive style could fluently integrate a subject with other disciplines or situate it into broader context. He could refocus from the details to illuminate the bigger picture."

Sharing an Office

For ten years, Phil and I shared an office located on the fifth floor of the Pollak building, a square, labyrinthine structure where even today I find myself disoriented and walking in circles to find an exit. Our desks sat side by side, facing windows overlooking a central courtyard. We often talked about how to subvert the space so that it might more closely resemble a suitable setting for design education.

On countless occasions, we sat facing each other in lively debate. We agreed about most issues, but he, ever mischievous, often delighted in playing devil's advocate. I still believe that his methods of forcing dialogue and encouraging others to reveal honest opinions and beliefs helped confirm his own thinking or clarify concepts he was struggling with. Sometimes, at the end of these red-faced but friendly bouts, we'd poke each other in the ribs and jostle a hug.

Extending beyond our office, Phil's sharing nature embraced collaborative efforts with many others. One early venture attempted to fill a void in typographic literature. Beginning in 1982 and continuing for three years, Phil, Ben Day, and I wrestled over typographic content to eventually forge the text *Typographic Design: Form and Communication.* Our contrasting personalities and differences in typographic attitude generated a unique synergy as we gathered before a first-generation Apple computer to word-process the text. Phil usually sat at the keyboard, giving form to a barrage of thoughts and ideas. The interaction created a magical and unforgettable experience.

Art and Design

In 1964, Phil graduated with a BFA in graphic design from the Richmond Professional Institute. Before entering graduate school, he was an art director at A.H. Robins Company, where he had total responsibility for concept, design, and production of corporate literature, packaging, advertising, direct mail, information graphics, and exhibitions. In 1971, seasoned already as a graphic designer and art director for a Fortune 500 company, he entered graduate school at Virginia Commonwealth University to earn an MFA in painting.

And paint he did. From his early days as a child, he profusely recorded and translated experiences into vivid and memorable images. Paintings executed while in graduate school reveal a visual language inseparable from the language of his graphic design, where visual economy, decorative restraint, and optimum clarity controlled his creative gears. Humor, whimsy, and juxtapositions of unlikely themes and images work their way into surrealistic settings. Modernist graphic designers as well as artists such as René Magritte, Willem de Kooning, and Giorgio de Chirico informed his drawing and painting. Ultimately, he was a pluralist with modernist roots, and from this point of view he formed his opinions about art and design, as well as his approach to design history and criticism.

Phil participated with incredible versatility in the graphic-design field. He was a generalist who wore many hats: educator, practitioner,

From left to right, Rob Carter, Ben Day, and Phil Meggs in 1985.

They had just completed the first edition of *Typographic Design: Form and Communication.*

theoretician, and critic. Whereas many designers are practitioners only, or critics who write design criticism and history but are lesser practitioners, Phil was engaged as a designer, effectively approaching the discipline from many angles. As practitioner, Phil rejected formulas, dogma, and stylistic trends. At the core of every problem was content, through which form emerged. Examples of Phil's graphic-design work in this book reflect his pluralist approach to visual problem solving and his command of visual media. For twenty years, Phil and Libby Meggs maintained an active design practice under the name Meggs & Meggs. Appearing in this book, Libby's essay, "The Collaboration," reveals the reach of their life-long partnership.

Writing

During the process of extracting material for this book, we encountered a small shard of paper upon which Phil had scribbled: "writing, rewriting, thinking, rethinking." These four words capture the essence of Phil's writing process – a cyclical process as inevitable as the passing of seasons. When Phil wrote, words poured.

In my opinion, Phil's writing represents his most significant contribution to the graphic-design field. I say this not to compromise his contribution as a practitioner, for he was an exceptional graphic designer whose work received national and international recognition, but to acknowledge that writing enabled him to contribute to graphic-design history's coming-of-age on a global scale.

Writing seemed to come easily to him: whether in a lightening-quick memo or a thoroughly researched scholarly essay, Phil delighted in the power of a well-chosen word or phrase. Rarely did I see him without a pen and pad, putting ink to paper at every opportunity.

Phil reminded me of a detective obsessed with detail and obscure facts that aid in solving crimes. His stories do not contain clinical descriptions devoid of emotion. They present accounts of real people, designers and artists, with real human traits and emotions. If dirt needed digging, Phil produced a shovel; if silver linings needed sewing, Phil stitched them.

For thirteen years (1989–2002), Phil served as contributing editor to *Print* magazine and generated a significant volume of work for this influential publication. His contributions to *Print*, the *Journal of the American Institute of Graphic Arts,* and other mainstream design magazines and journals reflect his gnawing quest to unearth new and emerging design developments and place them into historical contexts. They serve also as an attempt to further link the fragments of design history into a tangible continuum, fresh as clothes hung out on a line.

Phil's writings represent his expansive interest in visual culture and human communication. Including his tour de force, *A History of Graphic Design,* Phil authored 14 books and over 170 articles and chapters. The scope of this anthology makes it impossible to include everything. The selected writing presents a range of themes, from parodic and tongue-in-cheek commentaries such as "Recommended Reading for a New Millennium" and "Test Your Typographic IQ" to in-depth scholarly essays such as "The 1940s: Rise of the Modernists" and the classic *Print* series "Landmarks of Book Design." Readers have an opportunity to explore the sweep of Phil's topics and their relationship to greater social, political, and economic concerns. Above all, Phil championed the idea that design should improve the quality of life by advocating positive change for society and for the environment.

His writing efforts extended far beyond the world of graphic design. Between assignments and for amusement, Phil scribbled ideas for short stories. On one occasion while enjoying a few hours at the local swim club with his family, he dashed off the beginning words of a story about Farley, an irate man fed up with people stealing his deck chair. Phil had many writing projects stacked on the back burner, but time expired before he could get to them. One such project was a novel about the Civil War. "Imagine, Rob," he said, "what would it be like now if the South had won the war?" He explained in vivid detail the story's outline, while I stood in amazement as his enthusiastic and theatrical delivery brought the story to life. These stories and others never saw completion or publication, but they serve as a testament to Phil's profound curiosity, sense of humor, and observance of human nature.

In November 2002, Phil was inducted into the New York Art Directors Hall of Fame as design education laureate. Because he had just been admitted to the hospital, he asked that I attend the ceremony in New York to accept his award. After returning to Richmond, I visited Phil in the hospital and delivered his award, cradled in a small box with a red ribbon. He opened the box and lifted from it two stainless-steel letters – an "A" and "D" for "Art Director," and as he held them in his hands, he turned to Libby and modestly said, "These are nice enough to put out."

That was the last time I shook Phil's outstretched hand.

In his 1989 book, *Type & Image: The Language of Graphic Design,* Phil wrote a chapter on the subject of graphic resonance. In the introduction, he states, "Perhaps the most important thing that graphic design does is give communications resonance, a richness of tone that heightens the expressive power of the page. It transcends the dry conveyance of information, intensifies the message, and enriches the audience's experience. Resonance helps the designer realize clear public goals: to instruct, to delight, and to motivate."

To be sure, this quotation refers to graphic resonance, but it refers just as well to the rich tone of Phil's life, which enriched the experience of all who knew him and resonated to instruct, delight, and motivate others.

Growing Up with Phil

Bill Meggs

Philip Baxter Meggs was born on Memorial Day in 1942. Though I, William Joel Meggs, was there, my recollections of his birth are dim because I was only fifteen minutes old. We had shared a womb and even a placenta. The delivering doctor said that we were identical twins. Though our names were quite different, our nicknames, Bill and Phil, rhymed our identity. Very seldom did we hear just one of our names. It was always either "Phil and Bill" or "Phil or Bill." Like most twins we were premature – hey, it gets crowded in there – and were born scrawny. The doctor told our mother that she would never raise Phil, the scrawniest of the two, to be a year old.

We were born in Newberry, South Carolina, a small town in the Piedmont region of South Carolina, with red clay soil, gently rolling hills, and textile mills. Our parents were living in Whitmire, an even smaller town of three thousand people that did not even have a hospital. The seventeen miles to the nearest hospital must have been a horrific drive for a young woman in labor for the first time.

Our mother, Elizabeth Pruitt Meggs, was raised in Whitmire with three brothers and eight sisters. Our maternal grandfather, Samuel Baxter Pruitt, was gifted at mathematics and was timekeeper for the Whitmire textile mill in an era predating calculators and computers. He played a mean trumpet and led a band. Our maternal grandmother, Inez Mahaffey Pruitt, was a traditional homemaker who prepared dinner by buying a live chicken, violently wringing its neck, and tossing it aside to run around in circles with wings flapping until it collapsed. She then plucked its feathers, singed the fuzz with a lighted newspaper, cut it into pieces, dusted the pieces with flour, and deep-fried them. We were eighteen years old before we learned that there were other ways to cook chicken. Phil and I witnessed this awful process many times and preferred buying chicken parts at the supermarket many steps removed from the violence.

Bill and Phil Meggs at age two (1944)

Our father, Wallace Nat. Meggs, grew up on the Carolina coastal plain, a flat land of sandy soil, pine trees, and sand spurs. Our father's unusual middle name was legalized by the delivering doctor who abbreviated *Nathaniel* as *Nat.* on the birth certificate, probably because he did not know how to spell *Nathaniel.* Our paternal grandfather, Will Nathaniel Meggs, farmed in Sparrow Swamp, South Carolina, plowing fields of tobacco and corn with a mule. Don't look for Sparrow Swamp on a map. It is a crossroads with one structure, the Sparrow Swamp Baptist Church, a small wooden building with peeling white paint surrounded by crumbling tombstones.

Our grandfather Will gave up on farming during the depression and moved into the nearby town of Florence, a railroad center. He rose to a managerial position until his career with the Atlantic Coast Line Railroad was abruptly terminated when he went out on strike with the workers. At the end of the strike, all of the workers were rehired while his traitorous anti-company behavior got him fired. He then moved to Washington, DC, and worked at the Richmond, Fredericksburg, and Potomac Railroad yards across the Potomac River in Alexandria, Virginia.

Our paternal grandmother, Ruth Gardner Meggs, was a rotund woman who cooked enormous meals of fried meats and vegetables seasoned with fatback. She was determined to fatten her skinny grandsons. She kept piling our plates with food long after we were filled to satiety and insisted that we eat more and more.

Early on, Phil and I were easy to tell apart, because as the first born my head had to forge a way through the birth canal and suffered an interesting deformity. Phil, by contrast, came out feet first with a perfectly round head. As the days passed, my mother proved the doctor wrong about our prognosis. We celebrated our first birthday as healthy, bouncy, baby boys who were ahead of developmental milestones. We discovered the advantages of cooperation. Working together, we could escape cribs and playpens with ease. We discovered how to open a jar of deodorant and ate the whole thing. We blazed a trail to the top of the upright piano before we could even walk.

Throughout the preschool years, we were inseparable. If one of us accidentally dropped his ice cream cone, the other threw his on the ground. Once we were riding in a car holding our toy airplanes out the window so that the onrushing wind could spin the propellers. When the wind whipped one of our planes away, the other threw his out the window. Once one of us got his foot stuck between the wall and booth at a soda fountain. The extraction required great efforts on the part of many individuals. Immediately after the release, the other thrust his foot into the same space and got it stuck.

We were truly identical. Being dressed by our mother in identical clothes every day only added to the confusion. In the early years, only our mother claimed to be able to tell us apart. It is easy to ponder that we may have been switched back and forth several times. I may be Phil and he may be Bill. A small mole appeared on Phil's face, just to the right of and below his nose. When teachers and others used the mole to tell us apart, we would both lay a finger beside our nose to cover the spot.

Our first day of school was a near disaster for a twosome making inseparability a way of life. Our mother took us to the elementary school auditorium on the first day of school where first graders were gathered to receive room and teacher assignments. We objected after being assigned to separate classes. "We want to be together," we told the principal. "No!" he said. "It is school policy that twins be put in separate classrooms." On that cue, we both began to cry. Not low-key gentle sobbing, but loud, hysterical wailing.

Realizing that only one thing would mollify us, the principal relented. We literally cried our way into being together at school and quickly demonstrated a talent for academics in the days when the gifted program consisted of giving second graders the sixth graders' *Weekly Reader.*

When we learned to write, Phil declared himself to be a lefty while I was right-handed. This gave rise to our mother's theory that identical twins are mirror images of each other. Subsequent right and left brain choices reinforced her theory. We both had monovision, a condition where one eye differentiates for near vision and the other for far vision, but my right eye and his left eye were for far vision. Our hair naturally parted on opposite sides.

Drawing was a passion for the Meggs twins from an early age. In the first grade, we drew elaborate pictures of a host of war planes. Our B-29 bombers and sabre jets were easily identified by anyone who knew their war planes. In the summer before entering the second grade, our parents left our baby sister with our grandparents, who lived at 504 G Street, Southwest, in Washington, and took us on a trip to New York City. Our second-grade notebooks were filled with pictures of the Empire State Building, Chrysler Building, Statue of Liberty, and other New York City landmarks. The house at 504 G Street was a short walk from the mall, and throughout our childhood we spent at least two weeks a year visiting our grandparents and swarming through the museums and government buildings. Drawings of the Capitol, Washington Monument, Smithsonian, and presidential memorials filled our notebooks.

A great rift in our relationship came as we reached adolescence and wanted separate identities. We rebelled against wearing the identical clothes that our mother put out for us each morning. We were assigned separate classes when Phil chose art and I chose band for our electives in middle school. Consequently we developed separate friends. If one of us dropped his ice cream cone, the other laughed and kept on licking.

Phil took biology and became very upset at the contradictions between evolution and the fundamentalism of our neighborhood church where we religiously attended seven functions a week: Sunday school, Sunday morning worship service, Sunday evening training union and worship service, choir practice, a boy scout–like meeting, and Wednesday evening prayer meeting. We got a pin for going a year without missing a day of Sunday school. The second year we got a wreath that surrounded the pin, and then a series of bars that hung beneath the wreath for each subsequent year's perfect attendance. We went seven years without missing a day of Sunday school before our religious fervor was blunted by an inability to reconcile our expanding knowledge of the world with the teachings of the religious right.

Phil's great love of art became apparent early on. We attended art classes at the Florence Museum on Saturday mornings and entered our oil paintings into the Florence County Fair each year. The year that my painting of a clipper ship in full sail won the blue ribbon for best in show – Phil was quick to point out the great help I received from the instructor who had actually drawn the ship – was quite traumatic for the recognized artistic genius of Florence High School.

Florence did not offer the opportunities in art that someone determined to become an artist needed, so Phil persuaded our parents to pay for a mail-order Famous Artists School course. The bedroom that we shared with our baby brother Wally was turned into an art studio with drafting table, T square, and a taboret loaded with paints, brushes, and pencils. Phil diligently completed each assignment while still maintaining a high level of scholarship in the college preparatory curriculum. He was art editor of the yearbook our senior year, did professional layouts, and embellished each section with professional quality illustrations. The portfolio that he amassed got him into the graphic design program at Virginia Commonwealth University easily.

Our parents were horrified that one of their children would seek a career as professional artist. They were convinced that if Phil persisted and studied art, he would die of starvation on the streets of Richmond, and insisted that Phil study architecture or engineering and take up art as a hobby. Phil stubbornly refused to listen. Perhaps these concerns influenced Phil to study graphic design rather than fine art. Finally they agreed to send him to art school but insisted that he get a BA instead of a BFA which was perceived to be worthless. I was sitting beside our stunned parents at Phil's graduation when it was announced that he was being awarded a BFA.

After our freshman year in college, Phil and I got summer jobs at the Pee Dee Agricultural Experimental Station located in Florence. Our job classification was Insect Keeper Class II. We rode around in a van with four other college students and an entomologist inspecting hot, humid, muddy cotton fields for boll weevil infestations. We encountered thousands of mosquitoes and horseflies for every boll weevil we counted. One of the other students convinced me to go on a double date with him, his girlfriend, and a blind date for me. My date was described as the most beautiful, intelligent woman in South Carolina. He pumped my expectations so high that when I met my date, a short fat girl with buck teeth and average IQ, my disappointment could not be concealed and I was a miserable companion. At work the next day, we decided that we should switch off: that Phil should go out with the girl and pretend to be me. She did not guess that she was out with another person but reported that I was much nicer and sweeter on the second date.

I was the golden boy of the family when I chose to study physics in the post-Sputnik era. Ten years later, my hard-earned PhD in theoretical physics was worse than worthless – it made me unemployable in this country. By that time, Phil had been art director for major corporations, won design awards, and had his work in design annuals. The chair of graphic design at VCU offered Phil a sweet deal – to simultaneously be hired as a full-time instructor of graphic design while pursuing an MFA. Phil said he chose to get his MFA in painting rather than graphic design because painting is the basis for all of art, including graphic design. The chair said the reason he enticed Phil into academics is that Phil was the most intellectually gifted art student he had ever met. Phil's subsequent accomplishments proved him correct.

Phil and I again became best of friends after we graduated from high school and went our separate ways. As we married and had children, we kept in close touch and spent many holidays together with our families. My sons' favorite food was Aunt Libby's caramel cake. On one visit Phil told me that he was writing a history of graphic design. "Everybody writes art history books," he explained, "but no one ever wrote a history of graphic design."

Phil also told me that as he wrote the first edition of the book, he had no idea if it would ever sell or anyone would ever read it. After its adoption by most college graphic design programs and translation into five languages, he was convinced that he had a winner. The magnitude of his achievement, *A History of Graphic Design,* became clear from his obituary in the *New York Times* that was picked up by newspapers around the country, including my local newspaper.

Phil and I got in the habit of chatting on the telephone in the evening once or twice a month. We would talk for an hour or more, catching up on each other's children, spouses, and our professional endeavors. One day he called and simply said, "Bill, I'm sick." "Do you have a cold?" I asked. "No," he said. "I have leukemia." "What kind?" I asked after regaining my composure. It was unbelievable then, and still is, that Phil could have leukemia. By this time, I had given up on physics as a career and retrained in medicine, and was well versed in the many shades of leukemia. "Acute lymphocytic leukemia," he answered. I actually let out a sigh of relief. At least it wasn't acute myelogenous leukemia, the worst player in the leukemia family.

Phil was admitted to the hospital for chemotherapy. My wife, artist Susan Martin Meggs, and I dropped everything and immediately drove from our home in North Carolina to Richmond. We learned that his diagnosis had been refined, that he indeed had a more devastating form of leukemia, acute myelogenous leukemia. We also learned of his tremendous fortitude and emotional reserve. He faced the tribulations that were to unfold with courage and good humor.

His oncologist came through the cancer ward with an entourage of medical students, residents, and oncology fellows-in-training. I introduced myself, and asked if the hospital had the apheresis technology that I had used to harvest human white blood cells for research while doing a clinical research fellowship at the National Institutes of Health. In this technique, punctures are made in large veins in each of a person's arm, blood flows out of one arm into a machine with a rotating drum, and any desired blood component can be sucked off. All the other blood components are returned to the person's body. The brinksmanship chemotherapy used to treat leukemia can destroy the normal white blood cells in a person's body and lead to devastating infections. Donors can be put on an apheresis machine and donate huge amounts of white blood cells. Unfortunately, if the donor and recipient are not identical twins, the donated white blood cells can attack the recipient's body.

"Yes, we have apheresis," the oncologist answered. "Why do you ask?" "Because Phil and I are identical twins," I answered. "I can give him all the blood cells he needs if he

(continued on page 24)

1

2

3

4

1
Bill and Phil, second grade photographs (1950)

2
Phil and Bill, high school graduation photographs (1961)

3
Phil and Bill trying on their new birthday shirts in Syracuse, New York (1977)

4
Phil and Bill in Florence, South Carolina (1996)

Philip Meggs: Sketchbooks

Selected spreads from high school sketchbooks. Mixed media. Spread dimensions: 14 x 5 inches. (c. 1961)

Bank of Florence

crashes." "You say you are identical twins," the oncologist answered. "If we do the testing, we'll probably find you don't even have the same father." This retort triggered uncontrollable laughter from his entourage. After much discussion, including fights with Phil's insurance company about payment for the tests, samples of both our blood were sent to a lab to determine if I could donate white blood cells.

Two weeks later, Susan and I were packing the car to go to Florida for a wedding. The reports from Richmond were not good. Phil's bone marrow had not recovered from the first round of chemotherapy. He had developed a horrendous skin reaction to one of the antibiotics used to treat a host of skin, lung, and blood infections. There was even a fungus growing on his retina. His oncologist would neither take nor return my many phone calls.

"I don't feel good about being so far away in Florida with Phil so sick," I told Susan. "I am going to try to call his oncologist one last time before we leave."

Once again the oncologist's secretary refused to connect me, explaining that her boss was too busy seeing patients to talk to me. "I'm a doctor," I said. "And this is an emergency." At last I got to speak to Phil's oncologist. "Should I come to Richmond and donate white blood cells?" I asked. "I don't know what else to do," the oncologist replied. "He's very sick and getting worse each day. His bone marrow just isn't coming back. But I haven't checked your tests yet. Call me back in an hour."

An hour later I got the word. Phil and I were truly identical twins. We were a perfect match at every genetic site tested – which came as no surprise to our mother. Susan and I drove north to Richmond instead of south to Florida.

When we reached Richmond, I was injected with a drug that stimulated my bone marrow to release abnormally high numbers of stem cells and white blood cells into my bloodstream. I then spent several hours hooked to an apheresis machine watching movies. By that time Phil was in septic shock on life support in the intensive care unit, dying.

Blood bank computers block a person from donating blood components by apheresis more than once every six months. The computers had to be rigged so that I could undergo seven courses of apheresis over the next three weeks. But the therapy worked. The donated stem cells renewed his dead bone marrow, and the white blood cells fought off the infections until his new bone marrow started making cells. Amazingly, Phil recovered from the brink of death and was his old self again. He behaved as if nothing had happened and immediately got back to work.

It is said that people who live one year after a bone marrow transplant for acute myelogenous leukemia without a recurrence are cured. Our families celebrated Phil's cure thirteen months after he got out of the hospital at an oceanfront resort in Myrtle Beach. Our celebration turned out to be premature; the leukemia returned a few months later. Once again Phil was admitted to the hospital for chemotherapy.

I emailed the three doctors managing his case with an urgent plea. "Let's not let what happened before happen again," I pleaded. "On his last day of chemotherapy, let's do the aphresis and let me donate white blood cells before he gets sick."

All three answered my email with the same opinion: what happened before couldn't possibly happen again.

But it did. Only much worse. On his last day of chemotherapy, Phil went into septic shock. Shock so damaged his lungs that he died a respiratory death. His doctors just couldn't think outside of the box.

Phil got an extra two years of life after developing a devastating illness. During that time he revised *A History of Graphic Design,* coauthored another book, wrote a penetrating introduction for a new release of a Marshall McLuhan book, and planned what would have been his greatest work – a tour de force that would do for the digital age what McLuhan did for analogue media. The loss to the world is immense.

The Collaboration

Libby Meggs

We miss Phil terribly. We have a Meggs family email list that goes to three generations of the family. Every day we all got at least one email from Phil, filled with humor and insights that stimulated participation by every family member. Since his death, nothing is the same, not even the emails.

The loss to our family is terrible, but when Phil died, the whole world lost. His greatest works were yet to come but will never be. I am convinced that with vigorous exploitation of the precious gift of an identical donor, he could have gotten another two years, and maybe another two after that, and the works would have continued to flow from his pen.

Phil was an immensely talented artist, but his impact was not as an artist but as a writer with penetrating insights into art. It was always a great disappointment to me that he did not continue to make art, but not to him. He was very happy with his role as a chronicler of others' art. He had no regrets, other than losing life, for he treasured every day, every word, every image, and everybody. ⊷

We had no idea the long trip would so change our lives.

When we traveled from South Carolina to college in Virginia, he came 300 miles with his jam-packed trunk on a train from Florence and I rode 400 miles from Greenville in the back seat of my parents' loaded DeSoto. Neither of us had ever been away from home.

Everybody used to say we got together in the first place because we were the only people who could stand to wait for each other to finish a sentence. Maybe that was part of it: not only did we speak at the same pace, we also spoke the same language. We knew about Myrtle Beach, live oak trees laden with Spanish moss, dirt roads, Sunday dinners after church, and homemade peach ice cream. We understood the beauty of a sudden summer afternoon thunderstorm, iron grey over luminous, flat stretches of bright green tobacco fields. We had both caught lightning bugs, June bugs, and ladybugs, and had both drifted off to sleep on screen porches, listening to the lullaby of slow, sweet conversations among aunts, uncles, parents, and grandparents. It was almost as if we had shared a common childhood, just not together. Not yet.

He was sitting on a drawing board beside the pencil sharpener, the first day of the first class, the first time I ever saw him. I opened my tackle box and began to sharpen the brand new pencils that had been issued to each freshman majoring in what was then called commercial art at Richmond Professional Institute in 1961. I picked up a flat chisel-point pencil, baffled because I'd never seen one. "Gosh," I said, "how are we supposed to sharpen this one?" "You use a razor blade," Philip B. Meggs replied with confidence. He was nineteen, and an experienced transfer student. "A razor blade?" I repeated. I must have looked terrified. Never in all my seventeen years had I sharpened a pencil with something so dangerous. "Don't worry," he reassured me, "I'll be glad to sharpen all your pencils from now on."

So it began.

After developing personal passions about art, writing, design, and every other component of our separate youthful existences, often feeling out of step with our peers, we had each found the one person who would share and understand those passions, verbalize them, and nurture them. We went to museums and galleries, raided libraries, analyzed and discussed every detail of anything visual, any word we read, and any unsuspecting person we encountered. We gave each other small prints of our favorite paintings to tape to the walls of our rooms, exchanged copies of books we loved, from Dylan Thomas to Jean-Paul Sartre, and brought each other treats in the form of cookies from home or flowers "borrowed" under cover of darkness from the edge of a hapless yard. We tried to help each other in every way we could. Phil stretched my canvases and I ironed his shirts. He made suggestions about my drawing; I offered advice about his color. And we listened to each other.

Opposite:
Libby and Phil Meggs
Photographs:
Kuhn Caldwell (1964)

In each school subject, as soon as we were given our assignment at the end of class, Phil's active mind and ever-present sketchbook had combined to create at least twenty ideas before we left the room. By the time he had walked me back to my dormitory, he knew the medium, technique, palette, and typeface he would use. How could I do less than my best around such a person? Most of the class would still be thinking about lunch!

We were married for thirty-eight years, and in that time we were "co-conspirators" in every realm of our lives. We combined efforts in growing gardens, bringing up children, raising pets, rehabilitating houses, cooking meals, and doing work, though it often didn't seem like work. We had fun. Whatever either of us might write, design, draw, or paint, we involved each other. During the early years of our marriage, Phil was a graphic designer and art director at three different Fortune 500 companies, and I was the first art director hired by what quickly became the largest advertising agency in the Southeast. The professional success we both enjoyed helped to reaffirm our mutual respect for each other as capable, independent thinkers. Independent, but never far apart.

For eleven years we were a "career couple." We even had our own small business, Meggs and Meggs, that included conceptualizing, graphic design, illustration, photography, and copywriting. Everyone assumed our only child would be our adored cat Muffin, and then Andrew Philip Meggs came along. We were so thrilled to finally have Andrew that, when baby Elizabeth Wilson Meggs was born twenty-six months later, our happiness could hardly be contained. Phil and I changed diapers, changed our roles, and changed our lives, but our mutual appreciation, love, and respect remained constant. I stayed at home with our long-awaited babies while Phil taught at Virginia Commonwealth University.

Being an educator became Phil's first love, professionally. Teaching students about graphic design, he grew to be acutely aware that there was a need to be filled, a basis for the validation of graphic design as a respected profession. He had long loved history and possessed an insightful, analytical overview of the interrelationships of world events, big and small, throughout the past and right up to the minute. The importance of graphic design as an integral part of history had been largely ignored. Phil was changing that in his classroom, but his endeavor deserved a bigger audience. We had discussed this in earnest over a long period of time, and the day came when something seemed to click.

"Phil," I said, as he lugged his painstakingly researched notes out the door one morning, "you've already done so much basic groundwork. If you don't put this material together into book form, somebody else will write a graphic-design history. And you won't be happy with somebody else's text."

He stopped in his tracks, as if a light had come on. His competitive spirit kicked in. I knew he wanted to be the first, with the best.

"You're right," he nodded. "You're right."

It didn't take him long to get started, but the project itself proved to be grueling. Every morning, Phil worked in pre-dawn hours before driving to his job at the university. Every evening, he jumped up from the supper table to produce page after page at his typewriter, working until way past midnight. He spent untold hours obtaining permissions to use visual material from all over the world. Weekends and holidays belonged to the book.

A good portion of our personal savings and income went toward fees from museums and other sources that provided images for reproduction. We budgeted carefully. To augment hand-me-downs from cousins, I made clothes from inexpensive fabric remnants for Elizabeth and myself and haunted thrift shops to find little boys' pants and shirts for Andrew. A rare "eating out" treat might be spreading a tablecloth on the living room floor and bringing home fast food, if we had coupons, for an indoor "picnic." Andrew, Elizabeth, and I made and painted a beautiful puppet stage using an appliance box Phil had brought home, and the children crafted vivid characters as paper bag puppets, acting out their own plays. Every Thursday, I took them to check out new books and enjoy free movies at the public library. Every weekday, Phil took his lunch to school in a brown bag. Working together, we made ends meet.

Phil's tremendous undertaking meant creating a book that would contain over a thousand images within its five hundred pages. A publishing contract and deadline loomed large; time was a precious commodity. Besides discussing every aspect of the book's contents with him and proofreading and copyediting the text daily, I did my best to shield Phil as much as possible from routine, time-consuming distractions. For a while, I became the "detail man," making repairs, taking messages, settling squabbles, remembering birthdays, mowing the lawn, maintaining the house.

However demanding the book project might be, Phil took time every night with the children for a bedtime story, hugs and kisses, and tucking them in. A wonderful dad like this deserved special care himself. I tried to make sure he ate well and took his vitamins. I cut his beautiful dark hair, kept his closet and chest of drawers full of clean clothes, and, most of all, loved him.

Publication of *A History of Graphic Design* brought about a public awareness that, by golly, Phil Meggs could write, and, by golly, he knew what he was talking about. It changed our lives. Phil was in demand as a speaker, as a contributing editor, and as an author and coauthor of still more books from that day forward. My best buddy had quietly become a Force!

When Andrew and Elizabeth were older and more independent, it became evident that instead of continuing to do freelance work while accumulating more candles on my birthday cake, I could finally pursue writing and illustrating children's books. This had been a lifelong dream, postponed, but never relinquished. Because our situation had reached a point at which it was no longer so necessary for me to bring in additional, immediate income, I could allow myself the luxury of focusing every effort on my own book. The writing was easy, but the meticulous illustrations took over two hundred hours each to complete. This time, Phil became the "detail man." He shouldered household tasks and cheered me on, insisting that I keep submitting until the book was published.

Holding the printed, bound book in my hands, seeing it on bookstore shelves, and reading it aloud at book events was more thrilling than I had ever imagined. Phil's excitement made it a thousand times better.

He was present at every book signing and award ceremony, from Manhattan to San Francisco. He took me out to celebrate more times than I deserved. And then, in the middle of this happy time, he came home one day from a routine physical examination to stand in the middle of the kitchen and tell me in a calm voice that he could be dying.

So many years before, I had known that I did not want to live my life without this beautiful young man. I just never thought that one day this beautiful young man – and he will always be that to me – that one day he would die.

Everything, everything, came to a stop for both of us. Acute myelogenous leukemia became the focus of our lives.

The first night he was in the hospital, I slept on the floor beside his bed, reaching up to hold his hand. The next day, the kindhearted nurses provided a reclining chair. People tried to be helpful by bringing us stacks of information about AML. We read as much as we could absorb, then switched to Harry Potter, to escape.

Harry made us feel as if we were playing hooky from the illness. Giggling, we would shut the door, turn off the phone, and I would read aloud to Phil while he closed his eyes, smiling. We became students at Hogwarts, wand-wielding warriors, pilots on broomsticks. It was magic.

Andrew came home from California and Elizabeth came home from New York. They worked their own magic, surrounding us with love, help, and good cheer in every way possible. Of all the things Phil and I collaborated on, our children turned out best. Phil said this to the doctors, nurses, and anyone else who came into his hospital room. He was right. They were a big part of Phil's will to get well, and they kept me from sliding into darkness, though they, themselves, were devastated.

While all members of our family and most of our friends understood the seriousness of Phil's situation, some people had a difficult time accepting the fact that chemotherapy had left him with no immune system, and that he had to be isolated. My role in our partnership became protector and policewoman. Turning away so many insistent visitors was not easy, but it was mandatory. Phil's life was at risk, as much from possible infections as from the leukemia itself.

Phil nearly died three times during those five months in the hospital, then went into a miraculous state of remission and was able to come home. He was too weak to turn over in bed. New teamwork was in order for us. I helped him with his physical therapy, learned to give injections, changed dressings, and flushed the catheter in his chest every night, my mask and rubber gloves in place. He tried so hard to get well. He exercised diligently, swallowed barely palatable nutrition supplements, and bravely endured a multitude of medical procedures with never one complaint. His sweet spirit and determination were the greatest reward of all, next to his being alive. As partners combining efforts on the most important project we had ever undertaken, we managed to pick up where his excellent physicians and nurses had left off, and brought back a strong, healthy Phil.

It lasted nineteen months. From the soft spring morning of April 14, 2001, when he came home from the hospital, until that icy gray Sunday afternoon, November 24, 2002, when he went away forever, we treasured the precious gift of that time together.

During those nineteen months, we made little trips, held hands the way we had always done on all our walks, laughed a lot, and played jokes on each other, grateful he was alive, grateful for every minute we were able to share. I am still finding funny, loving notes he hid for me, falling out of books, tucked into coat pockets, pushed into the toes of my shoes.

Phil became well enough to go back to teaching, writing, designing, and painting. Though I wished he would retire following his survival of such an ordeal, he wanted life to be as normal as it could possibly be. Evaluating repeated tests and analyses, his oncologist pronounced him "cured." We were thrilled and relieved: we could actually count on a future. After years of working together in a cramped, converted furnace area, we bought a house with a huge, light, airy room that would be perfect for our joint studio space. During the six weeks Phil lived in the new house, he would disappear and then come bouncing out of that room, elated. "That room," he said, "is going to be great! You'll be doing children's books, and I'll become a house-husband." "Fat chance of your becoming a house-husband," I teased him. "I know that," he grinned, "and I have big plans for my half of the room."

He had so many big plans, so much exciting work already under way, such remarkable projects completed in his head, waiting to take form.

All he needed was time. Now, I sit in the huge, light, airy, quiet, quiet room, writing about him. What was it like, sharing my life with Phil?

Do this:

Take two kitchen matches and light them. Watch how they burn separately and then put them together side by side, flames touching. Their flames, combined, blaze with a brighter light than the light from the two apart. As one together, they enhance and sustain each other.

That is what it was like. ⊸

Phil and Libby Meggs (1964)
Photograph: Kuhn Caldwell

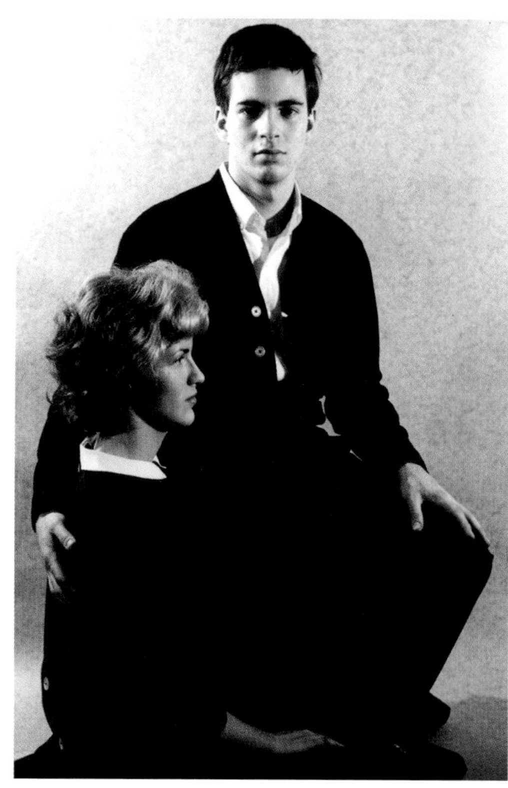

1

2

3

1
In his first year at the Richmond Professional Institute (1961)
2
As a senior at the Richmond Professional Institute
Photograph: Kuhn Caldwell (1964)
3, 4
A year after graduation from the Richmond Professional Institute (1965)

4

5

5
As a graduate student in Painting, Virginia Commonwealth University (1969)
6
Graduating with an MFA in Painting (1971)
7
A moment of contemplation (1971)
8
With letter Q (1975)
9
Posing in his Hawaiian shirt and new haircut (1987)
10
Wearing a "star" shirt and holding Charlotte
11
Photographing a piece of sculpture at Frank Lloyd Wright's home at Taliesin, Madison, Wisconsin Photograph: Derry Noyes (1999)
12
Holding the diploma for his Honorary PhD degree from the Massachusetts College of Art, Boston (1999)
13
At the opening of Denver Art Museum's exhibition, *US Design: 1975–2000,* which Phil co-curated over a period of five years (2002)

6

7

8

9

10

11

12

13

1

3

5

2

4

6

1
Wallace, Libby, Lib, Phil, Bill, and Susan Spring Meggs in Florence, South Carolina (1967)

2
Beth Meggs Lever, Wally, Bill, Phil, Lib, and Wallace in Florence, South Carolina (1996)

3
Phil, Lib, and Bill at Bill's wedding (1966)

4
Phil, Wallace, Bill (1999)

5
Libby Meggs in Jewett Campbell's painting studio, Richmond, Virginia
Photograph: Jewett Campbell (1964)

6
Libby and Phil Meggs at Phil's parents' home, Florence, South Carolina (1972)

7
The Meggs family clowning in a photo booth (1979)
8
The Meggs family on Easter Sunday (1981)
9
Andrew, Elizabeth, and Phil working on the old Chevy (1981)
10
Andrew and Phil Meggs putting down tent stakes (1987)
11
Andrew and Phil Meggs at Myrtle Beach, SC Photograph: Elizabeth Meggs (1998)
12
Elizabeth and Phil Meggs dancing at a family wedding Photograph: William Perry (2002)
13
Libby and Phil Meggs at Myrtle Beach, SC Photograph: Elizabeth Meggs (2001)

7

8

9

10

11

12

13

Life by Design: From Ephemeral to Historical

Elizabeth Meggs

As you read my father's writings on design, imagine what it might be like to grow up as the daughter of design historian Philip B. Meggs. At first, the idea of life with a scholarly researcher might seem dry, full of bibliographies, bland biographies, and dusty boxes of books. Nothing could be further from the truth.

Life with my father was always full of adventures, outrageous and outstanding people, amazing imagery, and fascinating stories, and that was without ever leaving the room. His sense of humor and fun, and his sense of the poetic, informed his approach to life. He was truly excited by history and its potential to provide insight and answers in the present and future on any subject. Dad could and would put anything we said or did into a historical context, including refrigerator drawings by my brother and me as children, and Dad didn't restrain himself from doing so. He seemed to have an innate ability to quickly observe everyday reality and put it into a dialogue of historical context, analogy, or funny anecdote. For example, on an evening walk with Dad in the summer, he would observe that the sky was "a Maxfield Parrish sky," or the clouds might be "N.C. Wyeth clouds." People he observed were not spared from this. A crowd of passersby might include a "de Kooning woman," "a Gibson Girl," "a Bosch creature," or "a Rockwell boy and dog." He could apply this historical contextualization and dialogue to any aspect of all that is visible in the world. Dad *was* history — he lived it, and made it current and alive for us. Somehow, it seemed that, like a sponge, Dad completely absorbed and then consciously and subconsciously understood all of the art and design he had ever seen or studied.

By teaching us that we were part of the ongoing historical narrative of human life on Earth, my father made us feel that what anyone does and says has the potential to be of great importance. Certain common denominators seem to exist in order for a person to do great work of historical significance in any field: a keen understanding of history is necessary, along with a scholarly and artistic spirit of exploration, a mind open to broad possibility that does not edit itself too soon when thinking of ideas, a willingness to face dissension and being misunderstood when one truly believes in one's work, an unwavering work ethic, a sense of wonder, an ability to be thrilled by one's work, and a deep analytical objectivity that does not negate spirit or passion or intuitiveness.

Dad's broad knowledge of the lives and backgrounds of historically significant designers and artists revealed that many factors people often think of as obstacles to doing great and noteworthy work are not real obstacles at all. In no way launching a platitude, but speaking with informed sincerity, Dad would say, "It doesn't matter where you are, it's what you do — your work — that matters most."

He then would cite numerous innovators of wildly different backgrounds in order to underscore that the work is what matters. One thing that made Dad such a consummate teacher was that he saw huge potential in every person from every walk of life to do great work, because he knew that was the truth of influential innovators. Dad always believed that through disciplined hard work and study, an answer to any problem, whether it was a design problem or an automotive concern, could be found. I admire my father's ability to be clear and communicative, with a complete lack of pretension.

Indeed, through being a historian, Dad showed his love for all that is ephemeral and fleeting in this world (which, according to scientific theories regarding the life of this universe, is ultimately all that exists as we know it), by recording it and presenting its significance within a historical context. He did this in many ways on a personal level for my family. In every role Dad played, as a painter, a historian, humorist, father, husband, son, educator, writer, or designer, he operated at a level of artistry. No matter what role he approached, he put his whole heart into it and took it to a level of high art. That's why, if I had to use one word to describe my father, it would be this: artist.

In 2002, my brother and I were both working jobs in California. October arrived, and we both knew the brilliant fall leaves back home in Virginia must be stunning. We didn't say anything about being homesick for the East Coast autumn, but my father must have known that where we lived, autumn was not the splendid display of color it is every year in the

Virginia woods. So, he went into those Virginia woods, and found the most beautiful leaves that had fallen on the ground. He gathered a spectrum of purple, magenta, red, orange, yellow, and green, in thin, veined shapes and brought them inside the house to press between wax paper in our family's big old encyclopedia. He was going to send us some color, send us some beauty, and send us a poetic reminder of home in the mail. My father was going to send us pressed Virginia autumn leaves.

He never got the chance. At the end of October, on Halloween, Dad's doctor discovered his leukemia had returned, in spite of a miraculous recovery and nearly two-year remission. Within weeks, he died.

When I came home, it was November, with autumn leaves brown and falling and dead. I found the pressed leaves on Dad's drawing board. My mother explained that Dad had been ready to send the beautiful pressed leaves to us.

Nothing made sense to me in the wake of my young father's death. I read, and thought, and looked. I wanted answers. I could see physical evidence of a large intelligent design to the world, from a miniscule spider building a web to the Blue Ridge Mountains; from the ocean to the stars; from the enormity of the universe to the microscopic order of atoms, and in the beauty of fall leaves. These natural wonders seemed too complex and awe inspiring to be explained except that there is an intelligent design to the world. "But spiders die, mountains erode, oceans dry up, stars expire, and fall leaves … fall leaves turn brown and dead and crumbling," I thought bitterly.

My next thought was, "Fall leaves turn brown and dead and crumbling … unless someone presses them, preserves them, and remembers their beauty. Gone forever … unless someone loves them."

My father loved. That is the biggest thing I can say about him. He loved art and design and people, and his work told everyone how important all the ephemera of the world is. The fleeting colors of fall leaves are worth preserving.

I looked at the stars one blue night. I remembered learning long ago in an elementary school science class that many stars humans can see from Earth died hundreds of years ago, but their light still travels out into the universe. Since the starlight travels at the speed of light, the light that may have been emitted centuries ago is just now reaching us from a very distant star, which is actually currently burned out. Of course, in the night sky, I couldn't tell the living stars from the dead ones. They all sparkled.

Every year since my dad died, the autumn trees glow – oh, you should see them! The fall leaves are a poetic reminder of something bigger than my father initially intended when he pressed them in the family's big old encyclopedia weeks before he died. Every year they are beautiful, and every year their glorious colors return in the fall, as if to say in my dad's voice, "Don't worry so much, kid! There is a continuity to life, and it is beautiful. There is a purpose for everything that happens, and for every life."

So, I leave grief behind, and I figuratively gather purple, magenta, red, orange, yellow, and green leaves from the ground to press, preserve, and send out to the world. That is what being an artist is to me, as my father taught me. The cycle continues. My father was sending his love to me; now I will send my love to others. We should never underestimate the long-reaching power of what we as humans do while we are alive, for, like the stars that died long ago but still twinkle in the night sky that is visible to us, our light can travel far beyond our own lives.

Seeing how my father's work has extended beyond his own life, which I was privileged to share for twenty-five years, I know that the light he brought to this world extends indefinitely and exponentially. ➺

A few days before leaving for the Netherlands in mid-November 2002, I called Phil and Libby to say goodbye, and, when Libby answered the phone, I inquired about Phil's health. She passed the phone to him, and Phil's first words were "Alston, the leukemia has come back." Reflecting back upon this moment, I remember that he was much stronger than I that evening, and paradoxically it was Phil who ended up reassuring and consoling me. He said that I should not worry and that he would defeat the illness just as he had before, and we made plans about getting together soon after I returned. Phil died two weeks later on Sunday, November 24, almost at the very moment that my return flight from Europe landed in Boston.

How do I remember Phil? Our acquaintance goes far back, and, except for his brother Bill, of all those included in this volume I probably knew him the longest. First and foremost, he was my friend, so this will be a personal memoir, and I will leave more extensive accounts of his considerable professional achievements to others. Many of my anecdotes will have little to do with graphic design, but they will, I hope, provide other glimpses into his life. It is my hope that they will even make some of the readers laugh. Phil, I know, would want this.

Although Phil and I attended the same high school in Florence, South Carolina, we did not see much of each other during this period. Since Phil was a class ahead of me, we moved among different circles of friends. Among my early vivid recollections of Phil was his arrival in the autumn of 1960 at my art studio above our garage at my home on Cherokee Road. Little did I know this visit would initiate a profound friendship that would continue uninterrupted for forty-two years. One of the motives for this meeting was that we were both enrolled in a correspondence illustration course that was then part of the now defunct Famous Artists School then based in Westport, Connecticut. In the following months Phil and I would critique one another's assignments, and although my interest in the course lapsed after beginning my university studies, Phil went on to complete all of the lessons. This was indicative of one of his enduring traits – total perseverance.

Several years before my father's death in 1960, he bought a 200-acre tract of land near the Pee Dee River about 35 miles from Florence. Although he had optimistically intended this to eventually become his dream horse farm, only about 50 acres was cleared land; the rest consisted of woods, scrub brush, and swamp. Phil and I would regularly go there on weekends to paint watercolors. A decaying cemetery containing monuments to long-departed owners of our property especially intrigued Phil, and this became one of his favorite subjects to paint. Even with the passage of time I can still vividly recall one of his paintings from these outings.

Once when we were exploring the woods looking for new painting motifs, Phil remarked that he smelled the odor of a hog pen. Even though I assured him that no such animals

Back: Kuhn Caldwell; left: Emmett Gowin; right: Alston Purvis, holding Alex Thompson; front: Phil Meggs. Photograph: Kuhn Caldwell (1964)

were being raised on our land, he was determined that we further investigate the pungent scent. After walking a few hundred feet we found ourselves facing a moonshine liquor still in full operation, the odor having come from fermenting mash used for making the whiskey. Fortunately, no one seemed to be around at the time, and we wisely made a rapid retreat. It was well known around those parts that liquor still operators did not view the presence of intruders favorably. Phil had always been fascinated by my father's extensive gun collection, and he always insisted that we take along several weapons on our visits to the property. Rarely if ever having fired a gun in his life, Phil soon became an exceptional marksman, but fortunately such skills were not needed on that day. Two weeks later, on our next visit to the property, we found the lock on our entry gate broken and were told by the owners of the country store across the road that the state police had destroyed a still on our land only a few days earlier. From the looks on their faces, Phil and I were convinced the still belonged to them. In spite of the obvious danger we returned to the site, and, as I nervously kept vigil, Phil insisted upon immortalizing the now-wrecked still with one of his best watercolors.

I had originally planned on becoming a painter, and it was Phil who suggested that I consider studying graphic design, or commercial art, as it was often called in those days. At that time I was investigating possible universities, and one day Phil brought with him a catalogue for RPI (Richmond Professional Institute), later to

1

2

1
Emmet Gowin
Photograph: Phil Meggs
(1964)

2
Richard Carlyon
Photograph: Kuhn Caldwell
(1964)

become part of Virginia Commonwealth University. We both decided to apply and began classes there in September 1961. There were few teachers who did not influence and deeply inspire us. Of special and lasting importance was a freshman course called Introduction to the Arts taught by a brilliant young painter named Richard Carlyon. He tossed us headfirst into modernism, avant-garde painting, theater, writing, and music and helped to release our ships from their provincial moorings. There were other equally important teachers, such as John Hilton, the chairman of the graphic design department, and the painters Jim Bumgardner and Jewett Campbell. Also, Leon Bellin, a regular illustrator for the "Ribald Classics" in *Playboy* magazine, especially intrigued us.

When I look back on those years I realize that both Phil and I were more or less neophytes enthusiastically absorbing everything placed before us. As we broadened our horizons, it seemed as if we were bursting out of a shell. Still soft at the edges, we were determined to seize everything we thought we had missed in our earlier youth, and for us the world was wide open.

After spending our freshman year in a dormitory on Franklin Street, Phil, Emmet Gowin, Kuhn Caldwell, and I decided to move off campus. We found a second floor apartment at One North Harvie Street, an address that still sounds like the title of a John O'Hara novel. Although unaware of it at the time, I realize now that we were truly blessed as we roared through those days with a confidence that seemed to have no end. I recall returning home to One North Harvie Street as always being a pleasure. Our dinners together during the weekdays were events we all eagerly anticipated. Libby's constant presence at the table always provided a welcome grace and elegance. On some weekends we had lively dinner parties with our teachers as guests.

Phil, Emmet, Kuhn, and I were in many ways similar and in other ways quite different. Yet somehow we seemed to have had one of the happiest and closest households of my memory. We fed one another's spirits and creativity like four blazing logs in a winter fireplace, as each day brought with it a harvest of discovery.

To me, Emmet seemed to be the most intense and spiritual of our group. Quite early it was obvious that photography would be his true medium. It was through him that we were introduced to the work of Walker Evans, who later became my teacher at Yale and also my close friend. Kuhn was the most naturally gifted: it all seemed to come so easy to him. While Phil, Emmet, and I would at times agonize over an assignment, Kuhn would have already completed it and be out on the town. His talent always amazed us. With a brush of the hand he would do what for us would take days. Kuhn was an ex-marine, about six years older than we, and far more a man of the world.

One of my important contributions to the One North Harvie Street household was a wire-haired terrier called Alex Thompson, a name that I borrowed from a dog in a John Steinbeck novel. Alex could be the source of endless anecdotes, but in this memoir I will narrow them down to a few. Phil delighted in swinging Alex around in a circle with the dog's teeth clenched on a sock tied on the end of a rope. During one of these sessions several of Alex's teeth suddenly appeared scattered on the floor. Unaware they were baby teeth, we were furious with poor Phil, thinking that the dog's chewing days were forever over.

Another memorable Alex Thompson incident occurred during one of our weekday dinners. Our dining room table was placed between windows overlooking the street and the back of a sofa where Alex would invariably be perched impatiently contemplating the food. One evening when we were having fried chicken the display became too much for him to bear. In one flying leap he landed in the middle of the table, snatched a drumstick and rapidly retreated under the couch. There he knew he was safe, for when we moved the couch he would simply shift his position along with it. Phil was not at all amused, since his plate was the one that Alex had successfully targeted.

At the university and afterward Phil was always an intellectual stimulus, and his probing mind motivated all of his friends. An erudite scholar from the beginning, he was brimming with curiosity and approached each new subject with an intense energy. He always wanted to know what lay on the other side of the hill. How well I remember those times when he would stride (he was usually striding) into my room with some new discovery or, being an omnivorous reader, a new book, saying, "What do you think of this?" This would usually result in a vigorous exchange of ideas that would sometimes evolve into a debate. Phil always seemed to instinctively know "where the center lay," a trait that so many have to learn.

We were all equally inspired by painting as by graphic design and would regularly drive to nearby Washington to visit museums. Our favorite was the Phillips Collection; where we digested paintings by artists such as van Gogh, Monet, Degas, El Greco, and Cézanne. Phil and I especially enjoyed sitting on the bench in the Rothko room where the paintings seemed to actually breathe. We also managed a few trips to New York when we could afford them, and wandered through the Metropolitan, Frick, Guggenheim, and Whitney museums with the open eyes of children in gardens of discovery and returned to Richmond laden with books, catalogues, and fresh ideas.

Like most of my anecdotes, this one does not concern graphic design, but it is one that I know Phil would not want me to omit. In fact, when he gave talks in Boston, he would often use it as an introduction when I was in the audience. The incident took place during a late-afternoon outdoor end-of-the-year party at a spot along the James River west of Richmond. I, having perhaps too heavily imbibed, proceeded to the top of a knoll and lay down in the grass to enjoy the river view. Unfortunately, I surprised a copperhead snake, which bit me in the jaw. Walking back down to the party, I announced my plight to the group and then collapsed. Phil and Kuhn quickly placed me in the car drove me to a hospital where I remained for five days. Phil was always amused at my mother's nonchalant reaction when he called to tell her that I had been bitten in the head by a snake at a party. "Well, this time he's really done it," she replied. For his efforts in helping to get me to the hospital I always credited Phil with saving my life. However, he remained convinced that I was only scratched by a briar, and the case is still open.

During my university years graphic design history simply did not exist as an academic field. Names such as Paul Rand, Herbert Matter, and Josef Müller-Brockmann meant very little to us. When I entered the graduate graphic design program at Yale University in the fall of 1966, I had many of these eminent designers as teachers but heard their names for the first time. Phil changed all of this for future generations, and graphic design studies have never been quite the same since. Of course, there had been many excellent earlier writers who had made brilliant contributions to graphic design history, but Phil transformed the subject into an actual academic discipline. Steven Heller aptly wrote after Phil's death: "Indeed, how many educators have used 'the book' as required reading? How many students have read the names Lissitzky,

Cassandre, and Rand for the very first time in Meggs' narratives? How many design scholars have cited Meggs in their own research? And at how many conferences did Meggs bring insight to all of us hungry for knowledge? Phil laid more than groundwork; he built a monument to graphic design's legacy."

Phil's and Libby's last visit to Boston was when Phil was awarded an honorary degree from the Massachusetts College of Art. On the Saturday before their return to Richmond, my wife Susan and I took them to meet our friend Bernice Jackson, the poster collector and dealer in Concord. It was a memorable afternoon as we saw many treasures that until then we had known only through reproductions. I remember that one of Phil's more minor purchases on that day was an excellent facsimile of El Lissitzky's 1929 poster, *USSR Russische Ausstellung.* Chuckling, Phil said he would hang it on the wall at his office in Richmond to see what visitors would say, thinking it was an original. We departed that evening with rolls of posters under our arms and plans for future visits with Bernice, who wanted to supply images for future editions of *A History of Graphic Design.* This was the last time I saw Bernice, for the next morning she was found dead at her breakfast table. It was also the last time that I saw Phil.

In the summer of 2003 I was contacted by Amanda Miller, vice president of John Wiley & Sons, and Margaret Cummins, senior editor. (Amanda had been the editor of my first book, *Dutch Graphic Design, 1918–1945* when she was working at Van Nostrand Reinhold.) To my surprise I was asked to consider revising *A History of Graphic Design* for the fourth edition. I was greatly honored to have been offered this task, one that I had neither sought nor even remotely anticipated. Soon afterward Amanda and Margaret came to Boston to discuss the project, and, in spite of what I considered to be a daunting deadline, I accepted the assignment with much enthusiasm. For Phil, *A History of Graphic Design* had been the result of thirty years of research and revision, and to have his most important book entrusted to me by both Libby and his publisher was an honor that I could never adequately express.

Phil often told me that each new edition of *A History of Graphic Design* was a special pleasure, as it gave him the opportunity to revise, improve, and expand previous ones. Long before I ever imagined that I would be entrusted with future revisions, we often discussed what should be included and what should not. Once, when I made a remark about a designer whom I thought should not be included, Phil replied, "With a book such as this, one cannot include only those designers whom one likes, either for aesthetic or personal reasons." How well I understand this today. Phil also said that the final chapter was the most difficult for several reasons. First, many designers felt they should be in the book, and rightfully so, but of course this

Alston Purvis
Photograph: Kuhn Caldwell (1964)

Alston Purvis and Phil Meggs, Boston (1997)

would not be possible. In addition, living in the midst of the period about which one is writing makes it difficult to reflect upon the subject.

Phil was not only a friend but a mentor as well. He always urged me to write, not only about graphic design history but also about any other topics that I considered to be of importance. I regret that he never saw the publication of my father's biography, *The Vendetta.* Always intrigued by the story, he was constantly pushing me to get it completed. Whenever I would say to him that I could find neither the time nor the courage to write it, Phil would reply by saying, "Alston, this is something you have to do. Enough said." Phil's encouragement acted as a catalyst in bringing the book to fruition.

Phil had an elegant gift for friendship, an incisive perception for where our wounds and triumphs really lay, a wonderful laugh if the problem was on the amusing side, and warm consoling words if it stemmed from a darker aspect. True friends live on in memory. Phil's photograph sits on a shelf above my desk at home where I usually write. I often imagine that I hear his voice. "Alston, come on, you can do better than that," or "Hey, that's great," or "Keep at it." He enriched my life more than I can express. Devoid of any affectation, he was a man of true modesty, patience, gentleness, and loyalty. His unquenchable curiosity, solid integrity, and commitment to excellence will forever be a source of inspiration. ••

The first time I laid eyes on *A History of Graphic Design* by Philip B. Meggs I was browsing a display table in Doubleday's on Fifth Avenue in New York. It was 1983. I was art director of the *New York Times Book Review,* where I routinely received books before their official publication dates, yet had no clue this one had even been planned. Where was the publisher who should have been promoting the book? Assuming the *Book Review* would never cover this, Van Nostrand Reinhold didn't even bother sending a review copy. Needless to say I was stunned – it was the first time I saw the words *history* and *graphic design* together on a book jacket – and as I flipped through the black-and-white pages crammed with reproductions of vintage posters and typography, I thought, This Meggs person has *made* history by recording a virtually unknown history. Although I hadn't yet read a word, I impulsively believed this was probably the most important design book ever published.

A few days later I lobbied my editor to assign a review, aware it was a long shot. "Okay," he abruptly said, "but you do it." I was nonplussed. Professional books are rarely reviewed, and graphic design was never considered a priority. Unconvinced by his quick – though admittedly disinterested – approval, I further stammered about how this book transcended the subject by positioning graphic design as cultural history and hurriedly returned to my desk to start writing the review. Although only a couple of hundred words, it was my first book review for the newspaper. But had I known Meggs I would have been disqualified – those are the rules. Fortunately, I had never even heard of him, in part because before reading *A History of Graphic Design* my primary historical interest was in illustration and satiric art (on which I had written quite a bit). By the time Meggs' book came out I was slowly turning my gaze toward graphic design.

I reviewed it favorably, of course, which I presume helped its recognition quotient (though I had doubts many designers read the *Book Review).* But more importantly, after it was published, Meggs and I met, became friends and colleagues. I don't mean to suggest that writing reviews is like placing personal ads in the *New York Review of Books,* but often a grateful reviewee wants to meet (to at least thank) his sympathetic reviewer. I was more than merely sympathetic: Meggs' work inspired me to expand my own research, and he encouraged me to find different ways to explore design history on my own terms. Other graphic design historians subsequently found their own respective niches and, while still in its adolescence, there are currently numerous ways to tell the stories of graphic design apart from Meggs' omnibus-like methodology.

Nonetheless, all roads lead back to Meggs' pioneering book, writings, and lectures. Without them graphic design history would not have been born – surely there would not have been as many college level design history classes, symposia, and books. For that matter, many educators have used what will be called "the book" as required reading and students have read the names Lissitzky, Cassandre, and Rand for the very first time in Meggs' narrative. Meggs laid more than groundwork; he built a monument to graphic design's legacy. He actually became an inextricable part of that legacy, and when he died on November 24, 2002, after a long battle with leukemia, I once again had the opportunity to write about his accomplishments in the *New York Times* – this time as an obituary.

Philip B. Meggs was born May 30, 1942, in Newberry, South Carolina, then moved to Florence, South Carolina, that same year. He attended Virginia Commonwealth University where in 1964 he received a BFA; in 1971 he earned his MFA. He began his career as a designer specializing in corporate identity and promotion working for Reynolds Aluminum and later became art director of A.H. Robins Pharmaceuticals before starting his teaching career in 1968 at VCU. He married his college girlfriend Libby Phillips Meggs and had two children, who are now grown. From 1974 until 1987 he was chair of VCU's Department of Communication Arts and Design and afterward continued teaching there until illness in 2000 forced him to take a year off in order to fight his first bout with leukemia, which he won. Meggs was a consummate teacher who made an indelible impression on his students (indeed, three of my graduate students who studied with him are quick to praise), not only through his mastery of history, but during the basic design and typography classes that he taught three to four times a week for over three decades.

The first educator to create a graphic design history curriculum that did not depend entirely on anecdotal experience and recollection, Meggs systematically culled through art and design texts to develop an original syllabus. His narrative traced the linear progression of a field that originated with movable type and was endemic to media, culture, and commerce through various eras and epochs. Massimo Vignelli often lamented that graphic design could not be a serious profession without acute criticism. Without historical research, criticism would be impossible. Meggs knew this and set out to create vocabularies and methods that both borrowed from other historical disciplines but were unique as well.

Meggs was, however, modest to a fault. He did not always accept credit for what was due him. "The belief that design history and criticism are new areas of inquiry is not correct," he once told me. "Design criticism and history have been around since the early 1500s; each era documents what is important and/or controversial. People are repelled by the shock of the new; much of my design history is simply recording what appalled the establishment, from Baskerville to the Bauhaus."

Meggs was not trained as a historian but nonetheless realized the need and accepted the responsibility to make history come alive. Art historians were repelled by the commercial arts unless affixed with twentieth-century avant-garde or modernist pedigree, so the field was wide open. At the outset of this ad hoc pursuit, he was not interested in spreading the gospel to other art and cultural disciplines but rather in exposing graphic designers to their ignored legacies. He rightly believed that a graphic design student's capacity to practice quotidian graphic design, no less transcending mere commercial service, was limited by an enforced ignorance of historical context. So he found a cure: "My goal, as a design educator teaching design history beginning in the early 1970s, was to construct the legacy of contemporary designers working in the United States," he told me in an interview we did a few years before his illness. "I believed this could help designers understand their work, comprehend how and where the semantic and syntactic vocabulary of graphic design developed, and aid our field in its struggle for professional status. Design education is advanced when young designers learn what is possible by understanding the philosophy and concepts that shaped graphic design."

Based on an undergraduate academic curriculum that began before the invention of the printing press and movable type, he took students on a journey through the twentieth-century modern era, with its revolutionary approach to typography and picture making, concluding with the computer's influence on contemporary methods and styles. His classes addressed formal, theoretical and aesthetic issues through a critical lens that had largely been ignored in most studio design classes. Because of the initial success of these courses during the late seventies, Meggs received a grant from the National Endowment for the Arts for an unprecedented series of lectures — a kind of movable feast of slides and discussion — offered free to any college or university that requested his appearance. Yet being an itinerant design historian necessitated developing standardized syllabi that later became the core of *A History of Graphic Design,* which for many years (until the 1994 publication of *Graphic Design: A Concise History* by Richard Hollis) was the only English-language textbook of its kind and is still required reading in courses throughout the country. (In 2006 a posthumous fourth edition, edited by Meggs' friend Alston Purvis, was published.)

Meggs had a profound effect on students and even veteran practitioners. "He was the first person I ever heard talk about design history in a way that seamlessly, warmly, and elegantly connected past and present," said Paula Scher. "He made me feel like I was part of a movement of my time, not an irrelevant practitioner grinding out trivial works for yet another bureaucratic corporation." Indeed his article in *Print,* "The Women Who Saved New York" about Scher, Louise Fili, Lorraine Louie, and Karin Goldberg, each of whom worked at the time in a "retro" typographic language (Meggs actually coined the term), was a story about how contemporary designers redefined past styles to underscore the zeitgeist. In this way Meggs brought history alive by routinely connecting it to current practice. Meggs' original quest for forgotten pioneers, movements, and styles, as manifested in his series of essays in *Print* magazine on the progressive book design and profiles of contemporary practitioners, is one of the key foundations for broader scholarship.

I admit we had a friendly competition to see who would uncover the most forgotten designers and obscure archives. We would often talk about who should carve out what territory (or take over the world) so as not to duplicate each other's work. But I always felt he was somewhat more methodical than I, perhaps because from childhood he was continuously challenged by his family (and especially his twin brother Bill, a scientist) to back himself up with facts. He followed a rigorous method of discovery and analysis, and at conferences we both attended I watched as he routinely took copious notes. Given his rational, almost scientific mind, he took pride in developing theories of design that he then arduously attempted to prove through uncovered documents and artifacts that others might think were junk.

He refused to accept anything at face value. "I found that an abundance of material existed; but it was in piecemeal form," he said about the research process. "Printing magazines and books from the early nineteenth through the early twentieth century stashed about in the Library of Congress always included design issues, and even reproduced and reported on work dating from the Incunabula and Renaissance. Unfortunately, there is a lot of contradictory and inaccurate data around, so I always try to corroborate information from at least two sources. It's so embarrassing when you learn that you depended on an unreliable source."

With post-modernism and deconstruction on the rise at hothouse academies like Cranbrook and Cal Arts, Meggs' Eurocentric and male-dominated history met with mounting criticism. Within certain academic quarters "the book" was considered limited by its acceptance (or codification) of a canon. Yet *A History of Graphic Design* was an expanding life form, which is why Meggs insisted on calling it *A History.* He often said the subtitle was acknowledgement that the book "was not the encyclopedia of graphic design but a concise overview for contemporary designers and design students." Each of the three editions (translated into Spanish, Korean, Japanese, Hebrew, and Chinese) he worked on was more inclusive than the preceding — a testament to his tireless investigation. Meggs also prefigured the wiki, as part of his process. When people suggested designers and works they thought should be added, he asked them to write a concise paragraph justifying their significance. Some of this "citizen history" wound up in his revisions.

In 2001 the New York Art Director's Club recognized Meggs' achievements with its Hall of Fame Special Educators Award. He was to receive it in fall of that year, after he went into remission from an earlier bout of the disease. However, the attack on the World Trade Center forced a year-long postponement of the proceedings. Although he was planning

(continued on page 48)

A History of Graphic Design
First Edition (1983)

A History of Graphic Design, First Edition: the first definitive text on the history of graphic design

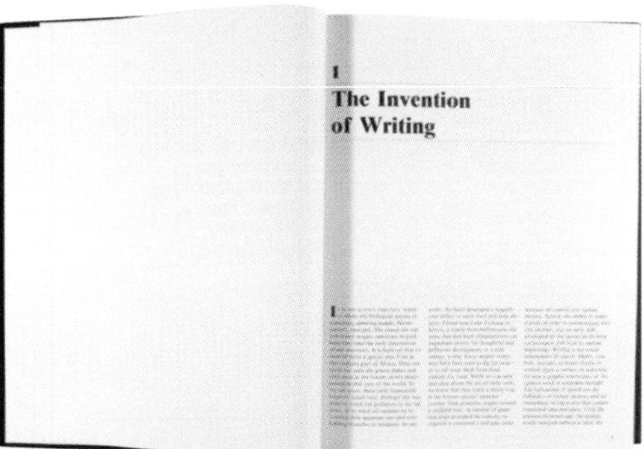

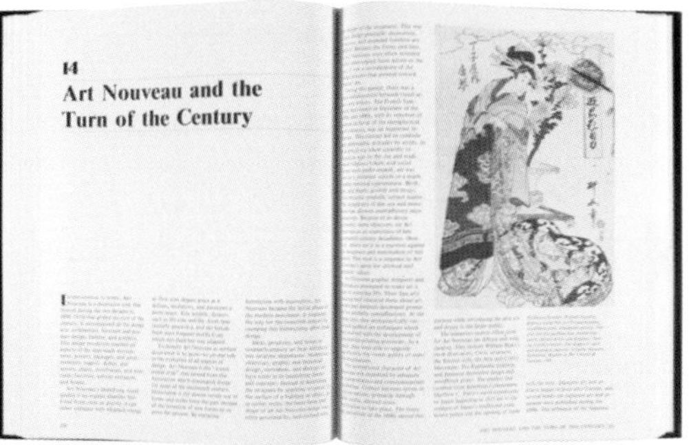

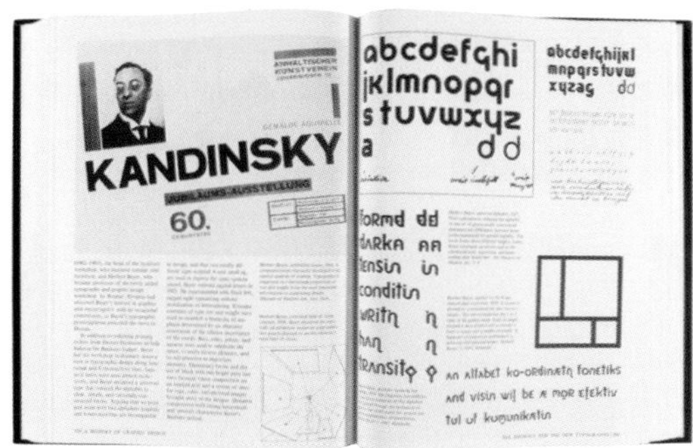

MEGGS

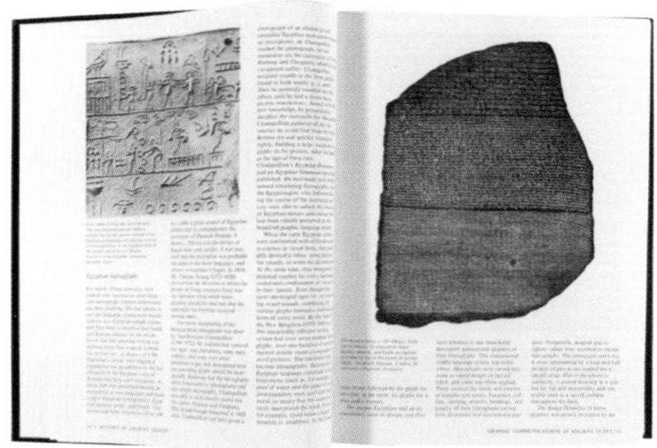

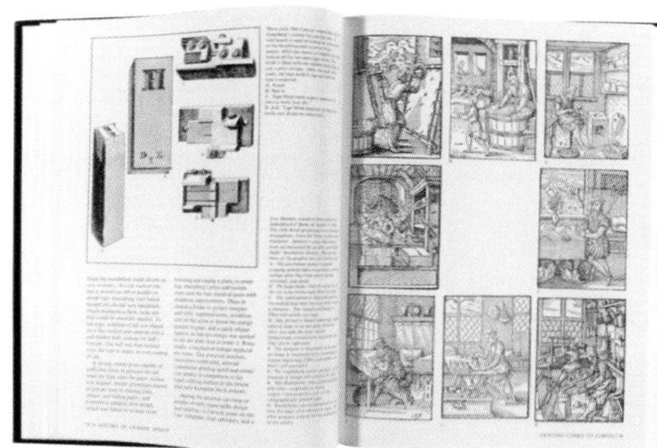

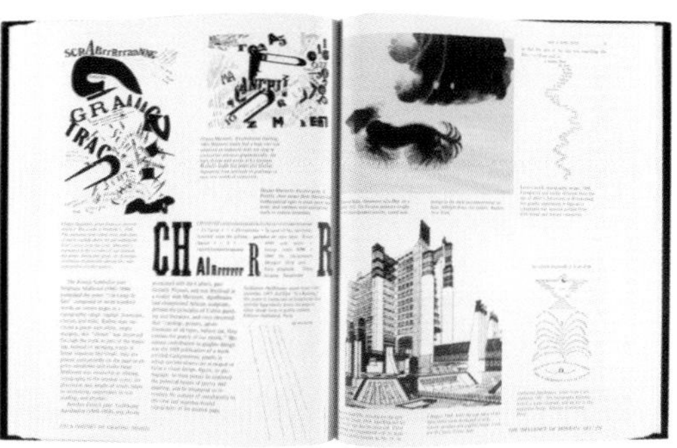

HERAUS!
Deutsche Luftkriegsbeute
KRIEGSANLEIHE
BRITONS
YOU

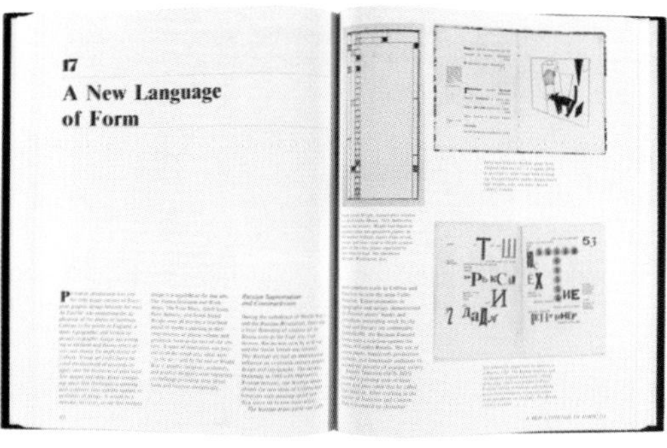
17
A New Language
of Form

Helvetica
Helvetica Italic
Helvetica Medium
Helvetica Bold
Helvetica Bold Condensed

ionesco
LA CANTATRICE CHAUVE

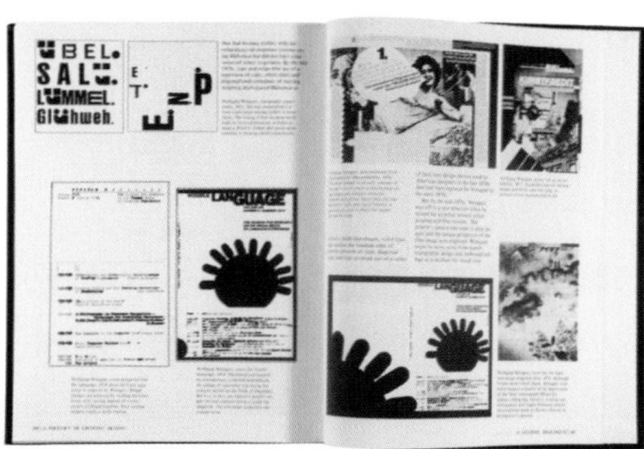

A History of Graphic Design
Second Edition (1992)

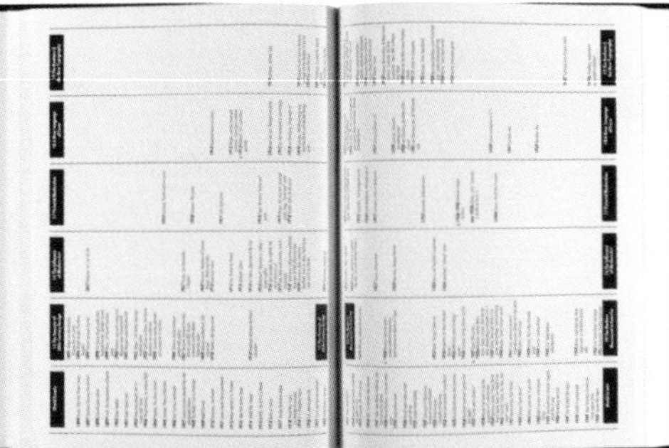

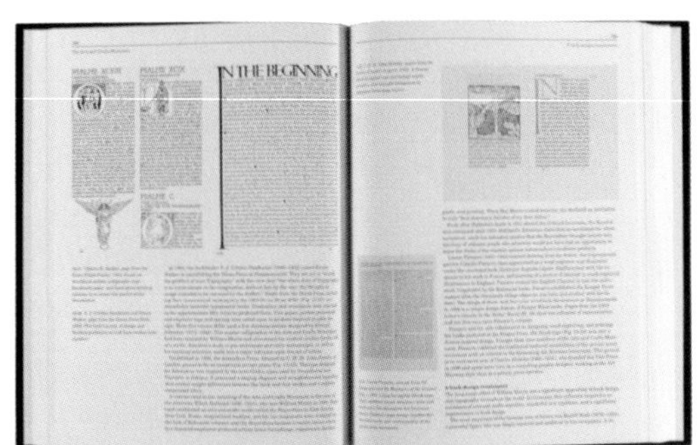

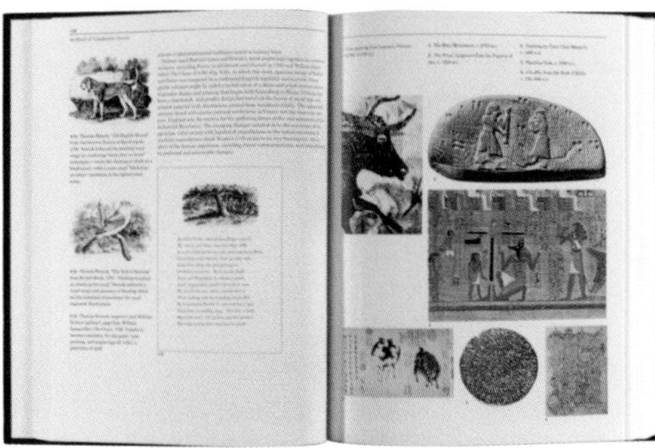

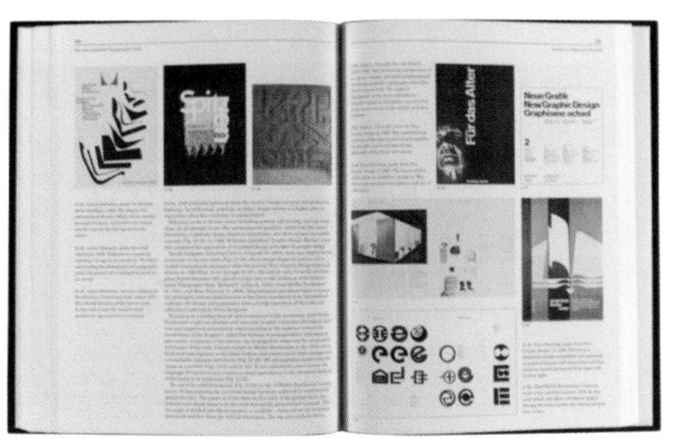

MEGGS

A History of Graphic Design
Third Edition (1998)

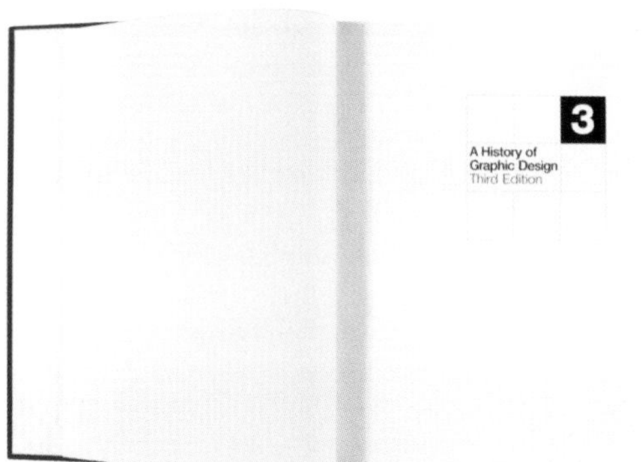

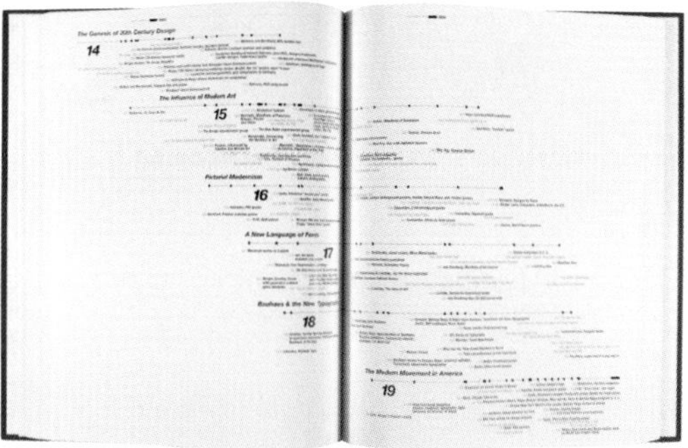

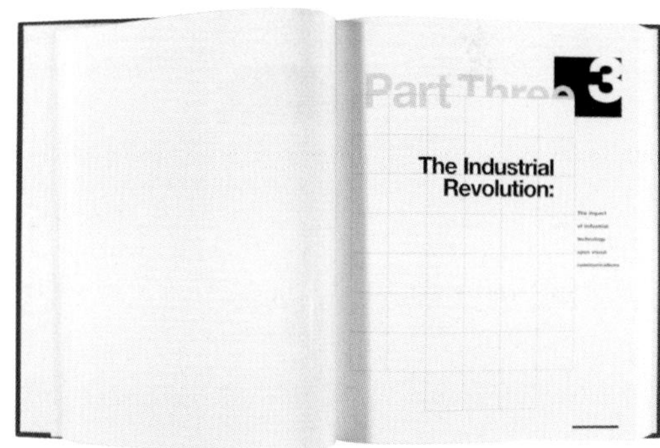

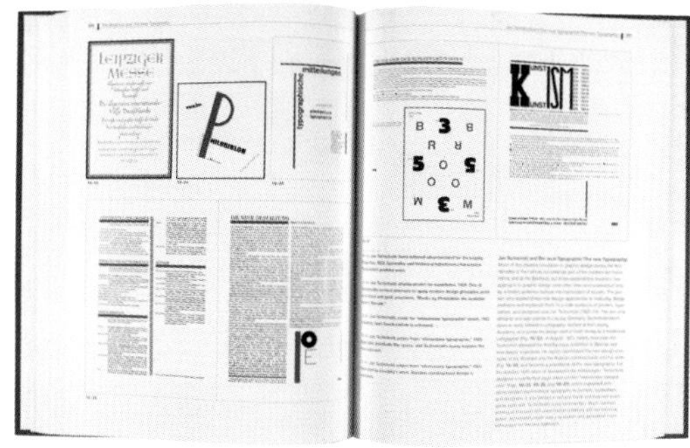

to attend the fall 2002 induction ceremony, the week before he learned the leukemia had returned and chemo would commence on the night of event. He never made it to New York. In 2003, after his passing, I naively thought *A History of Graphic Design* would simply be frozen in a suspended state, like the mythical history museum in H.G. Wells' *Time Machine,* which chronicled the world's accomplishments to the point at which the world ended owing to nuclear war. I didn't count on the genius of "the book" being its solid foundation on which a limitless number stories can be added.

Phil Meggs: Fond Personal Memories and Warm Professional Recollections

R. Roger Remington

In the 1980s two events launched an awareness of the importance of the history of graphic design. The first was the arrival of Phil Meggs' *A History of Graphic Design* at bookstores; the second was the symposium on graphic design history at Rochester Institute of Technology. Phil Meggs was a central player in both historic events. This essay will detail both in the context of my friendship with Phil Meggs.

New York and Fashion Institute of Technology were the locations for my first meeting with Phil Meggs. We were both participating in a utopian mission of establishing a national graphic design organization for educators, which ultimately became the Graphic Design Education Association. It was an important meeting for me because, like Phil, I had realized the importance of the history of graphic design as a central component to any professional education program in design. Around the edges of what I remember as long, wheel-spinning meetings of academics, Phil and I managed to share a few minutes of the common aspects of our design history research. I recall how happy Phil was to share his knowledge and how inspirational it was for me because Phil was already well into research and writing on his seminal work, *A History of Graphic Design.* These meetings continued over several years and along the way my friendship with Phil deepened and my knowledge of graphic design history became richer.

I recall how, over the years, I would eagerly await the arrival of *Print* magazine to read his latest article. Likewise, his regular contributions to the newsletter of the American Institute of Graphic Arts were inspirational. His research and writing style created a template upon which I would eventually publish.

By the early 1980s, design history was in the air among design educators as RIT colleague Dr. Barbara Hodik and I planned and delivered a national symposium on the history of graphic design. We called it, Coming of Age: The First Symposium on the History of Graphic Design, and it took place April 20–21, 1983, at RIT, amidst the final blast of that winter's snow in Rochester, New York. Looking back, it was a historic event in itself. I am still amazed how we were able to gather together just about everyone who was involved in design history at the time.

Massimo Vignelli gave the keynote address challenging participants to focus on history, theory, and criticism if indeed graphic design were to become a true profession. Of course, Phil Meggs was asked to participate. He gave an inspiring and very detailed talk, "El Lissitzky and the Visually Programmed Format." In his own unique manner, he clearly and systematically discussed Lissitzky's contribution, namely the concept of a visual program (to bring order, unity and clarity to complex graphic design problems) through an analysis of the books *For the Voice and Die Kunstismen.*

Additional educators, including Victor Margolin, Jack Williamson, and Sheila Levrant de Bretteville were present. Designers Rudolph de Harak, Keith Godard, Bill Bonnell, Lou Danziger, and others came to participate as well. Major historic figures from the field, such as Walter Allner, Elaine Lustig Cohen, and Morton Goldsholl dispensed their wisdom. Arthur A. Cohen gave a moving address about Herbert Bayer, followed by taped words of welcome to conferees from Bayer himself, followed by a showing of the beautiful "A Tribute to Herbert Bayer" multimedia program.

At the opening reception in the Bevier Gallery, while surrounded by a number of old friends, Phil proudly rushed up to me with a copy of *A History of Graphic Design* in his hand. It was hot off the press. He was showing it to everyone – it was such a perfect setting for the new book to be seen. Because of his manner of presentation, I thought he was making a gift of this first edition. It was awkward when he pulled it back, apologizing that it was his only copy. We all laughed together at the time and for many years to come, as we would recall the symposium and the appropriateness of the book becoming available concurrently with this historic conference.

Ten years in the making, Phil's first book, *A History of Graphic Design,* is his magnum opus. It is, without question, the definitive history of the field of graphic design and, as such, is the most required book for designers, teachers, and students. I consistently recommend it highly to my history students and enjoy warm feelings and memories of Phil as I do each year. In the past I kept a list in the inside cover of my copy. These were items, from my research, that Phil did not somehow include in the book. Then periodically as I would meet Phil, I would give him the list and we would have a jovial talk. After Phil completed work on the first edition of the book, he asked me if I would like to receive his research materials on Lester Beall for RIT's Graphic Design Archive. This attests to his instinctive generosity.

A History of Graphic Design first became available in 1983. Published originally by Van Nostrand Reinhold, it was a 500 page hardcover text with 1,200 illustrations and a dust jacket design by the author. Through detailed and well-researched text and profuse illustrations, it chronologically presented the history of graphic design. Its chapters include "The Prologue to Graphic Design," "A Graphic Renaissance," "The Industrial Revolution," "The Modernist Era," and "The Age of Information." The text is supplemented with a detailed bibliography (which attests to Phil's commitment to detail and accuracy) and index. Subsequent editions contained useful contextual timelines. In the foreword, the author wrote, "This chronicle of graphic design is written in the belief that if we understand the past, we will be better able to continue a cultural legacy of beautiful form and effective communication. If we ignore this legacy, we run the risk of becoming buried in the mindless morass of a commercialism whose molelike vision ignores human values and needs as it burrows forward into darkness."

The first edition was received with wide acclaim. It was critically praised by professional organizations such as the Society of Typographic Arts as "tracing the role of the designer as a messenger of culture." *Design Issues* journal praised the book "as establishing graphic design as a profession. Bravo!" *Print* magazine wrote "Now. . . a hefty, yet concise documentation of the entire field exists." *Communication Arts* magazine characterized the book as a "fortress work."

One of Phil's students wrote, "I was one of Philip Meggs' students at Virginia Commonwealth University in Richmond, Virginia. Our class was the first to use the first edition of this book as a classroom textbook for his History of Graphic Design class. He was a wonderful storyteller, with a true passion for graphic design. And more than that was the obvious joy he had in sharing that knowledge and those whimsical anecdotes in his own style of humor. Philip Meggs was an exceptional man who will truly be missed."

My own view of the value of this book mirrors those above. Design scholars have said that not until graphic design has a documented history can the field begin to be viewed as a profession. This book realizes that important goal. Its major benefit, of course, is to design education. *A History of Graphic Design* allowed design history courses to be added to curricula in many schools. Furthermore, it has brought attention to the formal study of design history, which has resulted in better scholars and teachers specializing in design studies work. The book is now available in its fourth edition.

Phil's close friend Alston Purvis, a design professor at Boston University, picked up the torch and produced the latest edition that is published now by John Wiley & Sons, under the title *Meggs' History of Graphic Design.* Images and complementary materials from the book are now also available online for teachers. Although expanded and updated, Phil's heart and soul are in the book, and it remains his masterwork.

Phil was a prolific researcher and writer. Over the years he produced a number of books by himself and with colleagues, including *Type & Image: The Language of Graphic Design* (1989), *Typographic Specimens: The Great Typefaces* with Rob Carter (1993), *Fotografiks: An Equilibrium Between Photography and Design through Graphic Expression That Evolves from Content* with David Carson (1999), and *Typographic Design: Form and Communication* with Rob Carter and Ben Day (1985). This book is currently in its fourth edition. All of these books add tremendous information to the resources available for students, teachers, and design professionals.

In 1997 I was invited to Virginia Commonwealth University and do a visitation, critique, and guest lecture. Being in residence at this fine school for several days and spending time with the outstanding faculty and students was wonderful. Phil asked me to do a talk on design history, and I remember how pleased he was that I decided to concentrate on the topic of the German typographers of the Ring Neuer Werbegestalter group (Tschichold, Dexel, Schwitters, et al.). The highlight of the trip was the final day when I was able to meet the Meggs family. Phil, Libby, and their children were very gracious to me as we all enjoyed a brunch together just before my return flight. This was the last face-to-face meeting I had with Phil, although we did correspond regularly.

This incident gives us a measure of the man. Ten years or so ago I heard from a colleague in Canada that one of their design historians had left the school suddenly just before classes began in the fall. Phil was contacted and an arrangement was made by which Phil would videotape his lectures at Virginia Commonwealth University and share them with the Canadian school. Later my Canadian colleague informed me about this and gave me copies of several of these lecture tapes. These videos have been a most valued part of my teaching resource library, and every time I show them to a group of students I am reminded of Phil and his impeccable knowledge of his subject matter, as well as his wonderful delivery methods in the classroom.

Upon learning of Phil's illness, I recall speaking to my graphic design history students about his situation. In class we watched one of his video lectures, and the students enthusiastically passed around and signed a get-well card, which I sent to Phil. Later Libby told me how much this had meant to him.

Several years ago I was in New York for the AIGA Medalist Award Gala at which Phil was honored posthumously. I had the wonderful opportunity of being placed at the table with Libby, her son and daughter, and Alston Purvis. It was a truly beautiful evening of celebrating great designers and educators, especially Phil Meggs.

In my research and interviewing work, I usually ask designers how they would like to be remembered. I am wondering how Phil would like to be remembered. I suspect that he would say in his mellifluous voice that he would like to be remembered as a guy who made a contribution to education by chronicling design history based on rigorous research and study.

I have always thought of Phil as a true Southern gentleman. He worked very hard to bridge the world of professional design and education. A consummate scholar in his field and an inspiration to many, he was a very generous and caring colleague. It has been a delight to reach back through the past and revisit my memories of Phil and to be able to share them with new readers.

Philip B. Meggs: A Personal Remembrance

Roy McKelvey

Like many, I first met Phil Meggs through the remarkable series of textbooks for graphic designers that began appearing from what was to me an unfamiliar school somewhere in Virginia named Virginia Commonwealth University. I was just starting my teaching career at my alma mater, Carnegie Mellon University, and these books proved an invaluable resource not only to me, but also to many of our faculty. The bookstore routinely received requests to stock *A History of Graphic Design; Typographic Design: Form and Communication* (which to us became simply, "Carter, Day, Meggs"); *Type & Image: The Language of Graphic Design; and Typographic Specimens: The Great Typefaces.* These served as the standard texts for many of our classes.

In the fall of 1994, I was looking for new opportunities as a teacher and came across a position announcement from Virginia Commonwealth University. I eagerly applied and was fortunate to be hired – and just as fortunate to be assigned an office space next door to Phil. My office-mate, David Colley, was also new to the department, but at a very different point in his career. David had been convinced to join the faculty after retiring from his position at the University of Illinois at Urbana-Champaign. (Coincidentally, I had learned of David and his work from Rob Carter's *American Typography Today.*) Within the first few weeks of our arrival, we came to know the flesh-and-blood Phil Meggs: a teller of fascinating (and usually hilarious) stories about the foibles of the famous and not-so-famous designers that he had studied or personally knew; the former department chair and passionate chronicler of the VCU Communication Arts and Design department, which he led into national prominence from 1974 to 1987; and finally, the generous and amiable man who always looked for the best in people and who always believed that achievement was there for the taking – at least for those who, like Phil, believed in their work and pursued it with humility, perseverance, and a complete lack of cynicism.

A History of Visual Communication class photographed by Phil Meggs while at the podium about to deliver a lecture.

Above all else, Phil loved to take risks. He saw no reason why he, and those he worked with, could not undertake any project, as long as the idea was sound and the work interesting and fruitful. Even though he had authored – and continually revised and improved – the world's seminal book on graphic-design history, he found the time to launch endless new projects and to inspire others to do the same. This book, for which I've been asked to write this tribute, provides a testimony and clear demonstration of Phil's devotion to work and the diversity of his interests. My task, in the short space I have remaining, is to write a little about how Phil influenced and inspired those he worked with and taught.

To state what should be obvious to anyone holding this book, Phil led by example. He passionately believed in what he was doing and I don't believe he ever knew what it meant to be "between projects." If he were not busy revising his history or typography textbooks, he'd be working on his next article for *Print* magazine. If you stopped by his office, he might tell you (after asking you how things were going in your life) that he was just completing a "small book" with Steven Heller called *Texts on Type,* or that he had just finished a collaborative project with David Carson (the book *Fotografiks*).

Rarely did our faculty know everything Phil was up to, for he rarely spoke about his accomplishments. I can recall only one exception: when he announced with obvious pride at a faculty meeting that he had been contacted by the Encyclopaedia Britannica to author its entry on the term *graphic design.*

For Phil, a true academic in spirit, this was just as cool as working with David Carson or Steven Heller.

My personal entrée into the inner workings of Phil Meggs came in fall 1999 when, after just completing a book on web design – a project offered to me due to a recommendation from Rob Carter, another prolific and generous member of the department – Phil stopped at my door one day and asked, "How'd you like to work on a book with me?" After grinning at me silently for a few seconds, Phil explained that he had been offered to lead a project exploring the evolution of various classic typefaces from their metal origins to their modern digital translations. The project stemmed from a recent review he had written for *Print* magazine, that compared several new releases of Caslon with their historical antecedents. The article had generated such favorable reader comments that the editors at *Print* thought a similar analysis could be extended to a range of typefaces and typeface families.

"I told them I'd do it," he said, "but only if I could collaborate with other authors." He then proposed that since he, Ben Day, and I were scheduled to teach in the graduate program the following semester, this could provide an opportunity to complete a significant project with the students. "How many graduate students can cite a book chapter in their resumes?" he wondered aloud. This book, entitled *Revival of the Fittest: Digital Versions of Classic Typefaces,* would hit the bookstores twelve months later.

MFA graduate workshop in design/visual communication taught by Phil Meggs, Ben Day, and Pino Trogu. Top row, left to right: Ben Day, Phil Meggs, Deborah Beardslee, Marty Watkins, Sandra Wheeler, Charles Tyrone, Elizabeth Neal, Christiane von Stillfried, Richard Woollacott; middle row: Gladys Brenner, Pino Trogu, Helene Benedetti, Paris Ashton-Bressler, Banu Berker; foreground: Terry Melton-Douglas. Photograph: Pino Trogu (1990)

During a frenzied semester (and much of the following summer) the students and faculty in VCU's graduate program researched, designed, and produced the material for a 186-page book analyzing the history and formal characteristics of twenty diverse typeface families and well over a hundred different digital revivals. First-year graduate students, under the direction of Ben Day and me, worked out the book design while both the first- and second-year students worked with Phil in the graduate seminar course on researching and writing the chapter manuscripts and selecting figures and design examples. Each student was given the opportunity to design his or her own chapter and the responsibility of obtaining reproduction permissions. During the following fall semester, Phil and I wrote and designed the book introduction and managed the details of the final editing and production phases.

The point of this story relates to those aspects of Phil's character and outlook that I mentioned at the beginning of this essay. Phil saw no reason why he, his colleagues, and the students he loved and respected could not accomplish such a daunting task. It only required a belief in the worth of the project, a willingness to work hard, and the dedication to ensure that the final product met the highest standards of scholarship. I learned halfway through the project that when Phil had agreed to do this book "with other authors," he had not told the publisher of his plan to produce the book within the department – or to trust the research to students.

Later in the project, Marty Fox, the editor-in-chief of *Print,* asked that the book be given a final editing pass by John Berry, who had recently stepped down from his long tenure as editor of ITC's *U&lc* magazine. Phil agreed, but privately felt that he could have accomplished this himself and that the publishers had nothing to fear from the quality of scholarship he had so carefully overseen. Perhaps more importantly, he worried that this would put the book behind schedule, something Phil took very seriously. To be fair, John Berry's comments proved invaluable in correcting a small number of historical errors in the book's content and in suggesting a few key typefaces he felt should not be omitted from the discussion. In spite of this, Phil complained to the end about having to submit his work for external authentication.

When I look back on these times, I am amazed at the courage and faith Phil exhibited in committing us to such an ambitious undertaking. But Phil believed in the power of doing, and his educational philosophy centered on the notion that work offers its own reward. When the students learned of our plans for them at the start of that semester, they felt understandably apprehensive (the second-year students were also working on thesis projects). Within a short time, however, Phil had convinced all of us that this project deserved our best efforts and that it most certainly *could* be done.

When Phil was diagnosed with leukemia less than a year later, he assured us all that beating this disease was also something that *could* be done. When he returned to the department the following year after fighting off the disease, he had demonstrated to us once again that an unyielding faith in oneself, a willingness to work hard and remain dedicated to the task at hand could accomplish miracles. A little over a year after his return, we had our last conversation – in a routine tenure committee meeting. Phil informed me, as chair of the committee, that after we had finished that day's business, he would have to miss our last meeting because his cancer had returned. He assured us as we absorbed the shock of his announcement that he would "beat this thing again," and I truly believed that he would.

Less than a week later, I received a phone call from Phil's wife, Libby, informing me that Phil had passed away. He had died, she explained, because his first struggle with the disease – one he had fought with his usual determination and courage – had damaged his body too extensively. He had died, I decided, not because he gave up or lost his will (Phil would never do that), but because his body could no longer withstand the strain of fighting this last battle, one that he felt so determined to win.

Phil preparing for his History of Visual Communication class with Charlotte.

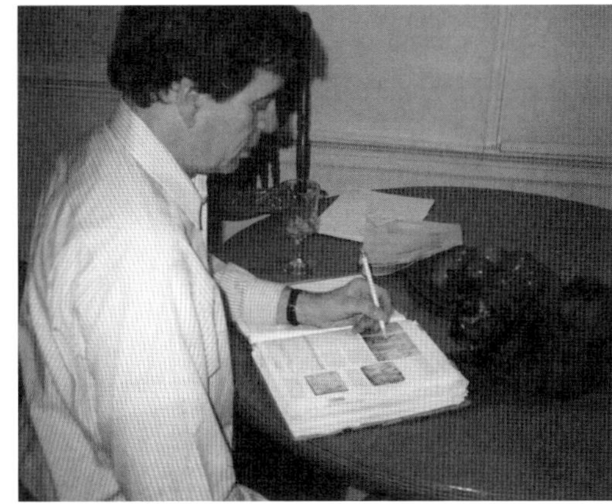

Duct tape holds this roll book together wherein Phil kept a record of his classes for 30 years. 12.37 x 9.75 inches. (1970s–2002)

Typographic Design: Form and Communication
First Edition (1985), Second Edition (1993), Third Edition (2002)

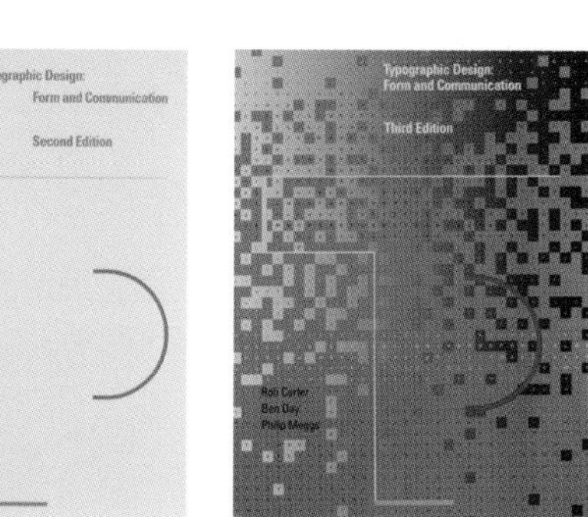

The first edition of *Typographic Design: Form and Communication*, written and designed by Rob Carter, Ben Day, and Philip Meggs.

The second and third editions were updated and designed by Rob Carter and Philip Meggs.

The fourth edition was updated and designed by Rob Carter in 2007.

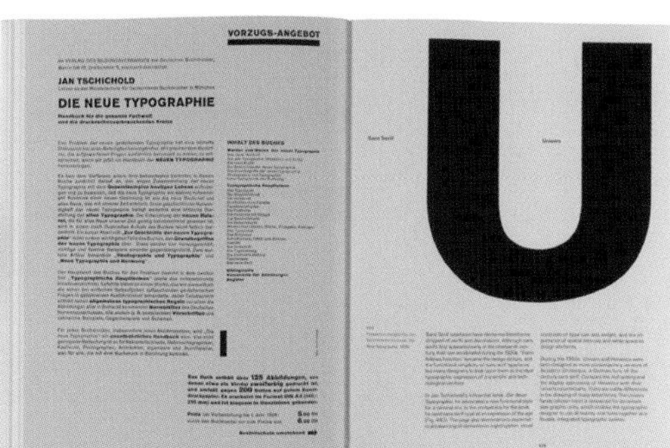

MEGGS

Type & Image (1989)

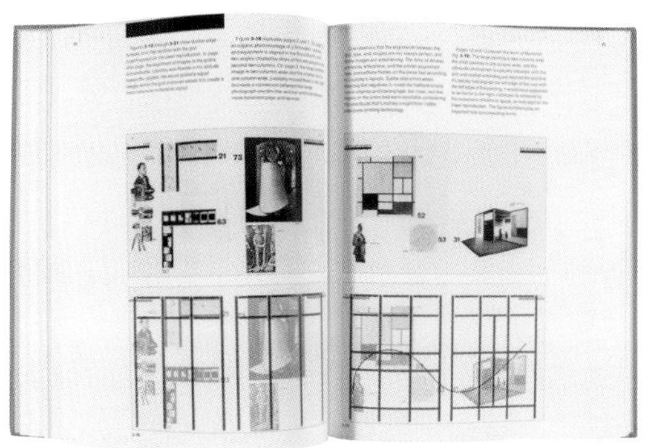

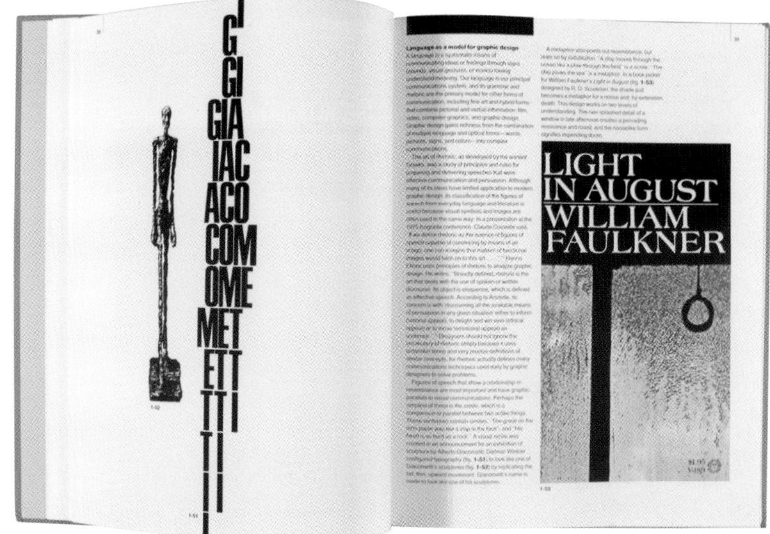

Typographic Specimens: The Great Typefaces (1993)

Typographic Specimens: The Great Typefaces, coauthored and designed by Philip Meggs and Rob Carter.

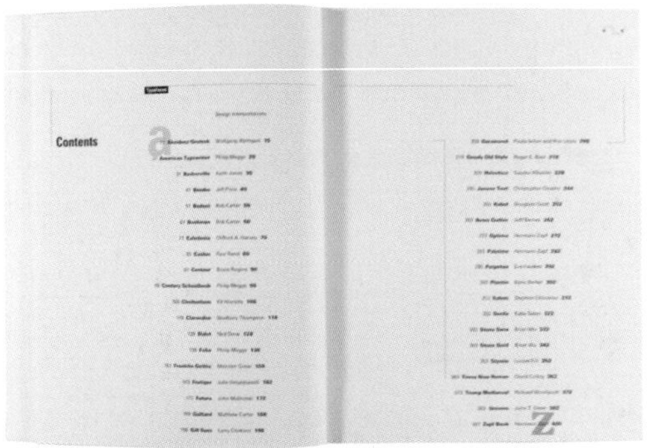

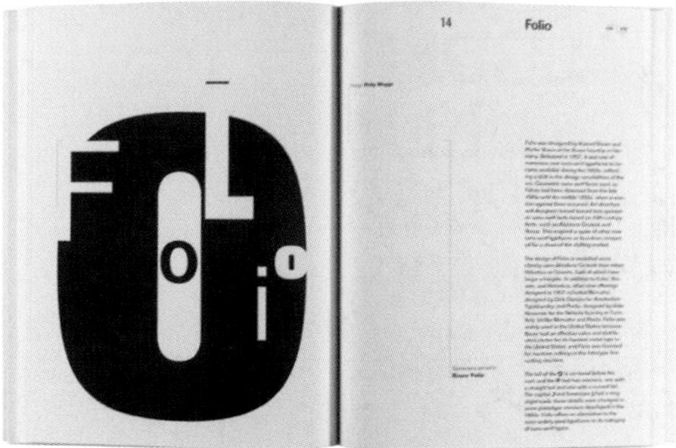

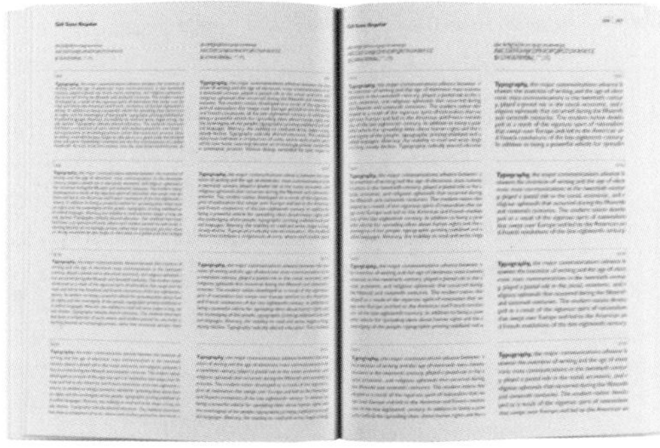

Revival of the Fittest: Digital Versions of Classic Typefaces (2000)

Revival of the Fittest: Digital Versions of Classic Typefaces, coedited by Philip Meggs and Roy McKelvey. Contributing researchers, writers, and designers were MFA graduate students in design/visual communication in the School of the Arts at Virginia Commonwealth University.

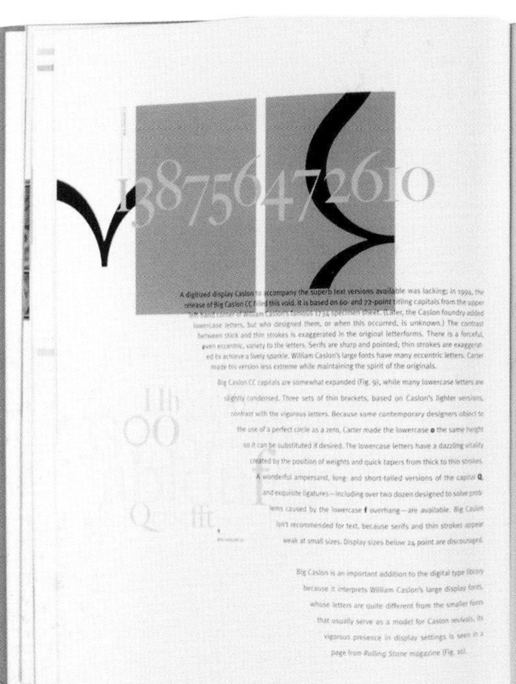

Tomás Gonda: A Life in Design (1993)

This monograph was researched, written, and designed by Philip Meggs.

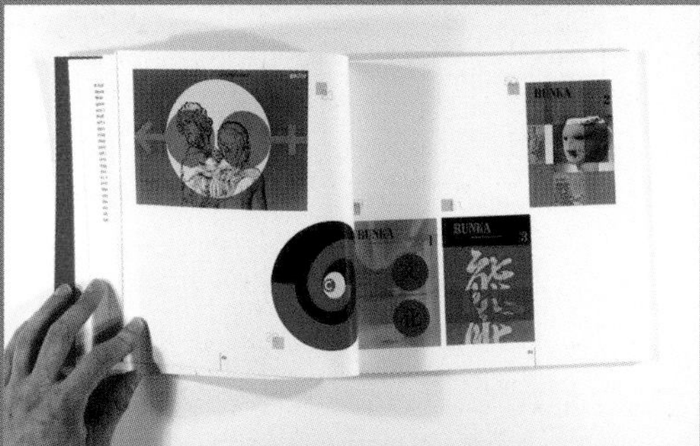

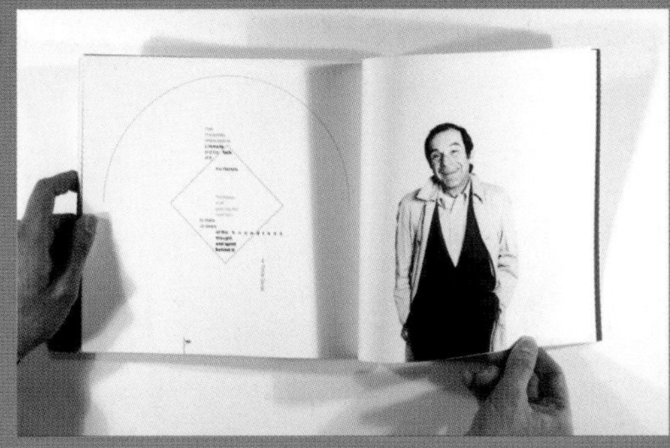

MEGGS

passion for photography respect for good photography. working on SD Women from 1980. thought what freedom for 2 years

304 696-2561

James Miho

NOTES/JAPANESE CONFERENCE
MARSHALL UNIVERSITY

Takenobu Igarashi April 5 7

1970 19 years ago - finish UCLA grad school, start prof. career as graphic designer in Tokyo with ... assistant. add environmental, product, & sculpture.

SAUL BASS on Lou Danziger
2-14-90
have to deal with background & context
design

April 27
Lou Danziger

started work in 1949.
ads for a lighting company
one at Eames House while ...

April 24, 1989

Noel Martin 67 (born in 1922)
George Rosenthal - died 10 yrs ago - partner on Portfolio magazine.
Began working in 1947 in Cincinnati

Interviewed by Philip B Meggs
February 15, 1991 4:20 p.m.
Ralph Ginzburg

I worked together like Siamese twins remarkable & rare relationship

Questions for Paul Rand
Late 1930s began as designer, form language of modernism

1976 age 25 joined Lubalin

Oct, 16, 1987

Cipe Pineles got out of Pratt
few jobs in field

Notes from lecture
October 17, 1987

Lou Danziger
1960s polarization between generations made fundamental changes:
simplicity → complexity
" indolence

Notes from Lecture
October 17, 1987

Steve Heller
60s in East Coast.
NBC–
Underground Press –

Lecture Oct. 18, 1987

MILTON GLASER

my work – vehicle for conveying ideas.
find appropriate form to convey a special idea.

Notes from lecture
October 18, 1987

3 Lorraine Wilde
Art Design + American Modernism

Hopes + Ashes Birth of Mode…

Phone Interview with Warren Lehrer February 1992
Philip B Meggs

I-25

doing a lot of street photography
found that he was more interested
in what people were saying in
conversation than the critical

Federico Interview Oct. 15, 1987

1918 –

1938 saw Cassandre poster 1st year high school

Marshall McLuhan Lecture Notes
(1972)

Marshall McLuhan is one of the most important thinkers of the current era. His ideas have radically altered many persons' attitudes toward the context of contemporary man's involvement in all aspects of society and environment. McLuhan's principal concept is the "the medium is the message." A "medium" is defined as all the things that man has invented to assist in his life – everything that man has invented that goes beyond his nude body and raw mind, which are the only devices that prehistoric man had to deal with his society and the hostile environment.

To clarify the thought "the medium is the message," we look to a few examples. Clothing is a medium that is an extension of man's skin. Skin performs a definite function. It is the outer protection for the body, and it regulates body temperature. When an individual is in a hot environment, the capillaries in the skin carry blood close to the surface to let heat escape from the body. In a cold environment, the blood flows deeper beneath the surface to keep body heat in the body. When early man invented clothes, it changed his life because he had extended his skin and gotten more protection and temperature control than ever before.

All the mediums can be viewed as extensions of the body or the nervous systems. Cars are extensions of the feet. Feet are used to propel the body from place to place. Invent cars (or trains, planes, etc.), and this medium now performs the same function as the feet, but faster and farther. fashion. In a sense, when one gets into a car, he has amputated his feet because they hang limply and unused while the car propels the body at 65 miles per hour compared to a usual walking speed of less than 10 miles per hour. McLuhan studies cars, or anything, not from the standpoint of how they pump the economy, how they work, what status symbols they are, how they're made, how they look, or any of the conventional methods in which man has looked at his accomplishments. Rather, he studies them from the standpoint of how they extend man's capabilities and make basic changes in his life.

McLuhan's greatest importance lies in the area of man's communications mediums, for we live in a communication-oriented society and communications media have profoundly altered our way of thinking and our philosophy of life. To clarify the statement "the medium is the message," let's take the example of television. The content – *Gunsmoke,* talk shows, what have you, is not the most important message on television. Rather, TV itself, and how it has altered our lives, is the important message. But before I get too far into TV I want to back up, take a look at pre-Renaissance man and how the invention of printing changed his life patterns and thinking processes. Then TV can be viewed as it influenced and changed Renaissance man.

Man, before Gutenberg's invention of movable type in 1457, lived in a verbal and auditory world. Few could read or write; therefore, society was communal. The individual saw himself as a member of a larger community, dependent on his fellows for all his information. One's knowledge was what one could commit to memory – songs, poems, bible verses, recipes, medicinal cures. Man felt a real relationship to the natural world and mankind.

The coming of printing exploded this auditory world. Printing and the resultant cheap books (incidentally, printing was the first mass production) allowed knowledge to be disseminated and made an illiterate culture into a literate one in a matter of decades. This ditto device changed man's thinking patterns and his self-image drastically. The auditory man became the visual man. Used to thinking in an overall manner, man now thought in linear, rational sequences. The communal man became the Western individual, the egotist, because his main gathering of knowledge was not from shared experience but the private experience of the individual reading his logical, linear book. Man became less emotional, more rational, and more scientific and orderly in his thought processes. The scientific revolution and the age of reason followed. The coming of printing preceded and informed all the rational creations that have created the technological society in which we live today.

Just as print exploded medieval society, television and other electric media are replacing the machine age (printing) with the electronic age, and are imploding Renaissance society. The TV viewer is worked over very differently than the reader. TV is a cool, or low-definition, medium. The viewer must fill in some of the detail as opposed to printing, where all the detail is clear, precise, and open to scrutiny. TV attacks and massages the nervous system both through sight and sound, so an overall involvement takes place. TV is returning man to his tribal origins and is making the world a global village.

Original manuscript pages
from Marshall McLuhan
lecture notes (April 11, 1972)

Marshall McLuhan
LECTURE NOTES
April 11, 1972

Marshall McLuhan is one of the most umportant thinkers of the current era. His ideas have radically altered many persons attitudes toward the context of contemporary man's involvement in all aspects of society and environment. McLuhan's principal concept is that"the medium is the message."A"Medium" is defined as all the things that man has invented to assist in his life--everything that man has invented that goes beyond his nude body and raw mind, which are the only devices that prehistoric man had to deal with his society and the hostile environment.

To clarify the thought "the medium is the message", we look to a few examples. Clothing is a medium that is an extension of man's skin. Skin performs a definate function. It is the outer protection for the body, and it regulates body temperature. When an individual is in a hot environment, the capillaries in the skin carry blood close to the surface to let heat escape from the body. In a cold environment, the blood flows deeper beneath the surface to keep body heat in the body. When early man invented clothes, it changed his life because he had extended his skin and gotten more protection and temperature control than ever before.

All the mediums can be viewed as extensions of the body or the nervious systems. Cars are extensions of the feet. Feet are used to propell the body from place to place. Invent cars (or trains, planes, etc.), and this medium now performs the same function of the feet, but on a faster, more distant fashion. In a sense, when one gets into a car, he has amputated his

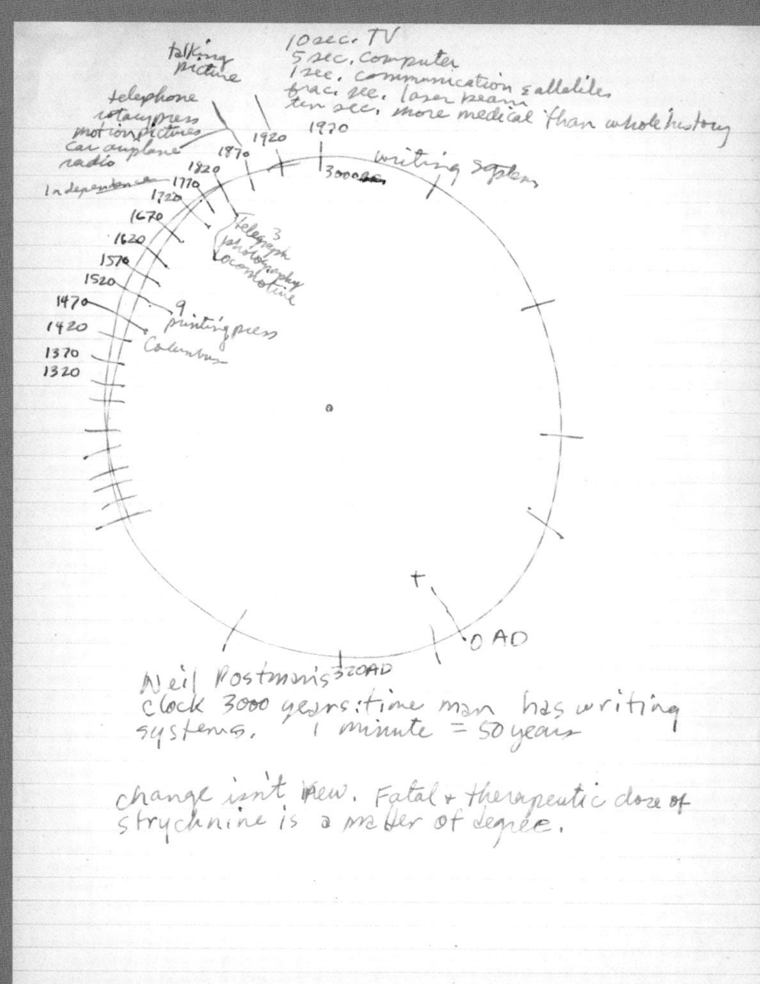

The TV-oriented person feels a communal relationship to other people – he watches individuals being killed in Vietnam and becomes committed to ending this conflict. The print-oriented individual of World War I read sequences of data – casualties, advance and retreats, and took in the logical, uninvolved communication of data very calmly.

McLuhan describes media as being either hot or cool. A hot medium is off high definition, focuses on one sense, and holds the attention of that sense: print, telephone, etc. A cool medium is off a low definition; the observer has to fill in the details, and frequently approaches more than one sense. Hot media promote concise, logical thinking, concentration, and rational, sequential thought. Cool media promote fantasy and all-pervasive involvement.

Media have changed society in many unexpected ways. The so-called sexual revolution, which took place in the 1920s and destroyed Victorian mores, was facilitated by two inventions – the radio and the motorcar. The radio, a modern tribal drum that unifies subcultures by rhythm, music, poetry (pop song lyrics), and news, puts physical and romantic notions into young peoples' heads. It provides influences beyond the individual's circle of friends, relatives, parents, and preacher. It creates longings to engage in physical passions. The motorcar, by providing mobility and privacy, proves to be an adequate location to escape from chaperones and neck, pet, and copulate.

The new electronic technology is easternizing the West because everyone born since 1950 is a Zen thinker. Ironically, Western technology is westernizing the Orient, but we are developing eastern thought patterns. The conquest is mutual, but just as in the case of Greece and Rome, the intellectual conquest is the more meaningful one.

Typographic man thinks in terms of linear sequences, labels, rationalizations, and compartments. Things are fragmented. A place for everything, and everything in its place. Biology, the study of life, is a separate entity from chemistry, the study of the structure of substances and the changes and interactions of substances. When we found that these two disciplines fuse, we created a new discipline with new categories and rules: biochemistry. By contrast, the Zen thinker sees the world as a unity. Rather than fight and re-create the world, the Zen master seeks harmony, unity, and a oneness with the universe.

Western art idealizes man and makes him big in the pictures. Superman, Flash Gordon, and Jesus Christ Superstar are our cultural heroes. Eastern art presents a vast natural panorama with small people, has no Superman, and uses the haiku poem as its main literary art form.

Definite signs indicate that McLuhan's idea is valid. Church attendance: 1960, 50 percent; 1970, 42 percent; 1971, 40 percent. Eight hundred thousand subscribe to *Organic Farming* and *Gardening* magazine.

Media interaction. TV does what mass mags do, but better. Magazines have declined. Mass media high-circulation magazines with emphasis on fiction were abundant in the 1940s. *Companion, Blue Book, Saturday Evening Post, Look,* and *Collier's* have gone to their graves. TV provides the fiction for Middle America now, and has captured the advertising revenue. However, periodicals for special-interest groups on subjects that do not have mass appeal have come upon the scene like gangbusters. *Psychology Today, Art in America, Skiing, Cosmopolitan, Intellectual Digest,* and *Scientific American* are just a few of the newer publications, plus hundreds of professional and trade journals. Print is undergoing a change; novels are generally shorter and less descriptive. However, rather than replace print, TV has tended to allow print to reinforce those things that it does best, while TV is about where print was in 1500.

To briefly look at your situation, the 1940s realistic illustration and the art editor who selected the illustrator and told the typesetter what size and style of type to use has been replaced, in two short decades, with contemporary visual communicators. These individuals are working with animation, filmmaking, editorial and advertising art direction, television still graphics, videotape, environmental design, and communications relative to social problems and education. The whole world is their visual workshop, the entire world culture of visual forms comprises their vocabulary, all the tools and techniques of the various communication media are their equipment, and in a post-McLuhan era the potential is limited only by the intelligence and imagination of the artist.

Novum Education: Virginia Commonwealth University, Richmond

From *Novum Gebrauchsgraphik* (November 1976)

The Communication Arts and Design Department of Virginia Commonwealth University in Richmond, Virginia, combines the advantages of an intense professional curriculum with the advantages of being part of a major urban university of 17,000 students. In the freshman year, all School of the Arts majors share a traditional basic program encompassing drawing, design and design theory, art history and English.

In the Sophomore year those students who enter the Communication Arts and Design program have another year of intense study. The core of the Sophomore program is a course entitled Problems in Visual Communications. In this course, students learn how to research, analyze, structure, resolve and present any design problem regardless of media. Other sophomore courses include: Visible Language, an exploration of the creative and communicative possibilities of letter forms and typography; Visual Thinking, a drawing course for designers that explores the expression of mental concepts in graphic terms; Photography, a thorough exploration of photographic processes and aesthetics; and Literature.

After this basic experience, the Juniors and Seniors are allowed to choose their studio courses from a variety of options. Included are print design, illustration, color photography, cinematography, animation, videographics, 3-D design, nature design workshop and university graphics, which is a professional studio for Seniors who work on design projects for the university and public service organizations. In the Junior year, students attend a lecture series called the Origins and History of Visual Communications. This course covers the role of design from prehistoric times to recent developments in visual communications. Juniors and Seniors in the Department must take Independent Visual Research. In this course the students define and solve design problems for which there is no preexisting solution. The purpose of this is to allow the student to become an independent thinker and problem-solver who can identify, structure and solve design problems on his own initiative in addition to being able to solve professional problems for clients.

The faculty do not adhere to any singular aesthetic philosophy. Through exposure to diverse viewpoints, it is hoped that students will be able to synthesize a unique individual approach to visual communications problem solving that will enable the student to make a meaningful contribution to society and the profession. The Department is deeply concerned with developing a social awareness of human and environmental problems as professional visual communicators. ➻

George Tscherny

From *Graphis 230* (1985)

During the last quarter of a century, American graphic design has witnessed a bewildering progression of styles and approaches. Revivals of Art Nouveau, Art Deco and Victorian ornament; the objectivity of the International Typographic Style, imported from Switzerland; the Push Pin Style; Pop Art influences; and the 'Postmodernist' reactions to the modern movement: these are some of the more significant graphic gyrations of recent times. In the eyes of its practitioners, each New Wave renders previous styles Old Hat. Yet throughout this period of flux, George Tscherny has maintained a remarkably consistent attitude and approach in practising graphic design. In a profession so susceptible to constant change – in which the discarding of ideas, styles and images is almost planned obsolescence – Tscherny's work has enabled him to remain at the forefront. What, then, are its ingredients?

One important aspect of Tscherny's work is an economy of means, addressing the essence of the problem at hand. Each project contains only those elements needed to convey its message, without the addition of any extraneous or decorative material.

When Tscherny solves a problem with photography, the image is often simplified by cropping. Only those components necessary for the photograph to tell its story, or expand the editorial content, are included. When the problem calls for drawing or illustration as the solution, Tscherny's freely drawn image-making approach presents his subjects as almost pictographic signs.

Black-and-white poster
on a new paper by
Monadnock Paper Mills.
Designer: George Tscherny

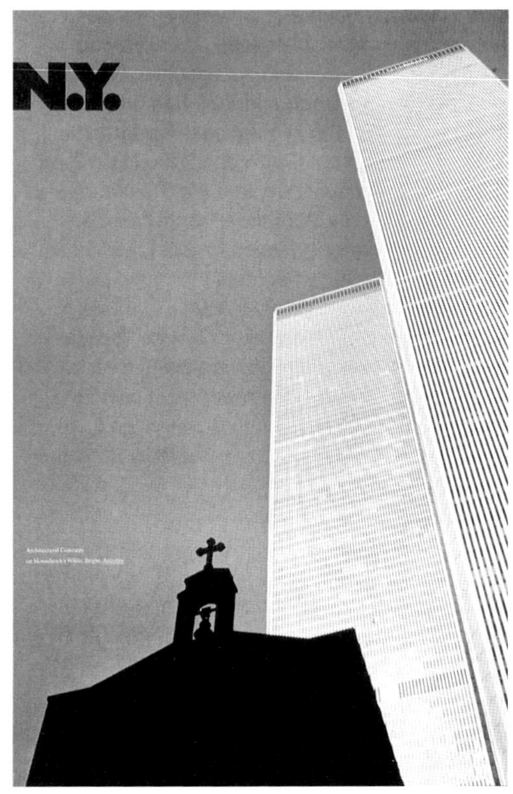

This economy of means does not degenerate into arid or bland communication, for it goes hand-in-hand with a gentle, human warmth. In the selection of photographic illustrations, Tscherny chooses images that project feeling and dignity. He achieves a similar human presence in his fluid gestural drawings as a result of their calligraphic and textural qualities.

Tscherny's bent toward an economy of means also figures in his work as a typographer. One is tempted to call him a classical typographer, not because his work imitates the grand tradition of the private press and the Renaissance book but because the basic attributes of classical typography are present in his approach. These include a concern for legibility and a meticulous attention to typographic detail. Also in evidence are appropriate typeface selections for the message and the audience, as well as a sense of rightness in determining sizes, weights and intervals. Refreshingly, the gimmicks, fads and eccentricities of much contemporary typographic design are absent. The result is that the message has a presentation which is direct and open, exemplifying two qualities of the Tscherny economy.

Graphic design can be a process of construction, resulting from procedures for building forms. Or it may be a process of visualization, realized through drawing and marking. For Tscherny, design is often a matter of selection, which is central to the design process. Perhaps the single most important aspect of Tscherny's approach to graphic design is the sensitivity of his vision, that attribute which, for more than three decades now, has enabled him to follow his own lights and yet maintain a remarkable level of quality. In the dozens of decisions made by a graphic designer in developing a project, one wrong choice in the *selection* of paper, typography, colour or photography can undermine the whole. Tscherny carefully weighs each element and its relationship to the totality with an unerring sense of the intended outcome. Clarity results. The intended message is conveyed to the audience unencumbered by irrelevant information or unclear forms.

George Tscherny's oeuvre provides reassurance that the work of the true communicator can rise above the cacophony of mass communications and transient styles, remaining authentic to the designer's vision, the client's purpose and audience needs. ◆

Issues: Demilitarization of Graphic Design

From *AIGA Journal of Graphic Design* Vol. 3, No. 3 (1985)

In the lexicon of pop psychology, the last ten years or so are known as the *Me Decade.* Me generation members are said to be very self-centered. Jogging, dieting, extending purchasing power in the face of inflation, taking self-awareness courses, and reading literally hundreds of self-improvement magazine articles are just part of the shift from public and social concerns to an involvement in our private little worlds. This is in marked contrast to the 1960s, which have been called – in the psychobabble of cultural analysis – the era of *Us vs. Them.* American social issues moved into the streets during that period of radical change. Born in 1967, today's 18-year-old college freshman has little memory of Vietnam, Martin Luther King, bra-burning demonstrations, or Watergate.

Public activism bore fruit. The Voting Rights Act, Affirmative Action, and the Environmental Protection Agency resulted from meaningful debate. The long and costly Vietnam War was wound down by a government unable to marshall the support of its people. The period that we now refer to as *The Sixties* didn't end on New Year's Day of 1970, perhaps because the social agenda was too full to be contained in one decade. Maybe August 8, 1974, the day that Richard Milhous Nixon threw in the towel and checked out of the White House, could suitably be called the end of *The Sixties.* Gerald Ford's presidency seemed to usher in more conservative clothes, less creative advertising, and a general malaise.

During *The Sixties,* graphic designers were very much involved in the major issues of the era. Professional design and illustration organizations had exhibitions of work by their members on such themes as ecology and the Vietnam War. Prominent graphic designers, notably the late Herb Lubalin, donated their time to create informational and public awareness graphics for causes in which they believed.

When thousands of people descended on Chicago for the 1968 Democratic National Convention to demonstrate against the Vietnam War policies of President Lyndon B. Johnson, Chicago Major Richard Daley unleashed his police against the demonstrators. While watching the violence on television, a Chicago graphic designer added a Hitler-like moustache to a photograph of Mayor Daley, set the headline "Heil Daley" in transfer type, and had the poster on an offset press the very next day. It sold out, and the proceeds were donated to a major anti-war group.

In the late 1960s and early 1970s, periodicals contained jarring juxtapositions. Such subjects as the March 1968 horror of the My Lai massacre – for which Lt. William Calley, Jr. was charged with the premeditated murder of 102 Vietnamese civilians in that tiny hamlet – were splashed in glowing color adjacent to sophisticated cigarette and beer advertisements in major magazines.

Design annuals and library stacks from *The Sixties* reveal the extent of the graphic design community's involvement in the issues of the time. Magazine covers became telegraphic statements on important social issues, and the poster provided graphic designers with a vehicle to circumvent the traditionally cautious media and make direct social statements. Memorable examples abound. A poster depicting a young woman, photographed while breast-feeding her baby, carried the ominous warning that mother's milk contained DDT and was hazardous to human health. George Lois' *Esquire* cover, with a photograph of a smiling Lt. Calley posing amidst a group of beautiful Oriental children, offended thousands of people. Yet, it reminded us that the social aberration of war changes the very soul of the individual. A Carl Fischer cover photograph for *Ramparts* showed American soldiers at the crucifixion.

Did the activism of graphic designers make a difference? Probably so. The power of words and images can work as effectively for social issues as it does for soda pop. Graphic statements can crystallize issues in a manner that is quite different from the transient television news account.

When the *Me Generation* arrived, the graphic articulation of social issues departed. During the late 1970s and early 1980s, the social agenda of graphic design was replaced by increased emphasis on surface style and technique. Often, the graphic designer becomes a performer, showing off the range of his or her visual vocabulary as an end in itself, rather than as a means to an end. Corporate America, with the help of its art directors, seized the environmental issue and made it their own. One memorable corporate advertisement showed an idyllic river scene and assured the public that the corporation was keeping the river clean. A college student investigated and discovered that the photograph was taken upstream from the advertiser's plant, which was polluting the river.

With the exception of illustrations by Marshall Arisman, Sue Coe, and others who are expressing their personal visions about the human condition, one is hard-pressed to find much evidence of social engagement in the design annuals from the past ten years. On Nuclear Freeze Day, over a million people marched in the streets of New York and memorable graphics were generated, but the energy was not sustained. The Hiroshima posters produced for The Shoshin Society are a rare exception today.

Arguably, graphic design does *not* solve social problems. However, it is one of the communicative means which helps shape public opinion. One prominent Washington pollster declared public opinion to be the most powerful force in the country, capable of inspiring presidents and the Congress to hop, skip, jump, and even flip-flop on the issues. Social issues in need of graphic articulation abound and are as pressing as the issues of *The Sixties.* By addressing them, visual communicators can fulfill an important public service. ➼

Ramparts cover, art direction: Dugald Stermer, photograph: Carl Fischer (January 1967)

Anti-Vietnam War poster, Design: Seymour Chwast (1968)

Design History: Discipline or Anarchy?

From *AIGA Journal of Graphic Design* Vol. 3, No. 4 (1985)

A heady enthusiasm greeted the emergence, a decade ago, of an interest in graphic design history which sprouted across America like mushrooms after a summer thunderstorm. The early stages of this movement were long on opinions and short on scholarship. Self-styled experts were suddenly available to deliver lectures to professional clubs and schools. Armed with reels of 35mm slides, their interpretations were loose and often highly opinionated. In art schools and universities, graphic design professors began to introduce design history as an informal part of studio courses, illustrated by images from such books as Herbert Spencer's *Pioneers of Modern Typography* and Dover Publications' *The Golden Age of the Poster* and *The First World War in Posters,* and so on. From this rather amateurish beginning, individuals around the country doggedly worked to bring substance to their research. A new field of inquiry – Graphic Design History – was coming of age. Symposia (notably the 1983 Coming of Age, A First Symposium on the History of Graphic Design at Rochester Institute of Technology and its 1985 sequel), books and articles, interest groups, and mailing lists have begun to create a network of passionately involved people.

What accounts for this growing interest in graphic design history? One factor is the shift in American society from an industrial to an information culture. Visual communications play a role in the emerging post-industrial society, which is similar to the role of automobile design during the 1950s, when America underwent the most rapid industrial expansion of any nation in the history of the world. The automobile was the tangible product and the visual icon of that era. Likewise, contemporary graphics are a major cultural manifestation of the information age. I am speaking of contemporary graphics in a comprehensive sense. Computer animation, video game iconography, and rock videos join more traditional graphics as expressions of this revolution. (The last ten years have seen a steady decline in sculpture and crafts enrollments in art schools and universities, accompanied by a steady growth in visual communications enrollments. This is an extension of the shift from industrial to information culture. The educational bureaucrats who believe these enrollment shifts are solely a reflection of a conservative generation's employment orientation miss the main point.)

Another factor is the graphic design discipline's quest for professional status and recognition as an important activity requiring specialized knowledge, skill, and even a measure of wisdom. If graphic design is to succeed in casting off the antiquated notion of "commercial art" taking a rightful place beside architecture and painting as a major visual expression of our culture, the "history void" must be overcome. A professional without a history is like a person without a country: a homeless refugee. The graphic design history movement bolsters the profession's quest for recognition.

Laymen develop an involvement in graphic design history through interest in its content. In its most populist forms, graphic design is history's *hard copy;* the documentation of revolutions and recording stars, politics and prosperity, real estate booms and Hollywood busts. On a more rarefied and aesthetic level, it can be an innovative, sometimes difficult art form. Its intrinsic value as design is one level of meaning; it also carries meaning as social message and historical artifact.

The design history experts are a lively and diverse group. But a unity of purpose and approach is lacking. Practitioners (notably those with a modernist, formal approach), design educators (who were trained as graphic designers and spend a significant amount of their professional week in teaching), and academicians (scholars trained in art history, philosophy, or other academic disciplines) have all joined the movement. Each group has a different agenda and brings a unique viewpoint to graphic design history. While the result may appear to be zoo-like to some observers, each group brings special insights and knowledge to the dialogue.

There is not even agreement, for example, on the historical scope which should be studied. Some advocate the shortsighted view and believe that graphic design is a new activity, born of the industrial revolution. Others advocate a farsighted view, believing the essence of graphic design is giving visual form to human communications, an activity which has a distinguished ancestry dating to the medieval manuscript and early printers of the Renaissance.

As yet, graphic design history is not a fully developed discipline in the sense that art history and architectural history are. The histories of other disciplines – science, medicine, architecture, and painting – have become important areas of human activity in themselves. Mixed in with the heroes and myths, the aspiring scientist or painter finds philosophy, values, and a sense of destiny. Formal, systematic opportunities to study graphic design history are not readily available. The University of Cincinnati is offering a master's degree in design history, and an increasing number of art schools and universities are offering courses. However, there is not yet a doctoral program for individuals who wish to make a lifetime commitment to researching and teaching design history.

Graphic design history must be studied in the complex context of its milieu. While we can speak of architectural history, painting history, product design history, graphic design history, etc., all of these are part of a larger *visual* history. Artists and artisans in each epoch freely borrow from one another. Ornaments in fifteenth-century French books echo architectural embellishment. The sinuous and organic lines of Art Nouveau lend unity to architecture, furniture, posters, jewelry, household objects, and fashions from the 1890s. The geometric stylizations of African masks and figurative sculpture, which were freely borrowed by Picasso and Braque as they pioneered Cubism, found their way into sculpture, architectural reliefs, book and fashion illustrations of the 1920s. While fashion and the excitement of the new shape this visual history, it may alsobe true that epochs embrace visual forms that relate to collective mythic needs born from historical circumstance.

The political and social circumstances of each time period have a significant impact upon graphic design history. The Depression and the rise of Nazism left an indelible stamp upon graphics of

(continued on page 72)

Philip Meggs: Selected artifacts from "idea" files

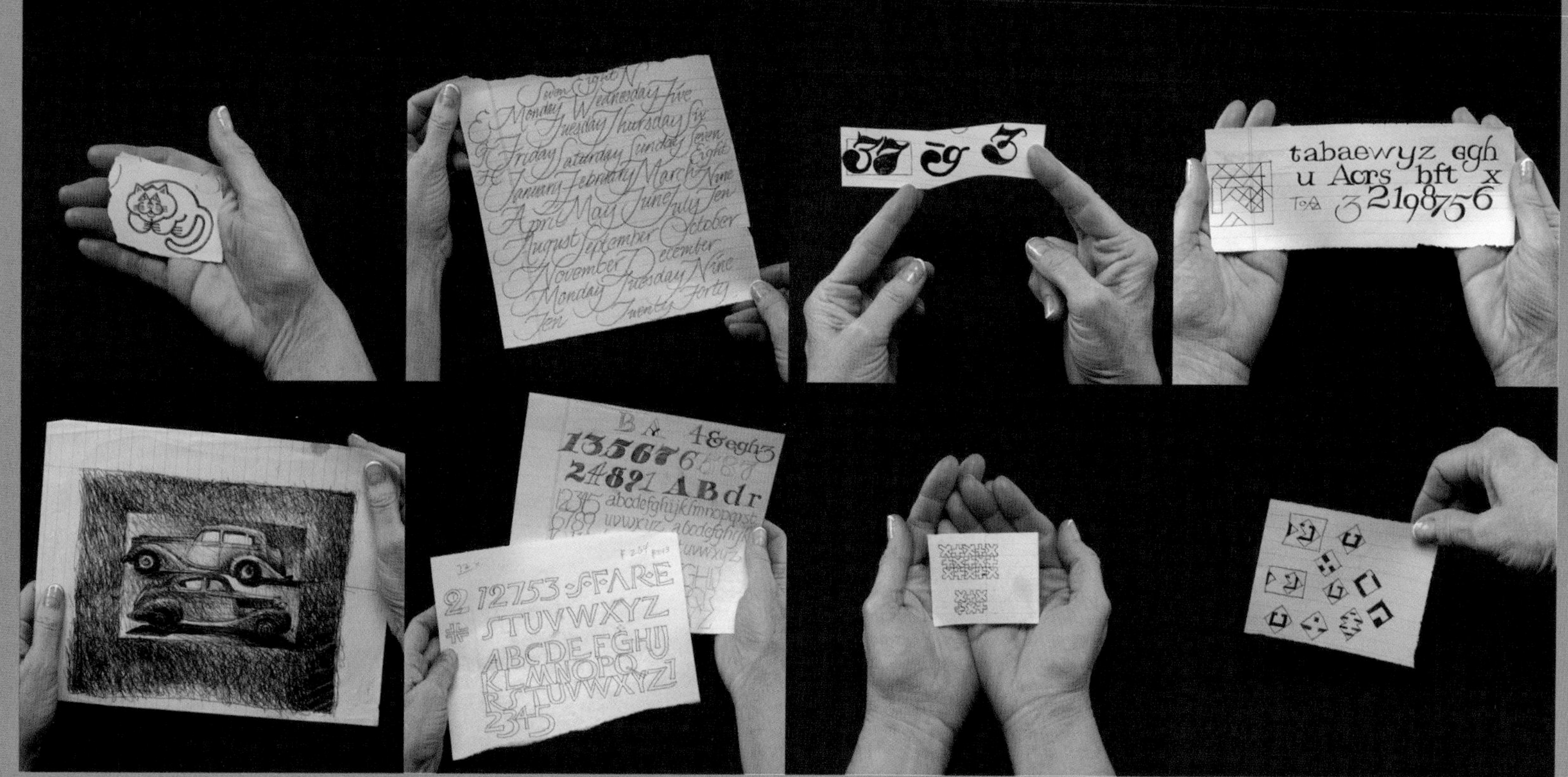

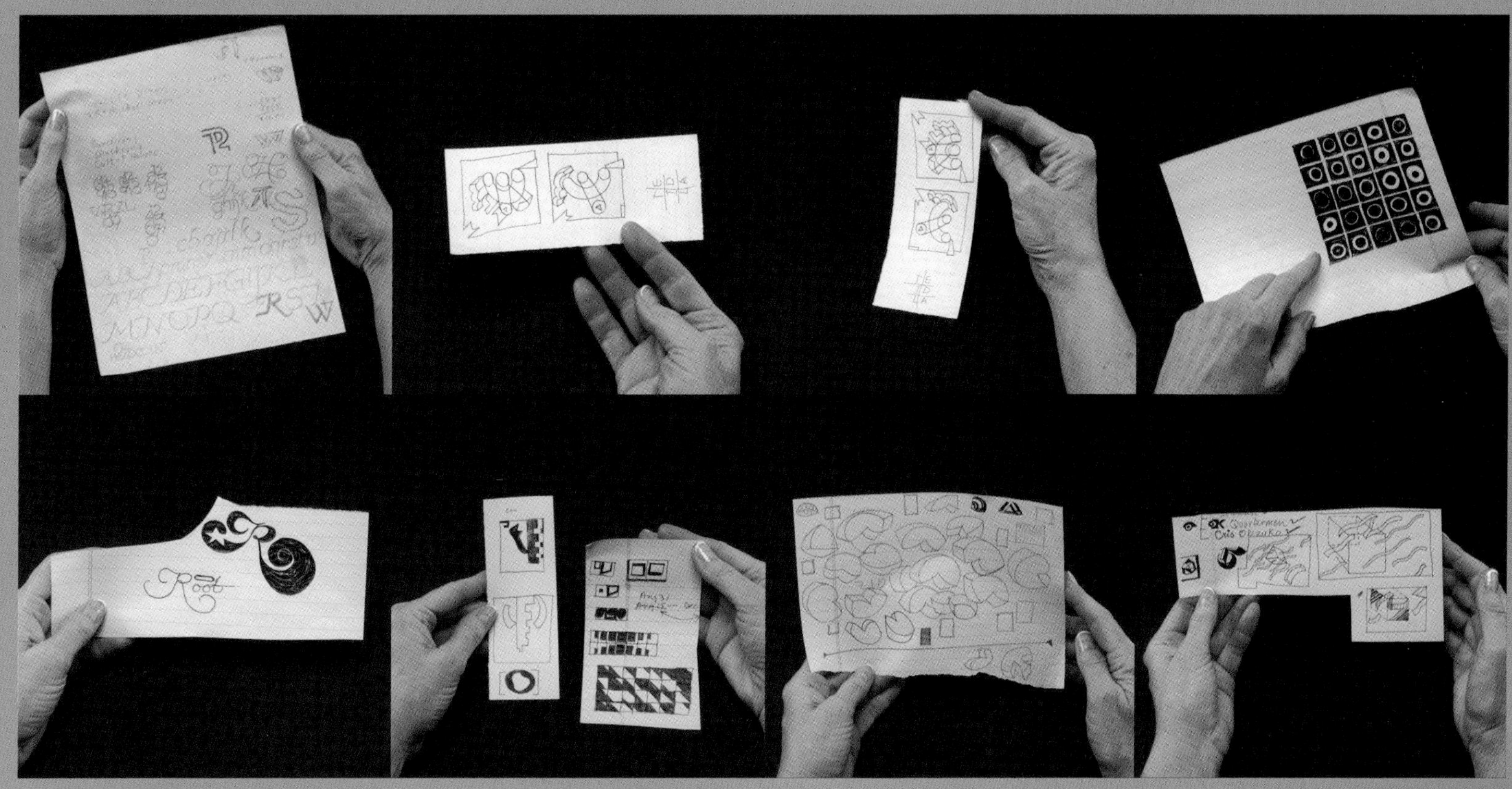
Root

the 1930s. In posters from that decade which are housed in the squeaky drawers of the massive poster collection of the Library of Congress, we find that fantasy and escapism commingle with strident political messages. Faith in the multinational corporation and its ability to address and solve problems was prevalent during the 1950s. This faith was badly shaken during the social upheavals of the 1960s. Graphics from each decade must be understood and interpreted in light of these and other historical forces.

Another connection is technological. Advances in graphic arts processes are sometimes as important as creative insight or historical circumstance in shaping the visual-communications vocabulary. An understanding of tools can lead to startling invention, with new forms and spatial configurations emerging from an engagement with advanced technology. During the mid-nineteenth century, the invention of color lithographic printing enabled imaginative visual artists to bring about a "color revolution" which radically altered mass communications and made graphics "every man's artform."

An important part of Herb Lubalin's contribution to American graphic design was his sensitivity to the new phototypography of the 1960s. Lubalin understood its potential for extending the designer's creative potential and opening new communicative possibilities.

One problem that is yet to be resolved is the criteria to be used when making judgments about historical significance. This is a key philosophical issue for any area of aesthetics, criticism, or history. At this point, the various experts do not agree. Logical criteria must be developed by those who make pronouncements about the value and importance of creative work. Two major, if unstated, approaches are the formalist approach and the socio-political approach.

Germanic in origin, the formalist approach sees design evolution in terms of its purity of form. Constructivism, de Stijl, and the Bauhaus are the genesis, the Swiss School is the realization, and the heirs of this tradition are seen as the significant designers of today. Graphic design, according to some advocates of this approach, is a new activity that did not exist until the twentieth-century visual revolutions. This view is myopic, for artistically trained individuals from Hans Holbein to hundreds of nineteenth-century artists of the chromolithography era were seriously involved in designing books, posters, broadsides, tins, and other printed matter from 1450 until 1900.

The socio-political approach sees this historical value of graphic design in terms of its political viewpoint and impact upon society. Political activists of several persuasions have embraced this approach. This dogma defines the value of graphic design in terms of its political correctness. The Solidarity logo becomes good; the logo of the multinational oil company becomes evil. This sociological approach is in direct conflict with the formalist approach. The logo or poster for the most worthy of causes might be graphically awkward, and work for the petrochemical monolith which creates the vilest of toxic waste dumps can be graphic invention of the highest order.

Graphic design is ill-served by a purely formal, or by a purely sociological approach. It is a pluralistic and complex activity. Responsible interpretation must consider form, content, chronological context, and social value. It must be viewed in relationship to what preceded and what followed it.

The importance of the late-nineteenth-century leader of the English Arts and Crafts movement, William Morris, offers a fascinating example of differing interpretations. Appalled with the mediocre quality of printed books of his time, Morris founded the Kelmscott Press in 1892 and attempted to recapture the quality of books from the early years of typographic printing. In *A History of Design from the Victorian Era to the Present,* Ann Ferebee writes that Morris' book designs had "little to do with the impending 20th century," while in *A History of Graphic Design,* I wrote of Morris' "extraordinary influence… upon graphic design." In *A History of Visual Communications,* Josef Müller-Brockmann reproduces a page from one of Morris' books, but does not mention him in the text. How can such different interpretations exist? Ferebee is operating from a vantage point of Victorian to Art Nouveau or Modern and is responding to Morris' lack of stylistic influence upon Modern design. *A History of Graphic Design's* reference is to the tremendous impact Morris had upon typography and the revitalization of book design through his influence upon Frederic Goudy, Bruce Rogers, and many others. Further, Morris had a strong philosophic impact upon the emergence of all forms of design in the early twentieth century through his call for workmanship, truth to materials, making the utilitarian beautiful, and the fitness of design to function. Possibly Müller-Brockmann did not feel that Morris was sufficiently important.

These different interpretations of design history are possible because, as mentioned above, a body of criticism and philosophy providing criteria and standards does not yet exist. Design historians take diverse vantage points based on their experience and interests. Although the design history movement is still in its infancy and suffers from growing pains, its emergence holds great promise for the future development of both graphic design and the study of history.

The design history movement should not lose sight of the fact that its subject is ephemera. Perhaps this is why the museum world has been so reticent to recognize the importance of graphic design, except for precious artifacts such as rare books and posters that relate to the twentieth-century avant-garde. Graphic design exists of and for its time, but its value – both to elucidate methods for creating messages and demonstrate the evolution of a visual vocabulary – endures.

The ultimate goal of design history study should be more effective practice. Its contribution should go beyond the use of design history as a vast data bank of forms and solutions to problems which can be accessible to the contemporary designer, expanding his or her vocabulary of possibilities. Graphic design history is a history of ideas. Eric Gill's 1928 *Gill Sans* typeface was based on the idea of using the proportions of Roman inscriptional letterforms in a sans-serif type design. Its geometric contemporary, Paul Renner's 1927 *Futura,* was designed in enthusiastic embrace of industrialism, standardization, and scientific rationalism. Gill, however, sought to retain values from the humanist tradition. Understanding such divergent viewpoints leads to greater awareness of the nature of form and its meaning, and brings conceptual understanding to professional practice.

The study of design history can support the development of professional ethical and value systems. The sense of purpose found in the scholar-printers of the Renaissance, who were unlocking the lost knowledge of the ancient world; the urgency of John Heartfield, using photomontage in posters as a propaganda weapon in the struggle against Nazism; and the wholesome commitment to commerce (in the best sense of that word) by the pioneers of corporate visual identification – these examples represent graphic design practice motivated by a dedication to exemplary human values. This sense of purpose must be present, if graphic design aspires to the professional integrity that we associate with the best impulses of the medical, legal, and teaching professions. Otherwise, it's back to commercial art. ➻

Design Education: Pedagogy vs. the Real World

From *AIGA Journal of Graphic Design* Vol. 4, No. 1 (1986)

Enthusiasm is decidedly *not* the attitude of many graphic designers toward the educational programs in colleges, art schools, and universities. Why does a dichotomy exist between the design profession and the schools? Why is the annual springtime ritual of reviewing portfolios by art school graduates so depressing for many professional designers? Is design education failing the profession and its students? Answers are elusive.

One problem is that there is no certification of the validity of design education programs or the graduates of these programs. Unlike architecture and interior design, which have professional certification by the American Institute of Architects and the American Society of Interior Designers, graphic design depends upon market forces to determine its level of competency. The result is lower educational standards, many marginally competent practitioners, and a lack of professional respect.

The arguments against certification include a belief that an examining board would somehow produce a creative straitjacket, licensing "Swiss" designers, for example, while denying young advocates of punk and post-modernist styles entry into the field. There may be some validity to a fear of abuse of a licensing process. Certification which establishes those minimum competencies necessary for entry into the field could set a minimum professional standard and force schools to address this standard.

Another difficulty is that design education comes in a multitude of configurations. Two-year community colleges and trade schools race to cover coursework which will provide the recipient of the two-year Associate of Arts degree with a portfolio of work to show prospective employers. Open admissions policies are often in effect, so that many of these schools take all comers. One two-year school has no portfolio requirements for entry and pays its recruiters commissions based on the number of new students who enroll. Talented students with strong potential often have no competition, and faculty members are forced to teach at the class level, resulting in low standards and sloppy portfolios.

The university art department presents a different problem. Frequently, this is housed in the College of Arts and Sciences and has the typical general-studies configuration, leading to the Bachelor of Arts degree. The curriculum spans the sciences, history, literature, foreign language, and about 30 credits of study in the major. Needless to say, many graduates of these programs end up with a well-rounded education, but lack sufficient visual training to be able to function in a professional capacity. Most university art departments, by tradition, are dominated by fine-arts faculty members who advocate a philosophy of "first you make an artist, then you give him or her the tools to do commercial work." Graphic design and typography are limited to a few courses during the junior and senior years. Unfortunately, sometimes students are led to believe that they are being prepared for the profession, when they are actually receiving a broad general education with a specific focus. The fine arts faculty attitude is condescending toward *commercial art,* as though it were something a *real* artist could do with his or her eyes closed.

At the top of the educational heap one finds four-year professional art schools, which house departments of graphic design (sometimes combined with illustration or other related disciplines and called visual communications or communication arts). These are found at independent art schools – such as Pratt and Art Center; also, they are housed in universities, including Syracuse, Boston, and Cincinnati. They grant the BFA degree, which means that a majority, usually about 60 to 65 percent, of the credits earned are in studio courses. Professional faculty teach in these programs and even have a reasonable measure of control over the curriculum.

Some art schools staff their classes primarily with part-time teachers, practitioners who come in once or twice a week to teach a course. While this can provide excellent practical training, it sometimes leads to erratic curriculum patterns when students study under a succession of professionals who teach what they do at their jobs. Unless great care is taken by the program administrators, students can receive a spotty education, lacking coordination between courses and missing critical fundamentals.

Why do professionals perceive design education to be out of sync with their expectations for entry-level graphic designers? The professional component of the curriculum must address two issues: technical or craft training and creative development. There is no justification for failure to prepare graduates for the craft aspects of graphic design. The preparation of art for printing, type specification, simulating type and image with markers, and using drafting instruments are pass/fail situations. Work either meets professional standards or it is wrong. By including technical training components in their curriculum, where the student either does things properly or repeats the course, schools can address this issue directly if the faculty has the will to do so. The only excuse for failing to provide appropriate craft training in a four-year program is educational incompetence. The four years required to earn a BFA in graphic design is the same length of time as for the BS degree in electrical engineering and computer science programs, so there should be no excuses.

More problematic is the issue of creative development. How does one produce a creative visual artist? The problem has plagued educators throughout this century. Creativity and insight come from the whole person. One's childhood impressions and feelings, concepts from art history class, the styles currently in vogue, styles from the past seen with fresh eyes, the chance glimpse of a green car passing a pink dress on the street – all of these play as great a role as the most carefully constructed classroom exercises. Methodologies abound, but probably the most effective approach to problem solving is knowledge-based intuition. By bringing an in-depth understanding of the problem and a thorough knowledge of design and graphic techniques to bear upon it, the designer somehow sweats out a solution. The broader the designer's background knowledge, the more likely effective solutions become. Awareness of design history plus films, theater, photography, and literature greatly aid the designer.

In looking for a program or method, many American design programs have turned to the German tradition of form generation. Student portfolios are filled with visual exercises in color manipulation and form development, reflecting hours of work, strong hand skills, and acceptably modernist taste. This relates to certain segments of design practice, particularly corporate identity and signage systems, but it creates a vast gulf between design education and the mainstream American design community. Simply put, while the schools are busy manipulating form, the profession is busy manipulating minds. Herein lies the crux of the dilemma. American design education has drifted toward European modernism, while American graphic design has maintained a pluralistic pragmatism. Students often suffer an intense culture shock after graduation, for they have been taught to be form manipulators, while the profession demands that they become message makers.

As critical as form and style are to graphic design, the bedrock of professional practice is communications. Schools should try to produce independent thinkers with critical judgment and personal approaches to problem solving. Chicago designer Ed Bedno observes that if a school succeeds at this, each student develops his or her individual vision; therefore, the school has no house style and does not build a reputation based on an easily identifiable visual "look."

In spite of the amazingly pluralistic scope of contemporary American graphic design, some design-program faculties have become so inbred that those who interview many job-seeking graduates joke that they can identify the school by the portfolio, as all the problems and solutions are the same.

The result is a house style, with cookie-cutter graduates cut from the same mold year after year. Inbreeding occurs partly because the American education establishment often values *education* over *experience,* in selecting faculty. A Master of Fine Arts degree, representing two years of graduate study, is the mandatory background for visual arts faculty at many schools. Some universities are loath to hire teachers without graduate degrees, no matter how strong their professional backgrounds might be.

Increasingly, "publish or perish" is becoming a way of life at American universities. Since the baby boom is over, higher education is no longer growing, there are fewer opportunities for young people to enter the professorate, and the faculty is getting older. It is incumbent upon faculty members in higher education to keep up with their discipline. For academics, this means publishing articles in arcane scholarly journals. Fine arts faculty members have fought for and won the right to produce works in their studios and exhibit it as a substitute for publishing in scholarly journals. For graphic design faculty, the "publish or perish" doctrine can pose a dilemma. It is not always so easy for educators to maintain practices. Client demands can conflict with teaching schedules, and some universities have conflict of interest and outside employment rules that classify writing and painting as individual research activity but call designing a logo or booklet outside employment, which is strictly limited. Lanny Sommese, head of the Graphic Design Program at Penn State University, passionately believes that people who teach graphic design should be *doing* it. Further, he claims that there are sufficient cultural activities at a university needing graphics, and nonprofit organizations everywhere need design services but cannot afford professional rates; therefore, there should be no excuses for design faculty members who are not professionally active, even in small college towns.

While some graphic design faculty members are able to maintain a practice, many turn to fine arts for their personal work and others embrace the realm of theory, turning to scholarly writing filled with jargon so unfamiliar to most professional designers that it becomes as undecipherable as Egyptian hieroglyphics. The professionals who ridicule educators' investigations into such esoteric subjects as semiotics, however, should remember that the Bauhaus teachers, whose ideas are now part of our common visual language, faced hostile criticism and were even run out of town by the Weimar government. Ironically, the semiotics movement in American design education may bring education and the profession closer together. Semiotics is the study of signs, symbols, and their meanings. Adding it to the design curriculum tilts the emphasis away from form exclusively, and focuses students' attention upon meaning and message.

Advocates of semiotics as a foundation for graphic design practice have not yet found a way to convey their message to the profession. Herb Lubalin, for example, was a master of semiotics, for he intuitively understood syntactics (the form of signs and symbols), semantics (the meaning of signs and symbols), and pragmatics (the relations between signs or symbols and their users). If someone had told Lubalin, "I am a semiotician, and your syntactic manipulation of signs for semantic intensification has definite pragmatic suasion," he would have probably scratched his head and walked away.

But if someone had told him, "I study visual signs and symbols and their meanings, and I think that you reinvent forms to heat up their content so people can understand them better," he probably would have said, "Thank you." These comments are similar, but the vocabulary is different. When the theory of semiotics is made accessible to designers, a richer awareness of human communication will occur.

Design educators – in fact, all college faculty – are faced with a serious conflict as they plan their time. Should the bulk of their discretionary time go towards research, be it professional practice, writing, or whatever, or should it be focused upon the educational process, putting in extra hours working with students, preparing teaching aids, developing better projects, and evaluating student work? It's not an easy choice, particularly when the "publish or perish" dictum implies that promotion and tenure might better be obtained by doing a fair-to-middling job in the classroom and an excellent job on research, rather than devoting most of one's professional energy to excellent teaching.

In defense of educators who are constantly bombarded by professional critics, however, it must be stated that teaching the complexities of graphic design is not an easy task. Students entering the freshman programs of art schools usually have very weak prior training, so faculty members are starting at ground zero. It takes a long time to develop perceptual skills, eye-hand coordination, and design fundamentals. And even when an educational program succeeds in adequately preparing young designers for the profession, it fails in the eyes of professionals who do not agree with the philosophy and/or visual style found in the graduates' work.

So how shall we work our way out of the dilemma? Faculty should be required to maintain their professional competency, and closer ties between the profession and the schools are needed to enable greater understanding. Curriculum must somehow reach a balanced equilibrium between visual form and communication. A serious effort to establish certification of educational programs should be made, for nothing is more tragic than to have students attend programs expecting to receive professional preparation, only to find after graduation that major gaps exist in their education.

And when will the dichotomy between practice and pedagogy end? It won't. The ideal of schools, to maximize the creative potential of students, and the specific needs of diverse employers, whose visions are firmly planted on the bottom line, can never be fully reconciled. ⊷

The Swiss Influence: The Old New Wave

From *AIGA Journal of Graphic Design* Vol. 4, No. 1 (1986)

Two generations of Swiss design educators have profoundly influenced the course of American graphic design. Swiss design, or The International Typographic Style, had its roots in Constructivist and Bauhaus design of the 1920s and emerged and spread from Basel and Zurich during the 1950s. It is characterized by sans-serif typography in flush-left, ragged-right configurations on a grid.

The April 1957 issue of *Print* magazine featured a large portfolio entitled "12 Swiss Designers" which presented fully developed works in the Swiss style by Armin Hofmann, Karl Gerstner, Josef Müller-Brockmann, Emil Ruder, and Siegfried Odermatt. Any American with a subscription to *Print* could easily copy the surface appearance of Swiss design, provided he or she had a typesetter with Standard Medium (American issue of Akzidenz Grotesque; Helvetica and Univers were not yet available) and a client willing to risk having customers suffering impaired vision from reading unjustified sans-serif text type. In 1959, *Graphis* magazine further spread the word with an article, "The Typography of Order," by Emil Ruder. Advocating typography as "an expression of our own age of technical order and precision," Ruder discussed and showed visual examples of grid systems, the deliberate use of unprinted white spaces as a lively and forceful pattern, and the use of "overall" design to create a very close interconnection of all the parts of a printed production. The portfolio of some 40 works, which followed, amply demonstrated Ruder's theories.

Back in 1947, Emil Ruder started teaching typography and Armin Hofmann began teaching graphic design at the Allgemeine Gewerbeshcule (Basel School of Design). The Basel program is intense, and a mystique has developed about it in design education circles. Highly developed hand skills, strong structural design, and a rigorous design process are emphasized. Basel and Zurich designers arrived at many basic aspects of the Swiss style before 1955–56, when Hofmann made the first of his visiting lecturer trips to Yale University.

During the Sixties and Seventies, the Basel influence steadily seeped into American design education. In 1965 Armin Hofmann's *Graphic Design Manual* was published in an English version, and Ruder's *Typography: A Manual for Design* followed in 1967. Both books are excellent presentations of these master teachers' methods and became widely used as texts, further expanding the Swiss influence upon American graphic design education. Hofmann's book has been misunderstood, for some have approached the 301 examples of work therein as a style manual, rather than as the end products of a protracted analytical process. Hofmann's teaching approach involves immersion into the problem, generating scores of solutions and variations, until further elaboration is not possible. Hofmann and Ruder were far more open and exploratory than some of their American followers, who hardened the Basel approach into a rational style.

American students began studying graphic design and typography at Basel, and a post-graduate course in graphic design was established in the spring of 1968. Alvin Eisenman, head of Yale's graphic design program, wrote a now-famous letter declaring the Basel course to be fully

(continued on page 80)

Typographic interpretation of a Marshall McLuhan quotation, from the Basel School of Design.
Design: Willi Kunz (1975)

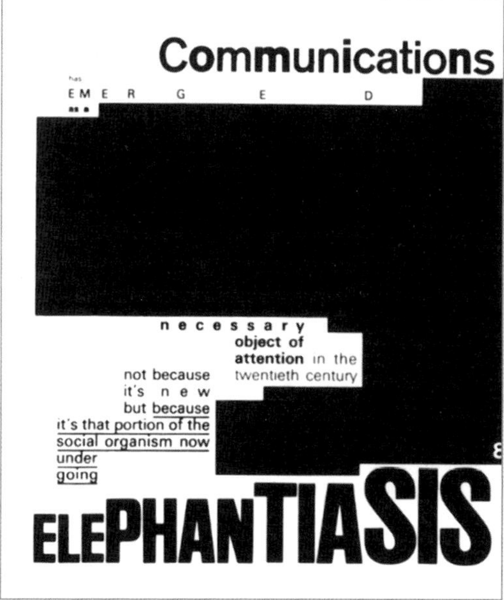

Philip Meggs: Sketchbooks

Selected spreads from a multilayered sketchbook that served as a repository for miscellaneous ideas and sketches.

Mixed media. Spread dimensions: 11 x 14 inches. (c.1970s–1980s)

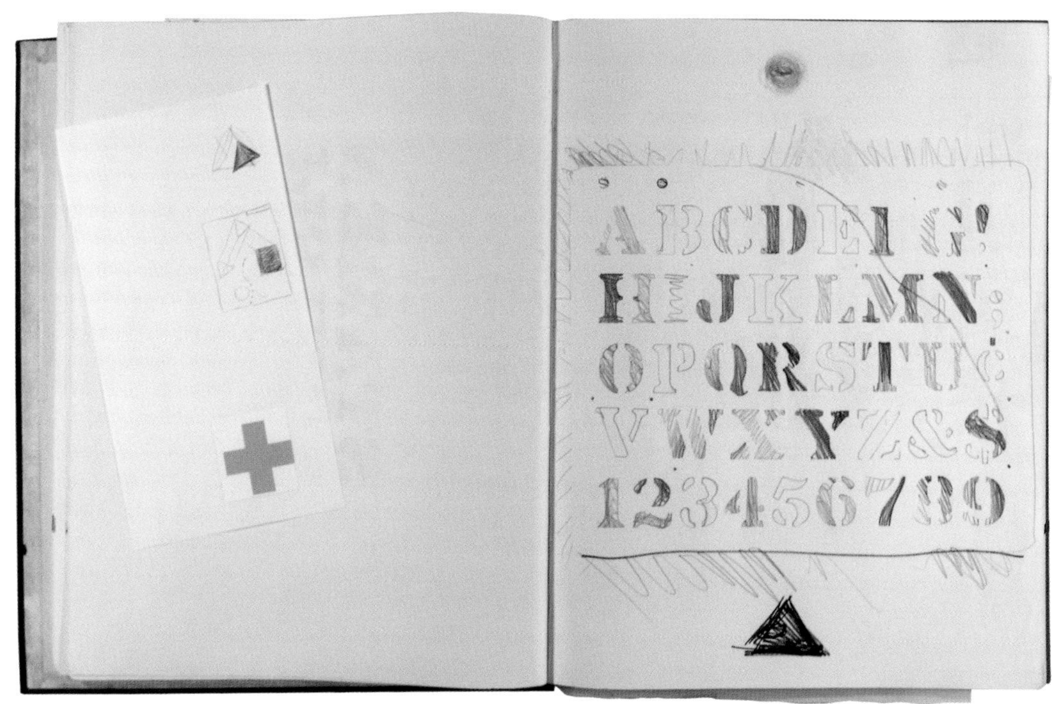

equivalent to the American M.F.A. degree. It then became quite common for American designers to make this Basel pilgrimage, then return to this country and teach.

In 1968, two years before Emil Ruder's death, young Wolfgang Weingart joined the Basel faculty. Weingart rejected the typography of absolute order and cleanness. His work and teaching introduced a lively, relatively free approach to typography. In the late 1960s and early 1970s, Weingart and his students broke with traditional rules and enriched the design vocabulary. Step rules, wide letterspacing (a convention that had vanished years earlier), mixing type weights within the same word, creating grids and then violating them, combining gestural and organic forms with precise sans-serif typeforms; a lexicon of typographic experiments were compiled which might, in retrospect, be called *Prototype New Wave* or *Early Post-Modernism.*

The second Swiss invasion of American design began in the early 1970s. Weingart made his first American lecture tour in 1972, speaking to design programs in Philadelphia, Cincinnati, New Haven, and Providence. Small, quiet infiltrations occurred on the east and west coasts as Weingart's students came to America to practice and teach design. April Greiman established a design practice in Los Angeles, and as her work became known in that area and influenced other designers, including some who mixed it with Pop and Funk imagery, it seemed that this New Wave was born in California. At the same time Basel-educated Willi Kunz established a design practice in New York, and it so seemed that this new attitude about typography was birthed in the Big Apple.

Most directly influential upon design education was Dan Friedman, who did post-graduate study at Basel, then taught at Yale University from 1970–73 and at SUNY Purchase from 1972–75. The Spring 1973 issue of *Visible Language,* a scholarly journal read by very few graphic designers except those in higher education, published a 16-page portfolio of Friedman's student work from Yale entitled, "A View: Introductory Education in Typography." A sequence of typographic designs, using a daily weather report as the message, ranged from simple functional presentations to unconventional and dynamic solutions. Friedman contended that "legibility (a quality of efficient, clear, and simple reading) is often in conflict with readability (a quality which promotes interest, pleasure, and challenge in reading). To what degree can a typographic statement be *both* functional *and* at the same time, aesthetically unconventional?"

Friedman's program ricocheted through American design education. Typography and design teachers from Michigan to Massachusetts and Ohio to Virginia developed variations of his weather-report project. The timing was right, for Modernism in architecture was under attack for being too rigid and arid by such dissidents as Robert Venturi, and many Swiss-influenced educators were beginning to feel that the rationalism of the grid was becoming old hat and were waiting for some new wave to replace it.

One school which enjoyed early publicity for its variations on Friedman's weather report project actually received credit for being the innovator; only subscribers to *Visible Language* knew better.

If asked what three individuals have had the greatest influence upon American graphic design education in the last 25 years, my answer would have to be Emil Ruder, Armin Hofmann, and Wolfgang Weingart, all from Basel. The course of American graphic design and design education has been definitely altered and expanded by this Swiss influence.

Toulouse-Lautrec: Superb but Not Alone

From *AIGA Journal of Graphic Design* Vol. 4, No. 2 (1986)

Henri de Toulouse-Lautrec, that dwarfed aristocrat who burned the candle at both ends, only to have it snuffed out at an early age, is credited with being a graphic arts innovator. His lithographs capture the exciting and decadent night life of Paris in the Gay Nineties, seen in his posters, illustrations for books, theatre programs, and menus. Thanks to Lautrec, the *high* art of an era became inescapably tied to applied art for printing.

The exhibition of Lautrec's drawings, lithographs, and posters at The Museum of Modem Art, New York, provided a rare opportunity to view Lautrec's fine and applied art together. The viewer was afforded an opportunity to see a majority of his posters in their original size and color. The Museum presented what have been called Lautrec's "more aesthetically brilliant and complex works than many of his contemporaries"[1] by hanging several of his posters upon a huge photographic mural of a poster-covered 1890s Paris wall. However, the mushy black-and-white tones of the mural – in contrast to the bright hues of Lautrec's originals put his contemporaries' posters at a distinct disadvantage. The Lautrecs were also preciously framed under glass, which removed them further from the drab photographic images beneath. This comparative exercise reeked of unfair competition.

Lautrec's impeccable credentials as a Post-Impressionist painter, combined with the romance of his era and subject matter, have exaggerated his contribution to the evolution of graphic design. One widely-used art history text lavishes high praise on his posters:

Henri-Marie-Raymond de Toulouse-Lautrec (1864–1901) revolutionized the art of poster-making by flattening illusionistic space in the Japanese manner and uniting the pattern of the pictorial elements with that of the lettering. The development of lithography into a polychrome medium converted posters, which had earlier been confined mainly to typographic announcements, into a new form of public art, which Lautrec brought to sudden maturity.[2]

The problem with this gush of praise is that the development of the modem poster was an extended and collective process. Lautrec's contribution was only one of many by designers and printers in Europe and North America. The 1880s American circus poster brought large scale and vibrant color to the medium, and French poster artists Jules Chéret and Eugéne Grasset blazed the trail ahead of Lautrec, whose moment of innovation was his 1891 first poster, *La Goulue at the Moulin Rouge,* which reduced images to flat iconographic shapes to a degree not yet seen in western posters. Following on the heels of Lautrec, the Beggarstaffs in England and Lucien Bernhard in Germany pushed poster design toward even greater simplicity and flatness.

Was Henri de Toulouse-Lautrec the guru of the modem poster, as some art history books would have us believe? Or was he the quick-sketch artist of the Gay Nineties, storming into the print shop with a hangover and using his brilliant gifts as a draftsman to bang out posters? Neither interpretation is accurate.

Toulouse-Lautrec, poster for the Moulin Rouge. In his first poster, he drew inspiration from the Japanese woodcut, taking the European poster one step further toward a symbolic iconography of flat shape and color.

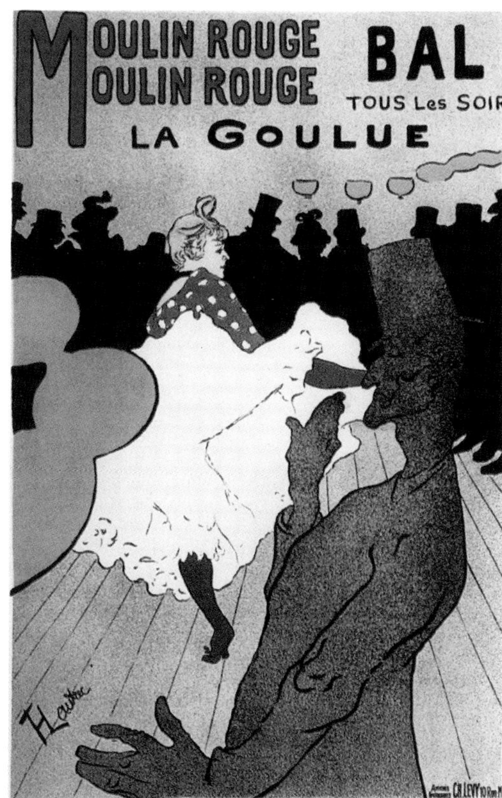

The brilliance of Toulouse-Lautrec's posters results from his unabashed mimicking of the Japanese print, combined with a master caricaturist's unerring eye for seizing the essence of his subject and articulating it with a stunning economy of line. Subtle nuances strip bare the personality and exaggerate the physical quirks of his subjects. Jaded decadence is expressed, but when photographs of his subjects are compared to his prints and posters, these qualities are not always found in the photographs.

In the best Lautrec posters, his casual lettering has an impetuous fervor which echoes the lines and shapes of the illustration, achieving a graphic unity. In other posters, he is unable to integrate word and image into a unified whole, and the lettering is amateurish. Added to the image almost as an afterthought, it lacks the vitality, spontaneity, and crudeness found in street graffiti and the gestured lettering of contemporary design. Neither does it achieve the controlled rhythm of calligraphy or lettering by a reasonably well-trained sign painter. The spatial integrity of his brilliant images is sometimes sabotaged by this awkward lettering, or by typography and/or professionally crafted lettering which is insensitively, plopped upon a lithographic illustration by others' hands at the print shop.

Eugéne Grasset preceded Lautrec in the use of bold, stylized black contour lines and flat planes of color, working with these Japanese-inspired elements as early as 1883. Grasset used flat planes in his backgrounds, keeping his figures dimensional while Lautrec slapped figures flat against the picture plane.

The attention given to Lautrec's posters also overshadows the large contribution of Jules Chéret, who produced over one thousand posters in contrast to about thirty-two by Lautrec. It was Chéret who introduced the large central figure, the bright, fairly flat planes of color, and an astounding range of lithographic techniques into the French poster. Comparison of original posters by the two masters reveals that Lautrec's celebrated splatter technique is limited and anemic when compared to Chéret's methods for hand-working lithographic stones. Through a staggering range of techniques – splattering, scumbling, scraping, scratching, smearing, smudging, gesturing – Chéret brought his work to life by then overprinting vibrant transparent color.

Certainly, Lautrec's small but superb production as a graphic designer is important and should be honored, but other figures are equally vital to the development of the modern poster. If Lautrec's posters are important art which warrant major museum exhibitions, many others deserve similar recognition. ➻

[1] Isselbacher, Audrey. Exhibition folder for "Henri de Toulouse-Lautrec," The Museum of Modem Art, New York. November 7, 1985–January 26, 1986.

[2] Honour, Hugh and Fleming, John. *The Visual Arts: A History.* (Englewood Cliffs: Prentice-Hall, 1982), p. 527.

High Style, Low Style, Vile Style

From *AIGA Journal of Graphic Design* Vol. 5, No. 1 (1987)

Over the course of this century, the corporation has been the American dream machine. It has provided jobs, technological advancement, stock-holder equity and philanthropy, such as supporting cultural programs, matching employees' charitable contributions and funding inner-city scholarship programs. Examples of corporate good citizenship abound. Westvaco Inc., for example, protects bald eagles in western Kentucky and red-cockaded woodpeckers in South Carolina by setting aside preserves of timberland inhabited by these endangered species.

Many – though certainly not all – major corporations have proven to be patrons of graphic design. "Good design is good business," proclaimed Fifties' designers as the corporate-image concept took hold and flourished. Yet a curious "high style, low style" ethic has developed in some corporate boardrooms and marketing departments. Graphic materials produced for stockholders, institutional ads in prestigious business and news magazines and sometimes even employee communications are "high style," produced lavishly and with taste and imagination. By contrast, materials produced for the consumer public are often "low style," strident and banal with little concern for design integrity.

One of the great folk heroes among corporate clients, Walter P. Paepcke, founder of Container Corporation of America, is lauded for his remarkable vision in understanding the contribution that design can make to a corporation. In the late Thirties, CCA appointed Egbert Jacobson as director of the design department and gave him the responsibility for developing a comprehensive design program. Initiated in 1951, the "Great Ideas of Western Man" advertising campaign was one of the most high-minded institutional advertising programs ever produced. Paepcke wrote that these advertisements "have made people talk about the company; have given the organization a tone of quality; opened doors for salespeople; interested college students in pursuing a CCA career; and perhaps even induced investors to study the company's stock."

The component of CCA's design activity not publicized, however, was produced by regional design studios that design grocery store and other packages for CCA's package manufacturing plants' clients. There was a real cereal-box mentality operating which addressed the infamous "least common denominator." Paepcke probably never paused to consider the contradiction of hiring outstanding designers and painters to interpret the "Great Ideas of Western Man" in business and news magazines in CCA's institutional advertising, while filling America's grocery stores with some of the most banal cigarette, soap powder and cereal boxes imaginable. Paepcke was a corporate aristocrat who possessed an exceptional understanding of the role that design could play in addressing the corporate audience, but his vision stopped short of the Bauhaus ideal of functional and aesthetic design for the working class.

Arguments that mediocre consumer graphics are necessary because "they sell" are dubious in product categories where the public is not provided a reasonable alternative. In some product groups only low-sales-volume, over-priced specialty brands give serious attention to well-designed products and packages. The corporate defense, "This is what consumers want," fell into disrepute when the Japanese automobile industry caught American automobile executives with their pants down in the late Seventies. These executives were producing luxurious, fuel-inefficient cars that appealed to themselves and their social strata. They were totally oblivious to the existence of a large segment of the American public which was rapidly changing its ideas about what an automobile should be.

More serious than corporate lapses in taste, or even misjudging the market with difficult consequences for workers and stockholders, is the problem of "vile style." When products defraud or injure customers, or do grave harm to spaceship Earth, star-crossed designers sometimes find that they have clothed the vilest companies or products in effective graphics.

The logo for an overseas investment firm was outstanding enough to warrant reproduction in a major design publication. After investors were bilked of millions of dollars, the firm collapsed and its founder fled the country to escape prosecution. The designer created an image of quality and reliability when the client was, in fact, a con man.

Environmental problems surface and cause serious soul-searching for graphic designers engaged in corporate design. An extensive list of toxic dumpsites, which were required by law to close on November 8, 1985, and file a closure plan 15 days later, was recently made public. The Environmental Defense Fund has discovered that many closure plans have not yet been submitted, most of those which were submitted are of very poor quality, and that some sites may be continuing to receive toxic wastes in violation of the law. Under the Reagan administration's Environmental Protection Agency, enforcement of these legal requirements has been lax. Designers working half a continent away can be totally oblivious to a client's toxic-waste dump. For example, the 28 toxic-waste dumps required to close in the state of Louisiana alone include such corporate giants as General Electric, American Hoechst Corporation, Kaiser Aluminum and Chemical, Uniroyal and Ethyl Corporation.

Allied Chemical caused one of the worst environmental disasters in history by dumping hundreds of tons of a highly toxic chemical, kepone, into the James River. After being convicted and slapped with a $13.2 million fine by Federal Judge Robert R. Merhige, Jr., Allied Chemical retained a design firm to develop a new visual identification program. It dropped the word *chemical* from its name, calling the renamed firm Allied Corporation. This is not unlike surgeons performing cosmetic survey on criminals to give them a new identity.

A personal close brush with "vile style" occurred when I was art director of the A.H. Robins Pharmaceutical Co. Inc. Shortly before I left that position I had been briefed and was about to begin work on graphics for a new product, the Dalkon Shield IUD birth-control device. Its inventor, an assistant professor of gynecology at Johns Hopkins Medical School, made wondrous claims for his invention. Problems were being reported with birth-control pills, and the IUD was touted as a major advance in safe and economical contraception. Today, A.H. Robins is in Chapter 11 bankruptcy to preserve its solvency in the face of thousands of suits from Dalkon Shield users whose problems ranged from chronic infection to death. Had I stayed in that position another six months and developed graphics promoting the Dalkon Shield, a difficult ethical dilemma would have arisen years later when problems surfaced.

Corporations are like people: While most are law-abiding citizens, criminals do exist. Designers usually lack the expertise to assess the ethical value of their clients' integrity on faith. When graphic designers provide an image of style and quality for corporate clients, sometimes we unwittingly put makeup over melanoma. High style can turn distressingly vile. ⊷

For a list of the toxic dump sites in your state, or to find out if your employer is on the list, write the Environmental Defense Fund Toxic Chemicals Program, 1616 P Street, NW, Washington, DC 20036.

An Oracle of the 21st-Century Book

From *AIGA Journal of Graphic Design* Vol. 5, No. 2 (1987)

Only a fool behaving like an ostrich with his head in the sand would deny that our day-to-day communications are shifting from ink on paper to the all-pervasive electronic bitstream. Writers process words electronically on microprocessors while their dictionaries sit idly on the shelf because an 80,000-word electronic dictionary is on-line, beeping every time a misspelled word appears. The encyclopedia, slowly growing more and more out of date, is being replaced by massive data banks, constantly updated and accessible by telephone and modem. What will become of the printed book? Will it perish after five centuries as a pillar of Western civilization?

The book may become obsolete as a major delivery system for information during the next few decades. However, it will survive and flourish during the 21st century as a major art form. A new book-art movement is in its infancy. Writers and artists are reverting to the Renaissance model exemplified by Aldus Manutius. Editorial decisions, design, production and distribution are controlled by an individual whose purpose is not merely to turn a profit, but to give birth to something important or beautiful.

Warren Lehrer, a multidisciplinary artist, has probed the nature of graphic communications in three books which stretch the normal parameters of the medium. Lehrer's works, though disguised in the traditional format of the book, are intermedia. While the pages can be read typographically, their space is both acoustical (having visual qualities which notate the properties of speech, sound and music) and plastic (possessing the spatial properties of 20th-century painting). These books serve several functions: to be read silently as literature; to be perceived as works of fine art; and to function as scripts for plays.

In approaching these scenarios for theatrical plays, the viewer has to suspend his or her normal attitudes toward typographic communications and graphic design. When I first confronted Lehrer's works, the inventive structure and unexpected typographic arrangements were compelling and fascinating, but my initial efforts to read his books were doomed to failure. I was trying to read *versations* as a traditional theatrical script, which it wasn't. Only when I became willing to suspend my preconceptions about how a book is read and understood, giving myself over to the characters, was I able to read and enjoy these books.

The reader develops empathy and understanding for Lehrer's cast. Some of them are: Ace Monroe, a slick British-born yuppie disc-jockey; Angelica, a 60-year-old black house painter from Alabama who has lived in a northern city for 40 years; and Carmen, a fast-food counter girl whose boy friend can't marry her because he married his sister's husband's niece as an expediency to establish residency in the United States.

Although Lehrer's books appear to be radical experiments, he has learned important lessons from the traditions of advanced 20th-century literature and typography. The visual interpretations of sound found in Futurist and Dadaist typography, the space-as-time pauses and visual/verbal rhythms of such poets as e.e. cummings, and the theatre of the absurd all

Spread from *French Fries,* written and designed by Warren Lehrer (1983)

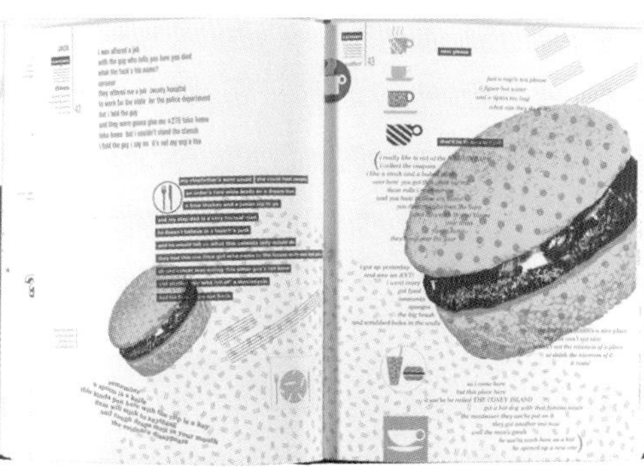

reverberate. Lehrer's tape recording and selection of verbatim dialogue have the relentless conviction of cinema vérité and oral history.

Versations, published in 1980, is a study in human dialogue. For readers perplexed by the design, Lehrer tells the reader how to approach it. The book consists of eight conversations with each character's words presented in a different type style or handwriting. This cues the reader to the speaker, and Lehrer has carefully selected the type or writing style for each character to express his or her nature. Seven of the dialogues are transcribed from candid tape recordings of real people, introducing a documentary element of oral history into the avant-garde book. Bold and italics are used for emphasis, and line endings are determined by breath pauses. The visual properties of the typography relate to the drama of the conversations, becoming a playbook for the reader. Lehrer's approach to page structure is unorthodox and sometimes challenging as he attempts a tightrope walk between graphic expressionism and an interpretation of the dialogue. The conversations loop in open arcs, cascade down the page in diagonal slashes, and often mix and intertwine.

The structure of *versations* is the structure of life, rather than the closed systems of art or literature. You can open the book and begin reading at any point, for the traditional opening, plot development, and final resolution, artificially developed by most theatrical drama, are absent. Instead, the reader is treated to characters who reveal their personalities and dreams as their statements and beliefs unravel.

Lehrer uses a lightweight, translucent paper for this book, enabling each page to interact with the pages which follow, resulting in some stunning juxtapositions. Some of the pages drift into chaos, paralleling the clutter and confusion, which result when everyone is talking at once.

The ideas contained in *versations* are expanded and enriched in his 1983 book, *I mean you know.* A sequence of stage directions and descriptions appears in a small column on the left-hand side of each page, and two of the characters are expressed as musical instruments. Lehrer advises us in the foreword that time moves from the top to the bottom of the page and that dialogue aligned horizontally on the page occurs simultaneously and should be read that way. Empty spaces are equivalent to silences, an idea dating back to Mallarmé's poetry of the late 19th century, and grey type is used extensively to notate hushed or whispered voices. Lehrer probes the relationship between theatrical performance, typographic arrangement, and page structure. Just how far can the author-designer go in his attempt to bring sound to the mute page, while letting it cue and direct the actors in performing the play?

The 1984 book, *French Fries,* coauthored by Dennis Bernstein and Warren Lehrer and designed by Lehrer, is one of the most fascinating books I have ever seen or read. To the typographic playbook format conceived in *versations* and developed further in *I mean you know,* Lehrer adds color and a range of illustrations, pictographs and photographs. The setting is the Dream Queen fast-food restaurant, where eight characters (employees and regulars plus Flash, which represents "a psychotic supermarket of fast-food personalities," the range of strange folks you might expect to encounter and hear if you spent your days in a fast-food restaurant) are joined by six additional characters who are heard over the radio when ghetto-blasters and transistor radios are brought into the Dream Queen. Printed in red, blue and yellow on a warm yellow stock, French Fries glows with the pervasive luminosity of all-night, fast-food restaurant light on colorful plastic surfaces: You can almost hear the fluorescent tubes buzzing.

The pages throb with energy and graphic vitality. When Jojo, the head clean-up man, is stacking trays, the page clatters with askew pictographs of orange fast-food trays. When post-doctoral student and divorced liberal Louise Giallanza (who is writing a book entitled *The Potato in America*) enters the Dream Queen, potatoes careen across the page, accompanied by bar charts on potato consumption and potato beetles.

(continued on page 88)

Selected spreads from a multilayered sketchbook that served as a repository for miscellaneous ideas and sketches.

Mixed media. Spread dimensions: 11 x 14 inches. (c.1970s–1980s)

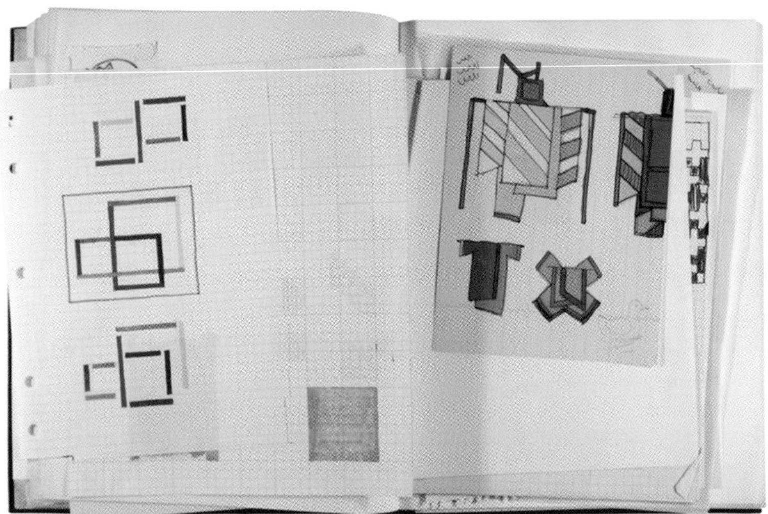

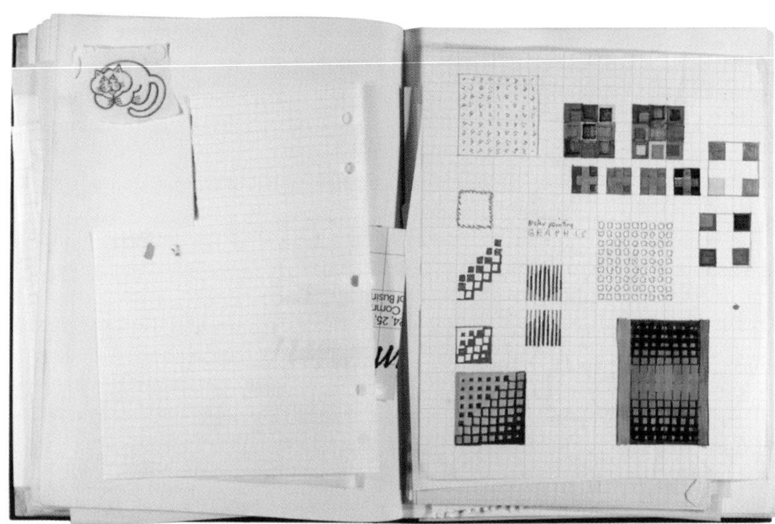

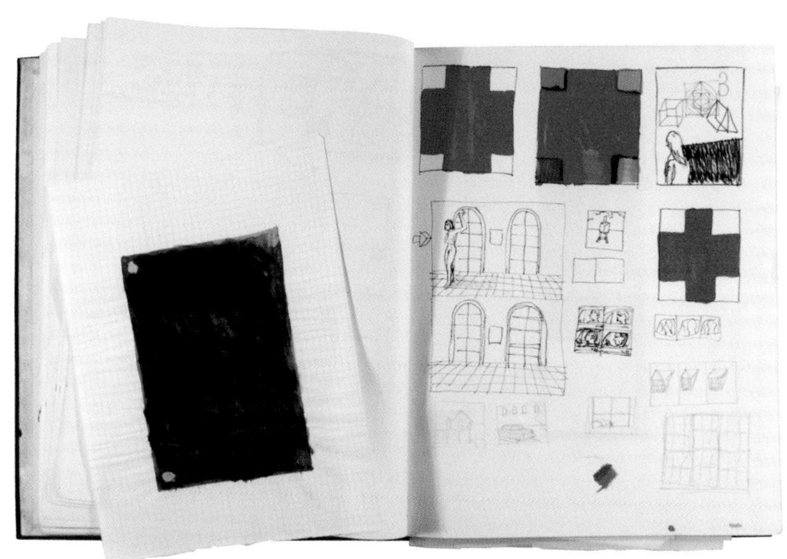

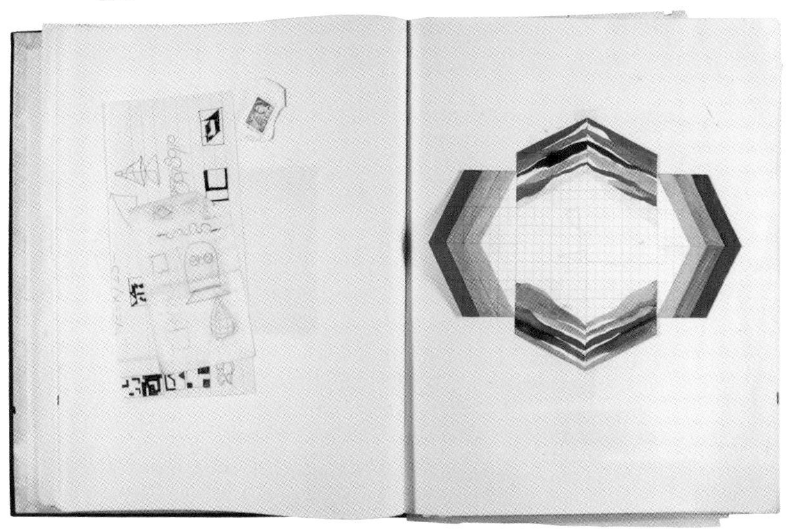

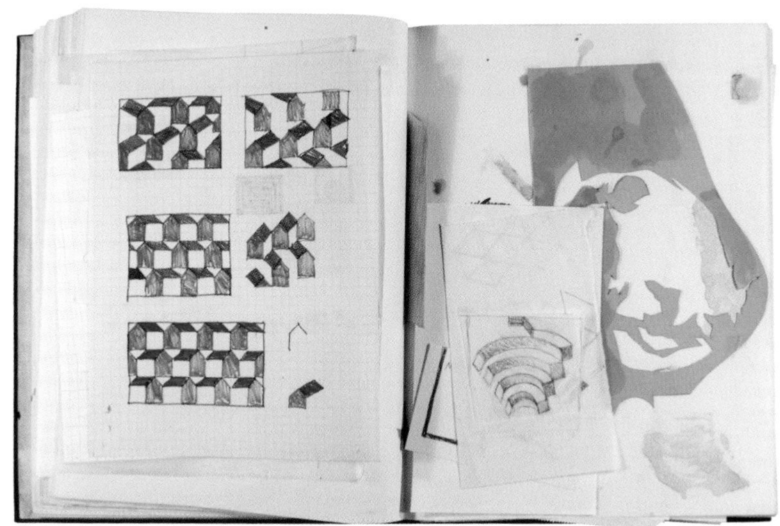

A murder occurs in the Dream Queen, and the radio gives updates on the case throughout the book. (A disclaimer advises us that *French Fries* was written before the McDonald's Massacre in San Ysidro, California.) A menu of terms in the back defines *mista* as a male customer in a fast-food restaurant, *the hole* as the graveyard for unsold burgers and fries, and *autopsy* as surgery after the fact.

French Fries proves that the book can be a movie, an existential visual feast, and a pastiche of literature and art. The entire book-art movement is rejuvenating the printed book faster than the pundits of the new electronic art can write its obituary.

Ultimately, Lehrer's books are about the human condition and human interaction, and they are definitely worth your attention as graphic design, as literature, and as observations on late 20th-century homo sapiens in the United States of America. ⊷

What Is American about American Graphic Design?

From *AIGA Journal of Graphic Design* Vol. 5, No. 3 (1987)

When it comes to design, does "Made in USA" have any meaning? What qualities or attributes are indigenous to American design, separating it from design in Europe, Japan, or the emerging Latin American design communities? It has been over 20 years since the distinguished German designer Olaf Leu wrote in *Print* magazine that German design had lost its national character and attributes. He observed that the purist geometry from Switzerland and the uninhibited freedom of American design coexisted as dominant influences upon German design as well as other design activities around the globe.

When Leu was writing, America could boast of an uniquely national, innovative school of graphic design. Bright concept-oriented advertising, accessible images, and a spatial dynamic combined with pragmatic but highly original approaches to communications problem-solving. America's turn at international design leadership began in the forties and lasted through the sixties. The catalyst was the sudden appearance of Modernism upon these shores as members of the European creative community flocked to the United States to escape the Nazis. But young American designers, raised on traditional illustration and comic books, saw the new form a bit differently. A synthesis occurred as European Modern design ideas were combined with a relaxed American vitality. The communication needs of a capitalist society and the egalitarian nature of this country were important forces which warped and reinvented European design Modernism. In American graphics from the forties, fifties, and sixties, advanced color and spatial concepts from European masters such as Klee and Kandinsky happily reside in combination with imagery as accessible as the Sunday comics.

Today, that uniquely American design vocabulary has mixed with ideas and concepts from around the world in a cultural blender. Instantaneous global satellite transmission, the multinational circulation of design periodicals such as the English *Design,* the German *Novum Gebrauchsgraphik,* the (until recently) Swiss *Graphis,* and the Japanese *Idea* have created a continuing international dialogue. It is hard to say where the "Italian Memphis Style" ends and the "California New Wave" begins, or "California New Wave" ends and "New Jersey Punk" begins, etc. ("New Jersey Punk" is "New York or Downtown New Wave" printed on black leather-look paper. See "The Right Face" by Paula Scher, *AIGA Journal,* Vol. 5 No.1, 1987; page 6.) In the eighties, design style has become a continuum of possibilities which leapfrog national boundaries. Recently, a Korean design periodical featured furniture designs which looked like Michael Vanderbyl graphics had been decoupaged onto contemporary Italian furniture. We can't even speak of Eastern or Western design anymore for the great divide between these two cultural mainstreams has become blurred.

Still, one can identify qualities in design which seem spiritually either American or European. Grid structures were developed in Europe, while the dense compression of typographic headlines by squeezing out the counterforms evolved in America. Certainly, the American sense of humor and a willingness to incorporate this irony and even sarcasm into visual communications is a national attribute. Many of the national qualities are fairly intangible: Push Pin graphics seem very American to us, while Folon's images have a European ambiance.

Because so much international cross-fertilization has occurred, perceptions of American vs. European design are in the eye of the beholder. To me, design in Chicago seems more European than design in Texas. Philadelphia design has a strong continental quality, while Los Angeles design is more homegrown. Others may perceive this differently. When Wolfgang Weingart spoke in America about Swiss design two years ago, he showed a range from traditional and New Wave Swiss to posters for McDonald's-style hamburger franchises. The range of sensibilities and approaches was similar to the range which can be found in most American cities.

The contemporary information culture is so fluid and pluralistic that variety, rather than any national attributes, is perhaps the most prevalent trait in design today. Instead of asking if there is a uniquely American color sense, we should inquire as to where the fashionable burgundy-and-grey fad – which popped out of nowhere around 1984 – in cars, fashion, and graphics came from. And where did it go?

While European design has traditionally had a strong theoretical aspect, many American designers, including some who graduated from the best art schools, brag about being "self-educated" and, until recent years, took a dim view of theoretical considerations.

In some Texas cities, the sense of individual freedom is so strong that no planning commission or zoning board can restrict the use of privately owned property. A trailer park, high-rise office tower, automobile junkyard, and luxury subdivision can be found adjacent to one another on an urban thoroughfare. American graphic design is like this.

Take Chicago design, for example. A visit to a typehouse there revealed that exquisite typography for designers such as John Massey, Joe Essex, and Jeff Barnes was being set along with a new back panel for Count Chocula™ cereal. When I asked if they did many cereal boxes, I was told, "Hey, didn't you know? Chicago is the cereal box and cents-off grocery coupon capital of the world!"

"Gee, I thought Chicago was the home of world-class architecture, Moholy-Nagy's New Bauhaus, Wright's Robie House, and national headquarters for Swiss design in America."

"Yeah," my host replied. "That, too."

This democratic pluralism of American design has resulted in the lack of any benchmark standards for professional practice or education.

Ten years ago, folk wisdom held that an illustrator could only make the big time if he or she relocated in New York, but a combination of overnight air express, instant faxing of layouts and preliminary drawings by telephone, and the creative excellence of illustrators such as Don Ivan Punchatz and Bart Forbes in Texas and Bill Nelson in Virginia has exploded the "only-in-New-York"

This Joffrey Ballet poster continues a European tradition of geometric structure and clarity that has roots in de Stijl and the Bauhaus. Design: David Colley (1977)

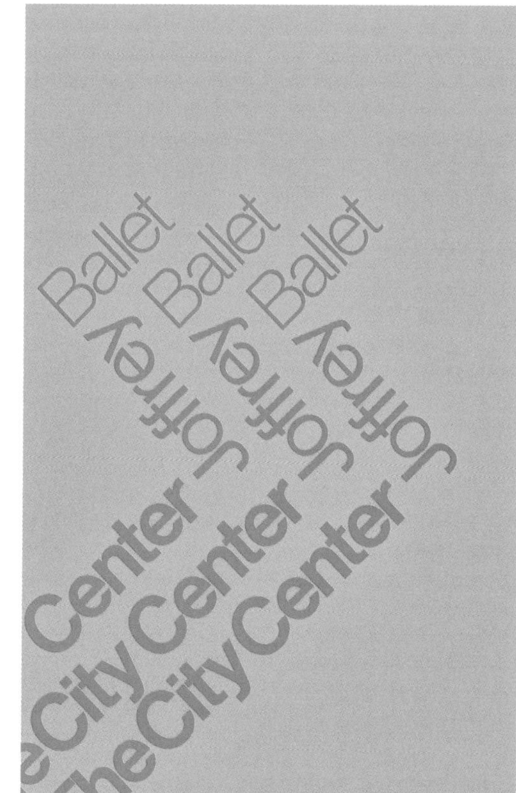

myth. Today, there is an international market for creative talent. Illustrator Paul Davis commented at a presentation several years ago that some of his assignments came from Tokyo, and that a Japanese art director had flown to New York to pick up an illustration the week before. After moving from London to New York some years back, Canadian-born illustrator Barry Zaid was commissioned to do a cover for the Australian *Vogue.*

More recently, the freely experimental, avant-garde, and even bizarre qualities of contemporary European illustration have been appearing in America, both in imported and homegrown varieties. *Esquire* and *The Atlantic* commission editorial illustrations from European illustrators, and the directory of artists in the back of the *American Illustration* annuals contain European addresses.

To test my attitudes on the question "What is American about American design?" against those of people who had practiced as graphic designers in both America and other countries, I called several designers. The first was Colin Forbes, the partner in charge of Pentagram's New York office, who has practiced design in London and New York.

"I'm terribly sorry, sir," the receptionist replied, "but Mr. Forbes is in London for a Pentagram partners' meeting and will not return to New York until the middle of next week."

"Well," I thought, "if anybody can respond, Massimo Vignelli ought to know." I dialed the number for Vignelli Associates.

"Hello, may I help you?"

"Yes, thank you. My name is Philip Meggs, and I wish to ask Mr. Vignelli a quick question for an *AIGA Journal* article, if he can spare a moment."

"I'm sorry, Mr. Mugs [sic], but Mr. Vignelli is in Italy at the present and will not return until the end of the month," the receptionist replied.

Remembering that the Swiss are pretty levelheaded about these matters, I proceeded to call Dietmar Winkler and reached someone at the Massachusetts university where he teaches. After explaining that the semester was over and faculty were pretty hard to reach, the youthful voice on the phone told me, "I don't know where Professor Winkler might be. I think somebody said that he might be going to Europe."

Design is now almost completely and totally international. Personally, I do not mourn or regret the passing of a uniquely American design style. Our nation has given to the world, and the world has given to us. International graphic design means international communications. This suggests a potential for international understanding, which can only lead to progress within the global village. ➻

Government Style: Design Consciousness and the Feds

From *AIGA Journal of Graphic Design* Vol. 6, No. 1 (1988)

The United States government has had an ambivalent attitude toward design over the decades. Some administrations understood and utilized the communicative power of the graphic artist. During other periods, federal design has languished, controlled by timid bureaucrats without visual training or concern for quality.

By 1972, the graphic identification of many federal agencies, along with tons of printed matter spewing from the central government, had reached a resounding low point. In stunning contrast to the historical role of the federal government in commissioning landmark architecture, many federal buildings of the 1950s and 1960s were executed in abysmal East Berlin modern: Mies' fabled "less," but without the "more." Many federal workers were spending their lives working in drab green offices whose lighting, furniture, ergonomics, and space plan were untouched by design intelligence. The Civil Service hiring process was blind, deaf, and dumb when it came to evaluating design talent. Many young designers and architects viewed the federal government as the employer of last resort.

Enter the presidential patron saint of design, Richard Milhous Nixon. To the howls of his detractors in the press, Nixon decked out the White House guard in epaulets and tasseled helmets and commissioned a custom-woven blue and gold rug with a giant presidential seal for the oval office. On a more meaningful note, Nixon responded positively when White House advisor Leonard Garment urged him to address the lackluster state of most federal design. Nixon charged Nancy Hanks, head of The National Endowment for the Arts (NEA), to steer the federal government toward effective design.

Under the leadership of NEA's Design Arts Program, the first of four Federal Design Assemblies was held in 1974. President Nixon's close friend J. Raleigh Warner, CEO of Mobile Oil, spoke eloquently about design and its potential role in public affairs. These blockbuster assemblies were enormously successful in educating government decision-makers about design's potential and importance. The design process was presented as an important tool for problem-solving. Suddenly, the designer working for the federal government was presented to the highest levels of government, not as a technician hacking out paste-ups next to the print shop, but as an involved professional with expertise in solving real communication problems.

A government-wide initiative was led by the NEA's Federal Design Improvement Program, directed by Jerry Perlmutter. In early planning, it was determined that most federal agencies lacked the sophistication and internal design staff necessary to maintain a flexible, evolving approach to visual identification and graphic design as found at IBM or CBS. Therefore, a strong systems approach was advocated. Demonstration programs included a redesign of the Senate papers by Massimo Vignelli. This typographic redesign proved without question that a designer could make documents more orderly and legible. Vignelli included wide margins for the notations that are made on proposed new laws and replaced a bland, centered format without a noticeable visual hierarchy with prominent headings and levels of information. The National Endowment for the Arts, rather than the Government Printing Office (GPO), paid Vignelli's design commission. This demonstration project was so convincing that the GPO internal design staff, headed by Lou Glessmann, former art director of *Time* magazine, was able to redesign the *Federal Register,* one of the two major government publications.

Leading design firms with expertise in visual identity evaluated various agencies' graphic image, then developed a visual identification program. After the first prototype program was created by John Massey for the Department of Labor, other agencies lined up for their graphic facelifts. Helvetica, whose medium weight has long been favored in corporate design programs, became the typeface of choice.

By some estimates 65 federal agencies significantly upgraded their graphic identity, and fully half of these developed a full-fledged visual identification system complete with a graphic standards manual and signage systems. Many of these were acclaimed for their excellence, including Danne & Blackburn's program for NASA, The National Zoo design program by Lance Wyman's office, and the Department of Agriculture program executed under the direction of internal design manager David Sutton.

The Design Arts Program published a newsletter edited by Nicholas Chaparos under a double-entendre title, *Federal Design Matters.* It reported on the latest architectural, graphic, and environmental design projects. In many issues, a timeline showed the progress of various federal agencies as they moved through the visual identification process. It was, according to Chaparos, "a subtle proselytizer, something staff designers could use with their supervisors to advocate effective design and show what other agencies were doing."

Chaparos edited several little books for federal designers, including a volume on photography for graphic designers by Norman Sanders, one about grids by Massimo Vignelli, and one explaining design standards manuals by Bruce Blackburn. To win over staff designers who were ambivalent about conforming to the requirements of a design manual, Blackburn used the analogy of a group of people working together to paint a barn. If each person went off on his or her own direction, painting one side of the barn red or green or purple, it would be a disaster. Likewise, if the Washington design office of a federal agency used Times Roman while the Houston office used Palatino and the West Coast used Futura, Garamond, or whatever they felt like on that day, there would be no unity.

The Office of Personnel Management developed new procedures for hiring architectural, interior, and graphic designers. Interested designers sent their applications and a slide portfolio to Washington, where teams of distinguished consultants reviewed them. The cynicism of designers toward civil service and the "insider-advantage" in federal employment that sometimes enabled clerks without formal training to move into design positions had to be overcome. Using the slogan "Excellence attracts excellence" in a nationwide initiative to attract top-flight architects and designers, the federal design initiative was an astounding success. Agency design managers formed an organization, The Federal Design Council, which maintained an ongoing dialogue about design issues. At its very best, federal design not only ran with the corporate pack, it helped set the standard of excellence.

When Nixon left office, the program continued under the Ford administration. During Jimmy Carter's presidency, the Federal Design Improvement Program began its decline.

During the Reagan administration, the Federal Design Improvement Program almost vanished. Only the portfolio review of external consultants – currently suspended while it is reassessed – and the Presidential Design Awards have continued. But, its legacy lives on. Those 65 federal agencies still have their vastly improved visual identities. The status of designers employed by the federal government is improved. New federal design programs still occur, though not with a central coordinating and motivating force. Siegel & Gale are redesigning forms for the IRS, and Anne Chaparos has recently developed an identity manual for The Geological Survey. After the initiative and vitality of the Federal Design Improvement Program waned, the Federal Design Council went out of business. One former member said, "The Council absolutely lost any reason to exist." It merged into the Washington Art Director's Club, a face-saving way to go out of business.

Before and after the Federal Design Improvement Program. Over 60 federal agencies had similar face-lifts. Design of updated logotype: Danne & Blackburn

Typographic format for Congressional acts and Massimo Vignelli's proposed redesign.

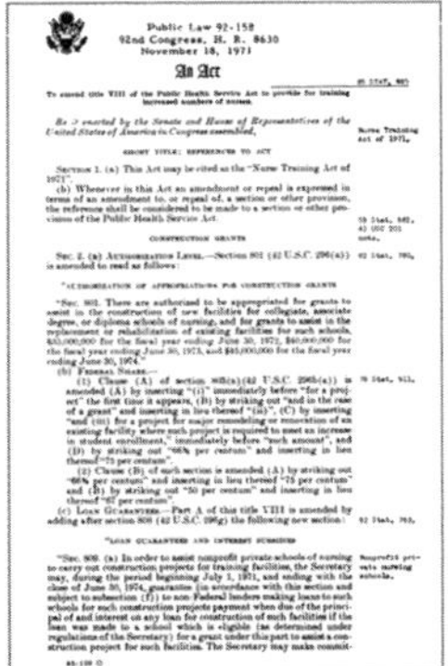

Public Law 92-158
92nd Congress, H. R. 8630
November 18, 1971

An Act

To amend title VIII of the Public Health Service Act to provide for training increased numbers of nurses.

Be it enacted by the Senate and House of Representatives of the United States of America in Congress assembled,

SHORT TITLE; REFERENCES TO ACT

Section 1. (a) This Act may be cited as the "Nurse Training Act of 1971".

(b) Whenever in this Act an amendment or repeal is expressed in terms of an amendment to, or repeal of, a section or other provision, the reference shall be considered to be made to a section or other provision of the Public Health Service Act.

CONSTRUCTION GRANTS

Public Law 92-158, 92nd Congress, H.R. 8630 Nov. 18, 1971

An Act

To amend title VIII of the Public Health Service Act to provide for training increased numbers of nurses.

Be it enacted by the Senate and House of Representatives of the United States of America in Congress assembled,

Short Title; References to Act

Section 1 (a) This Act may be cited as the "Nurse Training Act of 1971".

(b) Whenever in this Act an amendment or repeal is expressed in terms of an amendment to, or repeal of, a section or other provision, the reference shall be considered to be made to a section or other provision of the Public Health Service Act.

Construction Grants

The amazing thing about the Federal Design Improvement Program was that it accomplished so much with a very modest investment of tax dollars. As federal programs go, it was minuscule. Through its publications, seminars, and four design assemblies, it reached out to improve the quality and effectiveness of government communications throughout the country.

The federal design initiative was like a boat roaring along at high speed until someone cut off the motor. It still propels forward, but at a steadily diminishing rate of speed. Left in this condition, it will ultimately stop dead in the water, unless someone – the next administration or the National Endowment for the Arts – realizes that effective design is as vital to effective government as it is to effective business. Sinking back into the mediocrity of earlier periods is a real and present danger.

There may be hope for the future. Wayne Linker, Assistant Director of the NEA Design Arts Program, reports that the NEA is studying past design initiatives and is very interested in new programs in the federal sector. An informal assessment of the old Federal Design Improvement Program has been made. A more formal evaluation during 1988 will look at a number of areas, and new initiatives may be planned. The director of the Design Arts Program, Adele Chatfield Taylor, characterized the Design Arts Program as being "quite anxious to see if new efforts are needed." The book may not yet be closed on the involvement of the National Endowment for the Arts in improved federal design, for a rebirth may be possible under new NEA Design Arts leadership.

Information for this report was provided by Nic Chaparos, Lou Glessmann, Wayne Linker, Jerry Perlmutter, and Adele Chatfield Taylor.

ITC-Bashing

From *Print* Vol. 42, No. 6 (Nov/Dec 1988)

Typographic tastes are even more fickle than the fashion industry, so it is no surprise that the latest fad among some typographic designers is knocking the International Typeface Corporation. This latest spectator sport was launched last year at the Type 87 symposium in New York in a session dubiously entitled "The ITC Controversy." I wasn't in attendance, but according to eyewitnesses, the debate seemed to center on whether ITC is a force for good or evil in the typographic empire, and every designer who ever disliked an ITC typestyle was there to publicly bash it. This event has made ITC-bashing fashionable in some circles, so to restore the balance a cold eye should be turned toward ITC's contribution to typography.

One of ITC's major contributions is logistical, for it provided a mechanism for typeface designers – who cannot copyright their creations – to make their designs available to all distributors of fonts and receive a royalty for them. The old distribution method during the metal-type era was pretty sinister. A type foundry would commission typestyles from a designer, then invest heavily in matrices for a full range of sizes and weights. To protect this costly investment, the designs would not be licensed or released to any other firm. When Paul Renner's Futura was issued by the Bauer Foundry in 1927, it hit with a shockwave as designers and printers all over the world clamored for this new expression of the times. Its geometric simplicity and variety of weights fulfilled a yearning for modernistic graphics. Since the original was unavailable to other typefoundries, an outpouring of imitations and/or variations began. Ranging from exact copies to highly original variations, other fonts that could substitute for Futura included Airport, Atlantis Grotesque, Elegant Grotesque, Gill Sans, Granby, Kabel, Kristall Grotesque, Metro, Nobel Grotesque, Semplicita, and Spartan. What was going on? Economic survival! If a typefoundry's customers demanded geometric sans-serif typefaces and it didn't cast them, the customers deserted to the competition.

The dark side of this economic competition was that individual designers who invested months or even years in designing a type family could find that copycat faces were getting most of the business. When Hermann Zapf's Optima, Melior, and Palatino emerged as major typefaces, typefoundries and phototype-equipment manufacturers rushed to get a piece of the action. One typesetting-equipment manufacturer's specimen book has a chart in the front showing which of its faces are identical to well-known faces and includes: Musica … Optima; Patina … Palatino; Uranus … Melior. Another has an index which lists: Melior (see Medallion); Optima (see Zenith); and Palatino (see Elegante). Why bother to pay Zapf a royalty when typefaces can't be copyrighted in the U.S.?

When ITC was formed in 1971, it sought to address the needs of both designers *and* manufacturers. ITC would develop and publicize the designer's creation, then make it available to all manufacturers and pay the designer a royalty. This meant that designers could earn money from their inventions, and all manufacturers could have access to the name and master fonts of all ITC typefaces; so everyone benefited.

(continued on page 96)

Philip Meggs: Sketchbooks

Selected spreads from a multilayered sketchbook that served as a repository for miscellaneous ideas and sketches.

Mixed media. Spread dimensions: 11 x 14 inches. (c.1970s–1980s)

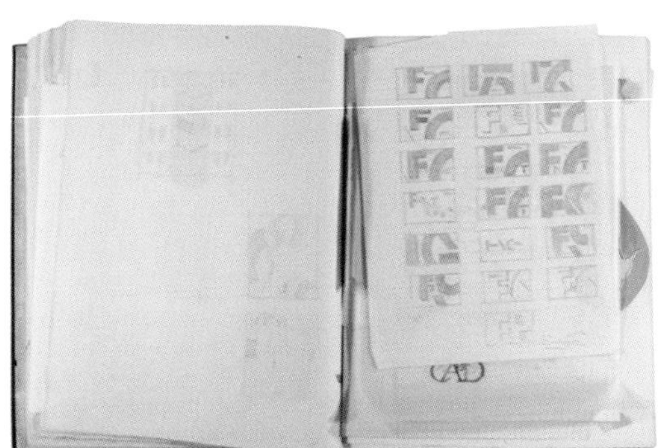

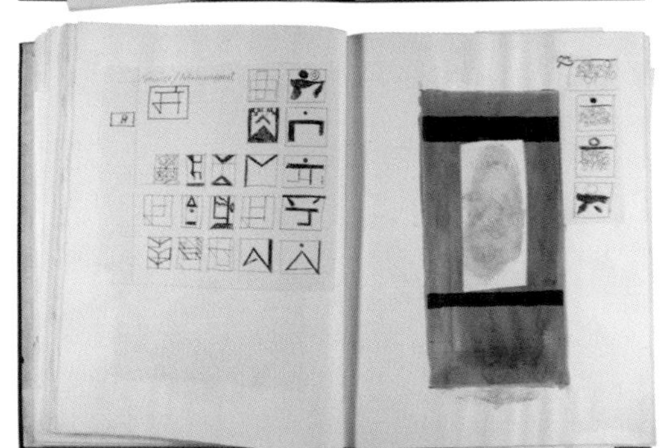

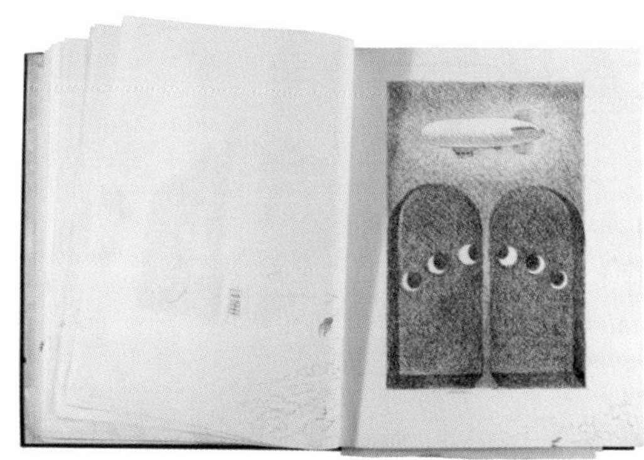

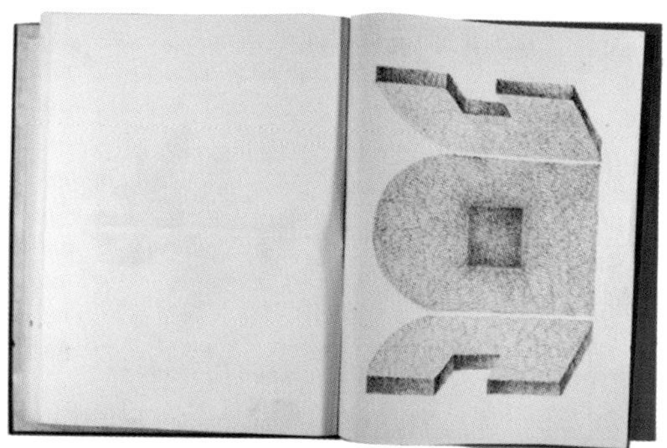
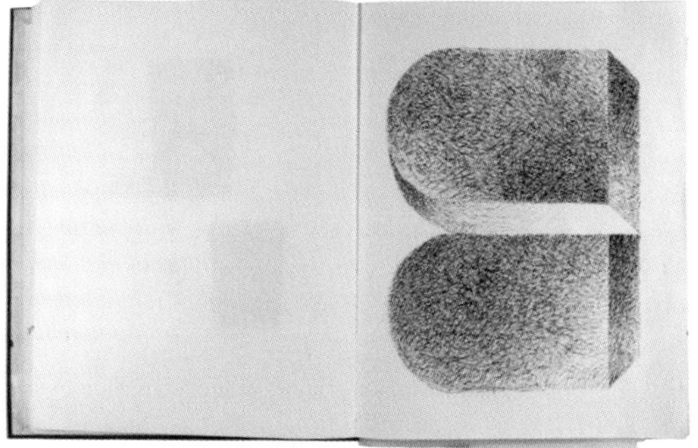

cite
cite
Special Esquire Offer:
10 Months of Esquire–Just 10¢ a Copy!

Looked at in terms of the technological revolution in typography, what ITC actually did was *reinvent the typefoundry.* Traditionally, a typefoundry was an industrial concern that cast metal types for printing, and typeface designs were developed to make its product attractive to customers. ITC understood that the typeface design itself was the product, so the company developed alphabets and then made them available to anyone, from the remaining metal-type foundries, to photo- and digital-typesetting-equipment manufacturers, to rubdown-lettering companies. The fortunes of great typefoundries seem tied to whether they realized that alphabet design – not metal casting – was the heart and soul of their business.

American TypeFounders dominated American typography in the first half of the 20th century and gave us Bookman, Century Schoolbook, the Cheltenham family, Franklin Gothic, Goudy Old Style, News Gothic, and important redesigns of Baskerville, Bodoni, and Garamond. But it thought it was in the metal-casting business, did not participate in the technological revolution, and is now a small subsidiary of a conglomerate, supplying metal types to hobby printers and leather workers. The Caslon typefoundry, opened in the 1720s by William Caslon and operated by his descendants until it went belly up in the 1960s, operated for two and a half centuries from the creative energy of its founder. Berthold in Germany, which realized that its business was alphabets and that it had to embrace new processes, remains a premier typefoundry and equipment manufacturer today.

Much of the criticism of ITC seems to be focused upon individual typefaces. All foundries have weeds in their gardens, growing alongside the flowers, and ITC is no exception. But one designer's weed is another designer's flower, and vice-versa. I once saw two design educators almost come to blows over whether Univers or Helvetica was a better typeface, yet 99 and 44/100 percent of the American public is unable to distinguish between them. One friend of mine worships Hermann Zapf and his typefaces, his fanaticism bordering on fetishism. Another friend, with an extreme modernist orientation, despises calligraphy, Zapf, and anything less geometric than his precious Univers. I've often contemplated inviting both of them over to have a beer and look at my collection of type-specimen books, but fear of the "accessory to murder" laws inhibits me. Lilly Kaufman, design editor at Van Nostrand Reinhold, once noted that probably no other discipline inspired such heated passions as those aroused when graphic designers expressed their feelings about typefaces.

ITC Garamond is especially controversial, for its large x-height combines with a refined regularity of character design to produce a totally different feeling from traditional variations. I often hear typographic purists complain, "They shouldn't call it Garamond because it isn't." In fact, they didn't call it Garamond; they called it *ITC* Garamond, which cues us that the visual ideas of Garamond got in bed with the contemporary interest in large x-heights, programmed type families, and systematized – rather than calligraphic – letterform construction.

"Shucks," says the owner of a high-quality typographic firm, who insisted that I not use his name since graphic designers provide his bread and butter, "I hear designers yelping about ITC Garamond vs. 'real' Garamond – whatever that is – and I just think this is silly. I can get a couple of dozen Garamonds for our various equipment, but the important thing isn't what Garamond you use, it's how you use it with letter and wordspacing, leading, line length, and so forth.

"You can order 10/12 Garamond Old Style and I can set you 9/12 ITC Garamond Light with 1/2-point reverse kerning to open it up a bit, adjust the processor to heavy it up slightly, and it'll look like an improved old-style font."

"The thing is, most designers aren't attentive to specifying the typographic details and expect us to be mind readers. Everyone says we're a quality typeshop, but really, our secret weapon is file cards on everyone who ever sent us a job. Most don't bother to tell us which Garamond they want – Old Style, No. 6, ITC, or something else – or if they want it kerned, and if so, 1/8-, 1/4-, or 1/2-point? But we really catch it if we guess wrong. These cards tell us what the client wants."

Pulling one out, he continued, "Here's one of the best art directors in the city. It says, 'Likes tight rags. Doesn't like letterspacing too tight, but hates loose settings, so try 1/2-point kern. Hang punctuation. Minimize hyphenation in ragged settings. Thinks Alphatype Helvetica has bad characters – use Linotron 202. Can't stand alternate characters, always use the regular ones.'"

"My staff calls this the 'quirk file,' 'cause it documents every quirk, preference, and idiosyncrasy in town. These guys think we're good because we set great type, and we do. But the real secret of our success is setting type, not the way they tell us, but how they really want it. Every time they complain, we reset the job and record it in the quirk file. We've got one client who likes his type ragged with, say, every other line 18–19 picas long alternating with lines that are 14–15 picas long. We give it to him and lose money on every other job, but he does two big annual reports every year with so many revisions that we make out like bandits."

Some of ITC's offerings are important. No less an authority than Wolfgang Weingart, instructor of typography at the Basel School of Design, declared that Adrian Frutiger's Univers and ITC's Avant Garde were the two most important typefont innovations of the 20th century. Perhaps he designated Univers because of its integrated family of 21 faces and Avant Garde for its array of capital ligatures.

For years, I have regretted that Berkeley Old Style, the exclusive typeface designed by Frederic Goudy in 1938 for the University of California, was not available; but now, thanks to ITC, this lyrical old-style face is available to everyone. ITC Baskerville is faithful to the original and can almost be called the face Johann Baskerville would have designed if he had had access to today's technology. Most of the other so-called Baskerville faces are really based on Fry's Baskerville, a 1768 variation that exaggerated the thick-and-thin contrast and the size of its serifs, which have the effect of Minnie Mouse's oversized shoes on skinny legs. ITC's excellently designed condensed Romans (ITC Garamond Condensed, ITC Baskerville Condensed, and ITC Century Condensed) have saved many an advertising and editorial designer's page when the copy ran long. Their handsomeness and legibility belie their economical use of space.

A contribution not sufficiently recognized is ITC's role in making available a new generation of "legibility" faces, such as ITC Weidemann. It leaves that old workhorse Times Roman in the dust when it comes to legibility and readability and should be receiving far more use for newspapers, technical manuals, dictionaries, and the like. ITC Weidemann has a more robust color, a slightly larger x-height, and better character definition. You can pack 49 characters of ITC Weidemann on a 16-pica line where only 45 Times Roman characters will fit. This 8 percent improvement in space economy can save 32 pages in a 400-page reference book while actually improving the reading experience.

ITC's tabloid, *U&lc,* which goes free to hundreds of thousands of persons at all levels of the graphic arts, has not only publicized ITC typefaces; it has upgraded typographic knowledge in America. Its editorial fare, notably Ed Gottschall's technology articles and Allan Haley's "typographic milestones" articles, is superb.

Now I don't mean to be a Pollyanna about ITC. It produced one typeface that strikes me as being so contrived that I actually asked the bookstore at the university where I teach to cease and desist in their practice of stocking it in rubdown lettering sheets. (This fascist curative was taken to protect my students' fledgling typographic sensibilities.) Some designers delight in ITC's mildly decorative faces such as Tiffany, Benguiat, and Korinna and use them heavily. These fonts give other designers visual nausea. That's design in America, and anyone who wants to impose his or her typographic sensibility upon the rest of us ought to be shipped to Siberia. ⊷

Test Your Typographic IQ

From *AIGA Journal of Graphic Design*, Vol. 6, No. 4 (1989)

Much debate has occurred about licensing and competency tests for graphic design. Advocates claim it would improve the profession; opponents believe it would stifle creativity and change. Allegedly, some professional licensing exams are esoteric and serve to limit entry. Tongue planted firmly in cheek, a professor of graphic design has prepared this typography portion of a graphic design competency exam. Answers are on page 99.

1. The European country that arrested a graphic designer for using sans-serif typefaces instead of blackletter is: (A) Germany (B) England (C) France (D) Italy

2. Renowned Swiss typographer Wolfgang Weingart said that the two major typeface innovations of the 20th century were the Univers family and: (A) Times Roman (B) Avant Garde (C) Eras (D) LED displays

3. When a noted design educator observed that there were no bad typeface designs, just typefaces that were not used effectively, he knew about: (A) Blimp (B) Stradivarius (C) Brush Bold (D) Daisy (E) All of the above (F) None of the above

4. Eric Gill named his typeface designs Joanna and Perpetua after: (A) King Edward's mistresses (B) Gill's second and third wives (C) Gill's two daughters (D) King Henry VIII's beheaded wives

5. If Helvetica married Garamond Old Style and had a baby, it would be: (A) A lemon (B) Optima (C) A turkey (D) ITC Garamond

6. Letraset purchased the Ready-Set-Go desktop publishing software because: (A) It's more fun to make letters on a Macintosh than to rub them down (B) So who's going to use rub-down letters in the year 2001 anyway, with computers taking over typography? (C) Why stock 100 different pattern sheets when you can store several hundred on a floppy disk? (D) All of the above

7. The famous typeface designer who couldn't be buried in a cemetery because he was an infidel and whose corpse was put on display in a warehouse was: (A) Firmin Didot (B) John Baskerville (C) Giambattista Bodoni (D) William Caslon (E) None of the above, you threw this one into confuse me

8. The following Egyptian city does not have a typeface named after it: (A) Cairo (B) Memphis (C) Karnak

9. The swashes on Bookman typefaces should be: (A) Used when appropriate (B) Torn from all typebooks (C) Carry a 50 percent surcharge when used, to raise funds for the homeless (D) Declared a national obscenity

10. The ultimate in elegant illegibility for the 1980s is: (A) 7/14 Garamond Italic printed in PMS 432 (B) 7/14 Caslon Italic printed in PMS 503 (C) 7/14 Bodoni Italic printed in PMS 567

11. The Futura Bold all-caps typography on Milton Glaser's posters is: (A) Too big (B) Too small (C) Just right

12. The great scholar of typography who insisted that no respectable typographer should use "condensed or expanded types, all 'sans serif' or (as they are absurdly called) 'gothic' types, all fat-faced blackletter and fat-faced Roman, all hair-line types" was: (A) Herbert Spencer (B) Daniel Updike (C) Stanley Morison

13. The best typographic design by a clothing merchandising firm is by: (A) Sears (B) K-Mart (C) Wal-Mart (D) Esprit

14. The "Helvetica" type from laser printers is: (A) Too round (B) Too soft (C) Too bland (D) All of the above

15. Which of these typefaces is NOT a pirated copy of Hermann Zapf designs: (A) Versatile (B) Uranus (C) Musica (D) Patina

16. The designer who uses the fewest different typefaces each year is: (A) Massimo Vignelli (B) John Massey (C) Bruce Rogers (D) Rudolph de Harak

17. The bottom counterform on this Helvetica 3 is so ugly because: (A) It's a Hong Kong–pirated font (B) It's from the new Macintosh/Linotron desktop publishing system (C) The Phototypositor operator was drinking on the job (D) The new co-op student left the rub-down lettering on the radiator

18. Which came first: (A) Univers (B) Helvetica

19. Mergenthaler Linotype is now owned by: (A) Ted Turner (B) A Saudi Arabian syndicate (C) An infamous polluter (D) A major computer company

20. Movable typography was invented in:
(A) China (B) Holland (C) Germany (D) Korea

Answers to the "Test Your Typography IQ!" Quiz

1. (A) Germany. In 1933, Jan Tschichold was arrested by the Nazis for being a "cultural Bolshevik" who created "un-German Typography." (5 points)

2. (B) Avant Garde. Weingart made this observation at the "Influences: Typographic Directions" Conference at Marshall University in March 1987. (5 points)

3. (E) All of the above. (And he said it anyway.) (5 points)

4. (C) Gill's two daughters. (5 points)

5. (D) ITC Garamond, which has the letterform construction of an old style face and the x-height of contemporary sans-serif faces. (5 points)

6. (D) All of the above. (5 points)

7. (B) John Baskerville. (10 points because we're using this irrelevant trivia to limit entry into the profession, and you got it right!)

8. (C) Karnak. (5 points) We tricked you! All three are Egyptian locales, and all three have typefaces named after them. Unfortunately for you, however, Karnak is an Egyptian temple and a village, but not a city.

9. (A) Used when appropriate, which may be never. (5 points)

10. (B) 7/14 Caslon Italic printed in PMS 503 (5 points). All three typefaces are highty legible, it's just that PMS 503 is a pale, washed-out pink with insufficient contrast. (You should have memorized the ink swatch book before taking this test.)

11. If you're a corporate designer who gets migraine headaches if you have to use type larger than 14 point, your correct answer is: (A) Too big (5 points). If you're an advertising art director who designs those car ads with 3-inch-high all-caps Machine Ultra-Bold Extra-condensed headlines, your correct answer is: (B) Too small (5 points). If you're Milton Glaser, your correct answer is: (C) Just right (5 points). Everyone else gets 5 points if you marked (C), but subtract five points if you marked (A) or (B) because it's not nice to criticize Uncle Milton.

12. (8) Daniel Updike, on page 243 of *Printing Types: Their History, Forms, and Use, Volume II.* (5 points)

13. (D) Esprit. (5 points, but if you put (A), (B), or (C), minus 20 points)

14. (D) All of the above. (5 points)

15. (A) Versatile (5 points). Patina, Uranus, and Musica are copies of Zapf's Palatino, Melior, and Optima, while Versatile is a copy of Univers.

16. (C) Bruce Rogers, because he died in 1956. (5 points)

17. (B) It's from the new Macintosh/Linotron desktop publishing system (5 points). This is true. The author of this quiz took a Pagemaker job down to the typesetter and the Linotron 100 output this 3 at 1240 dots per inch.

18. (A) Univers. It was designed before Helvetica, although both were released in Europe in 1957. (Also, Hydrox cookies came before Oreos.)

19. (C) An infamous polluter. (5 points) Linotype is now a division of the Allied chemicals conglomerate, which received the largest environmental fine in U.S. history for dumping toxic chemicals into the James River.

20. (D) Korea. (5 points) Pi Sheng invented printing from movable type in the 11th century; it was not until 1450 that Johann Gutenberg of Germany invented movable type *in Europe.*

Scoring: 100 = Expert, you may increase your hourly billing rate 20 percent. 80–99 = Professional, you may continue practice as a typographic designer. 60–79 = Apprentice, you may continue as a graphic designer, but only under the supervision of a Professional. 0–69 = Neophyte. Your license will not be issued. ••

Louis Prang: The Man Who Brought Out the Artist in Children

From *AIGA Journal of Graphic Design,* Vol. 7, No. 1 (1989)

For over a hundred years, children in America have enjoyed the creative experience of making art because one person, Louis Prang, cared. He is remembered primarily as "The Father of the American Christmas Card" because his Boston color lithography firm produced the first American Christmas cards in 1874. Birthday, Valentine, Easter, and New Year's Day cards soon followed. In the last years of the 19th century, his lithographic firm dominated the greeting card industry as Hallmark does today. Prang helped make color printing "every person's art form." Color and beauty entered the lives of ordinary citizens who had no hope of owning paintings, tapestries, or other art available only to the wealthy. Even children could own colorful images after Prang started marketing packets of die-cut pictures on subjects such as flowers, birds, fruits, kittens, or children. These were called "Scrap" and were avidly collected by 19th-century children for their scrapbooks. The quality of Prang's lithographic printing was so high that when French printers were shown examples of his work, they complained loudly that the prints were fakes, improved by hand-coloring with a brush.

Yet another contribution by this energetic man, the development of art materials and instruction for children, is neither collectible nor remembered, but is even more important than his printed artifacts. In 1856 Prang began to teach art to his young daughter and became aware that there were no safe, non-toxic art materials for children. Prang had become well-versed in color chemistry while apprenticing in his father's German fabric-printing business before immigrating to America to build a life in the New World. This knowledge enabled him to devise special formulas for non-toxic watercolor paints in bright, clear colors. After determining their safety for young children, he signed exclusive contracts with German pigment manufacturers.

Needing a safe and economical package for watercolor paints, Prang designed a special metal box with replaceable dry cakes of pigment. These slender, shallow watercolor tins, still in use today, were marketed under the brand names, "Prang's Palette Colors" and "Prang's Eagle Colors." Other art-supply products followed.

After discovering that the meager art-instruction materials available for children were abysmal, Prang set out to remedy this problem as well. Art training was limited to the private finishing schools for the upper classes, but Prang believed that many young men *and* women from working-class homes had native ability in art. If only the public-school system could have access to purposeful instructional materials and superb art supplies, unprecedented artistic activity could contribute immeasurably to the national experience. Prang resolved to address these deficiencies. During trips to Europe to promote his chromo-lithographic printing, he arranged visits to continental schools to learn about their art instruction. Results from German art schools convinced Prang of the value of a systematic and methodological approach to art education, building upon knowledge and experiences from previous lessons.

In the 1870s Prang launched a crusade in Boston by promoting art experiences in the public schools as a universal right. The Massachusetts legislature refused to endorse fine-art study for the public schools, but they decreed that practical training in those areas of art useful to manufacturing and industry should become compulsory. Gearing working-class students for factory jobs in the rapidly industrializing Northeast was a top priority, and art skills were perceived as being valuable for printing, advertising, product planning, and mechanical drafting. The new law could not be effectively implemented upon passage because trained teachers and useful instructional materials were nonexistent.

In 1874 Prang established an educational department within his firm. Earnings from the art-supply and lithography businesses were used to launch an unprecedented educational publishing company, which initiated a publishing landmark in American art instruction. This consisted of a series of art instruction manuals written by Walter Smith, an Englishman who had been wooed to Boston to become State Director of Art Education for Massachusetts. Prang produced a publication on color theory, complete with chromolithographic charts and diagrams for classroom use, including his system of relating a tonal scale of monochromatic grays to full-color art and a large color chart useful to teachers of painting and design. "Prang's Standard Alphabet" provided models of ancient, medieval, and contemporary alphabets for use by painters, engravers, marble workers, and industrial arts teachers in the schools. Eventually this set was expanded to forty-two plates, including fourteen in color. It provided an encyclopedic overview of letterform design.

Prang's 1876 art-supply catalog noted that "The importance of instruction in drawing in all public schools is becoming generally recognized throughout the Country.... The State of Massachusetts now requires such instruction as part of their system of instruction, while nearly all leading cities of this country have made provisions for the study." It noted that Smith's popular course was used at the two leading art schools in the country – the Massachusetts Normal Art School in Boston, the Cooper Union in New York – and in art programs of about three dozen major cities.

Prang launched a talent search for people to direct his art-education publishing program. John S. Clark was hired to manage the newly formed Prang Educational Company textbook firm. Later Prang discovered an outstanding supervisor of all drawing study in the Syracuse school system, Mrs. Mary Dana Hicks, and persuaded this young widow to move to Boston with her daughter. Mrs. Hicks enthusiastically developed Saturday classes for art teachers in many cities, including New York, Philadelphia, and Chicago, which were lagging in the growing public-school art-education movement. She became editorial director of the Prang Educational Company in 1882. Her time was spent writing accessible art instruction materials and training teachers for public-school art classes. Summer institutes were established in collaboration with state universities and art schools to prepare a new generation of art teachers.

After Prang's first wife of many years died, his friendship with Mary Hicks became closer and eventually they were married. Observers of their time noted that Louis and Mary Prang's most valuable contribution was their spirited effort to promote art and art instruction in the schools. In the late 1800s and early 1900s, most Americans firmly believed that art was too sissy an activity for boys, and perilously bohemian if a young woman wanted to pursue art other than as a pleasant pastime. The Prangs made a difference.

An early "coloring book" was published by Prang in 1894. Advertisements in children's magazines offered *Little Dot's Coloring Book,* with full-color pictures opposite outline versions that the child could paint. The total package – complete with a hinged metal box of Prang's nontoxic watercolors and a brush – was available postpaid for a quarter! Prang's lifelong study of color and color theory resulted in *Prang's Standard of Color,* published in 1898 when Prang was 74 years old. This pragmatic guide to color theory, harmony, and selection has had a lasting impact upon the study of color theory in American schools.

Cynics may say that Prang was merely a shrewd businessman who lobbied the Massachusetts legislature to create art programs in the schools, producing a large market for his art supplies and instructional materials. The record, however, shows otherwise. Prang invested time and resources in art education far beyond the call of duty, fostering and assisting emerging art programs and developing improved instructional materials even when he had a virtual monopoly.

Louis Prang died in 1909 at the age of 85. In 1918 the Prang company was dissolved and sold to the American Crayon Company, which continues to honor the memory of Louis Prang by using *Prang* as a brand name for watercolors. Some artists believe there is no other red as beautiful as the red in Prang watercolors. Apparently American Crayon Company has maintained Louis Prang's commitment to quality right into the 1980s. ➻

South Carolina landscape paintings. Gouache on illustration board 19 x 12 inches. (1962)

Cathedral. Two-color woodcut on rice paper 11.5 x 11 inches. (1962)

Miss Monroe.
Oil on board,
23.75 x 23.75 inches.
(1964)

Untitled.
Acrylic on wood,
7.31 x 3.5 inches.
(1969–1971)

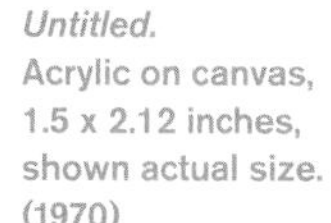

Untitled.
Acrylic on canvas,
1.5 x 2.12 inches,
shown actual size.
(1970)

A Pantheon of Design Eccentricity

From *AIGA Journal of Graphic Design,* Vol. 7, No. 2 (1989)

Graphics workhorse goes around in circles, even after retirement. In the early 1800s before the advent of steam-powered printing presses, Harper and Brothers powered their printing presses by a large draft horse that walked around a treadmill all day, turning a pulley system that powered presses on the floor above. When the plant converted to steam, the horse was put out to pasture on the Harper family farm. He promptly selected the largest tree in the meadow and walked around and around it all day – and every day – for the rest of his life.

Dinner at 2 o'clock in the morning. Ladislav Sutnar, the Czechoslovakian Constructivist who worked in New York during the 1940s and 1950s, detested the constant interruptions during the business day. He solved the problem by showing up at his office around three in the afternoon, taking care of clients, printers, telephone calls, and assistants until everyone called it a day, then working on his design projects until well after midnight. Noel Martin recalls that when he was in New York, Sutnar – who knew every good all-night restaurant in town – would invite him to dinner at 2 a.m.

Chicago designer changes with the times. A Chicago designer (name withheld by request) has only used Helvetica type and only eaten Wheaties cereal for 20 years. Recently he bought a box of oat bran cereal and used Times Roman on a project.

Illustrator makes midgets. Bill Nelson has begun to sculpt half-scale little men with pixie-like faces and real scaled-down clothes. These happy creatures spook the viewer by sitting around a room looking very real. One gallery that carries these figures reports that they are so life-like that some people think they are security guards.

Alvin Lustig slipped titles past their authors. According to Elaine Lustig Cohen, the legendary designer Alvin Lustig would often eschew aligning typographic elements such as the author's name and title on a book jacket. Lustig would slide one element past the other for a more dynamic spatial relationship.

Those bootprint patterns identify Cincinnati portfolios every time. At a Graphic Design Education Association conference at North Carolina State University last January, one of the speakers reported that a favorite technique of University of Cincinnati graphic design professor Gordon Salchow was to pull most of the work from the wall and drop it to the floor. Then he would walk back and forth over it while he critiqued the few remaining pieces, putting bootprints on the discarded comps. "Students went to great lengths to do work that would stay on the wall," she recalled.

Shucks, that's nothing. Paul Rand can critique a whole class in thirty seconds. A former student of Paul Rand recalls the week when everyone in the class was too busy to do much work on Rand's new assignment, redesigning the Parcheesi game. Rand arrived at class, paced up and down in front of the sketches, then turned to the class and said, "You mean I drove all the way to New Haven to look at this stuff?" He walked out, went to his car, and drove off. The next week, the work was their best of the semester.

Last will and testament leaves type to the Thames River. Thomas James Cobden-Sanderson, who founded the famous turn-of-the-century Doves Press with Emery Walker, did not want anyone else to print with the Doves Press type that he had designed. When Walker withdrew from the firm after disagreements with the aging Cobden-Sanderson, a legal agreement was worked out giving Cobden-Sanderson exclusive use of the types until his death; then Walker would retain possession. Cobden-Sanderson also drew up a will stating, "To the River Thames, the river on whose banks I have printed all my printed books, I bequeath the Doves Press Fount of Type." Cobden-Sanderson was not content to trust his executors to carry this out. Night after night, he would take as many types, punches, and matrices as he could carry to the Hammersmith Bridge and throw them into the Thames River.

Do Texas designers have harder heads? At a recent AIGA Washington meeting, a studio head was overheard discussing his differences with a recently hired young designer from Texas. "You can always tell a Texan," he remarked, "but you can't tell him much."

Guru wears eccentric hat. Reliable observers report seeing Milton Glaser walking around in a black hat with a perfectly round two-foot wide brim. It looks like something Ronald Reagan would wear if he played a kindly medieval monk in a movie, according to one eyewitness.

Farewell to the Opulent Eighties

From *AIGA Journal of Graphic Design,* Vol. 7, No. 3 (1989)

Decades provide us with a convenient means to map the woozy continuum of time. The Gay Nineties, The Roaring Twenties, The 1960s… mention of these decades conjures strong images and feelings. Other decades left a vague impression. The first decade of this century was an exciting time of airplanes, escalators, taxicabs, and submarines. Freud, Einstein, and Curie announced their unprecedented discoveries. The world of art was rocked by Cubism, Fauvism, and Futurism. The assassination of President William McKinley shocked the nation in 1901 as deeply as the assassination of Kennedy did in 1963. Yet, "The Noughts" (1900–1909) are locked between the Gay Nineties and war-torn Teens, with little residual public image.

Why do some decades live in the public mind, while others fade into oblivion? A suitable label must evolve, and potent graphic icons from photography, cinema, and graphic design are critical in crystallizing a collective public memory. The Noughts have no label, and its best graphics are extensions of the new art of the 1890s.

How will the 1980s be remembered? Economic expansion, a massive military buildup, and rapid technological innovation are the decade's legacy. Problems – massive public debt to pay for that military buildup, homeless citizens in the midst of plenty, environmental degradation, and the sleaze factor in Washington – were pushed to the back burner by a public enamored with electronic gadgets, powerful new cars, and the gilded affluence of the era.

What legacy does 1980s graphic design leave for the future? By any standard, the 1980s will be remembered as a golden decade for American graphic design. Design innovation exploded in cities beyond the traditional centers. Dallas, San Francisco, Minneapolis, Boston, and Philadelphia designers proved that innovation could transcend location. Pluralism was the spirit of the times, with a healthy diversity rather than a dominant style such as the 1920s Art Deco or late 1960s Psychedelia. The critics' labels – Postmodern, New Wave, and Deconstructionism – are hard-pressed to contain the exuberant spirits of April Greiman and Deborah Sussman in Los Angeles, the lush nostalgia of Joe Duffy and Charles S. Anderson in Minneapolis, or the dazzling California sunshine of Michaels Manwaring, Cronin, and Vanderbyl in San Francisco. The AIGA shook its image as an elitist New York club and emerged as a badly needed national organization for the profession.

Technology added to the excitement of the decade, permitting unprecedented new possibilities. Computer graphics allowed new approaches to typography and image-making, while making many design solutions more efficient and cost-effective. Six-color presses transformed traditional four-color process printing into lavish expressions as designers added special colors and varnishes. Early in the decade before oil prices collapsed along with the Texas economy, 12- and 17- color posters were produced by some Dallas designers. Even the most ardent critics of *USA Today* must concede that distributing this full-color newspaper all over America each day is an amazing feat, and its daily weather map is a graphic miracle of sorts. Express mail, fax machines, and color xerox all contributed to changes in the tempo and logistics of design. But all this technological innovation often resulted in nothing more than glitz, a superficial polish and dazzle devoid of meaningful content or form.

The decade feasted on graphic complexity as designers delighted in energizing and filling their space with texture, gesture, and vibrant color. If art moves forward by action and reaction, one might speculate that a "New Age" sparseness might emerge in the 1990s, making much of the 1980s graphics appear fussy and overwrought when seen from a later vantage point.

Information graphics came of age, and those most visually illiterate of professionals, the newspaper editors, actually discovered that they were producing a visual media that had to compete with television and magazines for the hearts and minds of the public. Graphic designers working in the broadcast industry started their own professional organization, complete with an annual exhibition. The Department of Labor declared graphic design to be one of the ten fastest growing professions in the country, and design education seemed to come of age with stronger standards and more cohesive curricula in many schools. One hears less bashing of design education from professionals than one heard ten years ago. The discipline discovered that it had a history, and fledgling efforts to forge a theoretical body of knowledge about graphic design began within the design schools. All in all, it was a heady decade for American graphic design. The optimism, economic expansion, and newfound national pride characterizing the Reagan Era seems to have permeated graphic design.

Although the most memorable graphics from many decades are those that address the pressing social and political issues of the time, 1980s graphic designers score poor marks for social involvement and concern. One is hard pressed to find many powerful graphic statements about the homeless, the drug problem (except public-service graphics of the "Just say No" ilk), or the social disintegration occurring in poverty-stricken inner cities. A blissful indifference toward pressing needs for environmental protection – from ozone depletion to toxic chemicals and acid rain – extended from Reagan's White House to Congress and rank-and-file citizens. Designers of the 1960s and 1970s made far more compelling and moving graphic statements about the plight of a fragile endangered planet.

Two poster exhibitions organized by Charles Helmken under the banner "Images of Survival" permitted designers to express their views about nuclear disarmament and AIDS. I predict that these two series of posters will endure, providing future generations with potent insight into attitudes and concerns about these horrible threats to the very existence of human life on this planet. This residual value to future generations will extend beyond these posters' contemporary impact.

The 1980s will be remembered fondly. Any fallout from its budget deficits, head-in-the-sand attitude about environmental issues, and the growth of poverty will fall, not upon the 1980s where it belongs, but upon the 1990s. It was an opulent, gilded decade.

Future Issues in Graphic Design Education: The Repositioning of Professional Practice

Presentation at the GDEA Conference in Raleigh, North Carolina (1989)

Only a fool would seriously predict what graphic design or any other cultural form will look like in the future. Even the young people in our classes who will invent the images, systems, and spatial arrangements of the twenty-first century don't have a clue about how they will break with our teachings to create new forms expressing their time.

During a Chicago visit in the mid-1970s, I heard hardcore Chicago Swiss design types emphatically state that the Swiss movement was out of gas. They were waiting for the next shoe to drop, unaware that in Switzerland the postmodern or new-wave design movement had already been launched by Rosemarie Tissi, Reudi Ruegg, Wolfgang Weingart, and others. New-wave designers educated in Switzerland were already at work in America. April Greiman was at that very moment designing in Los Angeles. Her ex-husband, Dan Friedman, was teaching postmodern or new-wave typography at Yale and SUNY Purchase. Willi Kunz had come from Basel to America, establishing his design office in New York.

Today, the seeds of 1990s advanced design are already planted and probably would look like weeds to most of us if we stumbled upon them. I won't touch future projections with a ten-foot pole. Rather, I wish to discuss forces at work that will impact and define the future. Some important forces are chips, China, and clients.

First, computer chips. The rapid computerization of graphic communications that is occurring will accelerate in the months and years ahead. Recent news reports tell of one-megabyte memory chips that can be stacked together for memory capability that will make current microprocessors obsolete. The Macintosh II, with its 68020 processor, is an incredibly powerful computer, but machines currently under development are ten times more powerful. But even this next generation pales, for heterojunction devices now under development for the mid-1990s are thousands of times faster. These can process data in 2 trillionths of a second and will be much cheaper because they are made by a microscopic, high-tech spray-painting process. Their ability to create and manipulate imagery goes beyond anything imaginable today. Paul Brainerd, president of Aldus, openly states that current marketing plans call for putting the design power of PageMaker into the hands of 4 to 5 million additional users. Every client, copywriter, and printer will become a graphic designer during the 1990s, repositioning the "real" graphic designer as a conceptualizer, imagist, and kinetic graphics specialist as media and graphics merge.

In a recent interview, designer Natasha Lessnik of *Spy* magazine noted that the art department waxer sits next to her Macintosh. "It's good for heat in the winter, but not much else," commented Natasha, who owns no X-acto knife.

Today, design education programs that do not embrace computer technology as a critical component at the center of the curriculum are as obsolete as Gutenberg's heavy metal. Faculty who do not upgrade their skills through an ongoing process of professional development are cheating their students and risk losing their tenure for professional incompetence.

New technologies generate new design possibilities because they alter our perceptions and thought processes. The computer must not be viewed as merely being the most powerful design tool ever invented. It must be seen as a catalyst for redefining the very nature of human communication. Those who resist the computer revolution are committing professional suicide.

The second factor is China. The most creative 1980s graphic design is made in Japan. The synthesis of two cultures, Western modernism and Japanese traditions, has yielded startling innovations. China is now opening the door to industrialism and modernization. The synthesis of Chinese thought and Western ideas will create unexpected new visual communications. And China will impact American civilization as well. China has been able to feed 1 billion, 53 million people on a manual labor, subsistence agriculture. She has a traditional culture based – not on the conquest of nature – but on people's close bond to the flow of nature. Just as Greco-Roman civilization survived the thousand-year dark age, Chinese culture has survived the forty-year Maoist stupidities; I believe that we will learn much from her. The startling industrialization of Korea is small potatoes compared to what we are about to see. Our design forms, philosophy, and world view will be shaped by Chinese thought during the waning decade of this century and the early decades of the next one. I am watching the Chinese.

My third factor is the client. Walt Whitman observed, "To have great poets, we must have great audiences, too." To paraphrase, "To have great designers, we must have great clients, too."

Applied design depends on patronage. After decades of design leadership, the collapse of CCA and CBS design excellence following management changes underscores this fact. Tomorrow's clients will be better educated, more sophisticated about graphics – they'll all have PageMaker, and expect much more from real-life designers – and will render decisions based on stronger, more comprehensive information. A designer's visual thinking ability and technical skills will have to be supported by strong literacy skills and reasoning ability. Our profession must develop a strong theoretical basis for its visual and communicative offerings if the graphic designer is to survive as a communications problem solver, not as a mere stylist or mouse-pusher.

There's more, but my time is up.

The Women Who Saved New York

From *Print* Vol. 43, No. 1 (Jan/Feb 1989)

To many outside observers, New York seemed to be losing its creative leadership in graphic design. But a new movement called Retro, led by female designers, shows that Manhattan is still a citadel of innovation.

Once upon a time, New York had competition. Early in the century, Philadelphia housed both the Curtis Publishing Company – publisher of the *Ladies' Home Journal* and the *Saturday Evening Post* – and N.W. Ayer, which pioneered the 20th-concept of a full-service advertising agency. The Big Apple and the City of Brotherly Love shared in graphic arts leadership. Many top-flight illustrators wisely established their studios in the beautiful hills near the railway linking these two cities. But Philadelphia declined, allowing New York to become the center of the graphic universe from World War II until the 1980s. In the present decade, creativity has literally popped out of the boondocks as Dallas, San Francisco, Minneapolis, and other cities including Philadelphia became centers for innovative graphic design. In advertising, Minneapolis agencies trounced New York by walking away with over twice as many awards in the latest CLIO competition. Defensive New York advertising executives declared their campaigns to be more effective albeit less original than those from Minnesota. This assessment was dismissed around the country as New York "sour grapes," as was Steven Heller's "Cold Eye" column in *Print* (November/December 1987, pages 133–134) blasting the AIGA for awarding its Design Leadership Award to a San Francisco clothing firm whose products and graphic designs exemplify the joyous, laid-back California style. Conversations with designers across America indicate that many are gleeful over New York's newfound competition. To be sure, New York's major publishers, corporate-identity studios, and creative design giants continue to maintain their high (but by now predictable?) standards. Chuck Byrne delivered a broadside in *Print* (March/April 1986, page 106) by writing that "seeing New York work is always reassuring. It's nice to know that *some* things never change." But those who applaud Pacific Basin innovation, Minneapolis creativity, and Dallas ingenuity and seek to write an obituary for New York's creative energy are premature. A new and unexpected movement has emerged from New York in the 1980s. General aspects of this new movement include an uninhibited eclectic interest in modernist European design from the first half of the century, a flagrant disregard for the "rules" of proper typography, and a fascination with kinky and mannered typefaces that were designed during the 1920s and 1930s, then banished from the profession after World War II. The formative innovators of this movement are female.

Efforts to name the movement so that it can be entered into the directory of design styles have floundered. Some people call it "Postmodernism." However, this umbrella term doesn't tell the whole story, because while architecture fits rather neatly into simple stylistic boxes (Victorian, Art Nouveau, Modern and Postmodern), graphic design is far too pluralistic and diverse to fit such a simplistic system of styles. "Eccentric typography" is a disparaging term used by some purists who are appalled by the revival of quirky typefaces. "Pluralistic reinvention" is a good attempt, because it suggests the diversity of influences as well as the differences between current work and the earlier models; however, it is a bit too dry and academic. Perhaps the term that has the best chance of sticking is "Retro." This prefix charges the words *retroactive* and *retrograde* with implications of "backward-looking" and "contrary to the usual." It seems to be the best effort yet to label this new approach. Like many good art and design monikers, it is slangy and a bit disparaging. Impressionism and Cubism were initially coined as putdowns, to connote fuzzy glimpses and cubed buildings, respectively.

Although new styles and movements appear suddenly and are as unexpected and pervasive as a dense fog, they can usually be traced to their founding fathers, or in this case, founding mothers. Retro was born in the hands of a small number of New York female designers principally working in the book-publishing field, which is traditionally known for its low pay and conservative design standards. These designers – Paula Scher, Louise Fili, Carin Goldberg, and Lorraine Louie – have rediscovered early 20th-century graphics ranging from the turn-of-the-century Vienna Secession to the modern but decorative typefaces from the two decades between the World Wars. They feel genuine affection for the kinky and eccentric typefaces from that period. Their attitudes toward space, color, and texture are extremely personal and idiosyncratic. Unorthodox attitudes about the rules and regulations of "proper" design and typography permit them to take risks and experiment. Jan Tschichold and Josef Müller-Brockmann, who wrote books about correct modern typography, would get eyestrain from these designers' work, for they exuberantly mix fonts, use extreme letterspacing, and print type in subtle color-on-color combinations. In many Retro designs, typography does not play second fiddle to illustration and photography, but moves to center stage to become figurative, animated, and expressive. Common influences and resources can be identified in their work, yet each of these four designers has an original viewpoint.

The self-consciously eclectic aspects of Retro continue a New York tradition. Scher credits Seymour Chwast of Push Pin Studios and his use of Victorian, Art Nouveau and Art Deco forms as an important inspiration. Fili worked with the late Herb Lubalin, who often called upon the extravagance of Victorian and Art Nouveau typographic themes in his more exuberant work.

If Retro has a pivotal figure, it is Paula Scher, who is known for her ironic sense of humor and outspoken attitudes. Scher began her career in New York after graduating from Tyler School of Art. During the 1970s, she worked as a graphic designer for CBS Records, where her work in collaboration with illustrator David Wilcox attracted national attention. Healthy budgets enabled her to commission outstanding illustrations and photography, and the music industry's interest in novel and original graphics provided opportunities to experiment with offbeat solutions. The high-flying recording industry crashed in 1978, as inflation, skyrocketing production costs, and slumping sales took a powerful toll. Scher recalls that her ambitions as a student were to become an illustrator, and she had struggled with typography in school. In her early years at CBS Records, she functioned as an art director who developed concepts, commissioned images, and designed typography to complement the image. The sudden collapse of funding threw her back on her own resources, for meager budgets limited business as usual. This adversity forced her to become a typographic designer. Her typographic design skills developed rapidly as she drew upon her imagination, art and design history sources, as well as her fascination with little-used typefaces in the back of type specimen books. Her typographic solutions used type in unexpected ways. Art Deco, Russian Constructivism, and out-of-style, little-used typefaces that many designers would be afraid to use were incorporated into her work.

When Scher first used graphic idioms from Constructivism during the late 1970s, the response to this work was underwhelming, and it was unanimously rejected from every exhibition. Only after these designs received some exposure did the professional community begin to warm up to them. She does not copy the earlier Constructivist style, but uses its vocabulary of forms and form relationships, reinventing and combining them in unexpected ways. Scher's attitudes toward space and color are totally different from those of her sources. Scher replaces the floating weightlessness of Russian Constructivism with a dense packing of forms in space that have the weight and vigor of old woodtype posters. The Russian Constructivists and Dutch de Stijl artists were deadly serious. The Russians wanted to invent new art and design in support of a new society to emerge after their Revolution, and De Stijl sought to invent a new order in art that would be a model for a new order in society. By contrast, a strong sense of humor runs through much of Scher's work, as Constructivist forms become whimsical faces and express a joyous outlook.

After forming the Koppel and Scher studio in partnership with Terry Koppel in 1984, Scher expanded her stylistic range in response to varied clients and assignments. Retro is but one approach in a vocabulary of possibilities.

The work of Louise Fili is highly personal and visibly influential. After graduating from Skidmore College, where an opportunity to work in the college type shop inspired a deep love for typography, Fili worked for B. Martin Pedersen and Herb Lubalin Associates. In 1978, Fili left the Lubalin studio to accept a position as art director of Pantheon Books. Her earlier work evidences Lubalin's influence. In her 1979 cover for *Ground Fog and Night,* for example, graphic devices used by Lubalin are clearly echoed: the letter *O* becomes figurative; and the all-capital typography is tightly structured into a rectangle. Fili's work grew in power and originality from this initial starting point.

Many people perceive the book-publishing industry as a laidback, low-pressure operation, but in reality nothing could be farther from the truth. Publishers market their books as two major annual lists, which are released in the spring and fall. These two major crunches are now three, for many publishers also have a winter list that is released between the two larger ones. Each project is produced on a hectic schedule that

(continued on page 112)

Selected pages from sketchbook with studies for larger paintings.

Watercolor and gouache, page sizes: 8.5 x 11 inches. (1969–1971)

SOFA + SHELL. SHELL + SKY ADVANCE
FORWARD – SOFA IS HIT BY LOW SIDELIGHT.
WALLS ARE PULLED FORWARD TO UNITE
WITH SOFA'S PLANE. FRONTAL
PROJECTION. SUSPEND TIME

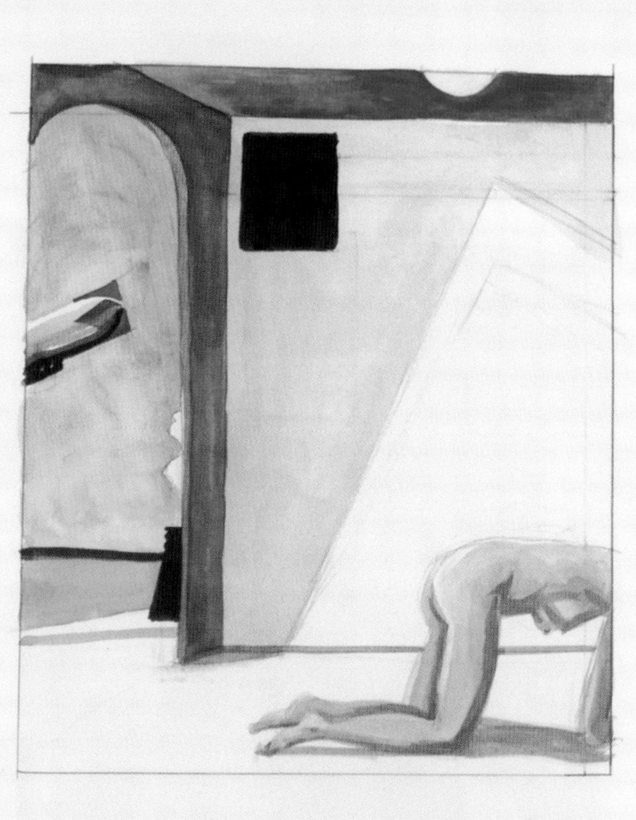

everyone involved must meet, resulting in extreme pressure as all books for a list are produced with concurrent schedules. Fili began to take her vacation and head for Europe each summer after completing the cover designs for Pantheon's huge fall list. It seemed an ideal way to recover from creative exhaustion.

Europe provided her with the inspiration that spurred the development of an original approach to American book-jacket design. The dimensional letterforms on the signs of little Italian seashore resorts built between the World Wars fascinated her, and she began photographing them. Her strong emotional attachment to Italy and France extends to their graphic traditions, and she started collecting European graphics from the 1920s, 30s, and 40s. These were found in the flea markets and used-book stalls of French and Italian cities. Between the wars, Italian and French graphic design took a curious twist as designers attempted to rectify the call for rational modern communication with their interest in sensuous and decorative visual effects. Modernistic sans-serif typefaces were decorated or given exaggerated proportions. Textured backgrounds were devised, and photographs were silhouetted. After World War II, design sensibilities shifted and these type styles and techniques fell into disuse. When typography converted from metal type to photographic and digital methods, the design sensibilities of the 1960s and 1970s considered these old faces to be outmoded, and they were not converted to photographic and digital processes. Fili responded to them with fresh eyes and began to introduce these inspirations into her work. As with Scher, Fili's eclecticism can more appropriately be called reinvention. She does not copy her sources, but uses them as background influences.

Fili's work is elegant and refined, possessing great subtlety and even softness. Seeking the proper graphic resonance for each book, she searches for the appropriate typeface, color schema, and imagery by producing volumes of tissue layouts. Sometimes, she will start with a vague typographic idea and a typeface will be suggested as the roughs become more focused. Often, that typeface will be a style she remembers from old typographic specimens or will have to be radically altered to achieve her objectives. Sometimes, it doesn't even exist. In those cases, lettering is commissioned. For Fili, the sad part of the death of hand-set metal typography is the loss of many old faces, which are simply unavailable. Fili has refused to let this limit her possibilities. She has worked around this problem when she wants to use now-forgotten and generally unavailable faces such as Iris, a condensed sans-serif with thin horizontal strokes, and Electra Seminegra, a bold, geometric sans-serif face with inverted triangles for the crossbar of the capital A, by restoring letterforms from old printed specimens, commissioning handlettering of the missing letters or even the entire title and message. Color and imagery also seem to resonate with the essence and spirit of the literature, almost as though Fili has developed a sixth sense for bringing visual correspondence to Pantheon's stable of authors. A division of Random House, Pantheon includes in its publishing list works of literature by authors of quality and distinction. The melding of Fili's unique sensibility with a publishing program that includes advanced and even avant-garde literature is a good match. She credits Scher as an influence, not directly upon the visual attributes of her work, because the work of the two women is very different, but as a role model demonstrating that a female designer could make a mark and become an influential and respected designer with a specific point of view.

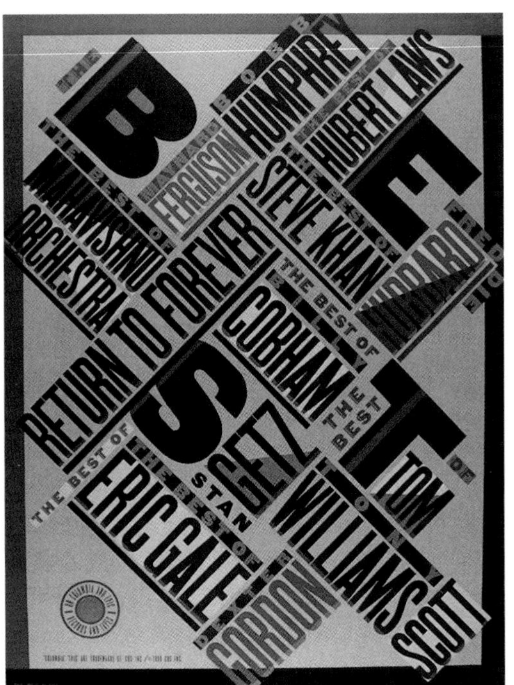

Promotional poster for CBS Records, inspired by Russian Constructivism. Design: Paula Scher (1979)

Scher and Fili are the wellsprings of the Retro sensibility, and this attitude and general approach to graphic design has attracted numerous adherents, among the best of whom are Carin Goldberg and Lorraine Louie.

Carin Goldberg graduated from Cooper Union, where she studied design and painting, which provided her with opportunities to experiment with color and space. Cooper Union alumnus Lou Dorfsman of CBS interviewed her after graduation, saw potential in her portfolio, and hired her as an assistant working under his tutelage. Later, after Dorfsman moved her to CBS Television's corporate design department, she realized that she had undergone an audition period. There, she learned a fine-tuned reverence for type and recalls that a type proof did not enter the offices that was not altered and improved. Later, she joined CBS Records and worked under John Berg and Paula Scher, who served as her direct boss. Emphasis was on innovation, doing whatever you wanted, and selling the most outrageous ideas possible. Goldberg recalls that Scher's commitment and involvement in design became a potent influence. When Goldberg opened her own design office, she began to focus on book jackets because her primary interest was in single-surface, poster-like areas.

Goldberg describes her work as being 90 percent intuitive and has no qualms about the influence on this work of early modernist posters. She has an enormous reverence for poster art, especially the work of Cassandre, and she approaches book jackets as small posters. "Without a sense of design history," she believes, "graphic designers

Book jacket for Pantheon Books. Art direction/design: Louise Fili (1983)

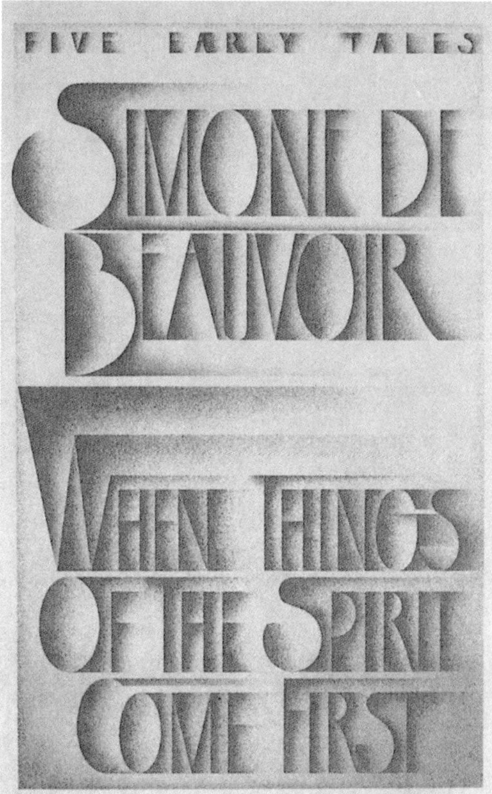

are lost in space." A striking image is needed in today's over-communicated environment, and art and design history provide her main resource. Goldberg's early experience as a painter informs her attitude toward space as does an architectural orientation, which comes from shared classes with architects in school and studio space adjacent to her husband's architectural office. Her ability to paint with her T square – functioning as a typographic precisionist with a painterly orientation – suggests the personal attitude that undergirds her work and transcends her myriad eclectic sources.

Goldberg recalls that Scher's effect upon her was not directly stylistic; rather, Scher's curiosity, her reverence for design history, and most of all her attitude toward her work and love of designing became vital influences. "Paula," Goldberg recalls, "really loves to design. As a young designer, I was as stiff as a board. Paula has this very happy, playful approach to design while being a very serious businesswoman and very serious about her work." Goldberg found Scher fair, noncompetitive and willing to help others, and she credits Fili with breaking new ground in book-jacket design. Goldberg thought, "If she can do it, so can I." When Goldberg opened her office, Fili was "kind of a door, proving that beautiful and original book jackets could be done."

Lorraine Louie migrated to New York six years ago from the San Francisco area, where she graduated from the California College of Arts and Crafts and worked for Kit and Linda Hinrichs for two and a half years. She recalls that during her first year in New York she really had to scramble. Six months at a small corporate design firm were followed by freelance assignments for CBS's advertising and promotion department, *Fortune,* and Vintage, for which she did book jackets. She then opened her own studio with emphasis on book-jacket design and publisher promotion. Louie declines to identify any specific influences, noting that her influences come from everywhere:

museums, other contemporary designers, and the 20s, 30s, and 40s. In the 1980s, she notes, "Everything influences everything." An intuitive designer, Louie strives to create individuality for her clients. She sees a reciprocal influence in contemporary design trends, but believes that designers do try to maintain individuality. "I work primarily with composition and color," she notes, "while Louise Fili is enormously innovative with typography and lettering."

Louie has developed an enviable reputation for her ability to create series of book jackets that have graphic distinctiveness as a group. At the same time, she maintains individuality for each book through imaginative color combinations and imagery. In addition to the heralded formats for the Vintage Contemporaries, Louie's covers for Peter Matthiessen's novels are unified by a vertical treatment of the author's name, geometric shapes, and eccentric typestyle.

When Scher and Fili first produced their Retro idioms, many designers raised on purity and typographic refinement were appalled to see the return of these exiled letterforms and eccentric spatial organization. Scher relates that, in the judging of a major design exhibition several years ago, two jurors of the "famous designer" variety approached some of her early Retro pieces and exclaimed, "Can you believe this (expletive deleted)!!!" But Retro – like the Postmodernism of Dan Friedman, April Greiman, and Willi Kunz in the late 1970s all early 80s – refused to go away, as more and more designers and clients responded to its energy and fresh approach. It has crept into the design vocabulary as designers, courageously or reticently, dare to use eccentric typefaces such as Empire, Bernhard Fashion, and Huxley. Many leading art directors now consider it part of their repertoire, along with all the other styles and approaches that are called upon as needed to express the proper character for a given assignment.

A 1920s poster by Paul Renner, designer of Futura, is reinvented as a typographic book jacket for Random House. Design: Carin Goldberg (1986)

Cover for a quarterly magazine by Vintage Books that features the work of new American writers. Design: Lorraine Louie (1987)

Paula Scher relates that designer/illustrator Richard Hess once told her "You're responsible for a lot of awful work." He was referring to the poor use of quirky old typefaces by her imitators who manage to locate the old fonts but fail to achieve the precise spacing, scale relationships, and color combination that make the best Retro designs stunning to behold. The late Herb Lubalin commented that he almost regretted designing the Avant Garde type family be cause the capital ligatures were created to resolve awkward spacing problems such as TVA, but that many designers and typographers used them poorly. Avant Garde capital ligatures were used throughout the 1970s in combinations that compounded and exaggerated the very misfit letter combinations they were meant to overcome. Scher, Fili, Goldberg, and Louie must surely be appalled at some of the Retro knockoffs that have been appearing without the concise sense of scale, space, and color.

In the usual way these things happen, art and design styles emerge from the hands of a small number of innovators, expand and become fashionable as more and more people climb on the bandwagon, then become part of the accepted vocabulary. Often, the innovators of a style continue to explore and extend its boundaries after the faddists have deserted it for other new styles and trends.

A willingness to take risks and a commitment to excellence are characteristic of the work of Scher, Fili, Goldberg, and Louie. This holds promise that, whatever course Retro takes, American graphic design will be enriched by the creative efforts of these four women for many years to come.

A Feminist Footnote

After completing my two-hour interview with Carin Goldberg, in connection with this article, I told her I had run out of questions. She looked me squarely in the eye and said, "Don't you have any questions about the fact that this article is about women?"

"It's interesting that you raised the issue," I said, "because I probably should have. But until you brought it up, I really didn't have any questions relating to that. Are you referring to problems that women have in the design profession?"

"Well," she responded, "you prefaced this interview with the information that people in other parts of the country have said that nothing new is happening in New York. Then there's this new movement and it's all women. Is this relevant?" "When I interviewed Louise Fili, the issue never came up," I said. "And if you hadn't brought it up, I wouldn't have. But let's discuss it. Is it relevant?"

Goldberg looked out the window and said, "I don't know that it is, and I don't bring it up because I'm sitting here chomping at the bit waiting to get angry in a feminist vein. I just think it's interesting that nothing in this interview really had to do with being a woman designer and I wonder if it really matters. Did this article come out of, 'Let's do women,' or did it come out of, 'Let's do New York?'" I replied, "It came out of, 'There appears to be a new movement in New York and the work is exciting.' It's very influential. If you pick up that new design annual over there, you find that condensed sans-serif types with funny Rs are being letterspaced all over the country. This is a Louise Fili, Paula Scher, Lorraine Louie, and Carin Goldberg influence. Maybe the gender issue is coincidental. If it happened to be Paula and Harry and Lorraine and Fred –"

"It would be a different article," Goldberg interjected.

"Maybe," I shrugged. "Or maybe it would just have a different title. But my interest is the design."

Goldberg ventured this would be a great way to do the article: "Calling it something as provocative as 'women'... then just writing about design."

I concurred.

The Obscene Typography Machine

From *Print* Vol. 43, No. 5 (Sept/Oct 1989)

At a recent Washington AIGA meeting, editors from four major design publications held a panel discussion. One of the shills in the audience asked, "Do the design magazines establish design trends, or do you merely follow and report about them?" After all of the editors replied that they weren't too interested in stylistic trends or the latest fashion, one editor commented that the one *real* trend that everyone in the room should watch closely is the increasing importance of computers in graphic design. Most designers who have overcome their computer phobia and learned computer-assisted design have become mesmerized by its possibilities. Text can be poured into columns, PMS matchcolor backgrounds can be changed instantly to try different color combinations, and type size and style can be changed at will. For thousands of organizations with publications budgets too small to afford design and typesetting services, desktop publishing allows a significant upgrade of routine printed material ranging from internal company publications to public-school study guides and church bulletins. But this wonderful new tool that is revolutionizing graphic design has its dark side.

Unfortunately, the ease of computer use puts potent graphic capabilities into the hands of people who are devoid of any esthetic sense about typography and have little or no understanding of the most basic principles of design. Powerful new software programs including Aldus Freehand and Illustrator 88 give the designer (or moron, as the case may be) the power to flip, rotate, stretch or bend typography with the click of the mouse button. This permits some of the most obscene type forms ever devised or imagined. Certainly, distortion can be a useful and innovative design tool when handled with sensitivity and intelligence, but we are seeing type distorted in violation of everything that has been learned over the past 500 years about making functional and beautiful letterforms. Newspaper advertisements are a major source of grotesque typographic distortion, as headlines are stretched or condensed to fit with about as much grace as a fat lady squeezing into a too-small girdle.

A principle from perceptual psychology is that when identical rectangles are placed on the page with one in a horizontal position and the other in a vertical position, the horizontal rectangle will appear heavier, even though it is identical to the vertical form. A typeface designer spends hours refining his strokes, shaving horizontal forms until they appear to have the same thickness as the vertical form.

Everyone who takes an introductory typography class learns that if a letter composed of curved strokes such as an *O* is the same height as a letter composed of vertical strokes such as an *E*, the *O* will appear too small. Typeface designers optically adjust circular forms, which must extend slightly above the capline and slightly below the baseline to appear correct.

One reason a typeface is considered a masterpiece is because the designer achieved optical harmony in adjusting the size and proportion of the parts – not mathematically, but esthetically and perceptually. Frederic W. Goudy's Goudy Old Style, Adrian Frutiger's Univers, and

John Baskerville's Baskerville: these typefaces are honored as great tools of communication and works of art because a virtuoso designer poured heart, soul and countless hours of work into creating harmonious relationships between letterforms.

Suddenly in 1988, anyone with a Macintosh or other computer and a $495 software program could wreak havoc on these beautifully crafted forms. Consider the four versions of Helvetica Medium above, executed on a computer and outputted from a Linotron 100 at 1270 dots per inch. The top setting is normal type reasonably close to the original font created by Max Miedinger and Edouard Hoffman 30 years ago, allowing for some alteration when converted to a specific digital output device. The second version was produced by grabbing the corner of the type with the mouse and squeezing it down into a shorter version, and the lower versions were produced by grabbing the corner of the type with the mouse and stretching it into taller condensed versions. The computer is a dumb robot, totally ignorant of the principles of perception mentioned earlier. In the lower versions, the horizontal strokes were stretched wider, while the vertical strokes maintained their original width. The result is grossly misproportioned letterforms. The optical adjustment of the *O* and *S* is exaggerated, making them seem too tall for the other letters. We are seeing typography approach this level of obscenity as students, neophytes, and even experienced designers, berserk over the new toy, violate well-drawn letterforms without bringing compensating values of expression or form to their work. Goudy and Baskerville must be spinning in their graves, and Frutiger and Miedinger must be quite depressed to see their artful letters, created as an act of love, destroyed by those who either cannot see or simply do not care.

One impact of this new graphic software relates to what is becoming known as Deconstructivist typography, whose integrated whole is taken apart. While some of the practitioners of this new typographic movement exhibit great sensitivity and originality, others are merely flitting through the collection of graphic procedures available with the new software. Operations that formerly required painstaking cut-and-paste work, such as setting type in an oval or along a curved baseline, can now be performed instantly by drawing an oval, a circle or a meandering line, typing in the text, then clicking the mouse on the word "Join" in the menu. The oval, circle or line instantly becomes the baseline of the type. These graphic devices provide a vocabulary of instant clichés, executed as simply as snapping one's fingers. Often, these techniques are used, not for thoughtful communicative or expressive reasons, but simply because they are there. The problem for designers exploring the elastic typography and/or the Deconstructivist sensibility on a computer is, "What do you do for an encore?" As with most specialized tools, a computer-graphics program permits one to do a limited number of things very efficiently, but only operates within a fixed range of possibilities. Its innovative graphic techniques will become old and tired very rapidly as more and more people hop on the bandwagon, transforming graphics that originally appeared fresh and innovative into hack work.

Another problem with all this graphic power is that tremendous capability is put into the hands of people who don't know an ampersand from a hole in the ground. A newsletter recently crossed my desk with each column of type linespaced differently, because the novice desktop publisher discovered that the page-layout program would permit automatic leading to fit the column depth. Columns in 10-point Times Roman with no leading were adjacent to other columns set in 10-point Times Roman with about 25 points of leading between the lines. Text columns were justified, producing gaping holes in each line of type due to poor wordspacing. He or she was too naive about typography to realize how the inconsistent wordspacing destroyed legibility and the tonal quality of the page.

Although equipment manufacturers and software developers have made modest efforts to educate their users about the rudiments of design through little booklets explaining effective page layout or newsletter design, complete with case studies of redesigned publications with notable improvements, a new generation of unschooled graphic designers – editors, public-relations agents, secretaries and other do-it-yourself desktop publishers – are totally ignorant of the rudiments of publication design and typography. Adobe, the company that developed the PostScript software that transforms crude bitmapped type on the computer screen into refined high resolution output, publishes excellent materials. Some software tutorials address design issues, but do it poorly. More must be done. There should be an ethical responsibility on the part of companies that put powerful tools into the hands of uninformed people without educating them about the proper use of these tools.

The obscene typography machine can also be the sublime typography machine. Professional designers can explore new creative possibilities and spend more time developing concepts and designing and less time laboriously executing their work. As this technology becomes available in third-world nations, their efforts toward education and development can take quantum leaps forward as a result of the economy of desktop publishing. The computer-graphics force is now with us, but its dark side must be controlled; otherwise, the obscene typography machine is going to inflict unimagined graphic atrocities upon the public. ●

Selected pages from sketchbook with studies for larger paintings.

Watercolor and gouache, page sizes: 8.5 x 11 inches. (1969–1971)

The 1940s: Rise of the Modernists

From *Print* Vol. 43, No. 6 (Nov/Dec 1989)

What is a graphic designer? During the 1940s, the scornful definition of anyone so conceited as to call himself a *designer* was "a slow layout man with an ego," recalls graphic designer Bruce Beck, who began his career in Chicago in 1946. The illustrator and the salesman dominated the 1940s art studio, and the copywriter and account executive reigned supreme in the advertising agencies. A layout man was a pair of hands doing what he was told. He had value as an artist with drawing ability and a sense of placement, but no one would consider asking him to solve a problem, or even ask him to think about the problem. Yet the 1940s was the incubator for the modern American graphic design profession: Forces were at work during the decade which would create a momentum for change by decade's end as designers persisted in pushing for a revised concept of graphic communications. The *layout man* – a facilitator who arranged writers' words and illustrators' pictures upon the page – was slowly replaced by the modern graphic designer, a conceptual problem-solver who engaged in the total design of the space, orchestrating words, signs, symbols, and images into a communicative unity.

A Watershed Decade

The decade of the 1940s was an epic watershed for America. The 1939 New York World's Fair established America's growing international leadership as the nation displayed its technological and industrial prowess. A dark cloud hung over this celebration, for Hitler launched World War II with his invasion of Poland on September 1, 1939. War and the postwar conversion to an industrial consumer economy formed the backdrop for this bellwether decade and for the ferment of revolution in American graphic design, architecture, and painting that it witnessed. Traditional illustration had dominated American mass communications during the first four decades of the century. This "Golden Age of American Illustration" began to draw to a close as the new breed of visual communicator – the modernist graphic designer – began to make his presence felt. Certainly, traditional illustration continued to dominate many mass-audience popular magazines and much print advertising until the early 1960s. But during the 1940s, modern design found a foothold at a handful of upscale and forward-looking magazines, including *Bazaar, Vogue,* and *Fortune,* in a small number of corporations, notably Container Corporation of America, and in a few advertising agencies. The legendary Alexey Brodovitch art directed *Bazaar* through the decade. His unerring sense of space, brilliant ability to design with photography – cropping and combining photographs in unexpected ways – and crisp arrangements of Bodoni typography became the model for postwar editorial design. At *Vogue,* the youthful Alexander Liberman replaced Dr. M. F. Agha as art director early in the decade, for Condé Nast reportedly had become disenchanted with *Vogue's* design in contrast to Brodovitch's design of its fashion rival. *Vogue's* image soon grew to resemble *Bazaar's,* with classic Bodoni type, generous white space, simple but elegant photography, and exquisite spatial balance. Throughout the decade, *Fortune* maintained its standard of excellence under several art directors. Among advertising agencies, N.W. Ayer & Son in Philadelphia and the Weintraub agency in New York City, where Charles Coiner and Paul Rand, respectively, held sway, were isolated citadels of design.

Most design and advertising of the 1940s project a numbing mediocrity. One can search in vain through periodicals of the period seeking the eye and hand of a designer, but find them in only a small fraction of the work. "Corny is the word for 95 percent of today's advertising," proclaimed art director James T. Mangan at a 1940 advertising convention in Cleveland. Mangan caustically declared it to be corny because it limited itself to cumbersome illustration and ponderous text. Advocating contrasts of scale and value and dynamic composition, he fought for a modernist approach to graphic design.

An opposing view was taken by the esteemed typeface designer Frederic W. Goudy in an address to the Advertising Typographers Association of America, published in the early 40s: "A great deal of modern advertising displeases me.... The fight is between formalism and modernism." After noting that "the traditionalist prefers, as a rule, the simpler forms of Roman letters and simple, straightforward arrangements of them, [whereas] the modernist prefers sans serifs – bolder, blacker and more erratic forms," Goudy blasted the modern designer for using "mere type spots of abstract design entirely unrelated to the text; his types contain nothing of romance or sentiment, and his arrangements follow no known law of order or beauty. His whole idea is that of a complete revolution of all the principles that have governed good typography since its invention....

The modernist gets attention value possibly by his bizarre types and arrangements, but not always favorably."

Modern designers faced an uphill battle, according to art director Charles Coiner of N.W. Ayer & Son, who wrote, "The tag 'modern' is misused by most people who try to use it. 'Advertising art,' too, is a much misused term. No one, in fact, seems quite sure what it means. Is it art or is it business? On one thing most advertisers agree – that they don't like 'modern advertising art.'" In the 1930s and early 1940s, this client and public attitude extended to modern fine art as well. When he was a New York high school student from 1939 to 1941, Lou Danziger – who has been a designer in Los Angeles since the late 1940s – remembers the Museum of Modern Art being virtually deserted on Saturday afternoons, with only three or four visitors looking at the work.

The European Migration

The lack of interest in advanced visual art and design began to change during the cultural ferment of the 1940s. In painting, architecture, and graphic design, the groundwork was developed for innovative new work after the war.
A major factor was the "brain drain," a wholesale emigration to America by leading European artists, scientists, architects, and writers. Their migration was caused by the rise of Fascism in Germany and Italy, ethnic persecution, and the growing threat of war. The masters of the modern European poster – A. M. Cassandre and Jean Carlu from France, Joseph Binder from Austria, and expatriate American E. McKnight Kauffer from England – arrived in America during the 1930s and early 1940s as part of this exodus seeking sanctuary in "the citadel of democracy." Leaders of the legendary Bauhaus school – the crucible where the modern art movements of Cubism, Futurism, Constructivism, and de Stijl commingled to give birth to a modernist design esthetic – arrived as well: architects Walter Gropius, Marcel Breuer, and Ludwig Mies van der Rohe; graphic designer and painter Herbert Bayer; painter and color theorist Josef Albers; and László Moholy-Nagy, whose activities encompassed design, film, painting, photography, sculpture, set design, teaching, and writing. Other major European graphic designers who immigrated to America included Will Burtin, Herbert Matter, Leo Lionni, Ladislav Sutnar, and Moholy-Nagy's close associate György Kepes. American practitioners were challenged by the presence of these Europeans with their avant-garde portfolios and innovative ideas.

Although some European graphic designers who immigrated to America experienced difficulty as they reestablished their careers, their acceptance by and influence on the American creative community was soon evident. Cipe Pineles recalls that she saw the portfolio of Will Burtin – who had achieved renown as one of Germany's leading designers – within two weeks after he arrived in America in 1938. *Vogue,* where she was then working as an assistant to Dr. M. F. Agha, was one of his first stops. Less than three years after he stepped off a steamer at the Battery in New York, Burtin was awarded the gold medal in the 1941 New York Art Directors' Club exhibition. His *Architectural Forum* cover expressed the passage of time through a decade of architectural design progress by a dynamic arrangement of signs and symbols rather than through narrative illustration.

Along with émigré designers, the creative ferment of painting in the 1940s provided an important resource for American graphic design. The center of the art world shifted from Paris to New York, and many European painters, including Marc Chagall, Piet Mondrian, and Fernand Léger, relocated there. Mondrian was inspired by the cool syncopated rhythms of boogie-woogie and jazz – along with New York's swift tempo, throbbing lights, and modern skyscrapers – to replace his black-line grid with a vibrant, colorful grid whose rhythms and form flickered across the canvas. Mondrian's New York work captivated artists and designers and demonstrated the energizing vitality that could be achieved through form and color.

By 1940, the avant-garde had split into two camps: Cubism – along with the geometric abstraction that evolved from it, such as De Stijl, Purism, and Constructivism – and Surrealism. American painters began to synthesize Cubism and Surrealism into a new visual style that evolved into the first major American art movement of the century, Abstract Expressionism. Willem de Kooning and Arshile Gorky sought to combine surreal imagery and forms within a Cubist compositional structure. The Surrealist technique of automatism – suspension of the conscious mind as a means to liberate subconscious imagery and forms – was used to create highly original forms and compositions. Automatism also served Jackson Pollock in his celebrated 1940s "drip" paintings, which redirected American painting with their rhythmic all-over compositions whose lyrical beauty and expressionist energy were unprecedented in world art. Painters had pushed subject matter aside and allowed color, form, and structure to become the focus of their work. Many graphic designers adopted this attitude, realizing that signs, symbols, and pictographs could function as both communicative and formal elements. Painters explored the textural and manipulative properties of materials and inspired designers to do so as well.

Many American architects embraced the International Style, with its emphasis upon functional design, simple geometric structure, and the banishment of ornament. Mies van der Rohe was the most influential architect working in America during the 1940s. His lean minimalism of steel and glass expressed his dictum that "less is more." For the new campus of Armour Institute (later renamed the Illinois Institute of Technology), Mies designed half a dozen new buildings with a steel-frame construction of exposed standard I-beams. The grid these created on the exterior surface was filled with a curtain wall of glass windows and beige brick. This construction method and the resulting clean geometric surface established the style for the high-rise office and apartment buildings that sprouted in American cities in the postwar decades. Two late-1940s buildings, Mies' twin 26-story apartment blocks on Lake Shore Drive in Chicago and the glass curtain wall of the United Nations Secretariat in New York City, designed by a collaborative led by Wallace K. Harrison in consultation with Le Corbusier, were enormously influential. This pared-down geometric simplicity influenced many graphic designers.

Bauhaus Ideals

After the war, as industrial production was redirected toward the consumer economy, product and industrial designers gained prominence and influence. Edgar Kaufmann, Jr., named head of the Museum of Modern Art's Department of Industrial Design, became a national spokesman for design excellence, preaching that form should be determined by function, structure, and materials. Kaufmann promulgated his Bauhaus-inspired ideals to the American mass audience through the museum's "Good Design" award, which became the seal of approval for contemporary good taste. Packaging and advertising for products achieving this distinction were quite naturally designed to convey the products' modern style. Late-1930s and early-1940s American automobile design had evolved into the *monocoque,* a shape resembling an upside down bathtub, as illustrated in Oldsmobile ads of the period. After the war, American cars were derided as being "streamlined into grotesque forms" with "bloated coverings" and suffering from "monstrous inflation." Some American car designs, notably Raymond Loewy's 1947 Studebaker, adopted European characteristics: tighter-skinned design that expressed function, less bulging sides, and less chrome ornament.

Even the venerable *Saturday Evening Post,* America's most popular and beloved magazine, flirted with the modern spirit as early as 1942. A new editor named Ben Hibbs sought to resuscitate the publication, which had grown a bit tired and set in its ways. Editorial changes were accompanied by a new typographic format. The traditional dense italic two-line logo was replaced. The large word "Post" was perched in the upper-left-hand corner, set in bold Bodoni-derived letterforms, with "The Saturday Evening" in small type above. This alteration occurred for the May 30, 1942, issue, promptly generating a storm of protest from readers, including some who wrote to illustrator Norman Rockwell to announce that the world was falling apart – the *Post* had been changed! This issue also featured one of the earliest photographic covers in the magazine's 214-year history. Although the *Post* experimented only sporadically with photographic covers during the 1940s, the once invulnerable domain of the illustrator had clearly been breached. Hibbs struggled mightily with competition from *Life,* whose photojournalistic approach gained momentum during the war years.

An inspiring advocate for modern design was Dr. Robert L. Leslie, director of The Composing Room, a leading New York typesetting firm. He set up an in-house gallery that regularly featured shows of modern graphic design and offered an opportunity for émigré designers to display their work. Leslie and Percy Seitlin edited a small magazine, *PM,* whose name was later changed to *AD* to avoid confusion with the progressive newspaper *PM,* that also provided a forum for creative work.

Many transplanted designers engaged in educational activities, becoming missionaries preaching the gospel of modern design. Herbert Bayer, for one, conducted classes in New York at the American Advertising Guild, where he practiced a European approach to design education. Visual properties – contrast, proportion, balance, harmony, space, color, and texture – were defined as the building materials of all artists and designers. Bayer's students worked exclusively in montage, the medium invented by the Dadaists which enables forms and images to be easily implemented.

László Moholy-Nagy had come to Chicago in 1937 to direct the "New Bauhaus." Although it closed after one year owing to the financial difficulties of its sponsors, Moholy operated his own Institute of Design from 1938 until his death from leukemia in 1946. This school offered the first complete modern design curriculum in America. Moholy's "first lieutenant," György Kepes, upset conservative design attitudes in workshops for professionals, and Chicago's top layout artists freed their minds and hands doing what a few disgruntled drop-outs dismissed as "doodles and dot patterns." Moholy made the Institute of Design a center for ideas, with open invitations to lectures, demonstrations, and exhibitions. These and other experiments in modernist design education laid the foundation for a postwar generation of American graphic designers. Emphasis shifted from naturalistic drawing and painting to concern for the visual elements making up a work of art or design; from traditional to experimental materials; and from representational illusion to a dynamic ordering of space. The new visual education became a major factor in tilting American graphics toward modern design concepts as the decade rolled forward.

Chicago had jumped to an early lead in embracing modern design during the 1930s. Lester Beall, perhaps the first native-born American modernist graphic designer, had freelanced in Chicago from 1927 until 1935, doing unprecedented work. Largely self-educated as a designer, Beall had majored in art history in college. During the Depression, on days when he did not have assignments to work on, he spent hours in the library studying and learning about modern art and design from Europe. Visual ideas from Cubism, Constructivism, and Dada were freely combined and integrated into his work. Working in New York during the 1940s, Beall would layer photographs printed in different colors of ink, mix typefaces such as Alternate Gothic and Bank Script, and combine drawing, symbols, and photography in the same design.

Walter Paepcke, founder of the Chicago-based Container Corporation of America, in 1936 hired nationally recognized art director and color authority Egbert Jacobson as director of the department of design. A new trademark formed the basis of a managed and consistent visual identification system that encompassed everything from invoices to vehicle identification and plant signs. Color was used in unprecedented ways, with the dull grays and browns of factories and paper mills yielding to vibrant hues. Paepcke's impact on American design, sharpened by his wife, Elizabeth, who significantly influenced his understanding of art, cannot be overestimated. In 1940, Hungarian art director and book designer Albert Kner arrived in Chicago and was promptly hired by Paepcke to create a package-design division. Kner called this design studio, whose pioneering approaches to structural and graphic design included the development of the ubiquitous "six-pack," the Design Laboratory. It boasted a newly invented ocular camera, which could photograph a viewer's eyes as they racked across a design, providing valuable information about visual hierarchy, focal points, and viewer response. Herbert Bayer was retained as a design consultant by Paepcke in 1945, and contributed to the evolution of Container's design thinking.

At N.W. Ayer & Son, Container's advertising agency, art directors Charles Coiner and Leo Lionni worked closely with the Paepckes and Jacobson in devising the company's legendary advertisements with imagery commissioned from outstanding painters and designers. During the war years, a seller's market existed as food was rationed and manufacturing capability shifted to armaments instead of consumer goods. Most manufacturers used their advertising budgets for institutional horn blowing to maintain brand identity and corporate goodwill. Container's wartime ads, in dynamic contrast to the bland conventionality of most editorial and advertising, jumped from magazine pages. Poster-like imagery and telegraphic messages were designed into a totality consistent with the best European modern design, but radically breaking with American advertising traditions.

In 1944, Container initiated a new advertising campaign consisting of ads saluting the Allied nations. Each ad was illustrated by an artist native to the featured country. After completing this series, Container initiated the "States Series," which paid homage to each of the United States and featured art by native-born artists. Why use an advertising budget to salute countries and states, and provide an esthetic experience for magazine readers with just a brief copy line about your company? Jacobson later explained: "The series began as a forthright bid for attention to the company's developing business, to its policy of integrated production and management, and to its awareness of the importance of good taste and top-notch design in any public statement." He also noted that Container produced package designs for its customers, and by practicing what it preached about good design, it would be taken far more seriously. (After running out of countries and states, Paepcke conceived the brilliant institutional advertising campaign entitled "Great Ideas of Western Man." Launched in February of 1950, this campaign featured important ideas of Western civilization selected by University of Chicago scholars and interpreted by artists and designers.)

Another inspired corporate understanding of design came from Sweet's Catalog Service, which retained Ladislav Sutnar as design director in 1941. Sutnar had achieved prominence in Czechoslovakia as a leading Constructivist designer in the 1920s and 1930s and was in New York as a design director for the Czech pavilion at the 1939 World's Fair when war broke out. Remaining in America, he wound up working for Sweet's, where he redirected the course of catalog and informational design. Sutnar organized pages with an underlying geometric structure, designed systems to permit readers to find data more easily, and stressed the concept of visual flow – the logical movement of information across the page. Sutnar made it easier for architects and engineers developing specifications to retrieve data by creating strong contrast between titles and headers and other text, and by using consistent page structure and prominent placement of page numbers. A pioneer of "systems design," he was far ahead of his time in addressing the problems of structuring and organizing massive amounts of information.

Designed for War

The momentum toward modern design was slowed during the first half of the decade, which was dominated by global conflagration. Graphic designers were heavily involved in wartime issues. Many leading designers served the government, including one German émigré, Will Burtin, who worked for the Office of Strategic Services and designed gunnery manuals for the U.S. Air Corps. Burtin's remarkable ability to understand complex information and express it in clear graphic terms was exploited to the fullest. Charles Coiner served as an important design consultant to the government, designing a systematic series of symbols for use in civil defense. He became a consultant to the Office for Emergency Management and art-directed propaganda posters designed to promote productivity and efficiency by America's workforce. The Office of War Information, headed by the eminent radio newscaster Elmer Davis, won respect for its handling of propaganda and official news. Bradbury Thompson, Tobias Moss, and William Golden also worked for the OWI, whose graphics were often innovative for their time. Its publications for distribution overseas were frequently designed in several languages. Young Noel Martin, who would begin his career after the war, was assigned to a camouflage battalion staffed by architects, painters, and designers. He remembers it as a valuable learning experience, as he was introduced by his colleagues to the modernism of Mies van der Rohe and de Stijl.

Mindful of the role illustrators played in producing posters during World War I, Norman Rockwell and Mead Schaeffer went to Washington armed with sketches of posters they were eager to contribute to the war effort. Rockwell presented a series of illustration concepts depicting President Roosevelt's "Four Freedoms," but he was spurned by numerous government agencies. "The last war, you illustrators did the posters," he was told by a bureaucrat at the Office of War Information. "This war, we are going to use fine arts men, real artists." Rockwell was told that he should offer his services producing pen-and-ink drawings for military how-to manuals. When a discouraged Rockwell headed home, stopping off in Philadelphia to present sketches for *Post* covers, he was commissioned to create the "Four Freedoms" series for its inside editorial use. The magazine was flooded with requests for reprints. Although "Freedom from Want" was criticized for portraying conspicuous abundance in a hungry world, the series achieved an iconic presence. Roosevelt's conceptualization was transformed into the reality of everyday life.

Rockwell's position in American visual communications is anchored to his ability to conceive, cast, light, and direct images that are "one-frame" movies charged with subjective integrity. His reputation as "America's best-loved artist" grew as his skills as a narrative genre artist expanded. Relying heavily on photography, which he art-directed to produce reference material, he became the best "single-frame film director" in America, with an uncanny ability to paint iconic statements about the human condition, addressing subjects ranging from the first date to the concepts of speech and religion. Needless to say, among the numerous federal agencies which reproduced "The Four Freedoms" thousands of times in posters and publications was the Office of War Information!

Despite the pronouncement of the OWI of its intention to use only "real artists," war graphics spanned the spectrum of graphic approaches and quality in a chaotic free-for-all ranging from vigorous modernism to amateurish cartoon treatments. Advanced design, traditional illustration, and fine art were all used with varying degrees of graphic quality and communicative effectiveness. Many works, such as the airplane identification poster, were executed anonymously by very talented designers.

After the U.S. and its allies emerged victorious in the global war, a new era began. The atomic bomb – "history's exclamation point" – made America the most powerful country on earth. Wartime production capability was rapidly shifted to peacetime consumer goods, creating unprecedented prosperity and affluence. Technological advances in electronics, transportation, and energy inspired a booming optimism after the anguish of war. Technicolor movies, air travel, streamlined cars, tabloid newspapers, big band rhythms, and television: the postwar tempo of life surged forward, leaving traditional ways behind. Although the first American public demonstration of a television broadcast had occurred on April 30, 1939, at the opening of the New York World's Fair, the development of this revolutionary communications medium was delayed because electronics factories were converted to the war effort.

Defining American Design

Three young American designers, Bradbury Thompson, Paul Rand, and Alvin Lustig, defined American approach to 1940s graphic design that drew inspiration from European modern art and design, but also represented original visions. Cultures require early warning systems to alert and prepare for the future. In the early 1980s, Pac Man and his ilk prepared us for the impending computer revolution, and concept cars in auto shows allow designers to prepare the public (and automobile executives who risk corporate futures on new designs) for model changes. For conservative graphic arts and communications professionals of the 1940s, the early warning system alerting them to the impending revolution in design was the "Westvaco Inspirations for Printers" series designed by Bradbury Thompson. With no budget for art – which had to be borrowed from advertising agencies and publishers – and limited to the resources of his time and the typecase, Thompson expanded the limits of typography and design in issue after issue. Delighting in complexity, Thompson was a tightrope walker pushing his page layouts to the edge of chaos, seeking a graphic complexity and order through his unerring sense of visual balance. Thompson worked to fuse word and image into an integrated unity having the immediacy and impact of the modern poster. His page layouts for "Westvaco Inspirations" reverberate with energy and vitality.

Thompson designed "Westvaco Inspirations" in the evenings and on weekends while working for the Office of War Information by day. After leaving that agency in 1945, he became art director of *Mademoiselle,* a position which he held for the next fifteen years. Especially in the design of covers, Thompson brought vigorous new design concepts to the consumer magazine.

Paul Rand was a catalytic innovator during the 1940s. Rand realized that most projects arrived from the client lifeless and with little visual potential; he defined his role as a designer to include a process of reinventing the problem. By discovering its visual and verbal essence, Rand could restate the problem, releasing its creative potential. He spent most of the decade working at the Weintraub Advertising Agency, bringing unexpected form and expression to 1940s

(continued on page 128)

Philip Meggs: Sketchbooks

Selected pages from sketchbook with studies for larger paintings.

Watercolor and gouache, page sizes: 8.5 x 11 inches. (1969–1971)

Untitled.
Acrylic on canvas.
54.25 x 54.5 inches.
(1969–1971)

advertising frequently stifled by lengthy pompous copy and traditional illustration. Rand combined the spatial instincts of a modern painter with a canny skill for producing graphic power in word and image relationships. He drew inspiration from the ability of modern painters such as Klee and Miró to invent signs and symbols, combine them in unexpected ways, and use them as dynamic compositional elements. A former Weintraub employee recalls an atmosphere filled with "screaming and conflicts.... Rand was redefining how advertising was created, forging the role of the designer.... It was heavy." A young advertising salesman named Bill Bernbach joined the agency, turned his hand to copywriting, and worked closely with Rand. Although this collaboration has been widely heralded as launching a new approach to advertising, careful review of work from the period indicates that visual/verbal synergy, a mutual interdependence of visual and verbal information, can be found in Rand's work before his collaboration with Bernbach. In 1949, Bernbach opened Doyle Dane Bernbach with Bob Gage as its first art director. This agency defined the "new advertising" of the 1950s and 1960s.

Alvin Lustig designed books for the Ward Ritchie Press in Los Angeles from 1937 until 1943. There he created intricate geometrical designs for letterpress printing, working directly with sans-serif type, geometrical ornaments, and rules. A complex and difficult designer, Lustig was an intuitive master who saw line and shape not as pure form but as a symbolic language of power. He did not see form and content as two entities to be somehow joined together; rather, he conceived of them as inseparable. Throughout the decade, Lustig did groundbreaking book-jacket designs for New Directions, a New York book publishing firm that held an exalted position in American literary circles for bringing challenging and often controversial literature to American readers. Lustig searched for signs and symbols that could convey the very soul of the literary subjects. He believed, like the abstract painter Wassily Kandinsky, that visual forms and colors possessed an inner life. Lustig designed many book jackets using line, shape, and texture as potent graphic phenomena that conveyed the emotive power of the author's work rather than specific information. He became a messianic figure in design whose electrifying lectures and presentations attracted a following of younger designers groping for an identity.

Record album design, in the meanwhile, was being revolutionized by Alex Steinweiss of Columbia Records, who searched the modern art and design vocabulary for new ways to package music. He achieved a delicate balance with his almost random scattering of forms, using a rich array of typography and imagery with organic and geometric design elements to express the mood of the composition.

Young illustrators introduced new approaches as well. Traditional illustrators such as J. D. Leyendecker and Rockwell painted narrative tableaus designed almost as little stage sets upon which the characters acted. Most illustrations were painted from the vantage point of the artist standing at his easel peering at the models arranged on the studio model stand. Making extensive use of photography for reference material, young illustrators such as Al Parker, Coby Whitmore, and Jon Whitcomb often used high or low vantage points, extreme closeups, and even distorted views of their subject or background. Shape, color, and the overall composition of the page or spread were important to these illustrators as they struggled to invent new ways to depict romantic young couples embracing in illustrations for women's magazine fiction. In addition to the growing presence of the graphic designer and the photographer, a threat to traditional illustration was the propensity to use fine artists for advertising and editorial imagery. Like the creative directors at Container Corporation, many art directors, including William Golden of CBS and Cipe Pineles of *Seventeen* often commissioned work from gallery artists instead of illustrators.

Art directors and designers began to make greater use of photography for imagery during the late 1940s, a trend that would continue steadily during the 1950s and 1960s. Advertising and editorial photographers with a personal, individualistic viewpoint were virtually nonexistent in the 1940s. Most photographers executing advertising or editorial assignments were employed by large studios. Their work was highly controlled and excellently crafted, but seldom evidenced imagination or feeling. The kind of photography Moholy-Nagy taught – a new instrument of vision that could give humanity "the power of perceiving its surroundings, and its very existence, with new eyes" – was slow to arrive in the arena of mass communications. Alexey Brodovitch at *Bazaar* was one of the few art directors breaking new ground in the use of photography. Herbert Matter, Irving Penn, Richard

Avedon, and Robert Frank stand at the forefront of photographers who brought an original vision to their work during this period. After the war, quantum leaps in the quality of films, cameras, and printing technology dramatically increased reproduction quality, allowing photographs to be reproduced with greater fidelity and detail. More prevalent use of hand-held cameras permitted location and action photographs from diverse camera angles as well as spontaneous, unexpected images that contrasted sharply with the static predictability of carefully posed studio shots. One reason photography replaced illustration as the major means of image-making was the belief of some young designers that photography was more compatible with their design approach than was illustration. The Bauhaus school, whose influence spread through American design and design education during the 1940s, advocated rational, objective design compatible with the scientific machine age. This encouraged factual machine-made images from the camera instead of hand-drawn illustrations that might allow the subjective vision of the artist to come between the message and its audience. Noel Martin remarks that it never occurred to him to use illustrators, because photographers seemed to relate much better to his modern approach to type and layout.

Today, the design profession has numerous female practitioners; this was not the case in the 1940s. Opportunities for women to enter the advertising and design professions were limited. Cipe Pineles recalls that after graduation from design school in the late 1930s, she experienced great difficulty finding a job because most potential employers simply were not interested in hiring women. Dr. Agha at *Vogue* hired her as one of his assistants. Only after she achieved national prominence as art director for *Glamour, British Vogue,* and *Seventeen* was she granted membership as the first female member of the New York Art Directors Club.

A New Generation

In the last half of the decade, a younger generation of graphic designers, many of whom had had their educations interrupted by military service, did the formative work that enabled them to emerge as major creative forces in the 1950s and afterward. These included Saul Bass and Lou Danziger in Los Angeles, Morton Goldsholl and Bruce Beck in Chicago, Aaron Burns and Gene Federico in New York, and Noel Martin in Cincinnati. Lou Dorfsman and Herb Lubalin quietly gained experience during the 1940s, preparing for their spectacular accomplishments in the decades ahead.

Trained as a fine artist, Noel Martin in 1947 became assistant director of the Cincinnati Art Museum, where his duties included graphic design. The resources of a modest in-house letterpress shop were used by Martin, and a rigorous self-education process enabled him to embrace broad influences including the theory and typographic design of Jan Tschichold, László Moholy-Nagy, and Max Bill. Principally a typographer, Martin brought great clarity and purity to his work, defining museum graphics in postwar America. As his typographic influence grew, he became widely acknowledged during the 1950s as a major influence upon American typography. Aaron Burns also began his career in the late 1940s, and during the 1950s and 1960s emerged as a major catalyst for typographic quality.

Bruce Beck remembers the 1940s "as a terribly exciting time. We believed that we were part of an era that was creating Design!" Lou Danziger recalls that when he began his career in the late 1940s, one did not simply have to convince the prospective client of the wisdom of assigning a project to you instead of someone else; rather, one had to sell the client on the very idea of design. "Most annual reports were done by the printers," Danziger recalls, "and clients had to be convinced that design was a worthwhile activity. In the 50s, that changed, and management began to recognize the value of design." Stationery, invoices, and brochures had usually been made up by job printers, who composed type and letterpress cuts to produce the graphic design. Designers like Danziger advocated the use of symbols and consistent typographic formats for more effective communications by their clients. The growing importance of offset lithography in the years after the war hastened the shift from compositor to graphic designer, as the paste-up of type proofs and position photostats gradually replaced metal locked in a letterpress chase.

The new conditions of postwar culture required a new approach to graphic communications. The kind and gentle small-town world of Norman Rockwell yielded to an urban society whose values and lifestyles changed as rapidly as its technology. Although graphic design in the 1950s,

1960s, and beyond is very different in form and communication from the 1940s work, a small group of pioneers working diligently during that decade charted the course of American graphic design in the information age and laid the groundwork for its explosive development over the next 40 years. ⊷

Excerpts from *Type & Image* (1989)

Introduction

What is the essence of graphic design? How do graphic designers solve problems, organize space, and imbue their work with those visual and symbolic qualities that enable it to convey visual and verbal information with expression and clarity? The extraordinary flowering of graphic design in our time – as a potent means of communication and a major component of our visual culture – increases the need for designers, clients, and students to comprehend its essence.

Traditionally, graphic designers looked to architecture or painting for their model. Certainly, a universal language of form is common to all visual disciplines, and in some historical periods the various design arts have shared styles. Too much dependence upon other arts – or even on the universal language of form – is unsatisfactory, however, because graphic design has unique purposes and visual properties.

Graphic design is a hybrid discipline. Diverse elements, including signs, symbols, words, and pictures, are collected and assembled into a total message. The dual nature of these graphic elements as both communicative sign and visual form provides endless fascination and potential for invention and combination. Although all the visual arts share properties of either two- or three-dimensional space, graphic space has a special character born from its communicative function.

Perhaps the most important thing that graphic design does is give communications resonance, a richness of tone that heightens the expressive power of the page. It transcends the dry conveyance of information, intensifies the message, and enriches the audience's experience. Resonance helps the designer realize clear public goals: to instruct, to delight, and to motivate.

Most designers speak of their activities as a problem-solving process because designers seek solutions to public communications problems. Approaches to problem solving vary, based on the problem at hand and the working methods of the designer. At a time when Western nations are evolving from industrial to information cultures, a comprehensive understanding of our communicative forms and graphic design becomes increasingly critical. I interrupted all other activities for a half-year to study the nature of graphic design; this book is the result.

Chapter One: The Elements of Graphic Design

The general public does not understand graphic design and art direction. Designers tell the story of a graphic designer trying to explain his job to Grandmother. The designer shows Grandmother a recent project and says, "You were asking me about what I do, Grandmother. I'm a graphic designer, and I designed this."

Pointing to the photograph in the design, the grandmother asks, "Did you draw that picture?"

"No, Grandmother, it's a photograph. I didn't draw it, but I planned it, chose the photographer, helped select the models, assisted in setting it up, art directed the shooting session, chose which shot to use, and cropped the picture."

"Did you write what it says, then?"

"Well, no," the designer replies. "But I did brainstorm with the copywriter to develop the concept."

"Oh, I see. Then you did letter these big words?" asks the grandmother, pointing to the headline.

"Uh, no, a typesetter set the copywriter's words in type, but I specified the typefaces and sizes to be used," responds the designer.

"Well, did you draw this little picture down in the corner?"

"No, but I selected the illustrator, told her what needed to be drawn, and decided where to put it and how big to make it."

"Oh. Well, did you draw this little, what do you call it, a trademark?"

"Uh, no. A design firm that specializes in visual identification programs designed it for the client."

The grandmother is somewhat confused about just what it is that her grandchild does and why credit is claimed for all these other people's work.

The Designer's Task

The conceptual nature of the graphic design process generates public confusion about the designer's task. The designer combines graphic materials – words, pictures, and other graphic elements – to construct a visual communications

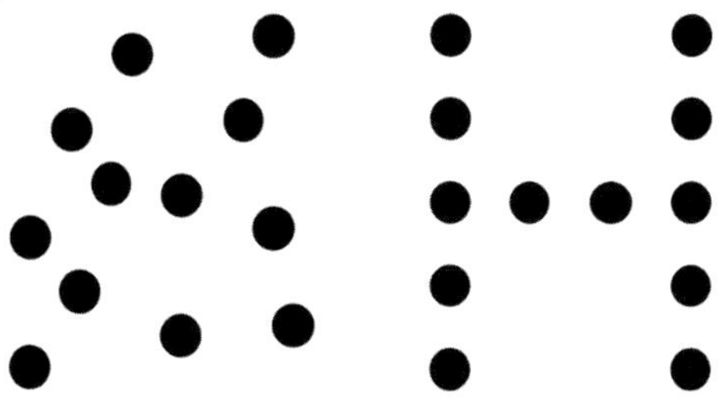

gestalt. This German word does not have a direct English translation. It means a configuration or structure with properties not derivable from the sum of its individual parts. The first set of twelve dots, randomly placed, has no meaning or content beyond the phenomenon of twelve dots printed on the page. By contrast, the second set of twelve dots has been consciously structured into a visual configuration with meaning as a common sign: the letter *H* from the Roman alphabet. In one sense, the letter *H* is not present, but the human eye perceives the dots, and the human mind connects them into a recognizable pattern – the structure of a letterform. In the first configuration, the viewer sees a random dispersion of parts; in the second, the viewer sees the whole.

Organizing these dots into a simple visual gestalt is symbolic of the graphic design process: The designer combines visual signs, symbols, and images into a visual-verbal gestalt that the audience can understand. The graphic designer is simultaneously message maker and form builder. This complex task involves forming an intricate communications message while building a cohesive composition that gains order and clarity from the relationships between the elements. Another aspect of the designer's task is to infuse content with *resonance.* A term borrowed from music, resonance means the reverberation or echo, a subtle quality of tone or timbre. A violin prized for its resonance creates music with a richness of tone that heightens the expressive-ness of sound. Graphic designers bring a resonance to visual communications through, for example, the use of scale and contrast, cropping of images, and choice of typefaces and colors.

Saul Bass on Corporate Identity

From *AIGA Journal of Graphic Design*, Vol. 8, No. 1 (1990)

Meggs: Let's start by discussing the design process. I've heard many graphic designers say that they avoid designing trademarks and symbols like the plague because it's so difficult. The designer has to invent a new form from scratch that has never existed in the world before. Over the years you have invented trademarks that have become real icons, celebrated for their originality. How do you approach the problem of designing a new trademark?

Bass: Trademarks are usually metaphors of one kind or another. The enterprise that you are communicating about has to explain itself in some way, the nature of what it is or does, what its areas of activity are. Communicating that is usually the starting point for developing imagery. Trademarks are, in a certain sense, thinking made visible. The process of defining what it is that you wish to communicate inevitably defines the objectives of the design process. Then, the search is for imagery or form that will adequately – and hopefully, interestingly – express this. Where one goes from this starting point can be unexpected and may not follow a totally rational methodology. But it's helpful to frame the problem in rational terms as a beginning point. From there, the designing will evolve on intuitive levels, and it may take peculiar turns.

As you go through the process of searching for a solution and alternative designs are generated, how do you select the appropriate solution?

It usually turns out to be something that satisfies the objectives as originally defined, and at the same time, is sufficiently interesting and hopefully provocative to separate itself from the cacophony of messages and visual phenomena that we wade through every day. In this respect metaphor and ambiguity are useful in enhancing levels of interest and attention. However, accessibility must be maintained when you are communicating with popular audiences – as is the case with many larger corporations. It's much more possible to employ richer metaphors and greater ambiguity when dealing with more defined activity and more specialized audiences and businesses.

Much has been said and written lately about the impact of computers upon design and visual communications. When designing a trademark, does the computer play a role in your design process?

Not in relation to the fundamental concept, the idea of what it is. Computers can respond quickly and efficiently to questions like, "How will it look if it's turned this way or that, made heavier or lighter, squeezed or expanded?" But these are secondary issues – modifying factors. The basic notion still has to come out of someone's head.

We have this old adage, "Imitation is the sincerest form of flattery." You havedesigned some very original trademarks, which have spawned many imitations. Original thinking seems to turn into a cliché as a result of plagiarism, which is rampant in design. What is your reaction when you see trademarks that look so very much like other trademarks, and what does this do to the original?

This happens in all pop-cultural areas. Hitchcock made a film a long time ago called *The Lady Vanishes.* In it, he juxtaposed two cuts: a close-up of a lady opening her mouth to scream and then a shock-cut to a close-up of a train whistle screeching. This device has been used in subsequent films, I don't know how many times. A student of mine once referred to this moment as a cliché when discussing it with me after he caught *The Lady Vanishes* on late-night television, not understanding that this is where it all began. Ironic! As we know, clichés become clichés because they do what they do extremely well. Then someone comes along and does something similar. And of course, it works well again…and again…and again. And voilá! A cliché! Clichés deserve study. There's something there working very well. If you understand what it is, then it may be possible to take the cliché, and turn or refresh it in some way, express it in new terms. I'm not terribly disturbed by seeing things pop up again and again, as long as they are not boring, and something is being added or changed in a significant way.

What is the value of visual identity to the client and culture?

It may be useful to look at the issue historically. Corporate identity as a clear discipline is a post–World War II phenomenon. It's only thirty or forty years old. During this period, it's grown from a cottage industry to an institutionalized form, has become an acknowledged component of business activity. Now – to whatever extent corporate managers believe in the value of design as affecting the so-called "bottom-line" – I think it exists where visual style has essential marketing values in relation to product or service. There's great commitment to the function of design, for example, in cosmetics, fashion, high-tech products, etc. Contrast this to the notion of design commitment in areas involving commodity products. Even those corporations that are willing to commit design resources to specific areas like product design or packaging don't necessarily commit to other areas across the board. We've been inundated with books on corporate excellence. What they don't say is that excellence is not selective. If it's not set as a standard everywhere, it's not going to happen appropriately anywhere.

Corporate identity has over the years taken an interesting form. Historically, its original expression involved the total image. In the original exemplars we admired – Olivetti, IBM, Container Corporation, and others – every manifestation of the company was aimed at excellence. Somewhere down the line, this got translated into corporate identity as consisting of a trademark, which is attached then to communications, which may or may not be excellent. So, despite loss of market and foreign competition, business hasn't really totally embraced the value of design. It seems that we've not really done as good a job as we ought to have in explaining the value of good design. Often I think it exists by default. From time to time, we see corporations embrace design where the chief executive officer sees it as a fashionable cultural phenomenon, neither a link to the efficacy of the business nor a life-enhancing cultural activity.... In a crunch, it's discarded precisely because it's neither.

How does one measure the economic value of a trademark and corporate identity program? Can its value be measured?

It's quite feasible to measure quantitatively – that is, measure recognizability and association. What is difficult to measure is what it may add to people's understanding and feelings about the company. We've measured recognizability and association with many marks we've designed for corporations. For instance, when I redesigned the old bell for the Bell System, the recognition level two years after the new redesigned Bell was introduced rose from 71 percent to over 90 percent. That is, people saw the bell and understood that it represented the phone company.

The economic value of a trademark is elusive. I don't know of any systematic means of arriving at a figure. I do know of cases where use of a new trademark was accompanied by a significant increase in sales. But it's difficult, if not impossible, to separate the contribution of the trademark from the rest of the marketing mix: advertising, sales promotion, packaging, distribution, pricing, etc.

I did hear a rumor a while ago that Coca-Cola once was involved in trademark infringement litigation and was asked to value their trademark. This is just gossip, of course, but the figure I heard they used back then was $3 billion. It doesn't seem unreasonable.

Let me ask if you have any thoughts on another process. When a company gets negative publicity, how does this relate to the reading of the mark and identity program? To take a recent example, I know many people who refuse to fly Eastern Airlines because they are sympathetic to the strike by mechanics and pilots. Do you know what happens, or has there been any research on what happens when a mark becomes a symbol – not of positive impressions – but of negative reactions?

The trademark has to be understood as simply one element in the communication mix. In and of itself, it doesn't change anything. Bill Bernbach once observed that an effective advertising campaign will kill a lousy product faster than no advertising at all. If a promise is made that can't be fulfilled, it's worse than making no promise at all. Whatever the manipulative power of design, the fact is that if you aren't basically accurate in what you say about products and companies, you will fail simply because, in the end, the performance of the product or company is the basic determinant of how the product or company will be viewed. With Eastern Airlines, the identifier will take on the coloration of what is happening. When Eastern straightens out, gets organized, and does a good job, the emblem will have another meaning. Certainly, changing it is not going to accomplish anything. We have to understand the limitations of what we do as well as the potentials.

(continued on page 136

Selected spreads from sketchbook with studies for larger paintings.

Watercolor and gouache, page sizes: 8.5 x 11 inches. (1969–1971)

Are these limitations and potentials of visual identification constant, or do they change?

Historically, identification was specific, literal, illustrative. The fire insurance company spouted fire or flames; the refrigerator company showed icicles. Then along came the highly reductive, abstract, formal visual work. It was startling, effective.

Which marks achieved this?

I'm thinking of the CBS eye, the Alcoa mark, the Chase Manhattan Bank mark. These appeared in a world of illustrative literal marks. They were quite powerful in this context and had tremendous impact. Reductive became fashionable. And designers created a flood of reductive, abstract trademarks. Slowly the visual uniqueness of the reductive mark diminished. And those expressions that are more specific, even illustrative, become contextually more interesting.

Why do we have this herd instinct?

The moment something "works," the pressure is on to play off it. Because the economic stakes are so great, everybody is looking for certainty. And things that have worked in the past are more likely to work in the future. And it happens very fast. The process used to take longer. Now, the new grows old without ever having had a childhood. What we have is a herd of independent minds.

We seem to be in a cyclical process in which context is significant and drives the situation. The form continues to change as the context evolves. This is an interesting contradiction in view of the logical definition of the trademark as fulfilling long-range strategic communication objectives.

And yet, we have some pictorial logos, such as the RCA dog, as well as reductive marks, such as the CBS eye, which are very potent and stand the test of time over several decades. What makes a mark powerful enough to sustain itself in a cyclical situation where context is shifting?

I might add the Mercedes trademark to this group, in terms of staying power. I'm a little dubious about the RCA dog. It's a lovely piece of nostalgia, but it doesn't tell you a lot about the firm. It certainly doesn't signal the technology. The theoretically ideal trademark is one that is ultimately reductive, but is still accessible, and yet is ambiguous in a formal sense. Ambiguity and metaphor add tension and interest to a form or expression. It keeps the mark alive. Ambiguity is even more significant in film and in some graphic forms, such as the poster.

Let's talk about these properties in some specific marks. For example, the mark you designed for Minolta. It has strong recognition value and has been widely influential upon the genre.

The intent was to suggest a lens. All of Minolta's products – cameras, copiers, etc. – use lenses in some way. The centerlines running through the blue oval were intended to do so, in as reductive a form as I could develop.

Your design of a reductive mark for Quaker Oats – starting with a very literal mark used for decades and expressing it in a contemporary manner – was a completely different problem.

The old Quaker man is a wonderful figure that we all grew up with. It sat on our breakfast table every day, and we learned to live with it in a very comfortable and friendly way. The impetus for this new mark was based on the fact that the Quaker Oats Company had diversified into chemicals, agricultural food products, restaurants, etc. The objective was to find a way to differentiate Quaker, the company, from Quaker, the cereal product, without giving up the values associated with that great American icon. At one point before we came into the picture, it was proposed that the Quaker company should adopt a stylized Q as its corporate signature. This was judged to be an inappropriate thing to do, and I believe it would have been.

The AT&T globe is another mark that has a powerful identification. Could you comment on the metaphor and symbolism of this mark?

Here we were transiting from the Bell System to a new company, from a system that could be described as "the national telephone company" to one that we wanted to suggest was "an international telecommunications company," with information bits circling the globe. An important component of the program is the tag we developed for television, where the information bits are gathered up by the globe. It's useful in the "seating" of this mark.

What do you perceive as the current dilemmas in corporate identification?

One of them has to do with the "generalization" of corporate logos, involving a loss of individuality and interest. A number of factors have contributed to this condition. The pressure of corporate development in the last forty years, I think, has changed the game. Large companies are no longer in a single business. They are involved with diverse products and diverse services. That differentiation makes it very difficult to be specific in the identity metaphor you create for a company.

Also, many large corporations have become cross-cultural, multi-national. This further defies specificity in the trademark. There is also the frequent desire to project stability, trust, good solid management, and so forth, further pushing towards generalization. Other factors affecting this issue have to do with the vast proliferation of trademarks, which simply have "used up" the generalized metaphors, and are making it more and more difficult to find original forms and ideas.

All of this pushes toward the homogenization of corporate identity. We're slowly getting to the point where we're talking about General Amalgamated International. I think that's a problem. Now, the challenge as I look ahead, is to, in a sense, push the clock back – how to do the communication job well and simultaneously maintain emotional components, individuality, and accessibility. ⊷

The Design Education Quandary

From *AIGA Journal of Graphic Design,* Vol. 8, No. 3 (1990)

The debate over graphic design education in America continues unabated. Neither educators nor professionals have been able to reach an agreement on what a design curriculum should encompass, or even how long the preparation time should be. By contrast, a pharmacist needs an accredited five-year curriculum for the Bachelor of Pharmacy degree and then must pass a rigorous examination before entering the profession.

An aspiring graphic designer might show up to the first job interview with the following: a two-year Associate of Arts degree from a community college or trade school; a Bachelor of Arts degree from a university with perhaps three-fourths of the course work in general studies and the remaining one-fourth in studio art; a Bachelor of Fine Arts degree from a private or university-related art school, where at least two-thirds of the courses are in studio; or even a Master of Fine Arts degree from an elite graduate school. The latter candidate has six years of education, in contrast to two years of study for the community college graduate.

The range of design curricula is bewildering. Some liberal arts–oriented Bachelor of Arts programs maintain that their "broader education" better prepares students for life, and deficiencies will be rectified after graduation. By contrast, professional art schools offering the Bachelor of Fine Arts program insist that anything short of their program produces dilettantes. Many graduate programs believe graphic design can only become a profession if a body of theoretical knowledge underpins professional practice, and they are developing this knowledge base. Students seeking a graphic design education face this bewildering range of options, with costs ranging from low tuition at local community colleges to some of the highest tuitions in the country at exclusive art schools. This is irrational. If a graphic designer can be produced in two years, why have graduate programs at all? And, if graduate training is needed, shouldn't two-year programs only prepare students to transfer to other programs?

Accreditation is a joke. The formal accrediting organization, the National Association of Schools of Art and Design (NASAD), examines such criteria as student and faculty contact hours; the integrity of the curriculum, measured by the balance between studio, art history, and academic courses; the general appropriateness of facilities; and whether faculty hold appropriate educational degrees. This process is acceptable as far as it goes and has helped many programs overcome administrative inertia to correct glaring deficiencies. However, a school or art department is reviewed as a total entity. Serious problems in the graphic design program can become a footnote near the end of the report renewing accreditation, or might be dismissed by the three educational administrators on the visiting review team. Once, after hearing a passionate plea by a graphic design program head about the need for typesetting equipment, an art school dean on a review team replied, "Yeah, we have that problem in graphic design at our school, too."

A specific accreditation process for graphic design programs by an organization such as the AIGA or the recently formed Graphic Design Education Association (GDEA) would give political clout to faculty and programs. Why do most engineering and architectural schools receive funding for computer labs to meet the challenges of the CAD/CAM revolution, while most graphic design programs become increasingly obsolete because their equipment requests are minimally funded year after year? Yet if an engineering program does not get appropriate equipment funding, its accreditation will be revoked. This can cause serious image problems for the school, coupled with significant enrollment loss if a program is spurned by students who learn about the loss of accreditation.

When the current bumper crop of young designers hits the streets, a chaotic game of musical chairs begins. In spite of the best efforts of school placement offices and career days organized by art directors clubs and AIGA chapters, the placement process is chaotic. Many suspect that the schools are now graduating far too many graphic design majors for the market, but apparently no one has made a national survey of just how many graduates receive degrees each year, and what percent are absorbed by the field.

Despite the problems, graphic design education has made incredible strides during the past decade. Ten years ago when design teachers attended a professional conference or art directors' club meeting, they could count on being criticized about the mediocre quality of design education in this country. Today, one is more often criticized for graduating too many students and causing the field to become overcrowded and overly competitive. The rapid growth, which doubled graphic design school enrollments, occurred in the late seventies, and many art programs have one-half of all majors in graphic design. The more recent change is not in the overproduction of graphic design graduates; it's that more of the applicants are qualified. While many programs have improved significantly, there are still far too many programs providing inadequate preparation. A major reason for the increase in the number of adequate programs is the growth in graduate education over the last decade. Graduate programs are producing teachers who are committed to education.

If this educational momentum is to continue, closer collaboration between the profession and the educational establishment is needed. This should start with a national survey of design graduates and the number and type of professional positions available. Basic certification of graduates – measured not by stylistic or creative assessment, but in design fundamentals and a basic knowledge of typography, computer software, design terminology, communication theory, and print production – would reform design education. Establishing national entry requirements for students applying to study at accredited design programs (SAT scores, grade averages, and visual aptitude measured by a standardized portfolio review) would reduce enrollments and improve programs.

Far too many art schools and colleges simply don't have adequate admission standards for a discipline requiring conceptualization and creative problem-solving. If the problems confronting design education are to be addressed effectively, educators and the profession must work together.

The Vitality of Risk

From *AIGA Journal of Graphic Design,* Vol. 8, No. 4 (1990)

A vivacious young woman from Rio de Janeiro moves to New York to study design and is later appointed co–art director of the world-renowned *Harper's Bazaar* magazine at age twenty-five. After ten years at *Bazaar,* she becomes the first art director of *Ms.,* the magazine of the women's liberation movement. Other accomplishments include designing award-winning books, working for *Rolling Stone,* and being chosen to art direct the revival of the 1930s classic, *Vanity Fair.* She is at the zenith of her career and celebrated for her work when cancer takes her life at age forty-four. This chronicle is not fiction. It is the story of Bea Feitler, described by friends and admirers as a "risk-taker," a "whirlwind persona," and "an unstoppable creative force."

Feitler's parents provided a European education, offering broad learning and stressing excellence. She showed talent and enthusiasm for art in her teens. Her parents encouraged Feitler's interest, made a global search for the right art school, and chose Parson's School of Design in Manhattan. Her uncle, Edward Newman, lived in the New York area and provided her with a transitional home.

Feitler was exotic and full of nervous energy. She thrived on the life of the city and her design-school experiences. Music, literature, and the ballet fascinated her. She would wait in line for hours to get standing room at the Met. Her initial interest in illustration yielded to a growing fascination with design. The fashion magazines, especially *Harper's Bazaar* – art directed by the legendary Alexey Brodovitch until his retirement in 1958, the year before her graduation from Parson's – held a special fascination for her. After graduation she made the rounds in New York, including a visit to *Bazaar,* where she was told to come back after she had more experience. She decided to return to Brazil and launch her career there. In partnership with two other graphic designers, she started Estudio G, specializing in poster, record album, and book design. She also collaborated on the design of the Brazilian magazine *Senhor,* which was revolutionary among Brazilian cultural and political magazines in its commitment to graphic concepts and progressive design. *Senhor* provided a wonderful opportunity for Feitler to experiment, to innovate, to succeed, and to fail.

Henry Wolf followed Brodovitch as art director of *Bazaar* in 1958. When Wolf left to become art director of *Show* in 1961, Marvin Israel, one of Feitler's teachers from Parson's became art director of *Bazaar.* Two issues later the names Beatriz Feitler and Ruth Ansel appeared on *Bazaar's* masthead as art assistants. Israel had contacted Feitler in Rio de Janeiro and invited her to return to Manhattan and join him at *Bazaar.* It was a fabulous opportunity for the twenty-three-year-old designer.

From their first meeting in the offices of *Bazaar,* Feitler and Ansel felt the mandate of Brodovitch's legacy and hoped to meet him. Though the opportunity never came, they absorbed his influence form Marvin Israel until he left *Bazaar* in 1963. In a move that received national press comment and surprised the media world, *Bazaar* promoted Feitler and Ansel, then in their mid-twenties, from art assistants to co–art directors. Pundits in the press who expressed open skepticism about their ability to manage the graphic destiny of one of the world's most sophisticated publications soon ate crow, for the synergy and energy of Feitler and Ansel occurred at a time when high fashion was colliding with pop fashion from the streets, rock music and experimental film were extending sensory experience, women and minorities were taking to the streets, and the new art movements, notably Pop and Op, were changing the face of aesthetic experience. Moon rockets, assassinations and the Vietnam War stunned the national psyche. Feitler and Ansel remained true to the best Brodovitch

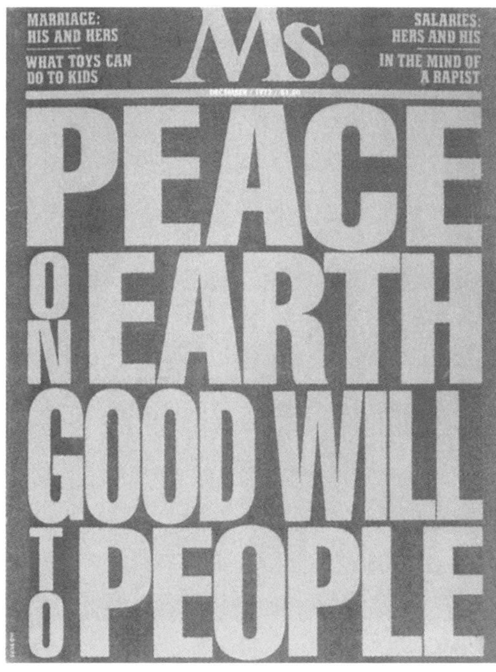

Cover for *Ms.* magazine.
Design: Bea Feitler
(March, 1973)

tradition of designing magazines as a harmonious and cinematic whole, while responding to events in the streets of the time, in a collaboration that was organic and mutually supportive. They were open to accidents, material around the studio and events surrounding them. In their office an inspirational wall collage would grow and change, providing an unending source for invention. Feitler once summed up her editorial design philosophy: "A magazine should flow. It should have rhythm. You can't look at one page alone, you have to visualize what comes before and after. Good editorial design is all about creating a harmonic flow."

Friends remember Feitler's energy as inexhaustible and her zest for life as exuberant and extravagant. A stunning contradiction was at the center of her being. She was a traditionalist with a deep devotion to her family and a sense of her cultural history. Yet she was filled with the spirit of the sixties. Close associates recall that she handled the dichotomy well. Her present was undaunted by any struggle between her past and her future.

In a 1968 *Graphis* article, photographer Richard Avedon recalled working with Feitler and Ansel on the April 1965 *Bazaar* cover. The deadline was past, it was after 11 p.m., and the photographs of Jean Shrimpton in a "space helmet" designed by one of New York's most famous milliners did not work.

"Ruth started to explain that we could cut the shape of the space helmet out of Day-Glo paper," Avedon wrote, "but she never finished because Bea was already cutting the shape. Rubber cement, color swatches. An eighth of an inch between the pink helmet and the grey background. No, a sixteenth. I was in the room and I don't know how it happened. And, it all happened in minutes? The moment was absolute magic, to watch Bea, the classicist, and Ruth, the modern, work as if they were one person."

The final cover with Avedon's photograph of Jean Shrimpton – now peering from behind a bright pink Day-Glo space helmet with the logo vibrating against it in acid green – won the New York Art Director's Club medal and has been often reproduced as an emblem of the sixties.

Bazaar of the 1960s was a dynamic statement of its time. Rollicking sequence photography, cinematic pacing, incredible scale changes, Pop art, and Op art often filled its uninhibited pages. It walked away with award after award in major designing exhibitions. Breaking precedent in 1965, Avedon, Feitler, and Ansel fought for and won the right to use a black model in the pages of a major fashion magazine. The reaction – subscriptions cancelled and advertisers withdrawing their advertising – was unexpected and frightened management, which did not use black models again for a long time.

Feitler worked well with photographers, who trusted her judgment and ability to select and design effectively with their images. In addition to close collaboration with photographers having long-standing relationships with *Bazaar,* such as Avedon and Hiro, Feitler and Ansel brought Bill Silano, Duane Michals, Bill King, and Bob Richardson to the pages of *Bazaar.* While working on a shoe portfolio with Silano, Feitler took him to see the French film *A Man and A Woman* six times. The lyrical romanticism and elegant cinematography from this landmark movie found its graphic equal in the pages of *Bazaar.*

Today a two-year tenure by an art director at a major consumer magazine is considered lengthy: the Feitler/Ansel ten-year occupancy of the office made famous by Brodovitch seems remarkable in retrospect. In the early 1970s, a new editor arrived and seemed somewhat unnerved upon inheriting two dynamic young art directors who carried considerable clout. It became apparent that the situation was not feasible. Feitler's final issue was May 1972. She left to join Gloria Steinem in launching the new *Ms.* Magazine. Ansel art directed *Bazaar* solo for five months, then departed after the October 1972 issue.

"In one sense, Feitler was always the original feminist," recalls her longtime associate Carl Barile, who worked with her at *Bazaar, Ms., Rolling Stone* and on the premiere issue of *Vanity Fair,* "but her decision to go to *Ms.* was made because she saw it as an opportunity to be creative and do innovative work." Her feminism was of the "treat everyone equally" school rather than the militant. And innovate, she did, with editorial designs as startling for the time as the articles appearing in *Ms.* Feitler used Day-Glo inks, established unique signature formats for various sections of *Ms.* and mixed photography with illustration. Her typography would be expressionistic and uninhibited. She was willing to cross the line separating the tried and true from the risky and unproved. Many art directors are unwilling to cross this line until fad and fashion certify its acceptability, but Bea Feitler would reach across and return with a novelty face, a decorated letter or a hopelessly eccentric form which happened to be just right for the message at hand. Conventional wisdom decrees that all-type magazine covers are newsstand disasters, but Feitler rattled marketing and outraged some with revisionist scripture on the all-type *Ms.* cover declaring "Peace on earth, good will to people" in pink and green Day-Glo. It sold out on the newsstands in December 1972. *Ms.* followed up with a neon-sign version in December 1973.

Her South American heritage influenced her design sensibility about color. She told assistants, "Trust me, listen to me, I know," while replacing their color selections with vibrant contrasting hues.

At *Ms.* Feitler made an indelible mark upon the face of American graphic design. Her deep interest in all of the arts was catalytic in expanding the magazine's scope to include cultural coverage. Perhaps she sensed that she was making history by graphically defining a movement and a cultural revolution. But she did not see *Ms.* and her graphics as the parochial product of strident feminism, she saw them as an all-people movement; not disenfranchising males who traditionally dominated the culture, but enfranchising those who had been left out. Not only did she commission art and photography from image makers of reputation and renown, she also commissioned art from fine artists, housewives from Brooklyn who made art or crafts and took the subway over to show her their work, and, yes, from men. She made time for those who showed her their work, and pondered whether their unique and even modest gifts might somehow make a point or provide a counterpoint.

Feitler's assistants were inspired but never governed by her approach to design. She was generous in allowing them to design their assignments and develop their own approaches. She had good judgment and intuition about people. Once a photographer or assistant gained her trust, she would let them fly, helping them to recognize their great potential. Many young designers who worked with her went on to become prominent art directors in their own right, including: Carl Barile at *Avenue;* Charles Churchward at *Vanity Fair;* Paula Grief at *Mademoiselle;* and Barbara Richner at *Ms.* Her charming personality touched everyone who knew her, but she could also be very demanding. Her standards of design excellence were not negotiable.

Even while art directing major magazines, Feitler had book jacket, album cover and book design projects under way. In 1974 Feitler left *Ms.* and worked on a variety of projects: Alvin Ailey's City Center dance posters and even costumes; record jackets including *Black and Blue* for the Rolling Stones; books; magazine designs and redesigns; and ad campaigns for Christian Dior, Diane von Furstenberg, Bill Haire, and Calvin Klein. Her book designs are superb examples of the genre, including *The Beatles, Cole, Diaghilev and the Ballets Russe,* Lartigue's *Diary of a Century, Vogue Book of Fashion Photography 1919–1979* and Helmut Newton's *White Women.* In this area of design notorious for its flat-as-a-pancake fees, Bea Feitler asked for and received cover credit with the author and/or photographer and negotiated a royalty from the books she designed. The book designer, she reasoned, gives life and joy and form as surely as the author or picture-maker does and should share in the rewards if the book attracted readers. She believed, "Modern books should be 50–50 in terms of visuals and words. People have to be hit over the head and drawn into the book. There is so much visual material in today's world that people can't judge what is good and what is bad. It's up to the graphic designer to set standards."

From 1974 until 1980, Feitler taught advanced students at the School of Visual Arts, where program head Richard Wilde remembers her as "one of the very best" teachers. Students fought to get into her class and she rarely denied entry, once commenting in an interview, "What really turns me on is the fifty-five students in my Editorial Design course at the School of Visual Arts." After declining to teach one semester due to an overwhelming workload, she called Wilde and asked if she could be assigned a class for the next term. He asked if her workload had lightened. She replied that on the contrary, it had increased, but she needed the inspiration and contact with students which only teaching could provide. As an instructor she was uninhibited, and nothing rattled her. Her interest was in encouraging each student's personal direction. As one example, Wilde recalls that student Keith Haring's graffiti-inspired work had detractors, but Feitler was enthusiastic about its vigor and potential. She

(continued on page 146)

Studies for larger paintings. Crayon on gridded paper, average dimension: 6.5 x 6.5 inches. (1969–1971)

Untitled.
Acrylic on canvas,
54.25 x 54.5 inches.
(1969–1971)

Untitled.
Acrylic on canvas,
78 x 78 inches.
(1969–1971)

Untitled.
Acrylic on canvas,
65.5 x 65.5 inches.
(1969–1971)

Untitled.
Acrylic on canvas,
66 x 66 inches.
(1969–1971)
From the collection of
Sidney and Evelyn Kessler

Untitled.
Acrylic on canvas,
66.25 x 66.25 inches.
(1969–1971)

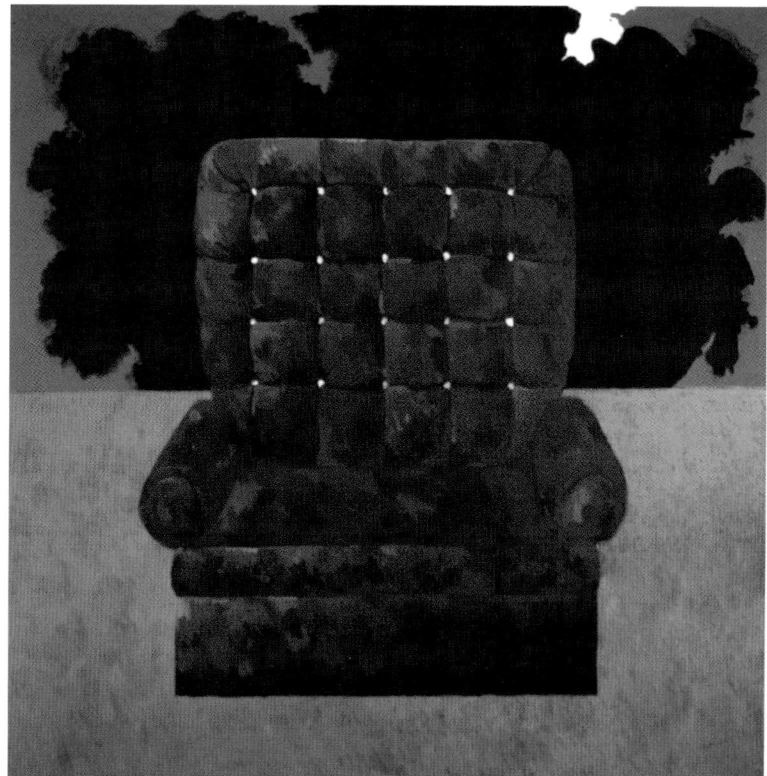

encouraged him to further develop his direction. And she was a wonderful role model for female students studying design.

A six-year association with *Rolling Stone* began in 1975. Feitler redesigned its format twice: in 1977 for its tenth-anniversary issue featuring the stunning photographs of Annie Leibovitz; and again in 1981 when it shifted from a tabloid to the current magazine format. In 1978, Feitler signed on as a consulting art director for Condé Nast Publications and created the graphic image for a new publication, *Self.* Editor-in-Chief Phyllis Wilson credited much of *Self's* distinctiveness to Feitler's experimental design approach and perceptive ability to work with photographs, "…seeing them and cropping them and moving them [until] you got something that would suddenly turn exciting…."

Her final project was the premiere issue of the revived *Vanity Fair,* which appeared after her death in 1982. She underwent surgery twice for a rare form of cancer. Her spirits were undaunted and many close associates at Condé Nast did not know she had been undergoing chemotherapy for several months. They thought her stylish turbans were a fashion statement. An associate took the mechanicals for the premiere issue of *Vanity Fair* to her apartment for her approval. After completing the issue, she went home to Brazil and did not live to see it published.

Bea Feitler only lived forty-four years, but filled them with energy, enthusiasm and a passion for life and design. Hundreds of people attended her memorial service, and as a living tribute her friends and family established the Bea Feitler Foundation, which funds a full one-year scholarship for a junior graphic-design student at the School of Visual Arts. She believed a graphic designer's work matters because the culture is expanded and enriched by those who shape and form information. She is missed for the vision, passion, and vitality she brought to each day's life and work and remembered for her profound contribution. ⊷

The Designer, Paper, and the Environment

From *Communication Arts,* Vol. 32, No. 4 (1990)

"We're tree killers," New York graphic designer Baker exclaimed to me on the telephone recently. "I just designed a CD box for a music group and it turned out well. But I realized, people are just going to throw this box away. It will become part of the waste in a landfill."

Many graphic designers share Baker's concern. Renewed emphasis on the environment has led many graphic designers to worry about being a prime source of environmental degradation. These fears are well-founded. Over 37 percent of the typical American household's garbage is paper, and it ends up in landfills. 500,000 trees are required to produce the 88 percent of each Sunday's newspapers that are not recycled. Estimates of the size of America's solid-waste stream vary widely, ranging from about three to eight pounds per person each day; therefore, each man, woman and child in America discards from one to three pounds of paper each day! Currently, only about ten percent of our solid waste is recycled. Since Long Island is exhausting its landfill sites, over 220 tractor trailers of garbage a day, or 80,300 a year, leave the island loaded with solid waste destined for landfills elsewhere.

When the University of Arizona Garbage Project applied archaeological techniques to the systematic exhuming of eight tons of garbage from seven landfills, they discovered that paper accounted for 40 to 50 percent of the contents both by weight and volume. What happens to all this paper? We have long assumed that since paper is biodegradable, it decays and returns to the earth. The Garbage Project, however, found

40-year-old newspapers whose level of preservation enabled them to be read. In a sense, materials in landfills are mummified, because pressure and the lack of oxygen and moisture inside a landfill prevent degrading from occurring. (It's sobering to realize that one's unsuccessful graphic designs, discarded income tax records, and old love letters survive intact in a landfill, potential research data for future archaeologists.) Perhaps the failure of a paper to degrade is fortunate, because if it did, it could release toxic chemicals from its inks into the groundwater.

Ten percent of our garbage now goes to incinerators, and this amount is expected to triple in a few years. Incineration is a horrible alternative: It pollutes the air with toxic metals, toxic organic chemicals and acid gases. Incineration operates on a simple principle: garbage in, toxic ash out. For every ton of solid waste incinerated, about 1/3 ton of toxic ash is produced and must be dumped in a landfill where it becomes a potential pollutant of groundwater.

Clearly, a massive recycling effort is needed. In Japanese municipalities, there is a systematic program to separate household waste, including metal, glass, paper, plastic and food wastes. Designer and educator Victor Papanek tells that after his daughter set up household in Germany, a municipal official brought two 10 x 30 inch screw-top canisters, similar in appearance to thermos jugs, for their weekly garbage. It took about a month to learn how to run their household to reduce their garbage to two small canisters each week. Many other industrial countries reduce their solid waste to a fraction of ours by taking reusable string bags to the market, using returnable containers, implementing recycling programs, composting and avoiding overpackaged products.

Recycling, reusable containers and making more sensible use of resources are the solutions to the back end of the problem. One aspect of the front end of the problem should also be a deep concern to graphic designers: destroying hundreds of thousands of trees each week to make paper. Trees can be a renewable crop. The American Forest Council points out that in 1920, the depletion of forestland led to predictions that we would exhaust our supply of wood in just 25 years. Fortunately, improved forest management averted this disaster. Today, six million trees a day are planted in America, we have 730 million acres of forestland and we have more trees than we had in the 1920s.

But there is a downside to this success story. Many native virgin forests have been turned into high-yield tree farms, with a loss of hardwoods and the extinction of many plant, bird and animal species. Massive amounts of toxic pesticides and herbicides have been applied to the tree farms. The forest-products industry wants to harvest many of the ancient native forests not currently protected by park and wilderness areas, and Federal restrictions expire this year.

An associate administrator of the Environmental Protection Agency recently observed that a big obstacle to paper recycling is ownership of huge forest lands by giant paper companies. For example, International Paper, whose paper lines include Hammermill, Beckett, and Strathmore, controls 6.2 million acres of forests through its IP Timberlands, Ltd. partnership. The partnership supplies about a third of IP's fiber requirements and sells timber to other producers.

If you ran a paper company and had invested millions of dollars into forests, paid property taxes on the land for 30 or more years, and now stood to recoup expenses and reap large profits by selling the trees to yourself, would you be interested in buying your raw materials from recycled paper dealers?

Paper industry resistance to recycling is further compounded by overcapacity. Pulp producers are expected to expand worldwide capacity by about 23 percent in the next three years, according to Salomon Brothers analyst Sherman Chao, while demand is only expected to rise 9 percent.

The overcapacity problem extends to recycled paper, too. With more and more American municipalities and citizens recycling, the supply of paper for recycling now exceeds demand.

For instance, New Jersey recently passed a law mandating separation of garbage into three categories of recyclable material. As a result, the ability of recycled paper dealers and their clients to process used paper has been overwhelmed. Newspapers were fetching $40 per ton, but in parts of New Jersey one now has to pay $25 per ton for someone to take used newsprint off your hands. Clearly, an expanded use of recycled paper instead of trees is needed, but this flies head on into the interconnection of the tree-growing and paper-manufacturing industries. In past years, paper merchant representatives calling upon me have denigrated recycled paper, alleging poor quality and printing problems. Whether this was sales hype passed on from paper companies or a reflection of problems, I don't know. I do know, however, that the reclamation and manufacturing processes have been dramatically improved, resulting in excellent recycled paper today.

There is evidence of a surge of interest due to environmental concerns and market demand. Recycled papers now available span the range of uses, including bond papers, book papers, copier and duplicator papers, cover and text papers, forms bond, writing papers and envelopes. Co-op America in Washington, DC, offers recycled toilet paper in its catalog. Other uses include soundproofing and insulation, the padding in automobiles (each automobile contains about 60 pounds of recycled paper) and paperboard packaging. If your cereal box is cold grey inside, it is made of recycled paper, but if it is a warm tan, it is made from freshly cut trees.

On June 22, 1989, the Federal government implemented a program requiring all Federal agencies and state and local governments receiving $10,000 or more in appropriated Federal funds to have a preference program favoring recycled papers. Clearly, the tide is slowly shifting toward recycled paper and other environmental initiatives as citizens, businesses and government all begin to feel their environmental responsibilities more keenly.

From fast-food chains to chemical companies such as DuPont and manufacturers including General Motors, a sense of environmental responsibility is growing. But there is also a lot of hype and profiteering involved as well. The recent surge of biodegradable plastic garbage bags is a case in point. Mixing a cornstarch additive into the plastic produces a garbage bag that will break down into many small pieces instead of one large piece of plastic in the landfill. However, more plastic is needed since the cornstarch weakens the material. The result of these "environmental" products is increased plastic waste.

In addition to actions required of all citizens, such as conserving energy, using energy-efficient transportation, recycling, voting for environmental candidates and supporting environmental organizations, what actions can graphic designers take? Collectively, designers exercise tremendous power over the paper industry through their specifications. This was brought home to me dramatically when I was an art director in the pharmaceutical industry and casually mentioned to our primary printer that we had been talking about changing the coated text and cover line we were using for all of our full-color projects.

"For God's sake, give me three months notice," he exclaimed. "We buy that paper for your work by the four-boxcar order, saving you and us a lot of money. We can't afford to be stuck with three or four boxcars of paper you don't want to use." Every designer has an environmental duty to maximize his or her specification of recycled papers to spur its production. By specifying recycled papers, including those now on the market, which are 50 percent recycled fibers, designers increase demand and spur the expansion of the recycling industry. Designers can urge their clients to use recycled business, copier and duplicator papers and implement company-wide recycling programs. The big paper companies will rapidly increase their interest in recycled products if the graphic design profession pulls paper sales toward recycled products.

National organizations such as the Graphic Artists Guild, American Center for Design and AIGA should set up environmental committees on their boards of directors. These organizations could go directly to the paper, printing and ink-manufacturing industries to advocate recycling and a reduction of toxic materials in manufacturing and end products. If ink swatches were required to carry a toxicity rating, designers could select colors that do not contain cadmium or other toxic heavy metals. Each local art director's club and AIGA chapter should implement environmental programs as well, focusing upon professional responsibility and public awareness projects.

Perhaps a new design ethic will emerge if graphic designers seriously become concerned about the environment. In recent prestigious shows such as AIGA Communications Graphics and the STA 100, one senses an aesthetic of technological perfection and conspicuous extravagance. One sees corporate publications with text pages printed on cover-weight stock with eight press impressions: four-color process; two PMS match colors; and both dull and gloss varnish. Such excess is wasteful of resources. Ironically, the content of these graphic extravaganzas is often vacuous. An environmental aesthetic might signal a shift of emphasis from style, surface and decoration to content, and from lavish to environment-friendly production. If major design exhibitions added categories such as "printed on recycled paper," "non-profit public sector design," and "one- and two-color," environmentally responsive design could be recognized and encouraged.

In this era of acid rain, global warming and toxic hazards, our current environmental situation isn't necessarily hopeless. As Buckminster Fuller pointed out, we don't have an energy and environmental crisis, we have a "brain power" crisis. Industrial society must develop saner lifestyles, seeking a new harmony between the human family and this fragile spaceship earth. Individually and collectively, graphic designers can be part of the problem or part of the solution. We have had our head in the sand during the environmentally oblivious Reagan era; the time to act is now. ➻

Landmarks of Book Design, Second of a Series: *For the Voice*

From *Print* Vol. 44, No. 5 (Sept/Oct 1990)

A chance meeting between a Russian poet and a Russian graphic designer in Berlin in the early 1920s led to the creation of a milestone in graphic design history. Late in 1921, the Russian constructivist El Lissitzky had traveled to Berlin in connection with a major exhibition of Russian art to be held there in 1922. Russia had been isolated from Western Europe by the battle lines of World War I and the turbulence of revolution, and this exhibition provided an early opportunity for Western Europeans to see works by Archipenko, Chagall, Lissitzky, Malevich, Rodchenko, and Tatlin. The new Soviet government had not yet turned against radically new art, and asked Lissitzky – whose German education and mastery of the language made him an ideal link between the two cultures – to stay in Germany and design a new trilingual publication called *Vesch (Object)* to introduce avant-garde Russian art to the West.

On October 8, 1922, Vladimir Mayakovsky, the leading poet of the Russian Revolution and early Soviet period, arrived in Berlin to join his mistress, Lili Brik. The Berlin office of Gosizdat, the Moscow State Publishing House, had decided to publish a collection of Mayakovsky's poems selected by the poet for reading aloud and titled *For the Voice*. Since Lissitzky was in Berlin, Mayakovsky recommended that he be commissioned to design and illustrate this volume. Their collaboration brought together two major creative forces in avant-garde culture. Both held the same ideas about Constructivism: Art should descend from the ivory tower to play a pivotal role in the restructuring of society. It should become a meaningful part of everyday life in the new socialist state.

Cover of *For the Voice* by Vladimir Mayakovsky. Design: El Lissitzky (1923)

Although Lissitzky and Mayakovsky had very different backgrounds, both had been closely associated with Moscow's avant-garde art and literature movements during the 1910s. Mayakovsky had been a teenage activist in the Social Democratic Worker's Party. The czarist regime jailed him repeatedly for subversive activity. While in solitary confinement in 1909, sixteen-year-old Mayakovsky started writing poetry. He was also keenly interested in art, and after his release, he attended the Moscow Art School.

There, he joined David Burlyuk and a few others in the Russian futurist group and became its leading spokesman. The form and content of Mayakovsky's poetry became increasingly assertive and rebellious. Wearing greasepaint, a yellow shirt, and a radish in his buttonhole, he frequented cafés where he recited poems written to be deliberately offensive to bourgeois audiences. He sought to "de-poetize poetry" through stunning technical innovations and by adopting the crude language of the common people. His work was declamatory and often written specifically for dramatic public readings before large groups. When the Russian Revolution erupted, Mayakovsky became an ardent supporter of the Bolsheviks, writing stirring poems in support of the Revolution, the workers, and the peasants. After the Revolution, he became an ardent spokesman for the Communist party.

Lissitzky had traveled to Germany in 1909 to study architectural engineering in Darmstadt, then returned to Russia when war broke out in 1914. After working at a Moscow architectural firm, he was appointed, in 1919, to the faculty of the revolutionary art school in Vitebsk by the headmaster, Marc Chagall. The painter Kazimir Malevich, founder of the Suprematist movement, which advocated the supremacy of pure geometric form and color over traditional representation, also taught there. Under Malevich's influence, Lissitzky began to paint geometric abstractions called PROUNS, an acronym for the Russian phrase meaning "project for the establishment of a new art." In 1921, Lissitzky became head of the architectural faculty at the new VKhUTEMAS art school in Moscow. He combined the nonutilitarian formal language of Malevich with the ethic of the Constructivist group, whose proclamations called upon artists "to construct" art and change the world instead of merely depicting it. Constructivist theory embraced applied design: It said in effect, "Go to the factories, this is the only task for artists." In his work during the 1920s, Lissitzky emerged as a major force in modern graphic design, exerting a powerful influence upon the Dutch De Stijl group, the Hungarian Constructivist László Moholy-Nagy, and the Bauhaus.

For the Voice proved to be one of Lissitzky's most influential designs. Mayakovsky selected thirteen poems, and Lissitzky developed a 19-by-13.5-centimeter (approximately 7 1/2" by 5 5/16") format of sixty-four pages. He resolved to "construct" the book working solely with elements found in a letterpress printer's typecase: wood and metal types; rules, bars, and bullets; a few dingbats; and one old engraved image of an imperial eagle. Layouts were developed as a guide for a German typesetter who could not read or write a single word of Russian. The printing firm's staff became fascinated by *For the Voice* and its unique format and asked Lissitzky to translate parts into German so that they could understand it.

As with most graphic forms, the shapes and images Lissitzky used in *For the Voice* have a dual life: They are perceived optical phenomena as well as communicative signs functioning with other signs to form a message. Western designers unable to read Russian have viewed *For the Voice* as a masterly arrangement of forms, apparently unaware that Lissitzky was translating the pure forms from his mentor Kazimir Malevich's Suprematist paintings into communicative signs. The broad influence of this book has been based solely on the impact of its visual aspect; Lissitzky's symbolic interpretations of the titles and texts of Mayakovsky's poems have not been comprehended by the reading public.

The cover of *For the Voice* reveals the resonance of the graphic approach used in the book. Mayakovsky's name runs horizontally and intersects the vertical placement of the title on a red bar. A large capital M composed of typographic rules balances the lower right placement of concentric circles.

Lissitzky illustrated the title page with a halftone reproduction of "Announcer," one of ten lithographs published in 1923 as a portfolio titled "Victory over the Sun." The book title and author are superimposed over the lithograph, and at the top left-hand page appear the words, Constructor of the book El Lissitzky. This attribution was chosen with care, for Lissitzky did not feel that he illustrated or decorated the book in the traditional sense; rather, he saw his role as a designer who "constructed" the totality of the book in an architectural sense.

Mayakovsky dedicated *For the Voice* to Lili Brik. For the dedication page, Lissitzky designed an abstract eye, which appears to look toward the viewer as a straight-on image while simultaneously appearing as a cross-sectioned side view. When read clockwise twice, the three Cyrillic letters placed around the eye read, "I love."

Each poem begins with a double-page spread containing the title and Lissitzky's Constructivist interpretation. Since the book was intended for oral presentations before audiences, Lissitzky wanted readers to be able to quickly find the next poem they wished to present without having to look it up in an index in the front of the book; thus he designed a series of thirteen diecut tabs down the right-hand margin, enabling readers to move their right thumbs down to the title of the poem they wished to read and easily flip the book open to its title page.

The first poem in the book was written in 1918 and is titled "Left March" (*Levy Marsh*). It is dedicated to the Red Marines. The title appears on the right-hand page opposite an iconographic ship constructed of typographic elements and flying the Soviet flag. With "Left March," Mayakovsky found his tone as a revolutionary poet. Suddenly, his work gained a dynamic boldness with a brilliant series of short, staccato images emphasized by a thundering repetition: "Left! Left! Left!" When Russian sailors march, they chant *"levoi"* ("left") over and over as their left feet hit the ground in unison. Mayakovsky used this as an auditory theme in the poem. A segment of the poem demonstrates Mayakovsky's new rousing style:

Rally the ranks into a march!
Now's no time to quibble or browse there.
Silence, you orators!
You
have the floor,
Comrade Mauser.
Enough of living by laws
That Adam and Eve have left.
Hustle history's old horse.
Left!
Left!
Left!

Whenever "Left March" was presented at a public poetry reading, the entire audience would rise to its feet each time the reader arrived at the refrain "Left! Left! Left! " In unison, they would raise their right arms and thrust their fists into the air, chanting, "Left! Left! Left!" A kinetic excitement would fill the hall as participation forged a communal bond. The political implications of a call to march to the left were, of course, understood by all.

Lissitzky expressed the auditory theme of the poem graphically in the top left area of the left-hand page. A sequence of three marching legs is constructed from metal rules and printed in red, and *"levoi"* is set three times in black sans-serif type of descending size.

The second poem in the book is entitled "Our March" (*Nash Marsh*) and was written by Mayakovsky for the only issue of the Futurists' newspaper, which appeared on March 15, 1918. This homage to those who risked their lives in the early stages of the revolution begins:

Beat your drums on the squares of riots!
Keep your heads higher with the
second deluge!
We are going to wash
the cities of the world.

The poem evokes city squares washed with the blood of martyrs who gave their lives in the struggle against the czarist regime: Lissitzky's large red square is not merely a decorative graphic element but a symbol of martyrdom during public demonstrations. Responding to the A and W in both words of the title, Lissitzky layered these letterforms to create a staccato graphic rhythm evoking the rhythmic beat of drums in the opening line. The typographic configuration below the large red square on the left-hand page demonstrates Lissitzky's delight in typographic play inspired by Futurist poetry. By selecting either the top or the bottom vowel, one can read two messages: *boy* means "fight" and *bey* means "beat them." The placement of this element creates a lively counterpoint to the diagonal accent on the upper right-hand page.

The title of the third poem, "My May One," is presented as an emblematic typographic configuration, taking advantage of the similarity of the Russian words "My" and "May" – they are spelled MON and AMN, respectively, to create a symmetrical design in a circle evoking arm patches and insignia. This poem is a celebratory ode to the May Day holiday, which is very important to Russians for two reasons: It was designated as an international labor day by the 1889 International Socialist Congress, and it marks the end of the long, severe Russian winter. Since over 90 percent of the Soviet Union is above the latitude of Montreal, Canada, the arrival of May Day is a real cause for celebration.

The title of the fourth poem, presented vertically on the right-hand page, is a Russian slang word

(continued on page 154)

Untitled.
Encaustic studies,
approx. 7 x 7 inches.
(1970)

Untitled.
Encaustic study,
approx. 9 x 9 inches.
(1970)

Untitled.
Acrylic on paper collages,
approx. 32 x 35
and 32 x 40 inches.
(1969–1971)

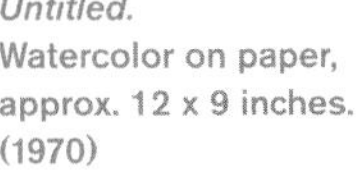

Untitled.
Watercolor on paper,
approx. 12 x 9 inches.
(1970)

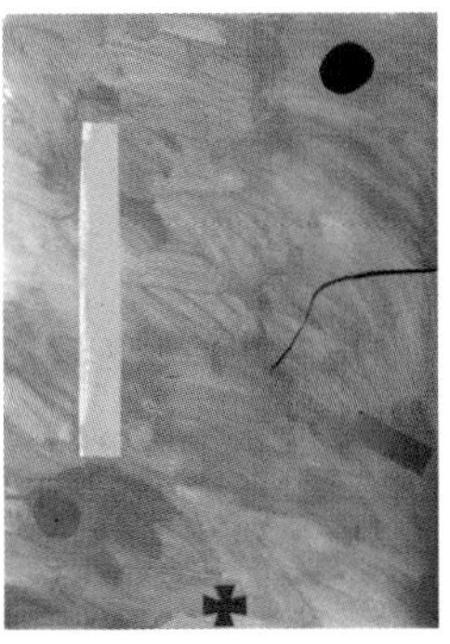

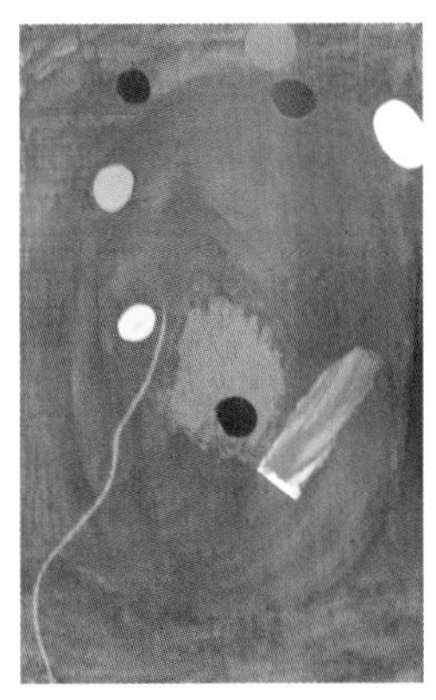

which has been translated as "rabble," "swine," and "scum." This poem is a rabid propaganda attack upon the evil capitalists. The four lines of text set in bold red sans-serif type on the title page read:

By the nailing of these lines
Stop mute!
Listen to this wolf,
Howling of this weak Poem!

On the left-hand page, dotted lines connect large dots, labeled with the names of major "capitalist" European cities, to skull-and-crossbones symbols from the typecase. Lissitzky used a connotative typeface for each of the cities: a sans serif reminiscent of Edward Johnston's London Underground type; an old-style Roman for Paris; and the blackletter still being used in Germany for Berlin. (The Bauhaus did not begin its extensive use of sans-serif type and Constructivist space until 1923, influenced in large measure by Lissitzky's Berlin work.) These diagonal lines are drawn at a 60-degree angle to the edges of the page. In contrast, the diagonals on the right-hand page are at 45-degree angles – a differential that creates tension between the elements.

On the following page of text, two lines of type are separated from the body of the poem and pushed to the right of the page number. They read:

You see?
Behind the naked digit…

A large pointing-hand dingbat from the printer's typecase dominates this layout. This is graphic humor on Lissitzky's part, offering a visual pun by permitting both the pointing finger and the page number to function as "the naked digit" of Mayakovsky's poem.

The fifth poem celebrates "The Third International." This was an association of national Communist parties formed in 1919 whose stated purpose was to foment world revolution and transnational class war, and to promote what Lenin called "civil war, not civil peace." Lissitzky used two printer's rules to form a huge letter that becomes the T in the words "Third" and "International." On the left-hand page, an overlapping complex – composed of a hammer, a sickle, and two Roman numeral threes – forms an appropriate symbol. The angle of the word "International" echoes and repeats the angle of the hammer handle, and the black Roman numeral three is placed at a right angle to it, creating a dynamic yet rigorously stable composition.

A poem to strike fear in every capitalist's heart, it begins:

We are coming
like a revolutionary lava,
above our ranks the red flag is burning,
our leader leads millions.
The Third International.
For older censors
the Third International is sounding.

The title pages for the 1918 poem "Orders to the Army of the Arts" are active and informal. The composition on the left, made of three letterforms and overlapping grids and rules, is graphic rather than symbolic. Scale changes and layering create a sense of dynamic movement and depth.

This poem, which first appeared in the periodical *Art of the Commune (Iskusstvo Kommuny),* on December 5, 1918, was written at a curious time in the evolution of Soviet culture. For a brief moment, the Futurist artists and poets, who had spent the decade of war and revolution calling for a clean sweep of the old order, seemed to be closely aligned with Bolshevik policy, which was also advocating a "clean sweep" of the past. Mayakovsky and other Futurists were installed as editors of *Art of the Commune* and sought to become the official cultural voice of the new society. Mayakovsky passionately believed that traditional art had no value to the workers, the communes, and the streets, and that all artists should join the revolution and revise their work to accommodate the new reality of Russian society. This poem calls Mayakovsky's Futurist comrades to "the barricades of heart and mind":

Out with cheap truths.
Erase the old from hearts.
Streets are our brushes,
Squares are our palettes…

In this poem, Mayakovsky and the periodical *Art of the Commune* were struggling with a dilemma. Unorthodox and experimental art is difficult to understand and therefore, by necessity, elitist; yet a proletarian culture requires art on the intellectual level of the masses. This posed a serious issue for Mayakovsky, Lissitzky, and all members of the Russian avant-garde.

In 1921, Mayakovsky wrote a sequel titled "Order No. 2 to the Army of the Arts." He opened each of the first four sections of the poem, addressed to actors, painters, poets, and musicians, with an exclamation to all artists: "This is for you." In his call for art that supports the revolution, Mayakovsky issues an urgent command:

I admonish you –
before they disperse you with
rifle-butts:
Give it up!
Give it up!
Forget it!
Spit
on rhymes
and arias
and the rose bush
and other such mawkishness
from the arsenal of the arts.

He closes by urging:

There are no fools today
to crowd, open-mouthed, around a
"master" and await his pronouncement.
Comrades,
give us a new form of art –
an art
that will pull the nation out of the mud.

On the title page, Lissitzky emphasized the No. 2 and illustrated this poem with two pointing hands from the typecase. One points to a red plus sign, while the other points to a black X symbol for crossing out or negating the old art. Each is accompanied by the caption, "This is for you."

The two large pointing hands echo the poem's accusatory tone, urging artists to reject or cancel out the old art and adopt new forms appropriate to the new society.

The poem "And You, Could You?" was first published in 1913 when Mayakovsky was a youthful and irreverent Futurist poet and painter. The shortest poem in *For the Voice,* it appears complete on its title spread and reads:

Suddenly I confused the everyday map,
by spilling paint/color from a
drinking glass.
I have shown on a plate of fish aspic
the crooked jaws of an ocean.
On the scales of a tin fish
I have read the calls of new lips.
And you –
could you play a nocturne
on a drainpipe flute?

This poem has been called a "Cubist still life in verse" (Stapanian, p. 69) for its nonlinear meaning and manipulation of imagery. The disjunctive imagery is open to varied interpretations and has been seen as a challenge by the poet (who can see the ribbed pattern of an aspic as a metaphor for the ocean) to the reader: The artist takes the mundane material of everyday reality and transforms it. Are you able to hear music in the clinking noise from downspouts? Lissitzky created a matrix of question marks and combined it with typographic elements from the title, including an inventive arrangement of the two forms of the word *Bbl* (you).

This is followed by a poem entitled "The Story of Little Red Riding Hood." It expresses a very different view of the revolution, for Mayakovsky issues a strong allegorical warning to the reader:

There was a cadet
who had a red hat.
Besides that hat,
he had nothing red in him.
If the cadet
hears about the revolution somewhere,
immediately he puts his hat on his head
and all lived well.
Cadet after cadet
and the father of the cadet
and the grandfather of the cadet.

But after a huge wind destroys the red hat, the wolves of the revolution take note. They decide the cadet is not true to the revolution, so they seize and devour him, cufflinks, trimmings, and all. Mayakovsky closed the poem with a stern warning:

When dealing with politics
my children don't forget
the fairy tale
about the little cadet!

Lissitzky illustrated this poem with a stylized – one might even say cute – little geometric figure with outstretched arms proudly showing off his red hat. This poem can be seen as a forewarning of the persecution of artists and writers who did not adhere to the state's official cultural policies during the Stalinist period.

The tenth poem is titled "The Story of How a Gossiper about Wrangel Was Engaged without Any Brains." The small subtitle within a ruled box adds, "Old, but Helpful Story." Written during the height of the civil war, this poem warns against false gossip. In 1920, an organized White force operated in the Crimea under Baron Pyotr N. Wrangel, striking northward at the Red Army, occupying parts of the Ukraine and Kuban, and posing a serious threat to the Bolshevik triumph. The gossiper in the poem told false tales about White Army victories. Eventually, Wrangel's forces were battered by the Red Army, holding out only long enough to evacuate 150,000 soldiers and civilians by sea from the Crimea. This ended the civil war and assured Bolshevik rule over Russia.

This title page lacks the structural cohesiveness of the others. Lissitzky used a decapitated engraving of a two-headed imperial eagle as a symbol of the opposition. This is an effective symbol, but it is an alien element in the context of the abstract geometric signs used throughout the book.

The eleventh poem, titled "Military Naval Love," is filled with sexual metaphors. Mayakovsky tells an allegorical tale about the romance between a male minesweeper and a female minesweeper. Once again, Lissitzky uses the Futurist technique of simultaneity, combining stylized images of an anchor and a heart with typography to make a smiling frontal face.

"Good Treatment toward Horses" is one of Mayakovsky's masterpieces. The opening verse uses an onomatopoeic device to initiate the sound of a horse's hooves on the pavement. Mayakovsky uses four words containing the basic vowels of the Russian language, each preceded by a guttural *gr* sound and followed by a short *b* sound. The Russian language sounds of the opening lines are:

Bili kopyta
Peli budto:
– Greeb
Grab
Grob
Grub –

The English translation reads:

Hooves beat
As though singing:
– Mushroom
Plunder
Coffin
Rude –

Mayakovsky used these four words for their sound, independent of their literal meanings. In combination, they become the rhythm of a horse's hooves. Lissitzky responded with a stunning graphic interpretation, using large black type for each of the three letters common to all four words. Then, four horizontal sequences of marks connect these letters to four different vowels, permitting the reader to decipher and understand the four words. Continuing the theme of shared vowels, Lissitzky uses a big red *0* as a common letter in the words for "good" and "treatment."

This poem was written in 1918, when war and revolution in Moscow were creating chronic shortages of food and fuel. The horse in the poem collapses onto the street from hunger and fatigue. A crowd gathers, ready to butcher it if it cannot rise. But the horse's owner coaxes it until finally it is able to rise and continue on its way.

The last poem in *For the Voice* is among Mayakovsky's most famous works. Lissitzky constructed one of his finest typographic compositions from the words in the complex title: "An Extraordinary Adventure Which Befell Vladimir Mayakovsky in a Summer Cottage." The subtitle at the bottom documents the location: "Pushkino, Akuslas Mount, Rumyantsev Cottage, 27 Versts on the Yaroslav Railway." (A *verst* – a Russian unit of distance – is slightly less than 1½ miles.)

In this poem, a desolate Mayakovsky is visited by the sun for tea and conversation in his cottage one hot July afternoon. He discusses his despair with his visitor, then vows to overcome it:

Always to shine,
to shine everywhere
to the very depths of the last days
to shine –
and to hell with everything else!
This is my motto
and the sun's!

Lissitzky needed only a large red circle on the left-hand page to signify the visiting luminary.

An unending argument in graphic design centers on the relationship of style to content. Designers who have definite stylistic approaches are sometimes accused of forcing their style upon the client's message. Designers without a recognizable or consistent style often assert that they let the solution grow out of the problem. In *For the Voice,* Lissitzky proved that a graphic designer can have a definite style and philosophy and effectively use it to interpret the specific message and content of the assignment at hand. In this and other works from the 1920s, Lissitzky pioneered a new approach to typographic art, which became a profound influence upon the evolution of twentieth-century graphic design. ••

Bibliography

Bann, Stephen, ed. *The Tradition of Constructivism.* New York: Viking, 1974.

Barooshian, Vahn D. *Russian Cubo-Futurism: 1910–1930.* The Hague: Mouton, 1974.

Blake, Patricia, ed. *Vladimir Mayakovsky: The Bedbug and Selected Poetry.* Princeton: Princeton University Press, 1975.

Charters, Ann and Samuel. *I Love: The Story of Vladimir Mayakovsky and Lili Brik.* New York: Farrar, Straus & Giroux, 1979.

Cohen, Arthur A., ed. *ExLibris 6: Constructivism & Futurism: Russian and Other.* New York: Ex Libris, 1977.

Lissitzky-Kuppers, Sophie, ed. *Lissitzky: Life Letters Texts.* London: Thames and Hudson, 1967.

Markov, Vladimir. *Russian Futurism: A History.* London: MacGibbon & Kee, 1969.

Nisbet, Peter. *El Lissitzky: 1890–1941.* Cambridge: Harvard University Art Museums, 1987.

Stapanian, Juliette R. *Mayakovsky's Cubo-Futurist Vision.* Houston: Rice, 1986.

Woroszylski, Wiktor. *The Life of Mayakovsky.* New York: Orion Press, 1970.

The Last Word on the Walker Show

From *Print* Vol. 44, No. 6 (Nov/Dec 1990)

When Minneapolis' Walker Art Center announced its exhibition entitled "Graphic Design in America: A Visual Language History," the design community was filled with enthusiasm. By some standards, this exhibition, which, after appearing in Minneapolis, traveled to New York, Phoenix, and London, was a smashing success. Over 200,000 people attended. Press coverage, including a lavish two-page review in *Time* magazine, gave the graphic design profession much-needed public exposure. The 1,200 artifacts in the mammoth survey included many extraordinary graphic designs.

However, for all its exceptional accomplishments, the exhibition was badly flawed. One of the sad ills of the Stalinist period in the USSR was its revision of history – the twisting of events to fit the party line. "Graphic Design in America: A Visual Language History" was a similar example of a history lesson told through biased eyes. If an alien from another planet had dropped in on the show, he or she would never have known that the illustrative tradition in American graphic design ever existed. From turn-of-the-century poster designers such as Penfield and Parrish; to the illustrative work of Rockwell, Leyendecker, and Kent; to the Push Pin tradition of Glaser, Chwast, Davis, and McMullan, this aspect of American design was almost completely ignored. When the omission of the illustrative tradition was raised at a symposium held in conjunction with the exhibit's New York opening at the IBM gallery of Science and Art, Walker curator Mildred Friedman simply dismissed it by saying, "It's my bias."

Certainly, anyone who curates an exhibition or writes a book must be accorded his or her viewpoint. The cumulative value of various viewpoints functions like the three-way mirror in the clothing store, providing a richer understanding based on diverse vantage points. Unfortunately, since American museums have virtually ignored graphic design, expectations for this exhibition were abnormally high. It could have provided a definitive overview of the evolution of graphic design in this country, or it could have been structured to provide the public with a badly needed understanding of the discipline. It failed on both counts. Americans live in a world of graphic information, yet they do not adequately understand the graphic tide crashing upon them daily. Instead of defining and interpreting graphic design, this exhibition delivered Friedman's preferences organized around themes: "Design in the Environment," "Design for Mass Media," "Design for Government and Commerce," and a timeline of American typography.

The outcry when this exhibition arrived in New York occurred because the graphic design community expected something the exhibition's title promised but did not deliver: a definitive overview. A more restrictive title would have better served the design community and the public. Although Friedman's diverse exhibition contained many brilliant works, it lacked focus. Fitting this exhibit into the limited space of the IBM Gallery necessitated a series of looping corridors, and the viewer could pass from one section into another without realizing it. This fault was compounded by the eccentric placement of artifacts into Friedman's categories. Logos such as the CBS "eye" and the RCA-Victor "His Master's Voice" dog were housed in the "Design in the Environment" section rather than "Design for Government and Commerce," which contained protest posters advocating social change that were designed against, rather than for, government and commerce.

Along with illustration, another area of graphic design receiving slight coverage was advertising design. A very poorly reproduced photographic blowup of the Volkswagen "lemon" advertisement was one of the few examples included. Advertising has earned its negative public image by a glut of obnoxious, distorted, and downright ugly ads; however, each decade has produced a small body of extraordinary advertising design. Better coverage could have demonstrated the potential of the medium to exhibition visitors. Additionally, posters from World Wars I and II, some of the most graphically intense American works, were not well represented. Overall, the exhibition had a predominance of work from New York, yet it almost completely omitted Manhattan-based innovators such as Milton Glaser and the late Herb Lubalin. The explosive creative accomplishments in graphic design from Texas, San Francisco, and Minnesota were also virtually ignored.

The "Design for Mass Media" section took an elitist posture, focusing upon affluence-oriented fashion and business magazines such as *Vogue, Bazaar,* and *Fortune,* while ignoring the real mass-media heyday of popular magazines like *McCall's, Life, Look,* and the *Saturday Evening Post.* In contrast, the vernacular of grocery store packaging held sway in the "Design for Government and Commerce" section. Here, Friedman took the line of least resistance, borrowing a mini-history of their packaging from the collections of Wrigley's gum and Nabisco cookies. Companies pay a promotional fee when actors drive Chevrolets or drink Sprite in the movies. One wonders if Nabisco or Wrigley's chipped in for the honor of art gallery exposure. To be consistent with the focus upon esthetic solutions found in "Design for Mass Media," Friedman should have exhibited brilliant modern package designs by such designers as Paul Rand, Saul Bass, Michael Vanderbyl, and Michael Mabry instead of Ritz crackers and Wrigley's gum, as ubiquitous and charming as they might seem. The curatorial goals seemed jumbled.

A golden opportunity for public education was botched in the "Design for Government and Commerce" section, where the whole area of corporate identity could have been explained. The big story should have been the shift from the illustrative trademarks of the first half of the century to Modernist visual identification systems after World War II. Friedman merely contrasted a few logos, offered a few bits and pieces, and showed a sensational metal 1930s Mobil flying horse in the "Design for the Environment" section. Adding a complete corporate identification system, from 2"-labels to large-scale environmental signs, would have been more illuminating.

The sloppy curatorial work, miscrediting scores of items, was most disturbing. The February 1939 *Harper's Bazaar* cover was inaccurately attributed to A. M. Cassandre, even though it is executed in Alexey Brodovitch's Surrealism-derived style and bears his initials. In the marvelous section of 1939 World's Fair graphics, three side-by-side cover designs were credited to "Designer Unknown," "Designer Unknown," and "Joseph Binder." The first "Designer Unknown" was Binder; the second "Designer Unknown," Bradbury Thompson (the piece was even signed by him in the distinctive script he used in the late 1930s), and the "Joseph Binder" was prominently signed by a designer/illustrator named Staehle.

A typographic panel correctly stated that Alexander Liberman became art director of *Vogue* in 1943; yet 1936 and 1940 *Vogue* covers were inaccurately credited to Liberman in the exhibition (might not Friedman and the Walker staff have had the presence of mind to check to see who the art director was, as listed on the *Vogue* contents page?). The November 1954 *Fortune* cover, designed and executed by Walter Allner, is prominently signed by him; it is also reproduced and discussed in a sidebar on the publisher's page. Yet Friedman erroneously credited the cover to Leo Lionni. The error was doggedly repeated on a huge color transparency of this cover in the IBM Gallery's Madison Avenue entry, in the color reproduction of this cover in the exhibition brochure, and on a reproduction of the cover that appeared in a *New York Times* article about the exhibition. Allner was one of the giants of 1950s and 1960s graphic design and deserves to be remembered for his contributions. These and dozens of other inaccuracies are inexcusable.

The errors and misjudgments continued on the typography timeline. Major typographic innovations – for example, the phototypositor, which radically changed the appearance of graphic design in the 1960s by allowing display type to be larger and sharper with letters overlapping and touching – were ignored, while relatively unimportant biographical bits were included. Typographic designs from Aaron Burns' 1961 book *Typography* – such as René Bittel's double-page Rover motorcar ad – were reproduced and credited "Typography by Aaron Burns," suggesting that Burns designed these works rather than chose them as examples for his book. Unaccountably, a handful of European works found their way into the exhibition.

The book accompanying the exhibition, also entitled *Graphic Design in America: A Visual Language History,* is a real lemon. For a book accompanying an exhibition, it has surprisingly few reproductions. It is a hodgepodge of disconnected essays, punctuated by short interviews with designers, including such people as Milton Glaser, who were virtually ignored in the exhibition. Some of the authors know little about graphic design. Others who do are error-prone. For example, on page 161 we learn from Lorraine Wild that Paul Rand visited Europe in the late 1920s and had first-hand knowledge of new European modern design. Rand was 14 years old in 1928 and though undoubtedly, a brilliant kid, he wasn't that precocious! The strengths, such as the narrative timeline by Ellen Lupton and J. Abbott Miller, and weaknesses, notably Estelle Jussim's essay, entitled "Changing Technology Changes Design," which is totally naive about major technological shifts and should never have been published, have been brilliantly chronicled by Scott Gutterman in his *Print* review of the book (March/April 1990 issue, p. 150) and need not be restated here.

How could this exhibition have been better? First, a clear goal – either chronicling the evolution of the discipline without bias, or educating the public about graphic design – should have been established. Then the pieces might have fallen logically into place instead of being forced into Friedman's arbitrary categories. By trying and ultimately failing to show everything, Friedman did little more than assault the viewer with great heaps of material. A brilliant public awareness exhibition was suggested by several very successful segments organized around themes, such as the displays of 1939 World's Fair graphics and 1984 Los Angeles Olympics graphics. An exhibition of exemplars (World War I posters, Columbia Records albums, IBM or Apple Computer graphics, etc.), with better explanatory text panels, could have provided a celebration of many of the finest accomplishments of American graphic design, while educating the public about the medium and its message. However, even a flawed exhibition of American design would have been cause for celebration and appreciation had Friedman honestly acknowledged her biases and followed them. She could have curated a lovely exhibition called "American Graphic Design: The Modernist Impulse." As an architectural historian and curator, she assumed she could apply her knowledge and approach to graphic design, but her Modernist design biases blinded her to the whole truth.

One curious footnote to the controversy stirred up by this exhibition is Steven Heller's "Cold Eye" column praising Mildred Friedman's curatorial skills (*Print,* March/April 1990, p. 136), followed by his letter to the editor (*Print,* July/August 1990, p. 323) repudiating his earlier view. In the "Cold Eye" column, Heller treaded lightly. He defended Friedman from her critics by asking, "Is 'Graphic Design in America: A Visual Language History' the definitive design exhibition?" Heller answered his own question: "No: nor was it intended to be. This was a curated show, the vision and decision of a very seasoned curator." In his follow-up letter, he blasted Friedman for creating an exhibition "sadly defined" by its flaws; "it was biased, prejudiced, and inaccurate. Its curator bit off much more than she could digest. She failed to reflect the real pluralism of American design." He closed by observing, "Its flaws invalidated it. Its history was skewed. It was a missed opportunity."

Heller is one of the few design writers seriously interested in criticism, and he often does it brilliantly. How could he have been so wrong the first time? He answers this question for us by asking. "How could I come down too hard on family?" Heller was an insider and participant in "Graphic Design in America," for he served as an informal adviser to the curator, moderated panel discussions, and did a series of interviews for the book. It became a conflict of interest when Heller also attempted to function as a critic, which must be an objective, outsider position. His courage in publicly recanting his position is admirable.

(continued on page 162)

Book Art.
Letters carved into a book,
12.87 x 9.12 inches.
(1980)

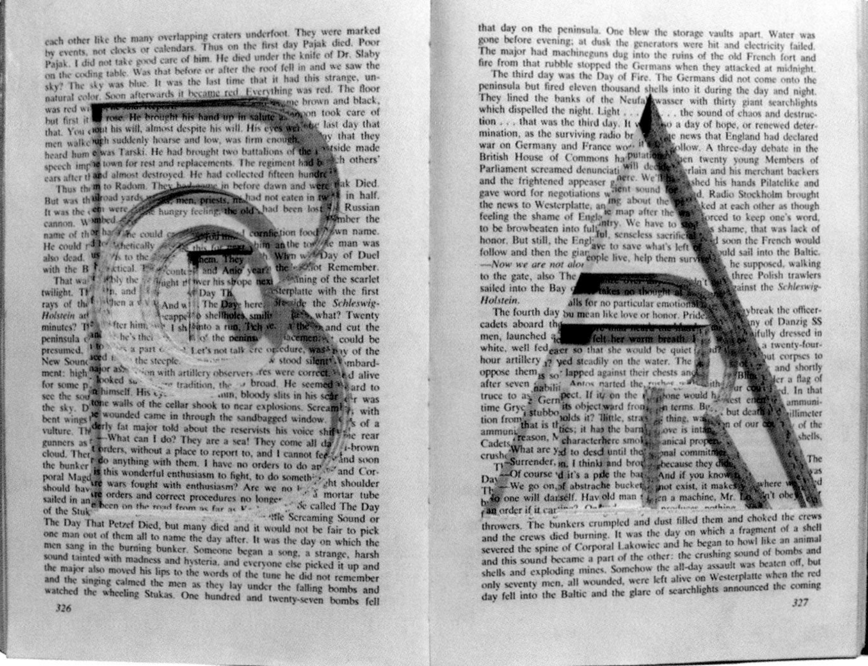

Untitled.
Watercolor on board,
8.12 x 11 inches.
(1990s)

In truth, however, "Graphic Design in America" was a worthwhile exhibition in spite of its stupid inaccuracies and curatorial biases. Public interest in graphic design has to some degree been cultivated. The museum world has been shown that graphic design exhibitions can garner strong public interest, large attendance, and positive media exposure. Many extraordinary accomplishments were documented, but the full story of the flowering of graphic design in America remains to be told. ➻

Women's Place: Two at the Top

From *Print* Vol. 44, No. 6 (Nov/Dec 1990)

Cheryl Heller

"Cheryl's going to replace this furniture very soon; you know, she's just been here a short time," her secretary told me as she ushered me into Heller's Wells, Rich, Greene office. The room was spacious (at least by New York's cramped standards), with a round marble conference table, wicker credenza, nondescript modern sofa, and eight assorted chairs. All available surfaces were occupied by comps, mechanicals, and photographs. A few minutes later, Cheryl Heller entered the room. She speaks precisely, projecting the confidence of someone who went from promising young upstart to legendary master of advertising creativity in the blink of an eye. After talking with her for a few minutes, one is struck by her openness and purposefulness.

Heller's road from unemployed college graduate who had worked part-time in a silkscreen printing plant while earning a liberal arts degree to executive vice president and creative partner at Wells, Rich, Greene was filled with 16-hour days and unshakable commitment. Despite the swirl of conflicting expectations that young people often endure – the clash between personal dreams, parental desires, and social pressures – she rose to the top of her field in a series of decisive, if unorthodox, steps.

For Heller, conflicting expectations included her strong desire to become an artist while her family in Ohio believed that "marrying a high school coach and having seven kids was an ideal outcome." She wanted to go to art school in New York, but her parents felt a small, private liberal-

Direct-mail piece for printer A. Colish suggests recipients will sleep better because they won't have to worry about the printing. Design: Cheryl Heller

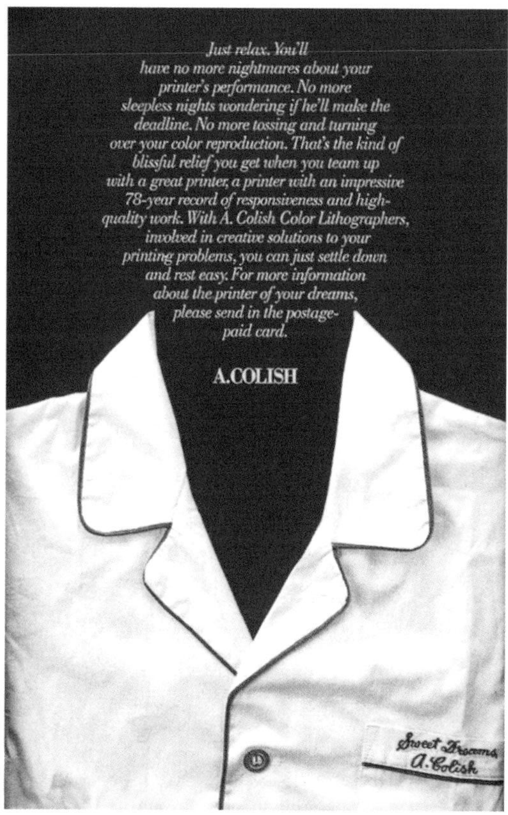

arts college would be more appropriate, so she attended Ohio Wesleyan University.

After graduating, Heller headed for Boston, where a random call landed a mechanical-artist position at the Giardini/Russell advertising and communications group. Her intention was to save money for graduate study in printmaking and drawing at the Boston Museum School. After a year as a paste-up artist, she was promoted to studio manager and spent a second year doing everything except design. From the beginning, she loved the business world, with its deadlines, pressures, and energy. When she did return to school for further fine-arts study, she found herself in a major life crisis. In spite of some first-rate teachers and the satisfaction of getting her work into a few galleries, she decided she would never make her mark in fine arts. In addition, she missed the professional environment. After leaving school, she was hired by Gunn Associates as assistant to designer Robert Cipriani and produced work for him for over three years. Eventually, she asked Gunn for an opportunity to design and worked hard to develop her creative abilities. After six years at Gunn, Heller was recruited by the HBM/Creamer agency to set up an in-house design department from scratch. Within three years, her one-person design office had grown into a fully staffed collateral division winning national attention and awards for its work for Reebok, Stride Rite, and the S.D. Warren paper company.

When HBM/Creamer was bought by the WCRS Group PLC, a British firm with annual billings of $2 billion, the new parent corporation offered Heller the opportunity to spin off her group, taking her staff and clients with her to form a totally new agency. Heller thus became president of Heller/Breene which, as New England's fastest-growing ad agency, doubled its billings to more than $35 million in its first year. Though it is unusual for a design division to become an advertising agency, Heller's group had already been creating complete ad campaigns. Her design-oriented approach made good sense. "To describe quality, you can't say 'quality,'" Heller observes. "You have to do it visually. Designers are much better trained than most advertising people to communicate visually because most advertising people are verbal. Our special skill is making those intangible things real."

In late 1989, Heller left the agency bearing her name. She was investing time and energy in building a company she didn't own and that would always be dwarfed by its immense parent. (Heller/Breene's billings of $30–40 million represented 2 per cent of WCRS's total.) Moreover, she had received an offer she couldn't refuse: Wells, Rich, Greene, one of the world's largest privately held agencies, sent scouts to Boston seeking Heller's services and recruited her to head their Image Group.

The origins of this group go back several years, to when Mary Wells, founding partner of Wells, Rich, Greene, returned from a trip to Europe with two shopping bags filled with magazines. "The Europeans are far ahead of us in print advertising," she told the senior staff after dumping the contents of her bags onto the center of a conference table. "We've got to do something about it." "Something" was setting up a nucleus of strong talent committed to creative and effective print advertising. The invitation to Heller to move to New York and take on the challenge of running the Image Group came at an opportune time.

Creatively, Heller sees advertising art direction and graphic design as the same activity. For her, advertising has provided the best forum for getting people's attention and communicating with them. I told Heller about hearing Victor Papanek speak to the Richmond, Virginia, AIGA the week before, and how he had declared advertising to be ineffective and a big waste of money. I asked, "If you had been there, how would you have responded?"

"I would have told him about Oil of Olay," she replied immediately. "It's a pink liquid in an old-fashioned bottle with a black label. My grand-mother's generation used it. Through advertising, this old, unexciting product has become the largest selling moisturizer in the world."

As president of Heller/Breene, Heller included among her administrative responsibilities personnel issues, ensuring that the rent was paid, and worrying about whether clients were paying their bills on time. As head of WRG's Image Group, her work is solely in the creative domain. Thus far, New York has been a boon; the Museum of Modern Art is down the street from her office, and the Metropolitan Museum close enough for lunch-hour visits. She concedes that the city has changed the way she works, but this is more the result of the agency environment than the Manhattan environment. It takes longer to do things at WRG, and on $60-million accounts, Heller's group might have to create 40 ads before a single one gets approved. It requires discipline and stamina to keep coming back under these conditions. But Heller is maintaining enough smaller clients and public-service work to balance the circumstances surrounding large national accounts.

Photography is a great love, and its innovative use has become a hallmark of her work. Handling the S.D. Warren account since 1980 has sharpened her approach to photography. Paper promotion offers overwhelming freedom, for there is no product to show and one has to create a communication about another subject, like fishing, whose essential story must be compelling. Throughout ten years of work for Warren, Heller has concentrated on the difference between "just photographs" and "photographs people have to look at."

Heller has a passion for ink on paper and has done only a small amount of broadcast work, though she anticipates doing more in the future. She believes that there are no mass markets anymore, and often television is not as efficient or controllable as print media in reaching diverse audiences with specialized interests. Yet, according to Heller, the level of print advertising in this country is horrendous, and she blames the big agencies and their clients for this problem, saying, "I can count on two fingers the big agencies that are doing fantastic print." Most are not committed to the medium and assign it to junior people or do it as an afterthought, she contends.

When I asked about the traditional conflict of design vs. advertising, Heller observed that unlike the situation in other areas of design, advertising's direct influence on sales provides a way to quantify results. For example, S.D. Warren's merchants always stock up before a promotion of a paper line in anticipation of the demand created by the promotion. She perceives a conflict between art and commerce endemic in advertising, but "chose to step right into the middle of this conflict instead of sidestepping it." She has to find value in the products and clients for whom she works, noting, "I absolutely believe in Warren and their products, their ethics, and their environmental positions." Heller has turned down political campaigns because of their negative approach and the tendency of political advertising to oversimplify complex issues. Another reject was a fake fireplace product, which makes a phony crackling noise.

Heller relates the relatively recent success of women designers to the importance of the portfolio in the design profession. "Having a tangible product that exists apart from one's person is a great advantage for any talented designer," she notes. She observes a tradition of raising American women to be "good girls" who do the assigned task and get it right. Yet she sees no difference in the way men and women design and notes the rarity of really good designers of either sex. In fact, she believes that "now it may be much tougher for men than women. Traditionally, much more has been expected from men for they have been the standard of how to work and achieve. Today, contributions from women heighten the competitive environment for men still further." Much of Heller's work has been for clients in industries where women are perceived as primary customers, making decisions about which products to buy. For an art director in those industries, being a woman is often seen as an advantage.

Yet marriage and child-rearing often create dilemmas for the legions of women working in design today, which has something to do, Heller observes, with the fact that women seldom rise to top executive ranks. Understanding and an acceptance of individual freedom for husband and wife are critical in a marriage when one or both spouses is in an intensely competitive field demanding long hours. Heller considers herself fortunate in this respect. When she was offered the opportunity to work in Manhattan, her husband, Gary Scheft, to whom she has been married for 18 years, left his job in real estate to relocate with her.

Much more than marriage, having children is often seen as changing the equation for working women, designers or otherwise. "The news is not yet in on how kids are raised today," Heller observes, pointing out that sacrifice – of outside interests and leisure time as well as the time one spends with one's family – is the lot of any dedicated careerist. Heller has no children, but whether that's the cause or result of her intense working life is, she says, "a chicken-or-egg question." What's important, she suggests, is that the balance is struck not merely between job and domesticity but between focused professional achievement and a less energetic, but perhaps more well-rounded, lifestyle. And this dilemma obviously transcends gender. "As you start to look at 40," she says, "there's a reflective process about life and the choices you've made that is unavoidable."

Soft-spoken and direct, without pretense or flamboyance, Cheryl Heller projects true conviction. She seems totally free of the hype and self-promotion one expects from New York advertising types. It is clear that for her, one's integrity resides in one's work. And Heller's work speaks for itself.

Deborah Sussman

Deborah Sussman is small in stature, but when she appeared at *Print's* offices for our interview, her energy and enthusiasm filled the room. She projects a sense of mission, a passion for design, and a genuine interest in people. Her dark eyes dart about, taking in everything. The reality of Sussman's reputation for modesty and humanity was immediately evident when she asked me to focus on the firm and its work rather than on her. She stressed that the firm thrived and expanded its environmental design involvement after her husband and partner, Paul Prejza, joined it. "The 35 employees at Sussman/Prejza work as a collaborative team on large-scale projects," she said.

In hindsight, the evolution of her career has a cohesive logic about it. She was born in 1931 of first-generation immigrants from Poland and Russia; her mother was a linguist who taught Sussman several languages and her father was a highly skilled airbrush illustrator. Sussman's elementary school, P.S. 99 in Brooklyn, was progressive for its time: Girls were taught shop and boys took home economics. Her early ambitions were to be an actress and an artist, and she explored both activities at Midwood High School in Brooklyn. She designed *Patterns,* the school magazine, in Futura, and used her own drawings in it. She was selected for the All City Radio Workshop and performed on the air. Design, she observes, combines both performance and artistry, for the designer must publicly present the product that results from a private creative activity.

Education and achievement were encouraged in Sussman's family, and her parents supported her interest in art and theater. But they were concerned when it became evident that she was going to pursue the creative arts instead of "marrying a nice doctor, settling down, and being normal." It was not until she married that they relaxed a bit. "Today," Sussman says, "it's normal for a young woman to want to become a designer. It's absolutely not an issue."

Sussman was educated at Bard College, the Art Students League of New York, Black Mountain College in North Carolina, and the Institute of Design in Chicago. While studying graphic design at the Institute, she received a summer internship at the design office of Charles and Ray Eames in Venice, California.

She arrived on July 5, 1953, and remained for four years of full-time employment, doing photography and graphic design. The Eames office left an indelible mark, and Sussman credits it as a major influence. Ray Eames possessed a painter's eye for form and color, and Charles Eames loved Mexican and Asian design and craft: He inspired Sussman's engagement with other cultures. Working on "Day of the Dead," the Eameses' award-winning documentary film about the Mexican day of homage, was a turning point for Sussman; living in Mexico for the duration of the project allowed her to become inspired first-hand by the colors and handiwork of traditional Mexican folk art.

Charles Eames's remarkable achievements in film, exhibition, and furniture design were not matched by his use of typography, which was often merely in the service of something else. Sussman recalls that he insisted on setting exhibition type in all capitals to "improve legibility." Nevertheless, she managed to pick up a good understanding of typography as she went along.

Sussman left the Eames office in 1957 when she received a Fulbright grant permitting travel and study in Europe and North Africa. Her extensive observation and photographic documentation of the urban landscape, especially the signage, colors, and textures of the streets, provided a vital resource for her design. In Europe, she enrolled in the Hochschule für Gestaltung in Ulm, Germany, where she was overwhelmed by the school's systematic approach to work and life. The doctrine of one universal design attitude that could be calculated in advance was on a collision course with Sussman's search for individual expression as it related to the larger community. She was passionately attracted to the art of the street, while HFG Ulm rejected this vernacular and historical expression, which could not be subsumed under the monolithic banner of Modern design. Sussman recalls, "At a different time in my life, I could have learned a lot more at Ulm," but at that time she was searching for a design of inclusion while Ulm preached exclusion. Upon her return to the U.S., she worked for Eames on a project-by-project basis during most of the 1960s, then started her own design office in 1968.

Educated as an architectural historian, architect, and planner, Paul Prejza was working in urban design at the Los Angeles City Planning Department when he met Sussman. From 1968 until 1970, he was a planner in the architectural office of William L. Pereira, and joined Sussman's design office in 1972, complementing her graphic-design expertise with his architectural and planning skills. In 1980, they incorporated as Sussman/Prejza & Co. The merger of architecture and graphic design has been a major thrust of their activities.

Models for sonotubes for 1984 Los Angeles Olympics. Design: Sussman/Prejza & Company, Inc. (1984)

How does it work, being married and principals of a large design firm? Sussman says she and Prejza are esthetically and intellectually complementary for "there's a yin and yang principle – maybe it's male and female operating – I'm extroverted, intuitive, and nonlinear and like multiple tracks; I change track in mid-sentence." On the other hand, "Paul is sequential, logical, and analytic. He's much more introverted and philosophical than I am. There are blessings and agonies in living and working together; sometimes it becomes difficult to separate work and play."

Sussman admits to a drive "to be a private and a general at the same time," and fondly remembers being closer to the tools of the design profession before the firm's explosive growth. Its work on the 1984 Los Angeles Olympics catapulted Sussman/Prejza into the international spotlight, and to many people, the firm appeared to be an overnight sensation. Yet Sussman undertook this project three decades after she began her professional career. She is also quick to acknowledge the many other participants in the Olympics design effort, especially The Jerde Partnership.

Sussman calls the Olympics project a rare opportunity where the needs and potential of the project synchronized perfectly with the studio's capabilities and approach. "It's something that only happens once in a lifetime, and for many designers it never happens," she remarks. The Olympics' environmental graphics demonstrated on a large scale the synergy existing between Prejza and Sussman. Prejza's aptitude for taking a large program, developing a conceptual overview of the system, and analyzing its needs dovetailed perfectly with Sussman's uncanny ability to grasp gossamer images from thin air. Prejza remembers Sussman solving the Olympics' color problem simply by opening the paper drawers and clipping out color samples.

Many people thought her color proposal was absurd, however. The Olympics were supposed to be white and clean and pure, but this exuberant designer arrived at the presentation with chrome yellow, magenta, orange, aqua, and purple! Sussman sold the color scheme by stressing its international character: The magenta and chrome yellow are the colors of wildflowers growing in Mexico; the aqua symbolizes Los Angelenos' affinity for the hues of Mediterranean sky and water; the intensity evokes the palette of traditional Japanese and Indian celebrations; and so forth.

Sussman finds color to be the most fleeting aspect of design, with the greatest potential for surprise when translated from the design proposal in the studio to the built environment. To many Modernist architects, color is an unnecessary element. Because of their purist sensibilities, they are attracted to the structural substance of gray steel. Other architects embrace the environmental potential of color and delight in working with it. Sussman's solutions combine an intuitive energy with compelling logic.

Sussman/Prejza now designs in several areas: visual identification, color schemes for interiors and exteriors, and the design of components for retail environments. The staff's capabilities span the disciplines of architecture, interior and industrial design, graphic design, and photography.

When I asked Sussman whether the term "Postmodernism" aptly described her work, she recalled her elderly cousin Samuel Susselman's observation, "'Ism' means 'think small.'" She rejects the identity of a label or movement, believing growth, exploration, and risk are key ingredients in a designer's ability to reach out and try new approaches. Sussman admits to approaching each presentation with an upbeat attitude. "I won't compromise my beliefs and I will always satisfy my client's needs." Even though changes may be made as a result of dialogue with the client, the final result seldom fails to satisfy her.

Once a major client, grudgingly going along with one of Sussman's unconventional proposals, grumbled, "Your reasons are always rooted in fact." Seldom are intuition and logic so well wedded as in Sussman/Prejza's work, and this may be a key aspect of the firm's growth.

Sussman sees graphic design as an expressive field, where one attends to others' needs and listens to their concerns. "Women tend to be better than men at this," she feels. "Graphic design has been an attractive profession for women and far less resistant than architecture." She believes that female designers still face problems – for instance, the skepticism of those who look askance when a woman heads up a large office or major project – but such problems are not insurmountable, as her own career has proven. "I've had to fight it out on a battlefield with men for many years," she remarks. Yet she finds an advantage in being a woman because, she believes, women have greater tolerance for the difficulties and conflicts generated in a high-pressure environment. "Women know what pain is and can bear it more than men. They can handle without anger the adversarial relationships of the marketplace. One of the reasons I've survived is because I've been able to negotiate through the Scylla and Charybdis of the professional world – with clients and collaborators and in-house staff.

Being in the right place at the right time, according to conventional wisdom, is often critical to significant accomplishment. As the career of the German artist, designer, and architect Peter Behrens (1868–1940) unfolded, fate put him in the "right place" several times with significant results. In graphic design, Behrens recognized the need for new typographic forms to express a new era, and he conceived and directed the first unified corporate identity program. His influence on product design was so significant that he has been called "the first industrial designer." His major buildings include a 1909 factory whose structure and glass curtain walls influenced the direction of architecture. The roster of architects who launched their careers as Behrens's apprentices includes such titans as Walter Gropius, Ludwig Mies van der Rohe, Le Corbusier, and Adolf Meyer.

At the beginning of the century, Behrens contributed to design curriculum reform by developing new approaches to introductory visual education. As a theoretician, Behrens's articles and speeches often crystallized and focused important issues about design in an industrial society, suggesting new directions. Behrens advocated functionalism, truth to materials, and standards of uniformity. Given the scope of Behrens's contribution, it might be argued that he occupies a position in 20th-century design somewhat similar to the positions of Cézanne and Picasso in painting: Behrens was a catalytic innovator whose work altered the course of design in this century.

(continued on page 170)

Kearny Street, San Francisco. Acrylic on board, 3 x 3 inches, shown at actual size. (2001)

This was Phil's last painting. It was exhibited at Art6 Gallery, Richmond, Virginia. He is pictured here studying details with his loop.

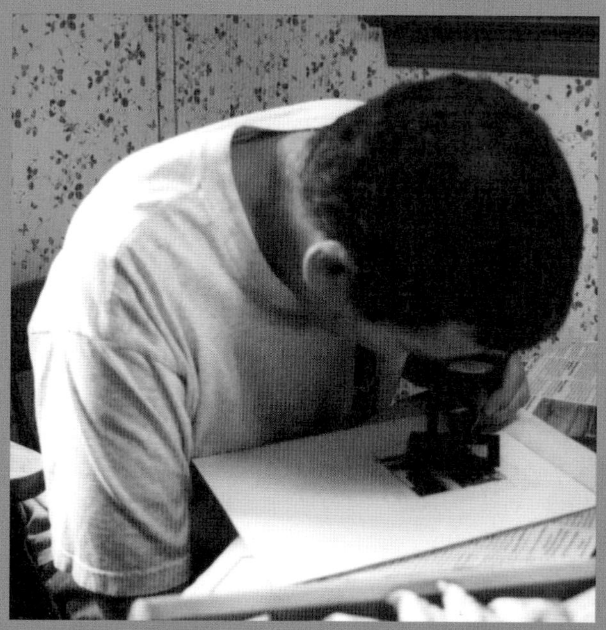

PEARL CITY SEAFOOD RESTAURANT
OPEN

Behrens was orphaned at age 14 and received a substantial inheritance from his father's estate, which provided ongoing economic independence. He chose art for his career and studied in his native Hamburg. Social realism became the focus of his early paintings, which depicted poor people and the industrial landscape. In 1892, Behrens was a founder of the Munich Secession, an organization formed by artists who, excited by new developments such as Impressionism and Post-Impressionism, broke with the academic tradition. In Munich, a renaissance in German arts, crafts, and design was emerging. In 1897, Behrens gave up painting for applied art and embraced the 1890s Art Nouveau movement, called *Jugendstil* (Youth Style) in Germany after the new magazine *Jugend* (Youth), whose pages were filled with Art Nouveau designs and illustrations. Behrens began to make large multicolored woodcuts inspired by French Art Nouveau and Japanese prints, and he became a frequent contributor of illustrations and decorative designs to *Jugend* and *Pan* magazines. New printing and manufacturing techniques and the excitement of Art Nouveau were creating tremendous interest in the applied arts, and many artists embraced graphic and product design. Behrens's close friend Otto Eckmann abandoned painting for design and illustration and, in November 1894, auctioned all his paintings. His letter to the auctioneer bid his paintings a "cordial farewell" and concluded, "may we never meet again."

In 1900, the Grand Duke of Hessen, who sought to "fuse art and life together," established a new artists' colony in Darmstadt, hoping to encourage both cultural development and economic growth in light manufacturing such as furniture and ceramics. The seven participating artists, including Behrens and Vienna Secession architect Joseph Maria Olbrich, all had experience in the applied arts. Each artist was granted land to build a house, and Behrens designed his own house and all its furnishings, from furniture to cutlery and china.

A sense of urgency existed in the German art and design community. A new century was at hand, and the need to create new forms for a new era weighed heavily upon artists. Typographic reform was one of Behrens's major interests and he struggled unsuccessfully for a time to develop a new typeface with a conservative type founder. Then he came into contact with 32-year-old Dr. Karl Klingspor, of the Klingspor Foundry, who agreed to manufacture and release Behrens's first typeface, Behrensschrift, in 1901. The Klingspor Foundry was the first German typefoundry to commission new fonts from artists, and it achieved international prominence when it released Otto Eckmann's 1900 Eckmannschrift, which created a sensation. Drawn with a brush instead of a pen, Eckmannschrift was a conscious attempt to revitalize typography by combining medieval and Roman attributes with those of Japanese prints.

In contrast to Eckmann's gestural vitality Behrensschrift was an attempt to reduce any "poetic flourish" which would mark the forms as the work of an individual hand and thereby reduce their universal character. Behrensschrift looks very calligraphic to the late-20th-century eye viewing this typeface more than 60 years after Paul Renner designed his geometrically constructed Futura. However, ornate Art Nouveau forms dominated new typeface design in the early 1900s, and Behrens's typeface looks very standardized relative to the typographic fashion of the time. Behrensschrift was an attempt not only to innovate a new typographic image for the new century but also to create a uniquely German type. Behrens combined the heavy, condensed feeling of black letter with the letter proportions of Roman inscriptions, while standardizing letter-form construction. Horizontals and verticals are emphasized and diagonals are completely eliminated and replaced by curved strokes in letters such as *W* and *V*. Some typographic authorities were outraged by Behrensschrift, but with its feather-stroke serifs and clarity – compared to the dense black-letter typefaces then in use in Germany – Behrensschrift was a resounding success for both book and job-printing typography.

In the promotional booklet for Behrensschrift, Behrens compared reading text type to "watching a bird's flight or the gallop of a horse. Both seem graceful and pleasing, but the viewer does not observe details of their form or movement. Only the rhythm of the lines is seen by the viewer, and the same is true of a typeface."

German art critics of the period were interested in the relationship of forms in art and design to social, technological, and cultural conditions. Behrens was deeply concerned about these issues and believed that, after architecture, typography provided "the most characteristic picture of a period, and the strongest testimonial of the spiritual progress [and] development of a people." Another attempt to express the spirit of the new era occurred in 1900 when Behrens set his 25-page booklet, "Celebrations of Life, and Art..." in sans-serif type. German typographic historian Hans Loubier suggested in the 1920s that this document might contain the first use of sans-serif type as running book text. All-capital sans-serif type is used in an unprecedented way on the title and dedication pages. The popularity of sans-serif types in the 20th-century vindicated Behrens's experiment.

In 1903, Behrens moved to Düsseldorf to become director of the Düsseldorf School of Arts and Crafts. Innovative preparatory courses preceded study in specific disciplines such as architectural, graphic, and interior design. Behrens's purpose was to go "back to the fundamental intellectual principles of all form-creating work," allowing "the principles of form-making to be rooted in the artistically spontaneous, in the inner laws of perception, rather than directly in the mechanical aspects of the work." Students drew and painted natural forms in different media, then made analytical studies to explore linear, pattern, and geometric structure. These introductory courses were precursors of the preliminary course at the Bauhaus, where two of Behrens's former apprentices, Gropius and Mies van der Rohe, served as directors.

A dramatic transformation occurred in Behrens's work in 1904 after the Dutch architect J.L.M. Lauweriks joined the Düsseldorf faculty. Lauweriks was fascinated by geometric form and had developed an approach to teaching design based on geometric composition. His grids began with a square inscribed with a circle and the numerous permutations made possible by subdividing and duplicating this basic structure. The geometric patterns thus developed could be used to determine proportions, dimensions, and spatial divisions in the design of everything from chairs to buildings to posters. Behrens's application of this theory proved catalytic in pushing 20th-century architecture and design toward rational geometry as an underlying system for visual organization. His work from this period reveals the tentative beginnings of Constructivism in graphic design, wherein realistic or even stylized depictions are replaced by an architectural and geometric structure. Often, Behrens used square formats, but more frequently he used rectangles in ratios such as 1 square wide to 1.5 or 2 squares tall.

In this electric lamp poster, Behrens has arrived at the typographic and spatial parameters of the mature AEG corporate identification program. (1907)

The major event in Behrens's career occurred in 1907, when Emil Rathenau, director of the Allgemeine Elektricitäts Gesellschaft (AEG) appointed him artistic adviser for the company. Rathenau had purchased European manufacturing rights to Thomas A. Edison's patents in 1883, and AEG had grown into one of the world's largest manufacturing concerns. A visionary industrialist, Rathenau sensed the need for a unified visual character for AEG products, environments, and communications. In 1907, the electrical industry was synonymous with high technology: Electric teakettles were as advanced as computers and videocassette recorders are today. As design adviser to the concern, Behrens began to focus intensely upon the design needs of industry, with design responsibility ranging from large buildings to stationery.

Otto Eckmann had been a designer and consultant for AEG, but he died of tuberculosis in 1902 at age 37. Behrens executed several graphic designs for AEG in 1906; then in 1907 was commissioned to design an important AEG pavilion for the 1908 German Shipbuilding Exhibition.

The year 1907 also marked the founding in Munich of the Deutscher Werkbund (German Association of Craftsmen), which advocated "a marriage of art with technology." Behrens played a major role in this first organization created to inspire good design in manufactured goods and architecture. The group's leaders, including Hermann Muthesius, Henry van de Velde, and Behrens, were influenced by William Morris and the English Arts and Crafts Movement, but with significant differences. While Morris was repelled by the products of the machine age and advocated a return to medieval craftsmanship in romantic protest against the industrial revolution, the Werkbund embraced new technology and advocated design as a way to give form and meaning to all machine-made things, including machine-made buildings.

With visionary zeal, Werkbund members advanced a philosophy of *Gesamkultur,* a new universal culture existing in a totally reformed man-made environment. Design was seen as the engine which could propel society forward to achieve *Gesamkultur.* Soon after it formed, the Werkbund split into two factions. One, headed by Muthesius, argued for the maximum use of mechanical manufacturing and standardization of design for industrial efficiency. Its adherents believed that form should be determined solely by function and wanted to eliminate all ornament. The other faction, led by van de Velde, argued for the primacy of individual artistic expression. A design philosophy is merely an idle vision until someone creates artifacts that make it a real force in the world. Thus, Werkbund members consciously sought a new design language to realize their goals. Behrens's work for AEG became an early manifestation of Werkbund ideals.

Behrens's work for AEG represents a synthesis of two seemingly contradictory concepts: neoclassicism and *Sachlichkeit* (loosely translated as "common-sense objectivity"). His neoclassicism grew from a careful study of the art and design of ancient Greece and Rome. Rather than merely copy the stylistic aspects of this work, he found a new formal language of harmony and proportion to achieve a unity of the parts with the whole. *Sachlichkeit* was a pragmatic emphasis upon technology manufacturing processes, and function. Artistic conceits and questions of style were subordinate to purpose. In concert, these two concepts guided Behrens in his quest for forms to achieve *Gesamkultur.*

The AEG graphic identity program made consistent use of the three linchpin elements present in corporate identity programs as the genre evolved a half century later: a logo, a typeface, and consistent layout of elements following standardized formats. Behrens designed a typeface for AEG's exclusive use to bring unity to its printed materials. At a time when graphic design in Germany was dominated by traditional black letter and decorative Victorian and Art Nouveau styles, Behrens designed a Roman-style letterform inspired by classical Roman inscriptions. Initially, this was not available in type, so display type on all AEG printed graphics was handlettered. In 1908, a typeset variation named Behrens-Antiqua was released by Klingspor Foundry, first for the exclusive use of AEG, then later, for general use. Behrens had three important goals in designing this new type: It differentiated AEG communications from all other printed matter; its forms were universal rather than individualized by the touch of an artist's hand; and it strove for a monumental character which could evoke positive connotations of quality and performance. Behrens-Antiqua possessed the solemn, monumental quality of Roman letterforms, tempered by the rhythm of the serifs. The ornaments were inspired by ancient Roman brasswork, whose geometric properties satisfied Behrens's belief that geometry could make ornament universal and impersonal.

In 1908, he designed the hexagonal AEG trademark. This pictographic honeycomb design containing the firm's initials signifies mathematical order while functioning as a visual metaphor that relates the complexity and organization of a 20th-century corporation to a beehive. Geometric spatial divisions based on Lauweriks's grid structures are one unifying graphic theme of Behrens's AEG publication designs.

The use of various graphic devices gave AEG materials a consistent appearance. In addition to modular divisions of space using Lauweriks's grid, these included: framing the space by a medium-weight rule; central placement of static elements; exclusive use of Behrens-Antiqua type; use of analogous colors, often two or three sequential colors on the color wheel; and simple, objective photographs and drawings with subjects isolated from their environments.

Industrial products designed by Behrens ranged from electric household products such as teakettles and fans to streetlamps and electric motors. He brought the formal eye of the painter and the structural approach and professional

ethics of the architect to product design.
The combination of visual form, working method, and functional concern in his work for AEG products enabled him to produce a body of work which has led to his being proclaimed the "first industrial designer." An innovative use of standardization is seen in the design of AEG teakettles with interchangeable parts: three basic kettle forms, two lids, two handles, and two bases. Three materials were used: brass, copperplate, and nickelplate; and three finishes: smooth, hammered, and rippled. All these elements were available to assemble three sizes of teakettles, and all the kettles used the same heating elements and plugs. This system of interchangeable components made it possible to configure 81 different teakettles, though only 30 were actually brought to market.

Beginning in early 1907, Behrens designed a series of AEG arc lamps that produced intense light by means of passing an electrical current between two carbon electrodes. These were 300 times brighter, used less energy, and were safer than the gas lamps of the time. Because the carbon rods had to be replaced every 8 to 20 hours, Behrens designed convenient exterior clips for dismantling them quickly. Their forms and proportions suggest Lauweriks's grid, while the overall shapes evoke the harmonious design and graceful curves of Greek vases. The arc lamps were widely used in factories, railway stations, and public buildings.

Behrens believed neutrality and standardization were appropriate in product designs created for machine manufacture. By designing street lamps and teakettles using simple forms shorn of decoration, Behrens stripped connotations of social class and wealth from these products. His work pointed toward a new sensibility about design, which matured in the 1920s. This rational approach decreed the need for form to emerge from function rather than being an added embellishment.

Between 1909 and 1912, Behrens directed the design for the AEG factory complex in Berlin. The Turbine Hall, designed by Behrens in collaboration with structural engineer Karl Bernhard, is one of the most influential buildings of the early 20th-century. A vast open space is formed by 22 giant girder frames enclosing an interior space 401 feet long and 49 feet high. In addition to the roof and glass walls, these girder frames support two traveling gantry cranes, each with a 50-ton lifting capacity for moving giant turbines under construction. The huge window areas are "curtain walls" floating in the space. The massive concrete columns at the corners are non-load-bearing. Except for the identifying logo and name on the end of the roof, there is neither ornament nor embellishment. The structure and proportion of functional elements are designed to convey the esthetic of the building. Its appearance suggests a massive industrial factory engineered for the assembly of giant steam turbines. This major architectural design by Behrens – with its exposed exterior steel girders along the sides, glass curtain walls, and form determined by function – became a prototype for future design evolution. Behrens's philosophy and the usual studio shop talk were surely a wellspring of ideas for his apprentices of this period: Gropius, Mies van der Rohe, Le Corbusier, and Meyer.

At the 1914 Werkbund annual conference, the debate between Muthesius's rationalism and standardization versus van de Velde's expressionism was soundly determined in favor of the Muthesius approach. Up until this 1914 meeting, Behrens played a key role among designers who rejected the ornament of both historicism and Art Nouveau design and advocated a spartan approach, stripped of decoration. The austere orthodoxy of the International Style was the evolutionary extension of these beliefs.

Behrens began to accept architectural commissions from other clients in 1911; graphic and product design occupied less of his time. In 1914, Behrens's contract with AEG was terminated, although he continued to work from time to time on AEG projects. Until his death in 1940, Behrens's design practice centered upon architecture. His buildings were often massive and ranged from expressionism immediately after World War I to modernist works in the late 1920s and early 1930s whose geometric simplicity and white stucco walls reflected the influence of Gropius and Mies.

One may ask why Behrens has not been more widely recognized or even lionized for his importance to 20th-century design. Perhaps the answer is yet another fact in the devastating impact of Adolf Hitler upon the century. Hitler's rise to power during the 1930s caused many of

Europe's leading modern artists and designers to join the flight of scientific and cultural leaders from the continent to the United States. When Gropius and Mies arrived here, they established architectural and educational programs that transformed American architecture. However, the aging Behrens remained in Germany. During his final years, he struggled to come to terms with the New Order and even signed correspondence, "Heil Hitler." Ironically, he was shunned by some longtime associates for his efforts to adapt even as he was being investigated and attacked by the Nazis for his artistic and political background and prior association with Communists and Jews, including Albert Einstein.

During the late 1930s, Hitler's architect, Albert Speer, planned the transformation of Berlin into an imperial city of the Third Reich, designed in a monumental Empire Style. One of the buildings planned for the grand boulevard stretching from a proposed Arch of Triumph to a domed Great Hall was a new administrative building for AEG to be designed by Behrens. Nazi cultural watchdogs were outraged "that this forerunner of architectural radicalism should be allowed to win immortality on 'the Fuehrer's avenue.'"[1] Hitler backed Speer in his decision to use Behrens, quelling the opposition. The design for the AEG building was completed in October 1939, but it was never executed, as the grand scheme for Berlin became an early casualty of World War II.

Behrens had been plagued with heart trouble since his mid-30s, and he died of a heart attack on February 27, 1940, at age 72. Neither the design professions nor the newspapers took much notice of his passing.

The neglect of Behrens's pivotal role in 20th-century design, at least in the United States and England, may relate to factors other than the taint of his accommodation with Nazism. Perhaps his drift away from Modernism in the later 1930s fueled the failure to fully recognize his earlier importance. Over the past half-century, the legacies of Hitler and Stalin have warped our perceptions of the human condition. But as the walls of the past crumble and a new era of international culture hopefully emerges, perhaps one small result will be a greater acknowledgment of Peter Behrens's impact upon design in this century.

Tibor the Pit Bull

From *Print* Vol. 45, No. 3 (May/June 1991)

Design conferences seem to bring out the pit bull in Tibor Kalman. At the 1989 AIGA conference in San Antonio, Kalman took part in a now well-documented lecture in which he called on designers to be "bad" and dismissed those who were "an accessory to the marketing process." To reinforce this polemic, he quoted from a recent Duffy/Peters Group *Wall Street Journal* ad, reading the last sentence in a sarcastic tone, while showing side-by-side slides of Diet 7-Up and Diet Sprite: "And as more and more competitive packages become more and more alike, a good package can become a packaged good's best if not only point of difference." Then, he lambasted designers for hiring themselves out "to give the appearance of a world (or a supermarket aisle) brimming with options" and for "being suckered by the allure of marketing." Duffy, whose design group has been acclaimed for the esthetic strength of its work, was cast as a flunky to clients.

In Duffy and Kalman's later *Print* debate (see March/April 1990 issue), Duffy asked Kalman, "Why didn't you use the work we referred to in the ad? We weren't referring to 7-Up and Sprite."

"Because I chose not to," Kalman responded. "I was not worried about being fair to you." This is the problem with Kalman's personal attacks upon members of the design community. This self-styled "bad boy" of graphic design simply isn't fair. Suppose Kalman had shown the work Duffy was referring to in his ad for Classico pasta sauce, for instance, presented side-by-side with a competing brand on the grocery shelf. The audience would have probably given Duffy a standing ovation for realizing one of the ideals of the graphic design profession – to improve the esthetic quality of the environment while serving the functional needs of client and consumer.

Kalman went on the warpath again at the 1990 "Modernism & Eclecticism" design history symposium sponsored by the School of Visual Arts in New York, where he spoke on the theme "Good History Bad History." This time, bad was *bad* instead of good, and Kalman and his co-authors, J. Abbott Miller and Karrie Jacobs, found plenty of examples to ridicule and attack. Renowned typographic posters for Columbia Records – designed by Paula Scher and inspired by Russian Constructivism – were dismissed as "so-called historicist eclectic work that has strip-mined the history of design for ready-made style." Scholarly design periodicals such as *Design Issues* were dismissed as "starchy little journals." Visual collections of trademarks and labels, such as Eric Baker's anthologies of trademarks of the 1920s and 1930s, were dismissed as "hack work in publishing." Kalman "proved" they constituted bad design history by presenting a contemporary trademark whose designer was influenced by an example in Baker's book. (Kalman's belittlement of Baker was contradicted by his own appeal, during the question-and-answer period following the talk, for someone to preserve the vernacular design from the 1950s and 1960s.)

I learned first-hand how Duffy must have felt when his words were illustrated by soft-drink cans, and how Baker must have felt when his meticulously researched books were called "hack work," when Kalman attacked my own book, *A History of Graphic Design.* This was dismissed for being about style. Kalman accused me of showing only "Modernism that is deceptively cool, deceptively pretty. Design used for selling expensive or tasteful luxury products." As he read this, a slide of a Cassandre poster appeared on the screen.

"What we don't see," he continued, "is the angry, frightening graphics of a tumultuous era," whereupon an anti-Nazi poster by John Heartfield appeared on the screen. I was dumbfounded by this accusation, for *A History of Graphic Design* reproduces six Heartfield works, but only four Cassandre posters, and it devotes 31 more lines of running text to Heartfield and his group than to Cassandre. (The Heartfield slide Kalman showed was even shot from *A History of Graphic Design!* I recognized the extensive retouching required for a faded area on the poster so it could be photographed for the book.) I wrote Kalman and advised him of his error.

When Kalman, in collaboration with Jacobs and Miller, published a revised version of his "Good History Bad History" talk in the March/April 1991 issue of *Print,* he removed some of the more outrageous errors and insults. In this sanitized version, Kalman states, "Even Ludwig Hohlwein's posters for the Nazis are neutralized by a lens that isolates only esthetic qualities," and suggested a re-reading of the *[History of Graphic Design's]* pages 299–300 (including captions) to verify this view. The *Print* reader who takes Kalman's advice will find – along with some biographical information and an analysis of the visual aspects of Hohlwein's work – the following: "After an unsuccessful 1923 attempt to seize power in the Munich Putsch, Adolf Hitler was sent to prison, where he spent his time writing *Mein Kampf* which set forth his political philosophy and plans to take over Germany. He wrote that propaganda, including the poster, 'must be aimed at the emotions and only to a limited degree to the so-called intellect.' Hitler advocated propaganda whose content level was directed toward the least educated in the audience using only essential, simple forms in stereotyped formulas. Hitler was convinced that the more artistically designed posters used in Germany and Austria during World War I were less effective than the conceptually simpler, but more illustrative work from England and the United States. Hitler had an almost uncanny knack for visual propaganda. The swastika was adopted as the symbol for the Nazi party. Uniforms consisting of brown shirts with red armbands bearing a black swastika in a white circle began to appear throughout Germany as Nazi storm troopers grew in strength and numbers.

"It seems almost inevitable, in retrospect, that the Nazi party would commission a steady stream of posters from Hohlwein, for the evolution of his work coincided closely with Hitler's concept of effective propaganda. As Hitler spoke in his passionate radio addresses to the nation about the 'master race' of fair-haired German youth and the triumphant superiority of German athletes, Hohlwein posters carried these images all across the nation. Hitler's ideas gained a visual presence, and… seeing the images over and over again reinforced them. As the Nazi dictatorship consolidated its power and the stormy holocaust

Black and white photographs of various subjects. (1975)

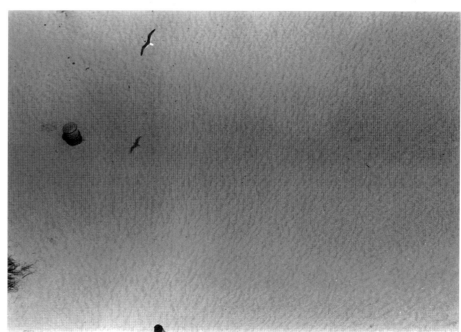

of World War II approached, Hohlwein moved toward a bold imperial and militaristic style of tight, heavy forms and strong tonal contrasts."

The preceding passage is from the two pages of *A History of Graphic Design* selected by Kalman and his cohorts to prove their premise that in this book, "Even Ludwig Hohlwein's posters for the Nazis are neutralized by a lens that isolates only esthetic qualities." If you take Kalman's premise seriously after reading this passage, you should consult your local adult education program to be tested for learning disabilities.

Kalman's "Good History Bad History" lecture and article are riddled with similar misstatements and misunderstandings. If Kalman knew more about design history, he would have known – as editor Victor Margolin of *Design Issues* tried to tell him during the question-and-answer period – that the debate about visual vs. social approaches to design history has been raging for years, notably in the "starchy little journals" he condemned. Books such as Steven Heller's masterly *Graphic Style: From Victorian to Postmodern* focus upon the visual and perceptual aspects of design, while others, such as Max Gallo's *The Poster in History,* concentrate on graphic design's relationship to the social, political, and economic life of the society in which it occurs. Just as biologists need to study organisms in their environment as well as under controlled laboratory conditions, design must be studied in its cultural context and as autonomous visual phenomena having syntactic forms and semantic meaning.

Kalman would have us believe a visual approach to design history is invalid, and the social approach is correct. I find his attitude disturbing. Graphic design is a visual medium; it is a primary source of esthetic and perceptual experience in contemporary culture. In opposition to Kalman's restricted view, we must demand pluralism from the design history movement. Neither graphic design's role as social message nor its role as visual art can be rejected.

Kalman hasn't been involved in graphic design long enough to comprehend the positive impact the design history movement of the last decade has had upon graphic design and design education. When we study the Bauhaus, for example, we learn about its forms, certainly, but we also learn about its philosophy, theory, and aspirations for society. As I wrote in my book, it sought to dissolve "fine and applied art boundaries… to bring art into a close relationship with life by design, which was seen as a vehicle for social change and cultural revitalization." One hopes this knowledge helps us to better understand our own work and role in society. (I invite the reader to read pages 329–41, about the Bauhaus, in *A History of Graphic Design,* to see if Kalman is correct about this being an example of history in which "style is a detachable attribute, a veneer rather than an expression of content.")

When Kalman says, "Modernism believed in itself, in its contemporaneity: It believed in the present," he shows a limited understanding of what Modernism was about. Perhaps the only consistent aspect of the numerous Modernist movements was their deliberate attempt to break with the past. Anxiety, dissension, uncertainty, and poverty were as prevalent as the lofty Bauhaus goal, stated above.

Kalman seems irritated when design historians coin terms such as Populuxe, Depression Modern, and Pictorial Modernism and bristles about design historians who categorize work according to its visual attributes. Terminology provides a conceptual handle for understanding works and their meaning. Thomas Hine's term "Populuxe" helped me understand the American design of the 1950s and 1960s, which provided an ambience of luxury for a mass market. Cars larded with chrome and crowned with padded vinyl tops mystified me – as did the reasons people paid extra for these models – until Hine's book explained the style and its audience. Often, design historians coin terms simply because an adequate term does not exist. The most controversial of the 24 chapter titles in *A History of Graphic Design,* "Pictorial Modernism," was chosen simply because I had an untitled chapter containing the illustrative graphic design influenced by modern art during the first half of the 20th century. All of the available terms, such as Art Deco, were too restrictive. I shortened the working title "Modernist Pictorial Graphics of the First Half of the Twentieth Century" to "Pictorial Modernism" when editing the final manuscript.

Design historians categorize designs by their visual attributes for the same reason biologists classify species by their visual properties: Visual attributes are the most readily identifiable characteristics. J. Abbott Miller fumes in one of his

"Good History Bad History" footnotes, in the aforementioned *Print* article, about "Ludwig Hohlwein's career (including his involvement with Nazi propaganda)" being placed by *A History of Graphic Design* "within the overarching framework of 'Pictorial Modernism.'" Returning to pages 299–300 of the book, we find Hohlwein's five-decade career described as evolving with "changing social conditions," from an early formal phase, where "he applied a rich range of texture and decorative pattern in his images," to his style during World War I, when he combined "simple, powerful shapes with more naturalistic imagery," to the "fluid and painterly" work he did for commercial accounts after the war, to his work for the Nazis. Organizing design history by visual attributes enables Hohlwein to be treated in one section, whereas historical organization by subject matter or decades would have split him into several different chapters.

Design history, art history, and "history history" have all developed research and evaluation methods and a theoretical basis for their work. Naive about this, Kalman mistakenly believes design historians merely make selections based on style. His blanket indictment of design historians for decontextualizing artifacts shows he does not know that design historians call upon a wealth of information from the era of the artifact and its creators. Right now, for example, I am researching a forthcoming *Print* "Landmarks of Book Design" article about William Pickering's phenomenal 1847 geometry book. A computer bibliographic search yielded an eight-page list of resources, including many from Pickering's time–lengthy obituaries written by knowledgeable close friends, "design criticism" by his contemporaries, and newspaper accounts of his revolt against gentlemanly price-fixing in the London book-publishing business.

Kalman pleads for a more inclusive history, and hungers for "ads for hemorrhoid products, retail handbills, license plates," and the cover of the "Charter paperback edition of *Eden's Gate*." Applying this reasoning to other disciplines, would Kalman and his sidekicks advocate literary anthologies supplementing works by Kafka, Shakespeare, and Mailer with trashy grocery-store novels? Or histories of art that include black-velvet paintings and those banged-out $49.95 oil paintings from cheap furniture stores alongside Rembrandt, Van Gogh, and Mondrian? All graphic ephemera aren't worth saving. Part of the design historian's role is to filter the past. It falls on him or her to separate the recyclable aluminum from the rotten apples and contents of cat litter boxes.

Kalman raises some important issues. Unfortunately, by seeing contemporary graphic design and design history in black-and-white terms, instead of in their full pluralistic spectrum, he brands people and their works as either good or bad, and his important issues vanish in a cloud of personal attack. Taking a position, then slanting the evidence to support that position, is ethically analogous to reinforcing the roof of a Volvo to make it look indestructible in a television ad. ➻

Landmarks of Book Design, Fourth of a Series: *The Elements of Euclid*

From *Print* Vol. 46, No. 1 (Jan/Feb 1992)

In 1847, London's leading book publisher and designer, William Pickering, produced a geometry book of astounding beauty – a startling precursor of modernist design.

"A feebler impress through the ear is made,/Than what is by the faithful eye conveyed," wrote the Roman philosopher Horace.[1] The English mathematician Oliver Byrne uses this quote in the introduction to his 1847 book, *The Elements of Euclid,* to justify the value of color in teaching geometry.

"The arts and sciences have become so extensive," Byrne's introduction states, "that to facilitate their acquirement is of as much importance as to extend their boundaries. Illustration, if it does not shorten the time of study, will at least make it more agreeable. This work has a greater aim than mere illustration; we do not introduce colours for the purpose of entertainment, or to amuse by certain combinations of tint and form, but to assist the mind in its researches after truth, to increase the facilities of instruction, and to diffuse permanent knowledge."[2] To accomplish this objective, Byrne developed a system of color coding to bring clarity to the intricacies of geometry. He cautioned, "Care must be taken to show that colour had nothing to do with the lines, angles, or magnitudes, except merely to name them. A mathematical line, which is length without breadth, cannot possess colour, yet the junction of two colours on the same plane gives a good idea of what is meant by a mathematical line."

Landmarks of Book Design, Fourth of a Series: *The Elements of Euclid*

For students struggling to learn geometry in the middle of the last century, the vibrant primary colors and crisp geometric shapes punched into thick papers by hand-cut woodblocks helped to avoid having an important subject "degraded by a dry and rigid course of instruction into an uninteresting exercise of memory."[4]

But from today's vantage point, as we study *The Elements of Euclid* with perceptions shaped by the geometric abstractions of 20th-century art and design, its remarkable pages provide not solely a geometry lesson, but an exuberant exhibition of graphic color and form. Although form was meant to follow the intended function of teaching geometry, *The Elements of Euclid* lives a second life a century and a half after its publication as book art.

This afterlife exists because Byrne, a mathematician, teacher, and surveyor (he was once dispatched to survey the Falkland Islands, the English colony located 300 miles east of the South American mainland), met with good fortune when his book was published by William Pickering. This English bookseller and publisher took full charge of the design of the volumes he produced, enabling him to become the leading purveyor of well-designed books during the first half of the 19th century. His obsession with book design and printing prompted him to spare no expense in translating Byrne's text and drawings into a masterly book.

Pickering was born in 1796, the illegitimate son of a book-loving earl, thought to be the second Earl of Spencer, and a lady of title. His name came

Page from book four of
The Elements of Euclid.
Designed and published by
William Pickering (1847)

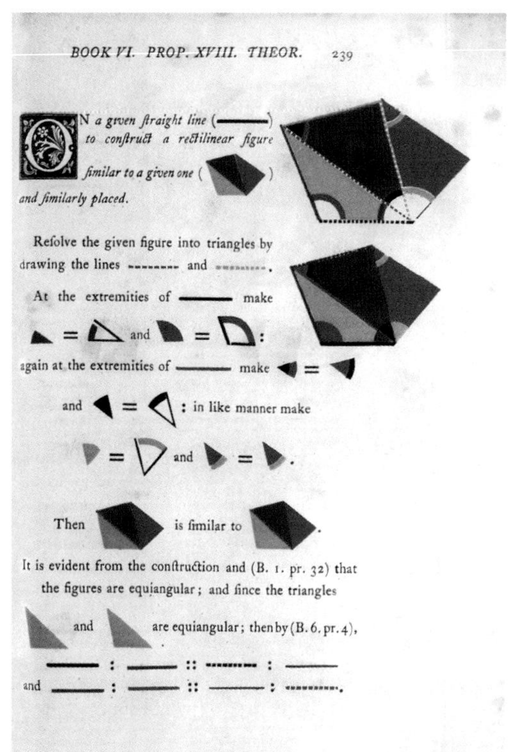

BOOK VI. PROP. XVIII. THEOR. 239

ON *a given ſtraight line* ( ) *to conſtruct a rectilinear figure ſimilar to a given one* ( ) *and ſimilarly placed.*

Reſolve the given figure into triangles by drawing the lines and .

At the extremities of make = and = :

again at the extremities of make =

and = : in like manner make

= and = .

Then is ſimilar to .

It is evident from the conſtruction and (B. 1. pr. 32) that the figures are equiangular; and ſince the triangles

and are equiangular; then by (B. 6. pr. 4),

: :: :

and : :: : .

from a tailor with whose wife he was put out to nurse.[5] At age 14, Pickering was apprenticed to Quaker booksellers John and Arthur Arch, where he gained expertise about books and literature.[6]

After a decade of employment with other booksellers, Pickering opened his own business as a second-hand or "antiquarian" bookseller. According to Pickering's biographer, Geoffrey Keynes, "One or the other of his parents retained an interest in his welfare, and 1000 pounds were placed to his credit at the bank."[7] Pickering immediately began to publish as well as sell books. Early in the 19th century, publishing was dominated by large London houses, and Pickering was part of "a new breed [of independent publishers who] arrived on the scene with positive and decided ideas on what they wanted to achieve" as book publishers.[8] The London printer Charles Corrall had acquired a stock of Diamond Type – which, in the terminology of typography before the point system was adopted, is very small type, about 4½ points – and Pickering was inspired to begin printing a series of "Diamond Classics," which he advertised as the smallest editions ever printed of such writers as Horace and Virgil.[9] His purpose was "the launching of comparatively inexpensive series for popular education in an attempt to reach the widest possible circle of readers, and match the growth of literacy."[10]

These small economic editions were extremely successful. Pickering saw a parallel between his publishing program and that of Aldus Manutius, the Venetian publisher who invented the pocket book in 1501 so that he could make available small affordable editions of the classics. In 1828, this "induced [Pickering] to adopt the device formerly borne by the Aldine family in the fifteenth and sixteenth centuries, attaching the words ALDI DISCIP ANGLVS," which is Latin for Aldus's English Disciple." For almost three decades, most of Pickering's books bore one of numerous woodcut versions of the anchor and-dolphin logo, which signified Aldus' motto, "Make Haste Slowly."

Pickering's ability to produce books of high quality at low prices incurred the wrath of other publishers and booksellers. A network of established publishers controlled prices through the Bookseller's Association,[12] and Pickering would often publish competing editions of books whose copyright had expired, offering superior editing, typography, and printing at lower prices. Other publishers refused to sell him their books at the usual booksellers' discounts, and a secret committee of publishers posted spies on his street and conspired to hurt his business by spreading rumors that his books were "not out," "out of print," or "discontinued."[13]

Pickering achieved an elegance of design and typography unique for his time, and often invested heavily in it. Wrote the scholar Bernard Warrington, "Pickering's own distinction lies partly, but not wholly, in his particular attention to appropriate typography, design, and ornament. His productions represent a high point in that they are the result not only of the role of publisher and designer being combined in one person, but also of the role of publisher and bookseller being integrated to an extent which is perhaps unusual."[14] By 1830, Pickering had formed a close working relationship with the printer Charles Whittingham the Younger. Publisher and printer became close friends and "met almost daily at the Crown Coffee House in Holborn to discuss work in progress and plan new projects."[15] Pickering "supplied the larger share of judgment and originality, while the printer provided the technical knowledge with which his excellent training had provided him."[16] The collaboration enabled these two men to restore standards of design and typographic excellence, which had been lost during the early decades of the Industrial Revolution. It seems fruitless to speculate on the relative importance of their contributions, for apparently a synergy developed between Pickering, a publisher who liked to design the books he published, and Whittingham, a printer who had the expertise and knowledge to realize Pickering's goals. It was a fruitful collaboration, for the relationship enabled each man to achieve more in the partnership than he could have on his own.

Caslon Old Style types had fallen into disuse because hairline serifed "Modern Style" types inspired by Bodoni and Didot dominated book typography. Pickering and Whittingham rediscovered the beauty and hearty legibility of Caslon and used it, first for title pages, then for entire books. Pickering is credited with innovating the use of dyed cotton cloth, in place of flimsy paper, to cover boarded books. One account holds that Pickering was dissatisfied with the lack of strength of the red paper used in bookbinding. One day, as he was walking along Holborn, he noticed some red-glazed cotton cloth on display in a draper's shop window. The idea came to him to substitute fabric for the paper, and he began to experiment with the material. As a result of his innovation, cloth binding was adopted throughout the book-publishing trade."[17]

His work as an antiquarian bookseller gave Pickering access to the design and typography of earlier printers. The printing historian Stanley Morison has written, "Pickering was the first to design books in an eclectic-antiquarian spirit: I mean he was the first to go back to XVIth century Venice & Lyons for inspiration. Before his time the development of the book shows no instance of atavism. If I am right, Pickering is the tribal chief of the Morris-Ricketts-Rogers school."[18] The "school" referred to by Morison had spurred typography and book design forward in the late 19th and early 20th centuries by championing Renaissance masters; Pickering was the first to rediscover a tradition of excellence.

His passion for design led Pickering to commission woodblock ornaments, initials, and illustrations interpreting works by leading painters of the period. During the 1840s, the attention Pickering and Whittingham gave to wood-engraved ornament became obsessive, and intricate blocks were commissioned from a masterly engraver, Mary Byfield. This emphasis on engraved ornament became "a labor of love rather than profit," for "Whittingham gave to it an amount of time, care and risk all out of proportion," notes Arthur Warren, Whittingham's biographer, who then observes, "It was gratifying, no doubt, to be praised for the best printing, but it could not be gratifying to know that the expense of woodcut work always equalled and sometimes exceeded its market value."[19] Ultimately, these production costs had to be absorbed by Pickering.

It was in the midst of their obsession with wood engraving in the 1840s that the opportunity arose to publish Byrne's color-coded geometry book. It offered a new challenge, a radical departure from conventional geometry books, and an unprecedented opportunity for color wood engraving. Pickering and Whittingham rose to that challenge.

One aspect of *The Elements of Euclid,* the juxtaposition of the geometric diagrams with Caslon Old Style types and ornamental engraved initials, seems incongruous to the late-20th-century viewer, for sans-serif type without decorative elements seems more compatible with Byrne's geometric diagrams. In 1847, the "modern" design sensibility was more than a half-century into the future; although sans-serifs had been invented, they had never been used for book text. Had Pickering used sans-serif type for book text, the audience would have probably howled in protest over this totally unfamiliar form.

The Elements of Euclid was published during a period when Pickering was struggling with financial difficulties and litigation. At the time, bills or invoices were commonly issued and used as credit, exchanged as though they were currency, and often deeply discounted. Pickering was in heavy debt to one John Joseph Thornthwaite, a bookseller, bookbinder, and discount agent who, like Pickering, had experienced financial problems during the depression of the early 1840s. Litigation between them dragged on for years, with a final hearing on April 22, 1854, which forced Pickering's bankruptcy. Pickering died five days later. His obituary stated, "Mental anxiety brought on a decline in health, and gradually sinking he died on Thursday, April 27, about half-past 11 o'clock, a.m., having completed his 58th year, and still bearing the respect and regret of many who knew him long and intimately."[20] It required 28 days of auction to sell 9,711 lots of Pickering's publishing and book-selling stock. His three daughters were left without resources and "totally unprovided for."[21]

Pickering's biographer, Geoffrey Keynes, calls *The Elements of Euclid* "a very curious work in which Caslon's old-face pica is associated with Chiswick Press initials and ornaments and with diagrams and symbols printed in brilliant colors, these being 'used instead of letters for the greater ease of learners'. Youthful learners would certainly be vastly amused, but probably rather bewildered, by the chromatic display of the handsome quarto pages. Pickering may, however, be credited with having fathered a gallant, if unsuccessful, experiment in education."[22] Writing more than a century after *The Elements of Euclid* was published, Keynes offers no justification for his negative reaction to its educational value. An opposing view was held by the book's author, Oliver Byrne, who wrote, "*The Elements of Euclid* can be acquired in less than one third the time usually employed, and the retention of the memory is more permanent; these facts have been ascertained by numerous experiments made by the inventor, and several others have adopted his plans. The particulars of which are few and obvious; the letters annexed to points, lines, or other parts of the diagram are in fact but arbitrary names, and represent them in the demonstration; instead of these, the parts being differently coloured, are made to name themselves, for their forms in corresponding colours represent them in the demonstration."[23]

After reading Byrne's book, I found the color coding easier to follow than the traditional cacophony of alphabetical labeling of angles, and believe Keynes's criticism is overstated. But whether or not Victorian students wrestling with the intricacies of geometric theorems found *The Elements of Geometry* useful, the book's spirited pages transcend its time and purpose, and the work is ultimately a captivating artifact.

Notes

1. Oliver Byrne, *The First Six Books of The Elements of Euclid* (London: William Pickering, 1847): viii.

2. Ibid., vii.

3. Ibid., xiii.

4. Ibid.

5. Arthur Warren, *The Charles Whittinghams, printers* (New York: The Grolier Club, 1896): 207.

6. "Obituary Notice for William Pickering," *Willis's Current Notes* (London) 41 (May, 1854): 43.

7. Geoffrey Keynes, *William Pickering: Publisher,* rev. ed. (London: Galahad Press, 1969): 10.

8. Bernard Warrington, "William Pickering, His Authors and Interests: A Publisher and the Literary Scene in the Early Nineteenth Century," *The John Rylands University Library Bulletin* 69, no. 2 (Spring, 1987): 572–73.

9. Keynes, *William Pickering,* 11.

10. Warrington, "William Pickering, His Authors and Interests," 574.

11. "Obituary Notice for William Pickering," 43.

12. Bernard Warrington, "William Pickering and the Book Trade in the Early Nineteenth Century," *The John Rylands University Library Bulletin* 68, no. 1 (August, 1985): 254.

13. Keynes, *William Pickering,* 33–34.

14. Warrington, *"William Pickering, His Authors and Interests,"* 626.

15. Keynes, *William Pickering,* 24.

16. Ibid.

17. "Obituary Notice for William Pickering," 43.

18. Stanley Morison, "Letter to Geoffrey Keynes," 1924.

19. Warren, "The Charles Whittinghams, printers," 194.

20. "Obituary Notice for William Pickering," 43.

21. Ibid.

22. Keynes, *William Pickering,* 37.

23. Byrne, *Elements of Euclid,* ix.

I Am Type! Revisited

From the Introduction to *Print's Best Typography* (1992)

"I bring into the light of day the precious stores of knowledge and wisdom long hidden in the grave of ignorance. I am the leaden army that conquers the world: I am type!" proclaimed a 1933 broadside designed and written by the great typeface designer Frederic Goudy. Were he alive today, Goudy would probably be alarmed at the turn American type design has taken a half-century after his death: His army of lead soldiers has been transformed into a fusillade of electronic bits, bytes, and pixels. Today's computer-based technology permits designers to extend the visual range of type into new directions that Goudy could hardly have foreseen.

Typography is no longer just a craft used to give visual form to the spoken language, for contemporary designers have reconstituted type into symbolic icons and expressive visual forms undreamed of by Goudy and his contemporaries. A number of significant changes in our modern culture have caused this revolution in the noble art of alphabets. In earlier times, the spoken word was ephemeral but the printed word remained fixed on carved stone or printed page. Electronic technology now makes possible the recording of speech, permitting the spoken word to survive just as the printed word does. Typography has thus been freed from a mindset that viewed it as the sole documentary record of human thought.

The kinetics of film, video, and animation have greatly influenced print graphics, resulting in a new emphasis on movement and energy. The ability of type to literally march across the video screen, zoom back into infinity, or rush forward until the dot of a lowercase *i* fills the screen has not been lost on graphic designers working with a static printed page. Capturing the vitality of kinetic energy and freezing it in printing inks is now commonplace.

Visual art has been redefined, and twentieth-century artists and designers have proven that colors, textures, and shapes – including letterforms – have lives of their own apart from their representational or symbolic meaning. In typographic design, this non-verbal level of expression can be teamed with the verbal meaning of words to intensify or enhance the message.

For over five hundred years, type marched in horizontal rows dictated by the relentless constraints of typesetting technology. Today, flexibility abounds. Technology places unprecedented control of space and scale in the hands of the designer. Both enormously large and minutely small sizes of type operate at extremes of scale that disregard the limitations of traditional technology. Spatial configurations warp, bend, fracture, and separate, defying the regimen of Goudy's leaden army. Type can run over, around, and through images with any desired degree of transparency. All of these new possibilities can be accomplished with the click of a mouse. Tracking of letterspacing in measurements of 1/20,000 of an em, using negative line spacing, stretching type, bending it back in space, and setting type in circles, ovals, and any configuration devised by the designer's imagination becomes routine.

(continued on page 186)

Philip Meggs: Proposal for a children's book
***The Tiniest Teeny of Them All* ©1970**

Prototype children's book.
Color marker on paper,
8.5 x 10 inches. (©1970)

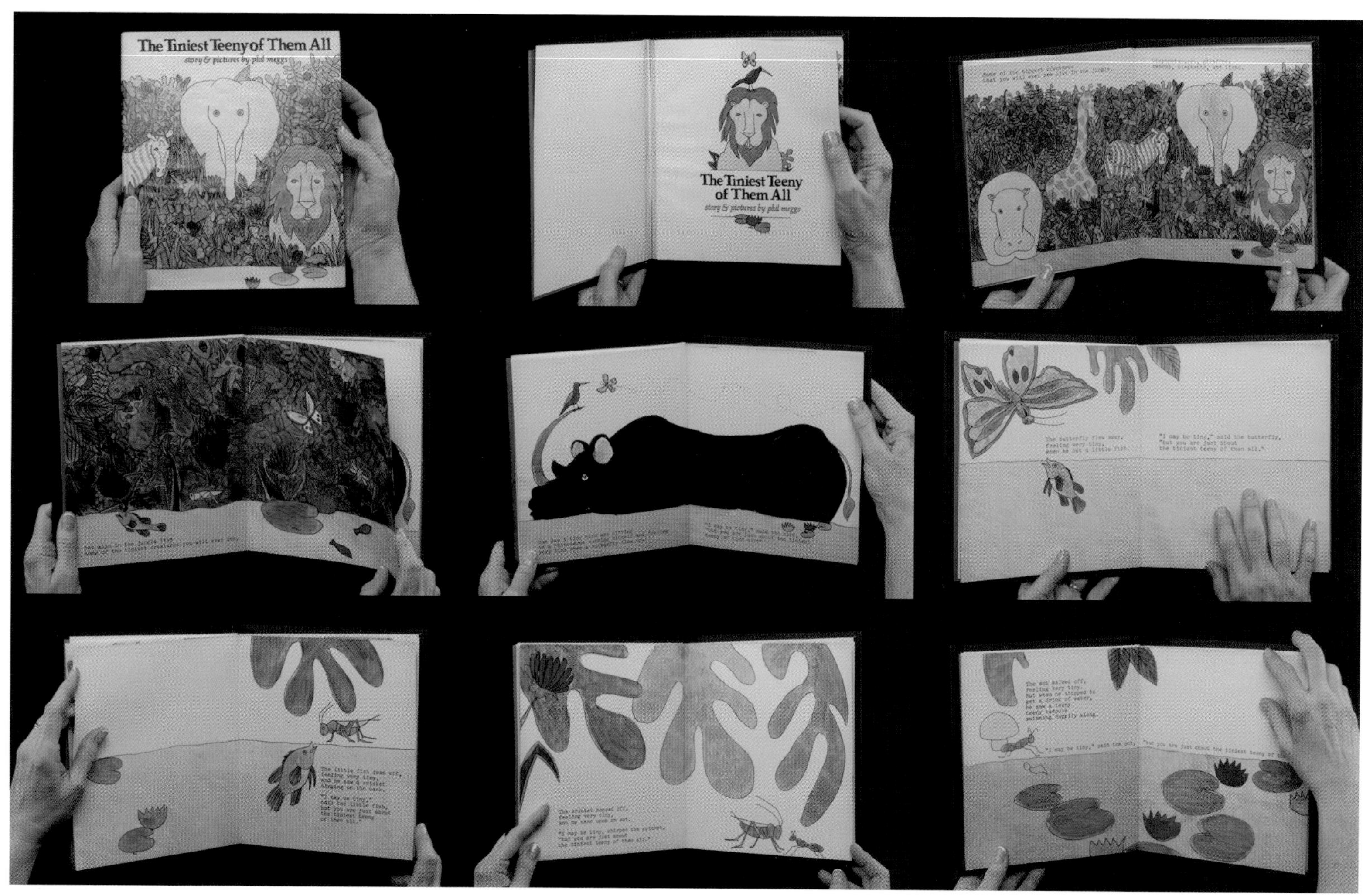

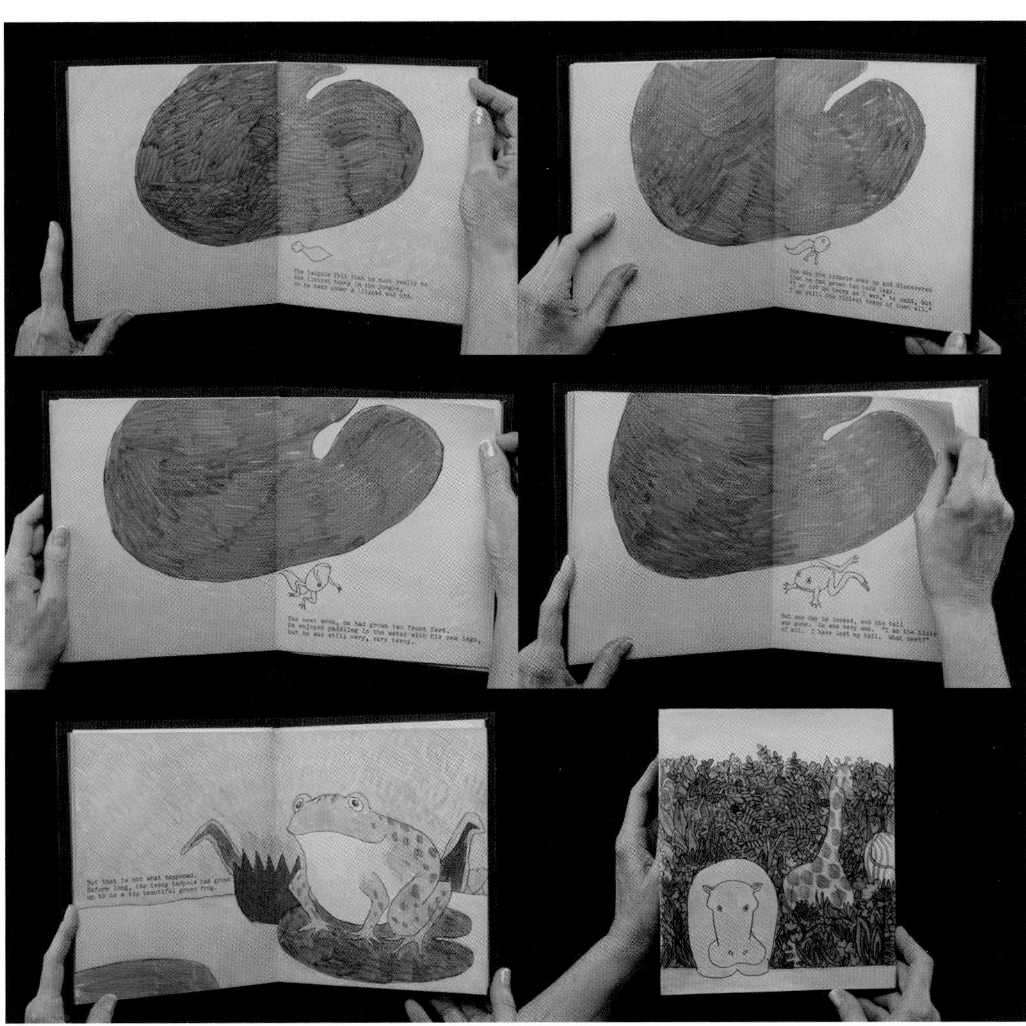

Some of the biggest creatures that you will ever see live in the jungle.

Hippopotamuses, giraffes, zebras, elephants, and lions.

But also in the jungle live some of the tiniest creatures you will ever see.

One day a tiny bird was sitting on a rhinoceros sunning himself and feeling very tiny when a butterfly flew up.

"I may be tiny," said the bird, "but you are just about the tiniest teeny of them all!"

The butterfly flew away, feeling very tiny, when he met a little fish.

"I may be tiny," said the butterfly, "but you are just about the tiniest teeny of them all!"

The little fish swam off, and he saw a cricket singing on the bank.

"I may be tiny," said the little fish, "but you are just about the tiniest teeny of them all!"

The cricket hopped off, feeling very tiny, and he came upon an ant.

"I may be tiny," chirped the cricket, "but you are just about the tiniest teeny of them all!"

The ant walked off, feeling very tiny, but when he stopped to get a drink of water, he saw a teeny, teeny tadpole swimming happily along.

"I may be tiny," said the ant, "but you are just about the tiniest teeny of them all!"

The tadpole felt that he must really be the tiniest teeny in the jungle, so he swam under a lily pad and hid.

One day the tadpole woke up and discovered that he had grown two back legs.

"I am not so teeny as I was," he said, "but I am still the tiniest teeny of them all."

The next week he had grown two front feet. He enjoyed paddling in the water with his new legs, but he was still very, very teeny.

But one day he looked, and his tail was gone. He was very sad. "I am the tiniest teeny of all. I have lost my tail. What next?

But that is not what happened. Before long, the teeny tadpole had grown up to be a beautiful green frog.

Technology alone cannot fully explain the creative freedom of contemporary graphic design. Art moves forward by action and reaction, and many designers seem to be challenging the ease and conformity permitted by computer technology. Some are experimenting with spontaneous – and even crude – yet beautifully designed hand lettering and writing. Collage is used to combine unlike and unexpected shapes, color, and texture. Many designers are fabricating words as solid dimensional objects, capable of being constructed from substances ranging from Plexiglas to cake icing or discarded pieces of wire or metal; anything that can make an image becomes a potential tool for the designer seeking to imbue words with expressive form.

An element of play has entered typographic design, pushing at the seams of conventional wisdom and traditional practice. Designers sometimes propel their work toward the outer limits of legibility, almost as if they were daring the client to reject it or defying the reader to decipher it. Although failures abound, many of the works included here proved that risk-taking can avert disaster and result in graphic design which fascinates the eye with new visions and experiences.

Each of the 175 designs selected for this book appeared in the 1992 edition of *Print's Regional Design Annual.* They are presented much larger and in a more detailed form than is possible in the *Annual,* and in a context that emphasizes their typographic distinction. The work ranges over the entire spectrum of print communications, and if Goudy were here to review it, he would doubtless amend his broadside to read: "I am the liberated letters that bring into the light of day the precious duality of form and message, freed from the grave of tradition and rigid technology. I am the electronic army that flows around the global village; I am type!" ⊷

Introduction to *Typographic Specimens: The Great Typefaces*

Coauthored with Rob Carter (1993)

Typographic specimens have been an important design tool since the first specimen sheets were produced in the early decades of typography following Johann Gutenberg's invention of movable type around 1450. Early printers and typefounders used specimen sheets to attract customers for their graphic services. Printed specimens provide an opportunity to study and learn about typefaces, to select and plan typography, and to increase one's understanding of letterforms. Specimens aid in the selection of fonts to be purchased for the font library used by a designer. Even though contemporary technology enables one to view typography on screen and study printed sample proofs in planning a design, specimen books introduce unfamiliar typefaces in printed form and aid in the development of connoisseurship. Comparative analysis of similar faces in printed form becomes possible.

There has been a phenomenal growth in the number of typefaces available over the past two decades, introducing many weeds into the typographic garden. The motivation for this book was a desire to combine in one resource the finest typeface designs. The criterion for design excellence in a typeface includes a harmony of form achieved by unifying diverse letters within the alphabet; this creates a rhythmic quality satisfying to the reader or viewer. This combination of unity and diversity creates legibility. Originality, the introduction of new forms into the typographic landscape, is often a hallmark of a significant typeface; however, even subtle innovations within a tradition can create an important typeface. A typeface gains distinction through unique proportions, characters, and shapes, but when these identifying properties are too exaggerated or pronounced, they intrude upon the integrity of the typeface.

First, the authors selected over one hundred type families whose properties seemed to satisfy these criteria. To minimize the influence of personal subjective judgement upon the final selection, over one hundred prominent designers and design educators were sent a ballot listing these typefaces and were asked to vote for the type families that best fulfilled their personal criteria for typographic excellence. They were also asked to write in any typefaces they felt should have been included on the list. This jury provided remarkably consistent viewpoints when selecting fonts they regarded as great typefaces. The typefaces contained in this book represent the results of this poll without alteration; certainly, each of the authors would have compiled a somewhat different selection, as would have each participant in the poll.

Originally it was our intent to select experimental or applied designs to open the section for each type family in the book. A number of designers returned ballots with a note expressing interest in developing an experimental page or submitting an existing design for one of the type families. We began asking designers if they would like to design a page and quickly found enough interest to cover the type families represented in this book. The diversity and originality of these design interpretations add a lively dimension to the book.

Traditional standard type sizes have become somewhat irrelevant since contemporary computer software enables type sizes and spaces to be altered in thousandths of a point, and the wide availability of enlarging and reducing copier machines lessens the need for a variety of specimen sizes. Three display sizes are shown of most fonts, and the point size appears in small flags adjacent to the specimens.

Researching the origins of each type family increased our awareness of the forces shaping the evolution of typeface design. These include handwriting, technology, the cultural milieu, marketing, and the original visions of creative type designers. Early in the evolution of typography, written forms provided models for typefaces; this influence continues today.

Technology and typeface design

Technological advances alter typeface design, and these influences are not always positive. Hand-set metal type was cast from matrices which were made by stamping hand-carved punches into a softer metal. Typeface design was dependent upon the skill and artistry of the punchcutter, while the limitations of this handcraft process ultimately determined the quality and nature of letterform designs.

The industrial revolution brought technical advances, including more precise carving, making possible such refinements as thinner strokes and sharper serifs. Mechanical routers enabled the manufacture of wood type for large display purposes, while mechanical punchcutters permitted very precise metal type based on the designer's drawings rather than carved punches. Expanded use of display advertising and posters led to the development of whole new categories of typeface design to satisfy the new applications.

The invention of Linotype and Monotype keyboard typesetting machines in the 1880s made text type far more economical and efficient than hand-set metal type. This reduced the cost of books, magazines, and newspapers. Typefaces were designed specifically for the limitations of these machines; for example, a Linotype machine held two fonts in its magazine, and they had to have the exact same set width. Regular, italic, and bold fonts mixed on the same line required identical set widths. Ironically, as machine-set type replaced hand-set type for text, an expanded need developed for new handset typefaces used in advertising headlines and editorial display type.

During the 1960s, photographic typesetting processes rapidly replaced hand- and machine-set metal type. The low cost of developing new photographic fonts created a new explosion in typeface design. Metal typefaces were redesigned for different sizes, because the thinner stroke weights had to be heavier in smaller sizes to appear optically correct. But phototype used one master font for all sizes, often causing thick strokes to appear too heavy in large sizes, while thin strokes would drop out in very small sizes.

Phototype yielded to digital type during the 1980s. Letterforms were generated by pixels, so the resolution of the output device became an important factor influencing typeface design.

The digital type revolution brought great flexibility to typographic design, but this was a two-edged sword, permitting subtle design nuance as well as extreme distortion of letterforms that often violated the integrity of the typeface designer's work.

The revivals

The Arts and Crafts Movement of the late 19th century looked back to historical eras of printing and designed typefaces modeled after early printed books. This inspired a period of revivals during the first three decades of the 20th century, when new versions of rarely attainable typefaces such as Garamond, Baskerville, and Bodoni were created. Metal type foundries including Berthold, Stempel, and Bauer in Germany, Deberny & Peignot in France, and American Type Founders in the United States – and typesetting machine manufacturers, such as Linotype, Monotype, and Ludlow, developed their versions of the classical typefaces. This proliferation of variations continued unabated when phototype, rub-down lettering, and digital type companies drew their own variations, altered existing designs, or pirated type designers' work.

By 1990, a staggering range of originals, revivals, adaptations, and copies created a confusing number of variations. Controversies erupted over the relative merits of a bewildering number of variations of traditional typefaces such as Garamond. Often the original font is not necessarily the best version, because later versions sometimes incorporate design refinements or exploit the superior capabilities of new technology. In other cases, some revivals or copies violate the design integrity of the original. The versions chosen for this book are based on often competing considerations: fidelity to the original design; subtle visual refinements or improvements incorporated in the redrawn version; and availability for contemporary electronic-page design. Versions that depart significantly from the original font by exaggerating distinguishing features such as serifs and proportions have been avoided.

The cultural milieu

Visual forms dominant during each epoch often had a pronounced influence upon the development of typefaces. This can be seen in the Victorian Era, when the same ornate gingerbread decorating houses and porches found its way into typeface design. These exaggerated designs have survived, not as typographic masterpieces, but as nostalgic artifacts evoking a historical period. On the other hand, geometric typefaces were designed during the 1920s and 1930s based on elemental forms such as the circle, square, and triangle. This paralleled similar forms in fine art as well as architectural, product, and graphic design of this period; however, these geometric typefaces, including Futura and Kabel, have survived the passage of time as important members of the typographic lexicon.

Typefaces have been designed during each era that capture the spirit and sensibilities of that time. Extensive use by many designers creates a market for specific typefaces and the equipment used to set them. This has led competing companies to develop copies and variations. For example, the popularity of Futura spawned a host of imitations, including Metro and Spartan. Font manufacturers have used extensive promotion to generate markets for their latest typeface designs. Typography often experiences cyclical changes not unlike the fashion industry. Typefaces become wildly popular, then after periods of extensive use, they are no longer used. Designers move on to the next innovation or revival.

Effective typographic design is dependent upon a broad perceptual and conceptual understanding of typefaces and their potential for communication and expression. One method of achieving this understanding is comparative study of well-designed fonts. We hope this book will be a useful resource for everyone who works with type. ➻

MEGGS

Yin/Yang and the Art of Graphic Design

Commencement Address, School of the Arts, Virginia Commonwealth University (May, 1993)

Last Wednesday, I tried to count how many commencements I've attended. Three of my own, about 20 as a VCU faculty member, high school and college graduations for brothers, a sister, nieces, nephews, in-laws – I've attended over sixty commencements. That's two months of my life; I've sat through over five-dozen commencement addresses. Most were dull and loaded with clichés.

Then three weeks ago, after I finished looking at Cookie Montgomery's work in my design class, she said, "Oh, by the way, the CA commencement committee wants you to deliver the address at the CA commencement."

And you know, I don't remember a thing those sixty commencement speakers said. Except one thing: the president of Georgetown University, located in the heart of Washington, DC, spoke about the relationship between cities and universities and noted that the Jesuits who founded his college had bet on a tiny Portuguese fishing village on the banks of the Potomac River and won, while at about the same time, Thomas Jefferson bet on Charlottesville and lost. Had Jefferson had the good sense to locate his college in a more central location, at the little trading town of Richmond, there would have never been the need – long overdue – for a great university to spring forth in 1968 to enable Richmond to realize its destiny, for a city can not become great without the resources of a great university.

The conservative old-line schools in Virginia – UVA, William and Mary, and Virginia Tech – avoided the arts like the plague, so the need for arts education was answered beginning in 1926. That's when a radical little Richmond school of social work hired Teresa Pollak to teach art classes. Inspired teachers and talented students created their own momentum, and they grew the VCU School of the Arts. I've always thought the VCU central administration was somewhat aghast at this turn of events, but has been helpless in the face of the sheer numbers and quality of our school. We're one of the two or three largest in America, our top graduates can hold their own with the best in the nation – and it was all a haphazard accident.

I've always considered it to be a great honor to be associated with the CA department; it is an island of creative energy, a visionary paradigm of what a university is supposed to be: a place where curious people come together to seek truth.

The faculty in this department are remarkably committed: to their art and design, to the philosophy of this program, and to their students. I have seen visual communications faculties at other schools tear the program apart at the seams with backbiting, infighting, and intolerance. Here a visionary artist like Dick Carlyon works in harmony with practicing designers and/or illustrators like Robert Meganck: Rob Carter, Ben Day and I collaborated on your typography textbook while agreeing that irreconcilable philosophical differences exist between us.

This department has been blessed with brilliant leadership. Our chair John DeMao did a fantastic job making the case for grant funds and alumni contributions for our computer labs. Some of you were a bit ticked off when John Malinoski refused to transfer that questionable course, or made you stick to the letter of the law in meeting degree requirements. But now, you'll take great pride in knowing that everyone who received a BFA in communication arts and design has to pass Malinoski's muster and meet those same high standards.

This department has become a magnet for talented students. Excellence attracts excellence. Each year we receive proof of your capability. This year Kim Norris won honorable mention in the *Print* magazine cover contest, Chad Cameron and Faith Fletcher were selected for the Society of Illustrators national student competition, and we swept the Wolftrap poster competition, with four finalists and the grand prize winner. Thirteen schools entered the Washington Art Directors Club annual student competition; only 25 pieces were selected from over 200 entries: five were from our department.

When I judged the Washington illustrators club exhibit a couple of years ago, one of the officers said, "DC used to be a punk illustration town; suddenly there were all these excellent illustrators all over the place, and they are coming from your school." Another said dryly, "We'll pay you to shut that program down; the competition is getting too stiff." When the design director of the National Geographic Society visited schools all over the country to select a design program for his son, he chose our program.

One thing I do remember about those 60 commencement speakers is they always told a corny joke. Mentioning those other colleges reminds me of one I heard in the graphics lab during basketball season. How many Virginia Tech basketball players does it take to change a light bulb? Answer: only one, but they give him a B in three credits of electrical engineering.

How many UVA undergrads does it take to change a flat tire? Answer: three, one to stand around and brag about how much better their old tire is than anyone else's new tire, one to mix the drink, and one to call daddy to come and fix the flat.

The reason I can't remember what those 60 commencement speakers talked about, not even the jokes, is simple. They failed to understand the power of visual communications, and did not provide a graphic sign or symbol to add an element of tangible, concrete image to their message. That's why you were handed a reproduction of the ancient Chinese yin-yang symbol as you entered the room.

In Chinese cosmology, yang and yin stand for the principle of polarity: heaven and earth, male and female, light and darkness. Yin was conceived as the earth – dark, passive, and absorbing. Yin is present in even numbers, valleys and streams; it is represented by the color orange, the tiger, and a broken line. Yang was conceived as heaven – light, active, and penetrating. Yang is present in odd numbers, the color azure, the dragon, and an unbroken line.

The yin-yang relates to the cyclical passage of time; day yields to night yields to day; summer yields to winter yields to spring; a seeds falls to the ground and dies so it can rise in the fullness of time to create a new plant. The yin-yang became real when a graphic designer – of course, they didn't call her that back in the third century BC – gave tangible symbolic form to the idea. It is a graphic metaphor, a symbol of balance. Visual balance, balance within nature, and balance in the living of a life. An old Japanese proverb advises not to overeat, for eight parts of a full stomach sustain a person; the other two parts sustains the doctor. Balance in all things.

We can expand the metaphorical meanings of the yin-yang, seeing it as a symbol for rightness and wrongness. This mixes the symbols of Asia with the philosophy of Persia, where in the sixth century BC, Zoroaster introduced a concept of duality into religious philosophy, defined forces of good and evil, declaring people's free will to make ethical choices. We can look to the yin-yang as a symbol for how we conduct our relations with other people, and the ethical values we bring to our work as professionals.

Yin-yang is about duality, about conflict, and about balance. I think it is important for visual communicators to contemplate these issues regularly, because visual communications have become a powerful force in contemporary society. Images define our view of our society, and of ourselves. Does television, film, and print media shape people's behavior? Contrary to the periodic protestations of the networks, evidence is abundant. After the first television screening of the movie *Bonnie and Clyde,* a young couple robbed a bank here in Richmond, and were captured holed up with their loot and guns in a local Quality Court motel. The advent of Joe Camel propelled the sale of Camel brand cigarettes among under-aged smokers from less than one percent to about 18 percent. Visual communications have the power to help form and shape our culture for good or ill.

We are living in what Glenn O'Brien in an *Artforum* article called the "Post Credible Era." Daily life in our post-industrial, electronic age has gone beyond that which can be called credible; we accept the incredible, the unbelievable, without batting an eye. Tabloid newspapers scream stories at the Safeway checkout line about the baby who was fed to the dog; tabloid television tells tantalizing tales claiming Marilyn Monroe was murdered by federal agents.

Ross Perot garners nearly 20 percent of the presidential vote in spite of a disinformation campaign alleging that he blew up a coral reef, hired detectives to spy on his employees – and claimed that he pulled out of the race because the Republicans were plotting to disrupt his daughter's wedding. When David Koresh, the leader of the Branch Davidians in Waco, Texas, said he was the second coming of Christ, thousands of Americans switched their television dials from CNN to MTV or Mary Tyler Moore reruns.

Concerned and aware visual communications can be one potent force for restoring credibility to messages and information. Your work can bring clarity, poetry, and truth into the mass communications dialogue.

Yin-yang has been interpreted by Zen Buddhist Philip Kapleau as representing the harmony between people and nature. Each of us should commit ourselves to the environmental movement and to spaceship earth, this fragile blue and green ball, a tiny rock with a wisp of water vapor hurling through space. When Buckminster Fuller spoke here a decade ago; globe and metal ball bearing. The Earth Day theme is, "Think globally, act locally." Everyone on the planet needs to honor this philosophy, especially visual communicators, because our work influences other people in powerful ways.

Maybe we can look at the yin-yang as a metaphor for alternating logic with intuition, for the world asks the visual communicator to be pragmatic and wildly creative at the same time.

You determine the future. In the sophomore lecture class, you may recall we discussed the photographs of Aaron Siskind, who photographed details of urban and natural environments, taking photographs of pure form and texture isolated from the subject matter. After his first one-person exhibition in New York, Siskind was leaving by the elevator, and the critic Clement Greenberg was leaving the exhibition at the same time. "Siskind," Greenberg said, "photography is a narrative art form. You shouldn't be doing what you are doing up there; it's all wrong."

"Listen, Greenberg," Siskind responded. "Let's get something straight. I'm the artist, and you're the critic. I can create anything I damn well please. Your job isn't to tell me what I can or can't do; your job is to write about what I did."

Always remember this. You are the artist. Members of your generation will determine the art and design of the twenty-first century. And you can do anything you want to, as long as you have the courage to create.

Yin-yang is about beginnings and endings, which are really continuums. I've always thought it curious that we complete our education at a commencement, but I guess termination isn't a very upbeat word.

Three years ago, or more, you selected the CA department, and we selected you. (You'll never forget the day of the CA portfolio review.) Your life, and the life of this educational program, have become inseparably bound together. And I do believe that a university department has a life – a spirit, and a mission that transcends any single person, group, or class. Even though you leave, we have been touched and changed by your presence. As your classmates spread around the country and even the world, they will take a bit of you with them, and you leave a part behind, because knowing you and working with you has influenced the faculty as well.

You stayed the course, learned what we had to teach, and now you go forth into the world. One thing I know about the faculty of this department is, we all care deeply about our students and our alumni. We appreciate our relationship with the alumni – they are willing to meet with and advise current students, both when graduates arrive in their area or at our career days; only last month a dozen came to Richmond and met with faculty to discuss the curriculum; alumni contributions to the department have been a significant source of funding for your education. As you leave us today, our relationship does not end; you are merely changing from CA students to CA alumni. We wish you the best, and hope that your dreams and aspirations can come true.

1

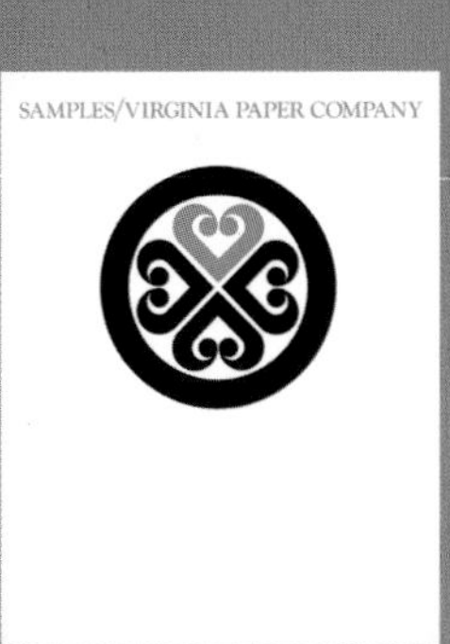

3

4

5

2

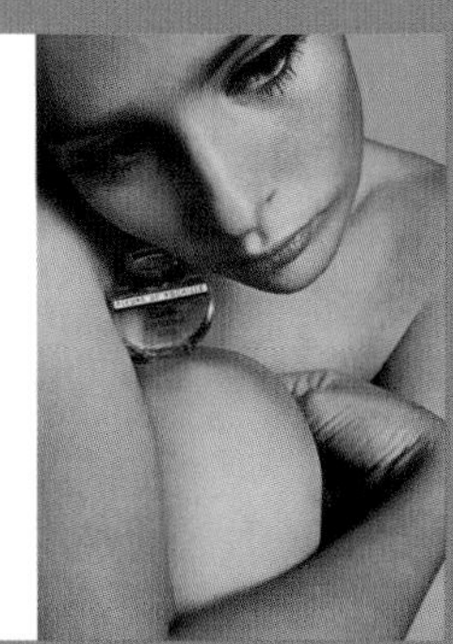

6

1
Brochure, Richmond Symphony. Offset, 4 x 8.31 inches. (1965)

2
Cover for holiday card. Four-color silkscreen, 8.81 x 3.81 inches (1966)

3
Brochure and logo, Virginia Paper Company. Offset, 9.75 x 12.5 inches. (mid-1960s)

4
Dimetapp Extentabs and Allbee with C packages, A.H. Robins Company, Inc. Offset, 3 x 5 inches. (mid-1960s)

5
"Limey" Allbee with C mailer, A.H. Robins Company, Inc. Offset, 8 x 12.06 inches. (mid-1960s)

7

8

9

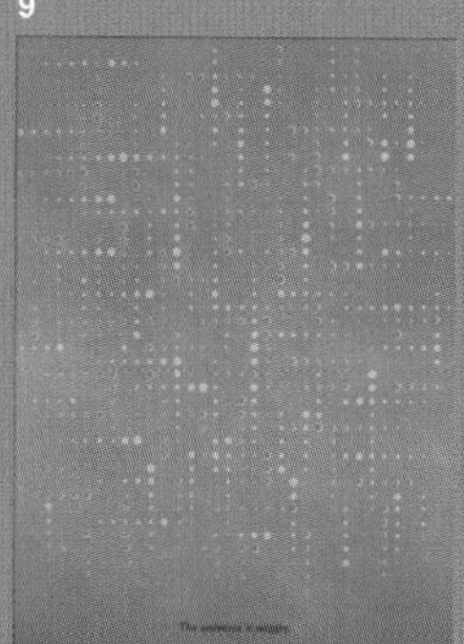

10

11

6
Annual report cover and spread, A.H. Robins Company, Inc. Offset, 17 x 11 inches. (1967)

7
Information packet, Allied Services, Department of Health, Education, and Welfare. Offset, 9.5 x 12 inches. (early 1970s)

8
Book cover, *Pattern Poetry.* Offset, 5.81 x 7.81 inches. (1976)

9
Logo designs. Various dimensions. (1960s – 1980s)

10
"The Universe is Wiggly," experimental poster. Silkscreen, 18.75 x 23.25 inches. (early 1970s)

11
"yesterday/tomorrow," experimental poster. Silkscreen, 18.75 x 23.25 inches. (early 1970s)

Landmarks of Book Design, Seventh of a Series: *American Typefounders Specimen Book and Catalogue, 1923*

From *Print* Vol. 48, No. 1 (Jan/Feb 1994)

This remarkable publication documents the profound influence on typography of America's greatest metal typefoundry.

Chaos and economic dislocation are stalking the typography industry.... Radical new technologies are rendering obsolete the old methods for setting type.... Highly skilled typesetters fear massive unemployment.... Once-prosperous companies confront bankruptcy, cutthroat pricing, and pirating of typeface designs.... Excess production capacity is causing havoc.

Although this scenario sounds like the sort of turmoil caused by the computer revolution that collapsed type houses into service bureaus and vaporized thousands of typesetters' jobs, it describes events that occurred a century ago. During the 1880s and 1890s, technological advances in printing dramatically changed the printing industry. Photoengraving – the use of photochemical processes to create line engravings, halftones, and lithographic plates from the artist's original work – replaced the labor-intensive, handmade printing plate. High-speed, steam-powered rotary presses caused the price of printing to plunge. In 1896, the press time required to print a thousand three-sheet posters dropped to 16 per cent of the press time needed in 1845, while labor costs plunged to 10 percent of their 1852 level. Wage costs for printing 10,000 copies of a 64-page magazine had been $302.50 on a hand press in 1852; by 1896, the same press run required a mere $4.63 in wages.

Linotype and Monotype machines reduced typesetting time and costs dramatically as well. The February 1899 issue of the *Inland Printer* reported that Frank Bevan, Linotype operator for the *Sydney (Australia) Daily Telegraph,* had set 11 full columns of type in one eight-hour shift; it would have required about two full weeks of hand composition to set this amount of type. Estimates of time and wage savings by keyboard composition vary widely; however, an 1896 Bureau of Labor study showed an eight-fold reduction in typesetting time and a ten-fold reduction in labor costs. A typesetting job that required 148 hours of labor at a cost of $41.60 when set by hand was completed by a keyboard-operated typesetting machine in 17 hours and 20 minutes, requiring a labor expense of $4.40. But dire predictions of widespread unemployment did not materialize, for this was a period of rapid economic expansion.

When the production costs of books, magazines, and newspapers plunged downward, a spiral of lower prices resulted, which created higher sales: This increased circulation fueled more advertising, thereby permitting lower prices and even greater production economy, spurring even higher circulation, etc., etc. Rather than face extinction, hand-set metal typography gained an extended life producing display type, especially advertising headlines, as typography became segmented. Linotype and Monotype machines were used to set body copy quickly and economically; hand-set metal type was generally used for display material.

The type foundries manufacturing handset metal type were hard hit as they lost the market for text type. Their industry was already suffering from excess production capacity and price wars that had pushed prices below production costs. There were too many type foundries, and middlemen played them off each other. Risky credit terms were used to garner sales; for example, entire typesetting departments were outfitted for printers with insufficient capital or business. Rapid depreciation of type prices rendered the value of printers' type stock – critical as loan collateral and insurance valuations – unstable.

Rumors of efforts to establish a monopoly were rampant, especially after a committee formed in New York in 1890 at a meeting of type founders prepared a report proposing the establishment of one large corporation to purchase all American foundries as a method to save the industry from financial ruin. On September 8, 1891, newspapers reported that within 24 hours an English syndicate would buy out all major American type foundries, and would then proceed to drive the smaller firms out of business. Apparently, the English financiers were unable to raise the necessary funds and the deal collapsed.

Of the 23 major type houses operating at the time, all but four or five were losing money; in an attempt to bring stability to the industry, 14 prominent type foundries, on February 8, 1892, formed the American Type Founders Company. Eventually, the number of foundries in the trust rose to almost two dozen, including most major American type foundries.

Printers, along with smaller foundries that did not initially join American Type Founders, feared a monopoly that would drive up prices and force out competitors. Obsolete and inefficient foundries joining the trust were closed immediately and replaced with sales offices; soon, all production was consolidated in a large manufacturing plant in Jersey City, New Jersey, across the Hudson River from Manhattan.

Leaders of the new trust reassuringly informed customers of ATF's plans to establish stable and uniform prices and adopt the point-and-pica system of measurement as a universal standard. The company promised to reform typeface design and the presentation of specimens. A first step was culling the bulky specimen books of the merged foundries to offer only the finest typeface designs, while banishing hundreds of useless, poorly designed, and obsolete fonts. In 1892, Joseph W. Phinney of Boston's Dickinson foundry, who was widely regarded as America's leading authority on type design, became the principal advisor in developing ATF's typeface library. Three years later, Phinney initiated a revolution in American typographic sensibilities, turning from Victorian ornamental designs to typefaces based on historical models.

American Type Founders kept its promise to reform typeface design and issue useful specimen sheets and books. The fragmented efforts of the separate foundries in typeface design yielded to a centralized type designing department established to create a steady stream of redesigned and new typefaces and related graphic material.

The typographic specimen book reached its high-water mark in 1923, when American Type Founders published 60,000 copies of *Specimen Book and Catalogue 1923.* This formidable 6¾"-by-10" volume, 1,148 pages and fully 3" thick, cost $300,000 to produce, or about $5 per copy. Three decades of accomplishment are documented through its presentation of type specimens, rules and borders, decorative material, and equipment.

Over 300 typefaces have a specimen page with a brief showing of every available size; the complete font is shown in a 14-to-18-point size range. In fonts with only a few sizes, demonstration layouts appear on the page. Other typefaces have full pages of sample designs, while major type families have lavish, fold-out inserts showing the fonts used with appropriate borders and ornaments. Two-dozen such inserts are printed in two or three colors on colored paper stock. These express the retro neoclassical design approach dominant in American typographic design during the first quarter of the 20th century.

Wadsworth A. Parker, who had been in charge of specimen design and printing at the Bruce Foundry, became manager of ATF's printing specimen department. As the company began to honor its promise to improve specimen materials, this department became widely regarded as one of the finest letterpress printing operations in the world. The craft in the production of *Specimen Book and Catalogue 1923* pays homage to this excellence. Intricate borders and repeat patterns of ornaments were set and printed with remarkable skill.

Specimen sections for major type families include inserts printed with colored inks on colored papers to demonstrate design possibilities

Spread from the *American Typefounders Specimen Book and Catalogue* (1923)

combining the typefaces with other graphic material. These coalesced and influenced the design approach for American job printing, publications, and advertising of the 1920s, which emphasized decoration, symmetry, classical typefaces, and a "traditional" feeling. The Modern design movement, with its asymmetrical page layouts, sans-serif type, and geometric forms, did not become a significant force in American design until late in the decade.

Specimen Book and Catalogue 1923 is an enduring monument not only to Parker and his staff, but also to ATF's director of general manufacturing, Lynn Boyd Benton, and his son, Morris Fuller Benton, who was hired in 1897 to set up the type designing department after his graduation from Cornell University with a mechanical engineering degree.

Landmarks of Book Design, Seventh of a Series: *American Typefounders Specimen Book and Catalogue, 1923*

Lynn Boyd Benton, half-owner of Milwaukee's Benton, Waldo & Company type foundry, had achieved fame in 1885 by inventing a matrix-engraving machine to automate the laborious process of hand-cutting the steel punches that were stamped into copper to make the matrices used to cast type. Before Benton invented his machine, a punch had to be hand-cut for every size of each character in a font. With Benton's machine, the artist had to make only one master drawing of each character. These were enlarged by a pantograph-like device capable of expanding, condensing, italicizing, or back-slanting characters, or making them lighter or heavier as required to compensate for enlargement or reduction. The enlarged drawing was scored onto a wax-coated metal plate; this was then electrotyped to make a pattern for Benton's machine.

Benton's machine was leased to Linotype and Monotype to manufacture the matrices for their keyboard typesetters; in addition, the speed and economy it introduced into manufacturing hand-set metal type made possible ATF's prolific introduction of typefaces. After ATF was formed in 1892, Benton, Waldo & Company's foundry was disassembled and replaced with a Milwaukee sales office. Benton's mechanical genius earned him a seat on the board of directors and the position of director of the general manufacturing department.

When Lynn Boyd Benton's son, Morris, was hired as director of the type designing department, he was assigned the awesome task of sorting through the thick specimen books of the 23 foundries absorbed into ATF and reducing thousands of fonts into a unified and manageable typeface library. His responsibilities were primarily technical at first because the chaotic variety of sizes and styles from the merged foundries had to be standardized using the American Point System of typographic measurement, adopted in 1886 but only partly implemented by the industry. As the company stabilized after the upheavals and plant closings of the merger, Morris Benton became increasingly interested in typeface design. During his career, he designed over 180 typefaces, making him one of the most prolific typeface designers of all time. Fonts by Benton and his staff were manufactured as hand-set metal type by ATF, and many were also issued by Linotype and Monotype for keyboard typesetting.

Although Morris Benton is often credited with developing the concept of type families, one can more appropriately state that he furthered and elaborated upon this concept; type families have existed since the mid 1700s, when the French typeface designer Pierre Simon Fournier le Jeune created a variety of weights and widths that could be used together. Benton took the type family concept a step further by creating extended lines of related typefaces, including Cheltenham, Century, Cloister Old Style, and Goudy.

About the sample layouts in *Specimen Book and Catalogue 1923* suggesting design possibilities, the foreword says, "[T]he examples of composition in this book were designed for the use of printers, as they may be found adaptable to their needs. The compositions are simple and practical in design. All of them may be duplicated without difficulty, with easily adjusted materials and without waste of time." *Specimen Book and Catalogue 1923* became a major resource for 1920s compositors and layout artists; it was part history lesson, part model book, and a source of ideas for using type, ornaments, and other graphic materials.

American Type Founders and Morris Benton played a major role in the development of enduring classical revivals, beginning with Benton's version of Bodoni, whose first fonts were issued in 1907. The inspiration for reviving outstanding typefaces from earlier epochs was initiated by William Morris at his Kelmscott Press, continued by the printers of the Private Press fine printing movement, then expanded into the mainstream of graphic design by Morris Benton and other designers working for type foundries. In 1908, ATF established its Typographic Library and Museum under the direction of typographic historian Henry Lewis Bullen. By 1923, this facility had acquired over 12,000 volumes of type specimens, including masterpieces of early and modern printed books and works on all aspects of typography and printing; it was the most comprehensive graphic arts research center in America.

Bullen urged Morris Benton to design a new version of Garamond. Specimens attributed to Claude Garamond – wrongly, it turns out – were selected as the prototype. (Beatrice Warde, the eminent scholar of typography, later proved these specimens to have been designed by French printer Jean Jannon, who was influenced by Garamond.) T. M. Cleland, a masterly and classical graphic designer, was retained to assist in the project and design an extensive series of borders and ornaments based on the graceful French Renaissance decorations found in books and buildings. ATF's Garamond launched an international revival of Garamond typefaces that still continues.

Typeface designer Frederic Goudy became art director of Lanston Monotype in 1920 and immediately produced a version named Garamont, adopting the spelling variation used in some chronicles of French printing. Linotype Garamond was released in 1925. Its design was a bit heavy-handed and Linotype designed a lighter, more graceful Garamond No. 3 soon afterwards. The Linotype specimen book stated that Linotype Garamond No. 3 was "reproduced primarily for advertising typographers to meet the conception of Garamond which has become established in their field." Translation: ATF's Garamond is so popular as a headline face that we have copied it to permit designers to have a matching style set on Linotype equipment for the body text.

Earlier, Goudy had created a typeface for ATF for which he received $1,500 in payment. There was no agreement for payment of royalties or a commission based on sales. ATF named the face Goudy Old Style and released it in 1915. Almost immediately, it became one of ATF's top-selling fonts. Morris Benton, true to his practice of producing extended families, designed a series of variations including Goudy Title, c. 1917; Goudy Bold, 1920; Goudy Catalogue, 1921; Goudy Handtooled, designed by Benton with Wadsworth A. Parker, 1922; and Goudy Extrabold, 1927.

Goudy Old Style made its creator a celebrity in the graphic arts, yet one can well understand his chagrin at receiving such modest compensation for one of the most widely used typefaces of the 20th century. Equally disturbing to Goudy was not being afforded an opportunity to design the other typefaces that bear his name. In Goudy's autobiography, he tells about a tour of the ATF plant by members of the American Institute of Graphic Arts. Bullen was serving as tour guide and paused at a casting machine, where he told the group that one of the fellow AIGA members had designed the type being cast. "Here is where Goudy goes down to posterity," Bullen proclaimed to the group, "while the American Type Founders Company goes down to prosperity."

Cloister Old Style established the standard for 20th-century revivals of the type designed by Nicolas Jenson in Venice around 1470. Morris Benton kept the tall capitals, minimal contrast between thick strokes and thin strokes, and subtle design attributes such as the diagonal cross-stroke on the lower-case *e* with a serif-like protrusion on the right. Since Jenson's typeface was designed a quarter-century before italic types were invented, it had no italic; therefore, Benton had to invent an italic for his revival. The resulting Cloister Old Style Italic has gently rounded letters at a 12-degree stroke angle and is far more compatible with the roman face than are most italics based on Renaissance models. As with ATF's Garamond, Cloister Old Style has abundant accompanying decorative initials, borders, and ornaments to satisfy 1920s Americans' passion for historical, Renaissance-derived designs.

One of the most widely used type families during the early 20th century, Cheltenham, was designed by the prominent architect Bertram Grosvener Goodhue for Ingalls Kimball's Cheltenham Press in New York. It has somewhat condensed lower-case letters but slightly expanded capitals, heavy strokes, and flat, stubby slab serifs with a gentle tapered transition from the stroke to the serif, similar to the serifs found on Clarendon fonts from the mid-19th century. Goodhue believed that the top halves of letters were more legible than the bottom halves; he responded to this theory with an eccentric decision to make Cheltenham's ascenders extremely tall and its descenders very short. Goodhue's original design had serious flaws; for example, the lower-case *r* popped up above the meanline and the upper-case *s* was too large. After Linotype introduced the design, ATF acquired rights and released it in hand-set metal in 1903. Morris Benton and his staff greatly improved the overall design of the face. Cheltenham – it quickly gained the nickname "Chelt" in composing rooms – has a warm, slightly offbeat character that made it an immediate favorite with advertising designers. The type designing department churned out an ever-growing Cheltenham family of expanded, condensed, bold, outline, and shaded fonts that eventually numbered over two dozen. *Specimen Book and Catalogue 1923* includes specimens of 23 Cheltenham fonts.

Cheltenham remains controversial almost a century after its introduction. In the 1937 edition of his two-volume *Printing Types: Their History, Form, and Use,* Daniel B. Updike, the conservative scholar of typography, said of

Landmarks of Book Design, Seventh of a Series: *American Typefounders Specimen Book and Catalogue, 1923*

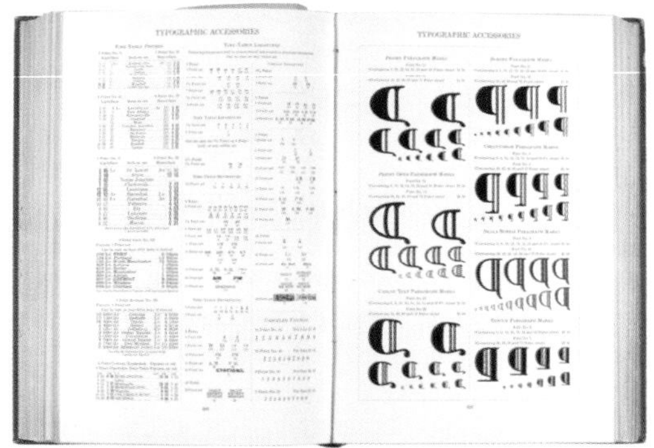

Spread from the *American Typefounders Specimen Book and Catalogue* (1923)

Cheltenham, "Owing to certain eccentricities of form, it cannot be read for any comfortable length of time. Its capitals are better than its lower-case, which is too perpendicular in effect – a fault appropriate to so distinguished an architect of Gothic buildings!" However, even Updike was partially won over, for he added, "It is, however, an exceedingly handsome letter for ephemeral printing."

In addition to the extended type families, many typefaces in *Specimen Book and Catalogue 1923* are available in only one weight, sometimes – but not always – accompanied by an italic version. These include Announcement Roman and Italic with dainty special characters that suggest lettering by hand, Bookman Old Style, and Souvenir.

Bookman has a complex provenance. To meet the need for a bolder face to use with their old-style fonts, the Miller & Richard type foundry of Edinburgh, Scotland, in 1858 issued a typeface much like Bookman, called Old Style Antique.

This new typeface found wide acceptance, leading many type foundries in Europe and America to design their own versions. When the merger into ATF occurred, the new conglomerate found itself with thousands of Old Style Antique matrices. After Wadsworth A. Parker chose the version from the old Bruce foundry, he recommended the name Bookman and the addition of Bookman's hoard of swash characters and ligatures that have caused that face to be praised and damned by typographic mavens for almost a century.

National Oldstyle, designed in 1916 by Frederic W. Goudy and manufactured by ATF, was created in response to a request for a typeface based on lettering commissioned from Goudy at the turn of the century for Nabisco (then called National Biscuit Company). *Specimen Book and Catalogue 1923* proclaimed National Oldstyle to be "a typeface of singular vigor and beauty which takes high rank among the types of distinction." Goudy held a dimmer view, saying, "As a display face it probably compares favorably with many others we could do without."

Souvenir appears as a single round-serifed typeface without an italic, stuck near the back of the type specimen section between Pin Print and Motto. Little used in the 1920s, Souvenir had its hour of fame in the 1970s when International Typeface Corporation acquired rights to the face from ATF and released it as a family of four weights with matching italics drawn by Ed Benguiat; Souvenir became one of the most widely used advertising typefaces of that decade.

The sans-serif section of *Specimen Book and Catalogue 1923* is titled Gothics, the curious name given to type without serifs by 19th-century American type foundries. Apparently, when the first sans serifs were released in England early in the 19th century, Americans associated their dense black color with "Old English" type based on manuscript lettering of the Gothic period. ATF's Gothic section included Morris Benton's Alternate Gothic, Franklin Gothic, and News Gothic, all still available today. These were accompanied by sans-serif fonts specifically designed for screaming newspaper headlines, including American Extra Condensed.

The Century family offers an interesting case study in ATF's penchant for extending a typeface into a complex line. Lynn Boyd Benton cut the punches for the original Century typeface in 1894 in collaboration with the famous printer Theodore L. DeVinne. Their goal was a blacker, more legible face than the thin, anemic text type used by *Century* magazine. The letters were slightly condensed for an efficient character count on the publications' two-column page format. Century Expanded was designed by Morris Benton around 1900 to conform to a system of typographical width specifications. In 1915, he designed Century Schoolbook as an extremely readable typeface for school textbooks; legibility and perception research guided its development. Stroke weights, character heights, and spaces between and within letters were carefully determined by designers who used vast amounts of research data in a quest for the world's most legible typeface for beginning readers. Thick and thin stroke weights are somewhat heavier than most serifed fonts and there are generous white spaces between and within the letters. The identifying characteristics of each letter are clear and even slightly exaggerated. The clarity and legibility of Century Schoolbook make it a "user friendly" typeface. It has maintained great popularity since its introduction, not only for educational materials, but for advertising, book design, and corporate work as well.

Following the 581 pages of type specimens, there is a 36-page section of typographic accessories including fractions, braces, printing hands, and perpetual calendars. The highlight of this section is an eight-page yellow-and-black foldout presenting perpetual calendars set in Cheltenham.

Colored papers are used for full-page section titles. Script, gothic shaded, and body types are relegated to small sections in the book, but one section of 179 pages is devoted exclusively to decorative material. It contains an incredible variety of borders, ornaments, and initials used with typefaces in the demonstration designs throughout the book. This section features a wide assortment of spot illustrations – the early 20th- century equivalent of clip art. These small cast-metal pictures were used to illustrate advertisements and job printing. Holidays, vocations, and sports, including golf and trap shooting, were among the available subjects.

ATF commissioned graphic material from leading graphic designers of the period. Ornaments and illustrations by Will Bradley, who designed typefaces, decorative material, and promotional booklets for the company, pepper the section. Bradley's paragraph marks appear on the page with Frederic Goudy's paragraph marks. Bradley's Wayside ornaments, first created in the late 1890s when Bradley owned and operated the Wayside Press in Massachusetts, share a page with a series of figures derived from the work of the English children's-book author and illustrator Kate Greenaway. The wide variety of initials includes special designs for major typefaces, including Caslon, Bodoni, and Cloister Old Style.

The back of the book consists of a 70-page section of brass rules, followed by a 252-page catalog of printing presses and equipment and an 18-page index.

American typography would not have been the same without the incredible accomplishments of American Type Founders. Its legacy includes standardization of the industry, raising the caliber of typeface revivals, and creation of a host of original typefaces that are now part of the universal typographic vocabulary. This contribution is eloquently documented in *Specimen Book and Catalogue 1923.* In 1934, ATF published another typeface catalog, titled *Book of American Types.* Comparison of this 207-page, 1/2"-thick volume containing about 200 fonts with the 1,148-page, 3"-thick *Specimen Book and Catalogue 1923* containing over 300 fonts and thousands of ornamental items offers dramatic testimony to the changes in typography and the American economy. The old typeface standards are still present, joined by moderne Art Deco–era faces, such as Bernhard Modern and Broadway. But the lavish ornaments and demonstration designs are gone. *Book of American Types* is printed in black ink, except for five pages in the front that have spot printing of blue ink and four pages in the back showing two-color initials with spot red added.

ATF remained America's premier metal type founder until the rise of phototype in the 1960s ended the reign of metal type. In 1941 – almost as a harbinger of the foundry's eventual decline – it sold its priceless library of printing and typography to Columbia University. ATF continued as a small company making metal type for hobby printers and punches for leather craft work, until it was forced into bankruptcy in 1993. On August 24, 1993, its remaining matrices and equipment were sold at auction. Although the era of metal type has ended, American Type Founders' legacy of typeface design continues, preserved in the masterly *Specimen Book and Catalogue 1923.*

1

2

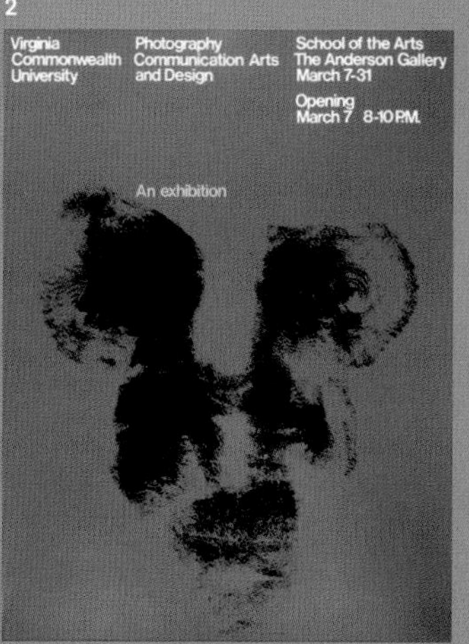

3

1
MFA promotional folder, School of the Arts, Virginia Commonwealth University. Offset, 27 x 10.75 inches. (1978)
2
Poster, "ART." Silkscreen, 23 x 17.5 inches. (Late 1970s)
3
Exhibition poster, Anderson Gallery, School of the Arts, Virginia Commonwealth University. Silkscreen, 17.5 x 23 inches. (Late 1970s)

4
Bicentennial stamp proposals. Color-key presentation, 1.56 x 1, and 1 x 1.56 inches. (1976)
5
Brochure cover, "Letterforms," high school teaching aid. Offset, 8.5 x 10.56 inches. (1978)

6
Book covers, Higher Education Leadership & Management Society, Inc. Offset, 5.93 x 9.18 inches. (1978 and 1979)

4

Letterforms.
A visual awareness project for high school art classes.

5

6

Tribute to an Unrepentant Modernist

From *Print* Vol. 48, No. 1 (Jan/Feb 1994)

The career of Tomás Gonda spanned five countries and five decades, but his contributions are not widely recognized.

A small number of designers become well known during their lifetimes; many others do not, in spite of producing exemplary work, and their contributions are not widely recognized. Tomás Gonda (1926–1988) did not achieve renown in a career spanning five decades that took him from his native Hungary to Argentina, Germany, Italy, and the U.S. Five countries helped shape his work, but a more profound rationale – commitment to visual form and a sense of integrity that he refused to compromise – underpinned his oeuvre. His idealism consistently led to disappointment, pushing him to move to yet another country every eight to ten years to begin anew in another socioeconomic climate.

Tomás Gonda clearly belongs to the post–World War II generation of European designers who embraced geometric form and the rational application of design to purpose. No person is an island, especially if he or she has access to *Graphis* or *Gebrauchsgraphik,* and Gonda's evolution reflects the environments in which he worked as well as the evolving sensibilities of postwar Modern design.

Gonda was born and educated in Hungary, where he studied at the Budapest Academy of Fine Arts with Álmos Jaschik. His excellent drawing skills are evidenced in 1943 pencil illustrations for traditional Hungarian folk tales, done when he was 17 years old. These drawings show great potential, and cause one to wonder what would

Cover for *Le Alpi e l'Europa.*
Design: Tomás Gonda
(1973)

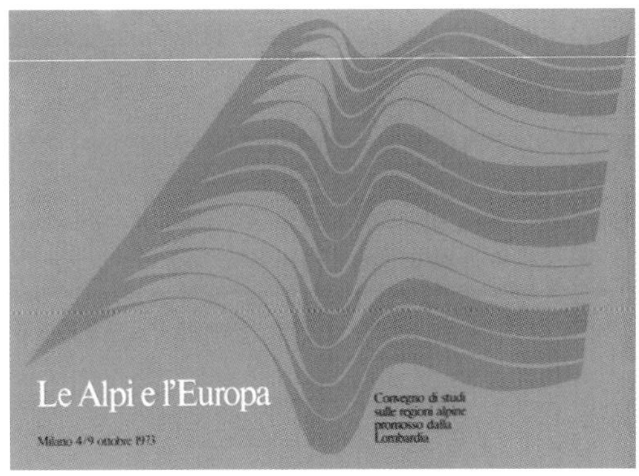

have happened had Gonda chosen to pursue traditional illustration or painting instead of moving in the direction of Modernist design. The early illustrations project an openness of space and simplicity of form characteristic of his later work.

The Hungarian economy was devastated by the war; graphic design, printing, advertising, and professional schools virtually vanished. Hand-painted comps for a photography exhibition and vacation resort from Gonda's early twenties reflect a mature conceptual understanding of the form and imagery prevalent in European Modern design of the 1930s and 1940s. Since design opportunities were virtually nil, most of Gonda's professional work from 1945 until 1948 was photographic.

As Soviet control over Eastern Europe tightened, Olivetti, employer of Gonda's father, offered relocation to Argentina in 1948. Tomás joined his parents in that country, where a stronger economy enabled him to practice graphic design. But graphic design was not well defined as a professional discipline in Argentina, and in fact, Gonda helped establish the profession there. Pharmaceutical graphics for Gador Laboratories, promotional materials for Cuyo printers, and various publishing, magazine design, and exhibition-catalog assignments for cultural clients were often limited to forms and imagery he could construct at his drafting table. A support structure of production services, photographers, and illustrators did not exist, and in 1950s Argentina, printing was characterized by coarse papers, low halftone resolution, and poor color registration. Later, Gonda lamented that he was 40 years old before he received his first full-color assignment. In 1956, he opened his own design office in Buenos Aires, and his typographic work, such as a series of annual covers for a number guide for machinery, received international attention.

In 1958, Gonda was asked to become a design associate at the Hochschule für Gestaltung Ulm (HfG), the School of Design at Ulm, Germany. With aspirations to be the new Bauhaus, the HfG sought a design language based on rational and functional concerns, replacing the subjective vision of the individual with a universal objectivity. It made major contributions to design education, introducing semiotics and the hegemony of science over design into the curriculum. But the HfG rejected continuance of the Bauhaus in a literal sense. That would have meant restoring the past, and HfG had a progressive, down-with-convention attitude. It addressed the specific historical situation of its time, applying postwar technology to the needs of contemporary life.

Institutes for Industrial Design and for Industrialized Building undertook large design projects for industry. Though separately run, they were closely associated with the HfG educational program. Strong relations with German corporations allowed the school to play a role in the re-emergence of German manufacturing and product design during the postwar reconstruction. The HfG sought a new industrial culture.

The Institute for Industrial Design was divided into development groups headed by faculty members. Gonda joined Development Group Five, led by Otl Aicher, which created corporate images, printed graphics, advertising, packaging, and exhibitions for clients including Lufthansa, Braun, Herman Miller, and Wilkhahn Sitzmöbel. The visual identification programs made a major contribution to the development of grid-based corporate design systems with every detail carefully calculated and specified.

The influential Lufthansa program was detailed right down to the packets of cream and sugar served with coffee on planes. After considering a new trademark, the design team retained the crane symbol that Lufthansa had used since the 1930s, but placed it in a circle and made it subordinate to the signature. Grid structures were developed for every conceivable advertising and informational graphic possibility; paper formats, including dimensions and folds, were reduced to an economical number. The colors used – yellow and blue – were totally unlike any other airline's colors.

Gonda's trademark for Wilkhahn Sitzmöbel evoked the fundamental essence of a chair – the major product of this German furniture manufacturer – while serving as the basic modular unit used to develop grid structures for all Wilkhahn graphics. Bright orange and olive green were selected for the identity program.

In addition to its application to systematic design programs, Gonda's personal vision emerged in posters for exhibitions and films, and in graphic ephemera such as typographic greeting cards. His typographic work often showed an almost playful interest in form. He demonstrated a fascination with the square, and explored sequence, both in series of related designs and in sequential forms on a single surface. Gonda taught courses in the Ulm visual communications program from 1963 until 1966, and in 1966 he accepted a one-year appointment at Ohio State University's industrial design department.

The HfG received financial support from the privately endowed Scholl foundation, industrial commissions, and public appropriations. Its politics were left-of-center, based on an idealistic sense of designing for humanity, not just for the affluent and powerful. While the West German government supported the Vietnam War, HfG became the site of antiwar protests. Eventually, political controversies, hostile press coverage, and devastating budget cuts led to the school's closing on December 5, 1968.

In 1967, as the Ulm situation became untenable, Gonda left Ulm for Milan, Italy, to become design director of the Rinascente Upim department store chain. After a decade of the production limitations in Argentina, followed by ten years within the rigorous programmed methodology of the HfG, Gonda felt liberated and his creativity soared. In his posters, he brought vibrant, sensual color to elemental formal arrangements using photographic images as symbols. His mature work is characterized by a joy of color and form, combined with an ability to bring a sensuous fullness rarely found in minimalist work. Simple objects gain a symbolic richness.

American design schools, including Carnegie Mellon, Ohio State, and the University of Cincinnati, developed design curricula influenced by the Swiss schools. William S. Huff, a guest instructor in the HfG basic course from 1963 to 1968, brought Gonda to Carnegie Mellon to design Huff's series of booklets on symmetry.

In 1972, Gonda returned to Italy to become design consultant to Pirelli, a manufacturer of tires, sports equipment, flooring, paper, and office machinery. This proved a good match, for Gonda's graphics projected advanced technology and a restrained dynamic. He developed sophisticated new ways to promote Pirelli products, using complex geometric forms as imagery and as informational graphics. A prolific photographer, he used scores of his color transparencies in Pirelli printing paper specimens.

The astounding volume of work Gonda produced during about six years with Pirelli included a steady stream of innovative formats for Pirelli calendars, conference graphics, and a stunning booklet for trail bikes. Photography in cinematic layouts conveys the essence of the trail-bike experience; the typography is pure sound poetry – or noise, depending on one's attitude toward motor bikes. During this prolific period, Gonda even found time to redesign the format for *Casabella,* Italy's oldest architectural magazine, combining a Modernist grid with elegant serif typography.

In 1977, Gonda left Pirelli and realized a life-long ambition to live in the U.S. He joined the Plumb Design Group in the New York City area and designed a trademark and comprehensive visual identity program for the Connecticut-based copier company Savin. The Savin logo used subtle letterform construction to create a unique word image in a visual identity program spelled out with the same elaborate detail found in the programs for Lufthansa and Wilkhahn.

In 1978, Gonda launched his own New York–based studio, Gonda Design. His clients included IBM – to whom he was recommended by Paul Rand – Champion Paper, and Booz Allen Hamilton. IBM was one of several clients with whom Gonda developed conflicts, however. He possessed a very low tolerance of mediocrity in any form, and adherence to his principles was far more important than good client relationships. The bottom line was never Gonda's highest priority, and he was willing to tell prestigious, highly profitable clients to go away.

In 1985, two decades after Gonda and his Ulm colleague Nick Roericht first worked on Lufthansa's visual identification program, they were asked to provide updated designs. Gonda proposed aircraft tails in the colors of the German flag and designed stunning posters featuring an exuberant diagonal shift across photographs of German landmarks. Unfortunately, these proposals were never realized. For Xerox Corporation, he designed more user-friendly control panels for copiers. Icons and symbols made copier equipment easier to operate. The resulting designs have proven a blessing – not only to users of Xerox equipment, but also users of competitive copiers, who embraced Gonda's underlying principles.

By 1985, Gonda's reputation in American design was growing as works such as his Tanagraphics calendar – with die-cuts in colored paper stock creating a new design for each month – were admired. His self-published posters made strong editorial statements, including "In Gold We Trust." Throughout his career, Gonda designed personal greeting cards, notably his annual New Year's cards. These were often explorations of pure type and form. An exquisite personal project was a 5 5/8"- square booklet entitled "Impressions," presenting photographs Gonda took during a trip to Japan with his friend Jim Miho. In the text, Gonda wrote:

Japanese books, objects, and friends always found a way into my life. Like something that was happening again, I visited Japan this past summer.

The following pages, a partial documentation of this trip, is to be shared with my friends. It confirms many of my dearly held beliefs and convictions regarding what constitutes excellence in design, what is beauty: for me it is a source of joy and inspiration.

Gonda saw Japan as a remarkable manifestation of functional and esthetic design used in every aspect of daily living, not merely as superficial decoration or as a marketing tool. Gonda was so impressed by Japanese design that he considered moving there. He wrote:

The echo, not the sound
the shadow, not the object
the restraint
the simplicity
the discipline
the improvisation
the minimal
the essence.

Personal works, including sketchbooks, paintings, prints, banner design, and photography, played an important role in Gonda's evolution. His paintings were a continuing study of form and color, as his photographs were a constant dialogue with his environment (he left thousands of carefully boxed and labeled color transparencies). Explorations of the square and serial art were echoed in graphic design projects. Gonda loved and was fascinated by the square; he felt its harmony and wholeness to be an end in itself

Gonda's final personal works were a series of collages made from receipts, packaging, and printed ephemera collected during his travels to China and Japan. These have an openness and vibrant optimism in poignant counterpoint to the illness he was experiencing, although he was not yet aware of its seriousness. Gonda had always used his left hand to steady his right hand when working. A loss of control over his left hand was an early symptom of a brain tumor. Tomás Gonda died in New York on Saturday, March 5,1988.

His close friend from Buenos Aires, Carlos Mosquera, wrote after Gonda's death: "Tom was genuine. He did not accommodate differences with the world. He believed in true professional quality… in the ethic of design. Everything was for him, unavoidably, a moment or an act of design…." ⊷

Landmarks of Book Design, Eighth of a Series: *The Bald Soprano*

From *Print* Vol. 48, No. 5 (Sept/Oct 1994)

In 1964, Ionesco's revolutionary play was reinvented on the printed page by means of graphic experiments far ahead of their time.

In 1948, Eugéne Ionesco decided to learn English by copying sentences from a conversational manual. The Rumanian playwright, who was working in Paris as a proofreader, became fascinated by the stilted, commonplace phrases of the characterless characters in the *Assimil Manual* who dutifully told one another that the floor is below, the ceiling is above, and there are seven days in the week. Although Ionesco had always hated theatrical plays because he felt embarrassed for the actors, this dialogue prompted him to write a one-act "antiplay," *The Bald Soprano.* Two proper middle-class English couples, Mr. and Mrs. Smith and their visitors Mr. and Mrs. Martin, are joined by a maid named Mary and a Fire Chief in an encounter defying time and logic. These characters chat, argue, and restate the obvious until it becomes inane, exposing the inadequacies of verbal communication. The puns and nonsense of vaudeville humor bob along the surface of a deeply serious message about the dilemmas of contemporary life. In a decade scarred by World War II, the Holocaust, atomic weapons, and the Cold War, Ionesco realized, "One can speak without thinking; for this we have clichés, automatic expressions."[1]

As he contemplated the deep mysteries of the universe and of life, he concluded that "science is not knowledge, rhetoric and philosophy are nothing but words, sets of words, strings of words…. When we have learnt everything, or if we could learn everything, we should still know nothing."[2]

Spreads from Ionesco's play, *The Bald Soprano.* Design: Robert Massin (1964)

After *The Bald Soprano* was first performed, in 1950, it inspired a revolution in dramatic techniques and helped inaugurate the Theater of the Absurd. This theatrical direction of the 1950s and 60s was based on a belief that the human condition made no sense, and that European and American dramatists were presenting a vain struggle to find meaning in life. The naturalistic conventions of the theater that were used to tell stories and offer social messages were supplanted by surreal, nonrepresentational techniques representing human powerlessness. Plot was eliminated; the traditional ending or summation was replaced by a wandering, often circular movement in time.

The French text for *La Cantatrice Chauve* was first published in 1954, and the English translation, entitled *The Bald Soprano,* appeared in 1956. Characters shouting and talking simultaneously, actors facing away from the audience, and other expressive aspects of Ionesco's drama were lost when his play script was printed in monotonous lines of type on gray pages. This breakthrough play needed the intervention of a graphic designer capable of reinventing Ionesco's dramatic techniques on the printed page.

In 1964, Robert Massin, the art director of Editions Gallimard, took on the project. Acting as "a sort of stage director," Massin translated "the atmosphere, the movement, the speeches, and the silences in the play, trying at the same time to convey an idea of duration of time and space on the stage by the simple device of the interplay of image and text."[3] The unprecedented brilliance of Massin's design can be fully appreciated only when one looks at it in relation to the play's meaning and content. Graphic invention was not an end in itself but grew out of a serious effort to understand and interpret the play.

Massin's design called upon the techniques of the comic strip and cinema to express time and sequence. The actual faces of the actors in Cohen's photographs "acquired the importance of an ideogram"[4] by becoming symbols identifying the speaker. High-contrast photography reduced the actors to black shapes on the white page. This technique robbed the characters of their individuality, turning them into stereotypes – cliché-people living in a cliché-world, filling time with cliché-ridden conversation.

The covers, shown here from the 1965 English-language edition, are illustrated with front and back views of the cast. Opening the book, the reader encounters the cast staring out from what would normally be the half-title page. The tight cropping of the photograph and the actors' posture, leaning forward toward the viewer, create a feeling of confrontation. Rather than invite the reader into the book, this image becomes a barrier to entry. The title page follows, jolting the reader with its large-scale, crude type. Massin achieved a rough, tattered typographic image by extreme enlargement of metal type, which had not yet been replaced by phototype in the early 1960s.

The next two spreads introduce the actors through full-figure photographs that serve as a legend for the reader, since photographs will identify the speakers throughout the book. Each actor and actress has a unique characteristic – Mr. Smith has a mustache; Mrs. Smith, a turtleneck sweater; Mrs. Martin, a hat; Mary, a hairbun; the Fire Chief, a hat – enabling the reader to quickly identify the speaker. Massin selected a different typeface for the words spoken by each character. Stage directions and explanations, set in an 8-point light, slab-serif font, are clearly delineated from the other typography. As the play opens, Mr. and Mrs. Smith are in their suburban London sitting room. Mrs. Smith prattles on about food and setting a good example for the children, while Mr. Smith reads his newspaper, paying no attention. Her conversation is filled with blatant contradictions; for example, the soup had too many leeks and not enough onions. The Smiths leave to dress when their guests, Mr. and Mrs. Martin, arrive for dinner.

In the play's most famous scene, the Martins chat while they wait for the Smiths to return. Mrs. Martin tells her husband that she believes she has met him somewhere before. Mrs. Martin's dialogue is layered over her image on the left-hand page, opposite her husband's dialogue and image on the right. As the conversation unfolds, they discover coincidence after coincidence: They're both from Manchester, took the same train to London, reside at 19 Bromfield Street, and have a two-year-old daughter with one red eye and one white eye. They suddenly realize they must be a husband and wife named Donald and Elizabeth; they embrace and fall asleep entwined on a chair.

Mary, the maid, enters quietly and addresses the audience in a soliloquy taking the shape of her body. She devastates Donald and Elizabeth's carefully constructed logic used to prove their relationship by telling the audience Donald's daughter has a white right eye and a red left eye, while Elizabeth's child has a red right eye and white left eye; therefore, their daughters can't be the same child. She concludes by announcing that her real name is Sherlock Holmes and leaves the room.

After Mr. and Mrs. Smith join the Martins, the two couples sit stiffly, looking out toward the audience. A long silence ensues, periodically broken as the actors utter interjections and clichés totally disconnected from earlier statements. To illustrate the passage of time, Massin showed the four actors seated in their chairs over and over for twenty-two consecutive spreads. One actor utters a sound and phrase on each spread.

The couples begin to share stories of extraordinary things they have seen – a man tying his shoelace; a man quietly sitting on his seat in the Underground reading a newspaper – when their conversation is interrupted by the doorbell. It rings twice, and each time Mrs. Smith goes to the door, only to find no one there. The repetition of this incident is conveyed through a dynamic layout. Each page is dominated by a full-length image of Mrs. Smith standing before the other three characters, who are seated in the background, as she tells them that no one is at the door. An argument begins over whether the doorbell ringing means someone is there, or whether recent experience teaches that no one is there.

This time, the Fire Chief is at the door, wearing his uniform and shiny helmet. An extraordinary layout records the dialogue as the Fire Chief tells Mrs. Smith that she looks angry and the group explains to him over Mrs. Smith's protestations that she is miffed over losing the argument. To achieve the warped lines of type, Massin had metal type set and proofed on sheets of rubber. These were stretched and bent into the configurations shown here and photocopied using high-contrast film.

Although this graphic technique is simple to achieve with contemporary computer software capable of stretching, bending, and skewing type, it was truly innovative in the early 1960s, when typesetting was still locked in the straitjacket of the metal letterpress.

The small pictures and open spaces of this spread are followed by large images of the Fire Chief and Mrs. Smith – then the senseless argument about the meaning of a doorbell's ring resumes on the right-hand page, in a format used for numerous pages in *The Bald Soprano.* By replacing the speaker's name set in type with small photographs of the actors, Massin enlivens the page. A different indentation is used for each actor, imposing a random yet rhythmic downward movement into the space. White space, contrast, and scale change were important design considerations in the pacing of the book.

After helping resolve the dispute, the Fire Chief informs the Smiths and Martins that he has come to see if they have any fires to put out, lamenting that business is bad. While there, he begins to tell them stories – nonsensical fairy tales and fables – each set in a contrasting typeface. The storytelling culminates in a tale, "The Headcold," in which the Fire Chief delineates a long series of relationships ("My brother-in-law had on the paternal side a first cousin whose maternal uncle had a father-in-law whose maternal grandfather had married…"). Four-dozen relationships into the story, the Fire Chief concludes with "an old woman who was the niece of a priest whose grandmother, occasionally in the winter, like everyone else, caught a cold." The playgoer or reader becomes hopelessly confused by this convoluted mockery of gossip and people's fascination with relationships. Massin set this tale in all-capital condensed sans-serif type to express its incoherence. The typography also introduces a dense textural contrast into the visual flow of the book. Jamming the lines of justified type together by squeezing all leading from between them further intensifies their verbal confusion and visual tension.

The storytelling ends when Mary, the maid, interrupts, calling "Madam" and "Sir" in a loud voice. Mr. and Mrs. Smith reply, "Why have you come here?" and "What do you want?" By positioning Mary's image across the center of the spread, Massin causes a visual interruption, suggesting a break or shift in the play. Discussion begins about the maid's behavior and her desire to tell the group a story.

After Mary recites a poem, the Fire Chief goes to the door, turns to the group, and exclaims, "Speaking of that, the bald soprano?" Massin conveys the Fire Chief's impending departure by cropping his image on the far right of the spread. This device also signals another shift in the tone of the play.

On the following spread, Mrs. Smith remarks that the bald soprano "always wears her hair in the same style." The Fire Chief exits, and a nine-page sequence begins with four or five images of the actors on each page. Their unconnected proclamations, placed above their heads at a

(continued on page 210)

Posters, National Endowment for the Arts, Washington, DC.

Offset, from left to right: 21.5 x 33 inches; 23 x 35 inches; and 23 x 35 inches. (1977–1978)

Poster, Communication Arts and Design Department, MFA in Design Program. Offset, 20 x 32 inches. (1978)

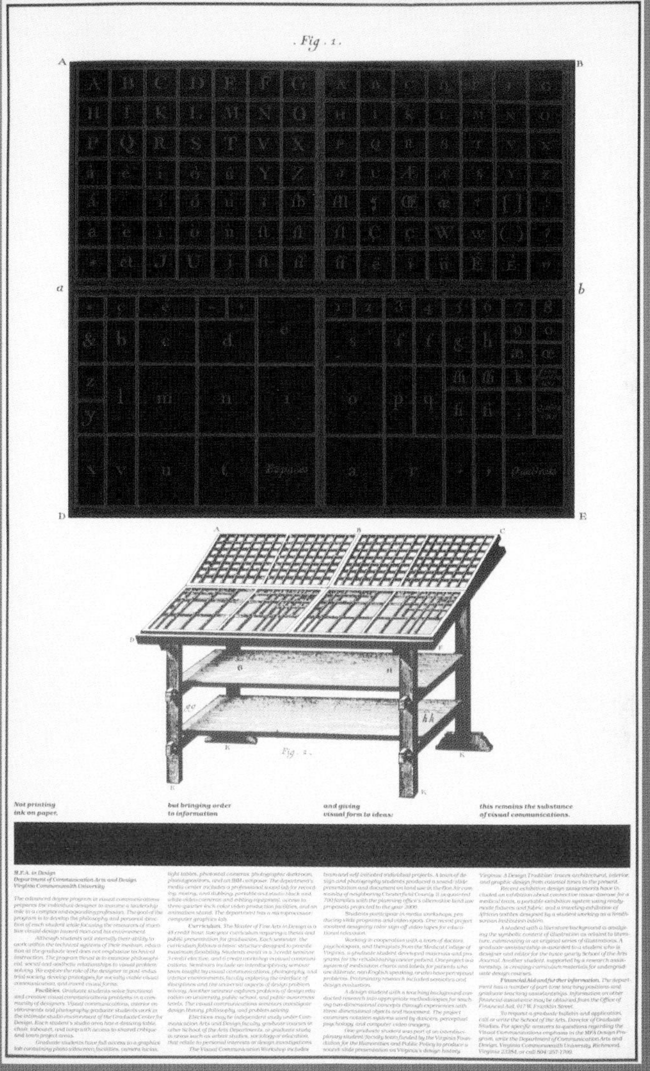

diagonal, include lines from the language manual, clichés, and nonsensical proverbs. This reaches a summation when Mr. Smith rises and shouts, "To hell with polishing!"

Following this proclamation, the actors fall silent for a tense moment. The script directions tell us that a new series of speeches begins in a "glacial, hostile tone. The hostility and the nervousness increase. At the end of this scene, the four characters must be standing very close to each other, screaming their speeches, raising their fists, ready to throw themselves upon each other."

Over the next fourteen spreads, Massin gives visual articulation to this steadily intensifying confrontation by increasing the scale of the type and disintegrating the lucid graphic order present in even the most dynamic of the earlier spreads. Each spread provides a new opportunity to increase the level of chaos. The first seven spreads have typography and photographs of the actors, with a dynamic structure created by lively diagonals and careful use of white space. Overlapping words can still be deciphered by the reader. The eighth spread dispenses with the images, using only typography to suggest the actors' increasingly incoherent shouting.

The graphic entropy moves toward a crescendo as Mr. Smith shouts the vowels *a, e, i, o, u* over and over; Mrs. Martin responds with the consonants *b, c, d, f, g*; and Mrs. Smith repeats the sound of a puffing train, *"teuff, teuff, teuf...."* Massin creates a series of typographic abstractions to express this chaos.

Suddenly, the actors become completely infuriated and begin shouting in unison into each other's ears, "It's not that way, it's over here." The stage lights are extinguished, and from the darkness the actors continue chanting, "It's not that way, it's over here," in increasingly rapid rhythms. Massin illustrates this by reversing the field and layering white type on the black void; the chant becomes bigger and overlaps more as it moves down the page.

The next spread expresses this auditory frenzy with even bigger type, followed by a spread decomposed into an abstract pattern formed by details of the letters.

The words cease abruptly, and the lights come on again. Mr. and Mrs. Martin are seated like the Smiths were at the beginning of the play. They begin to recite the same lines spoken in the opening scene as the curtain softly falls.

This marked the end of the play in the original version, but in the 1964 edition Ionesco offered three alternative endings. The first has Mary return and lead the actors off for dinner, and the stage remains empty for a long time. The annoyed audience begins to boo and whistle, and a dozen actors planted in the audience storm the stage, only to be machine-gunned by policemen in the dark corners of the stage. The director, author, and police commissioner appear on the stage. The director tells the audience, "Let this be a lesson to you.... We'll defend [the theater] against the public by keeping it away." He then tells the policemen who gunned down the people who stormed the stage to kick the audience out, and they clear the theater.

Another version has Mary return to the stage and introduce the author, who is praised by a shill in the audience. The author then shakes his fist at the audience and proclaims, "Bunch of idiots, I'll kill you!" as the curtain falls.

Ionesco's third alternative ending, illustrated by Massin, has the actors literally explode or collapse like their language, with heads detaching from their bodies and arms and legs flying to pieces. Ionesco commented wryly that this ending could be possible only in a film version.

When Ionesco's plays were first performed, many critics derided them. Jean Jacques Gautier, influential reviewer for *Le Figaro,* wrote that Ionesco was "a fraud whose activities could best be summed up by the following telegram: 'Fake surrealism now defunct. Stop. Ionesco follows.'"[5] Others understood Ionesco's message. Jacques Lemarchand "was won over by *The Bald Soprano* when he observed with amusement the audience's puzzlement and rage."[6] He wrote, "Within its walls, the theater holds a stock of dynamite which might blow sky high every other theater in Paris."[7]

Ionesco was a visionary who believed "the renewal of language could bring about a fresh vision of the world;"[8] Massin is a graphic designer "whose primary concern has been to give visual reality to the literary content."[9] To achieve a genuine expression of the absurd, Ionesco had to

Spread from Ionesco's play, *The Bald Soprano.*
Design: Robert Massin (1964)

invent his "own language and create forms that are not those of rational discourse."[10] Massin was able to reinvent his graphic-design language to create an appropriate vehicle for Ionesco's imagination. ➻

Notes

1. Eugene Ionesco, *Fragment of a journal* (New York: Grove Press, 1968), p. 30.

2. Ibid., p. 32.

3. Robert Massin, *Letter and Image* (New York: Van Nostrand Reinhold, 1970), p. 226.

4. Ibid.

5. Rosette C. Lamont, *Ionesco's Imperatives: The Politics of Culture* (Ann Arbor: University of Michigan, 1993), p. 245.

6. Ibid., p. 246.

7. Ibid.

8. Ibid., p. 260.

9. Nancy House, "Robert Massin," in *Contemporary Designers* (Chicago and London: St. James Press, 1990), p. 375.

10. J. S. Doubrovsky, "Ionesco and the Comic Absurdity." Reprinted in Rosette C. Lamont, ed. *Ionesco: A Collection of Critical Essays* (Englewood Cliffs: Prentice Hall, 1973), p. 12.

Bibliography

Hayman, Ronald. Eugène Ionesco. New York: Ungar, 1976.

Ionesco, Eugène. *Fragment of a journal.* New York: Grove Press, 1968.

______. *La Cantatrice Chauve.* Paris: Editions Gallimard, 1964.

______. *Present Past/Past Present.* New York: Grove Press, 1965.

______. *The Bald Soprano.* New York: Grove Press, 1965.

Lamont, Rosette C., ed. *Ionesco: A Collection of Critical Essays.* Englewood Cliffs: Prentice Hall, 1973

______. *Ionesco's Imperatives: The Politics of Culture.* Ann Arbor: University of Michigan, 1993.

Massin, Robert. *Letter and Image.* New York: Van Nostrand Reinhold, 1970.

Woods, Gerald, Philip Thompson, and John Williams, eds. *Art without Boundaries.* New York: Prager, 1974.

Required Reading for the Millennium

From *Print* Vol. 48, No. 6 (Nov/Dec 1994)
The Parody Issue

Print's *editors submitted the following question to Philip B. Meggs, the distinguished design historian: "If you were rocketed to a station in space, which books about design and visual communication would you take with you?" Meggs quickly retorted: "If I were rocketed to a station in space, I wouldn't take any books about design and visual communication with me." To which we counter-retorted. "Well, then, if you weren't rocketed to a station in space, which books about design and visual communication would you stay at home with?" "I'll have to give that some serious thought," said Meggs, adding, "Okay, I've thought about it. Here's my list." Whereupon he rattled off the names of the books presented here, all of which he feels would be a great help to designers trying to cope with fin-de-siècle angst. It turns out that these are books that Meggs was asked to do jacket blurbs for. We reproduce his blurbs in full as a service to our readers.*

That's Obscene! by Massimo Vanilli

Massimo Vanilli, the pope of good-taste design, looks at the American design landscape and doesn't like what he sees. "Back in the 60s," he writes, "we were working like beavers trying to replace American-style commercial art with Eurodesign. We were trying to clean up the mess. Ford was using the Victorian script, JC Penney panty-hose packages were using the brush script, and Memorex was using the [shudder] Olde Englishe. What's an émigré to do!

"We straightened it all out by getting 5,000 corporations to use the Helvetica on grids. We

That's Obscene!
By Massimo Vanilli
Rizollivani Pressi

165 pages, 8" by 12"
no illus., you can't bear to look at this stuff; $49.95

Retro Confidential Designewsletter
Edited by Paul A. Sneer
Spendagrand Press Monthly

64 pages
subscription prices vary based on exclusive franchises

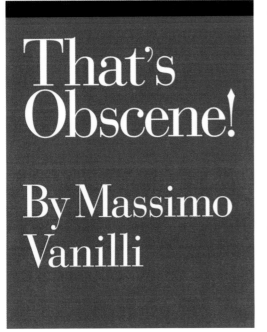

That's Obscene!

By Massimo Vanilli

sold everybody grids and even bought a penthouse laid out on a grid. But now, in the 90s, the whole scheme is coming undone through these desktop publishers using the Victorian, the brush script, the [shudder] Olde Englishe, and worst of all, the reprehensible California computer bitmapped corrupt degenerate deviate masochist nymphomaniac pervert psychopath sodomist typefaces." Vanilli offers several legal methods to be used to stamp out what he describes with Italian subtlety as "the crap." For lovers of finely designed clothing, this book is a real bargain, because it comes with a coupon offering a one-hundred-dollar discount on a thousand-dollar Vanilli-designed sealskin Nehru jacket, available only at Bloomingdale's.

Retro Confidential Designewsletter by Paul A. Sneer

The vicious cycle of heartbreak associated with retro design goes something like this: 1. Big-city museums hold exhibitions of beautiful but little-known works, such as turn-of-the-century Viennese posters or native Alaskan pottery. Designers in Chicago, Los Angeles, or New York attend these exhibits, and ~~plagiarize,~~ er, appropriate the motifs into their work. 2. Exhibition juries see this fresh new creative work and award big-time prizes. 3. Designers in smaller locales ~~plagiarize,~~ er, appropriate these now second-hand Viennese or Alaskan motifs into *their* designs. 4. By the time smaller-city designers' works reach the national juried shows, it is too frigging late. Yesterday's innovations are now old hat.

Retro Confidential Designewsletter breaks the cycle of despair. Each month, it goes behind the scenes to uncover the influential museum exhibitions, new furniture, and fashion designs that will not be made public for six months. Designers in Oklahoma City can now ~~plagiarize,~~ er, appropriate this material long before big-city designers even see it.

You can get an *exclusive* subscription to *Retro Confidential Designnewsletter* for your city, state, region, or for the whole country if you like! The national exclusive subscription will cost you $5,000 a month, but it is guaranteed to keep you

ahead of the crowd and will allow you, finally to ~~plagiarize,~~ er, appropriate your way to fame and fortune.

The Corporate Search for Corporate Anonimity by Chewmeinoff, Gismo, Lippincutt, Margarine, Landfill, Seagull & Guile

Studio head Rich Seagull's cunning was displayed when he announced, on the same day that his design office merged with its three main competitors, that the newly formed monolith would be the first design firm listed on the New

The Corporate Search for Visual Anonymity
By Chewmeinoff, Gismo, Lippincutt, Margarine, Landfill, Seagull & Guile

Business Weak Books
375 pages, 9½" by 12"
2001 illustrations;
price: if you need to ask, go into book design

York Stock Exchange – a fact that evoked a positive buzz among corporate clients. To celebrate the momentous merger of Chewmeinoff & Gismo, Lippincutt & Margarine, Landfill Associates, and Seagull & Guile, the principals have joined forces to produce this coffee-table book presenting their most representative work. In a stupefyingly bland introduction, they discuss the fine art of designing visual identity systems that blend into the polite, unobtrusive world of corporate image. Documentation is provided by over 2,000 logos featuring modern-y lines in a ½" circle, all designed by what is now the planet's, perhaps even the universe's, largest corporate image firm.

Many employees of the merged firms have been laid off, mainly due, according to an appropriately anonymous spokesman, to "hang-ups about quality." But after a decade of declining employment in corporate design owing to clients merging into oblivion, CGLMLS&G – as the new firm is known – is now hiring. "Only students with C averages from second-rate art schools need apply," cautions Rich Seagull, who believes "corporate clients are anxious to achieve mediocrity at great cost."

The Secret Erotica of Norman Rockwall Introduction by Jesse Helms

The Secret Erotica of Norman Rockwall
Introduction by Jesse Helms

Pleasure Publications
169 pages, 6" by 9"
69 illust. in living color
$69.96

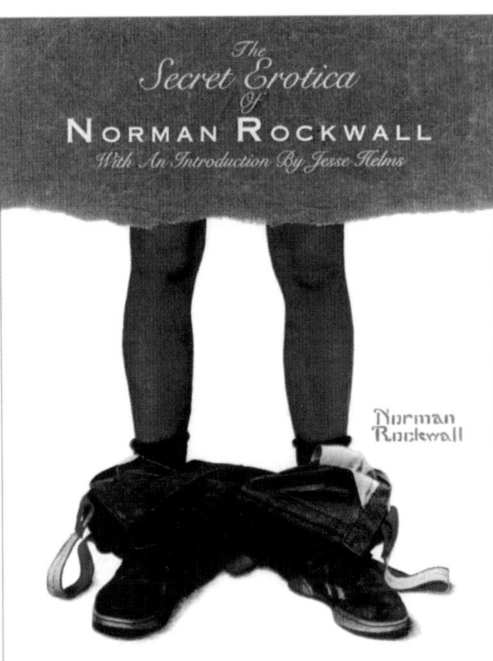

If you thought Andrew Wyeth's secret series of nude paintings of Helga, his farm-woman neighbor, was a jolt, you ain't seen nothing yet. During the half century when Norman Rockwall was winning accolades from the family-values crowd for his homey depictions of small-town life, America's most beloved artist was spending his off time recording the steamier side of everyday folk. Now, a hoard of 69 of these hidden-away Rockwalls have been brought to light and published in this lavish coffee-table tome. No *Saturday Evening Post* covers here!

The Secret Erotica of Norman Rockwall shows small-town America as it really was during the early decades of the 20th century, without any candy coating. The warts, bunions, corns, corsets, and overbites are all here; nothing is left to the imagination.

This book is a sociological treasure trove. You will see for yourself the undergarments worn by the straight-laced parson and his choir leader. You will discover what the freckle-faced kids actually did behind the barn or at the swimming hole after school. And you will find out what the kindly bespectacled doctor was really examining on his round of house calls. A flood of long-suppressed memories will wash over you as you make your way through this remarkable collection.

Me. How I Changed the Course of American Design
By Michael Michael Michaels

West Lite Books
201 pages; 8½" by 11"
291½ illustrations,
141½ in color; $49.95

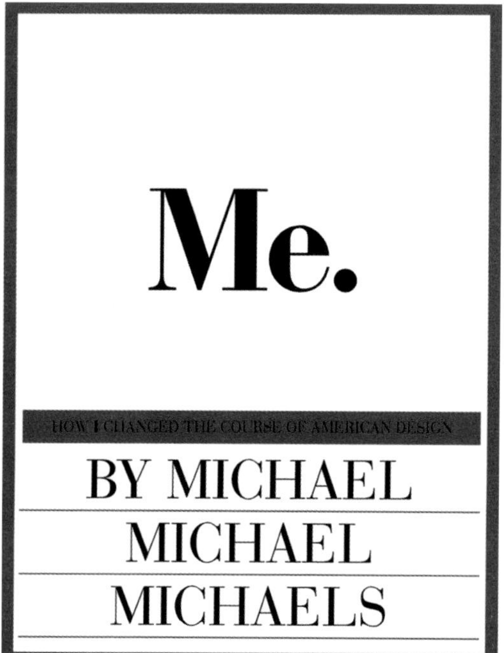

WITH APOLOGIES TO CHIP, KATHARINE, MICHAEL, MICHAEL, AND MICHAEL

Me. How I Changed the Course of American Design by Michael Michael Michaels

Michael Michael Michaels has become the most eloquent practitioner of the flamboyant Postmodern California Surfer style. In this stunning book, he shows why the Hermitage in St. Petersburg honored him with its first one-person show for a thirtysomething American. Luxuriating in his luscious West Coast esthetic, the reader easily understands why Michael has won over 500 prestigious design awards.

"It should have been a thousand," Michael opines, "but you know how mediocre the juries have become lately. They're actually using designers from the Midwest to judge these shows."

In the occasional paragraphs of text, set in 7-point Matrix with 84 points of lead, Michael unloads about the problems of contemporary design.

"New York! What a horror show!" he proclaims. "Dirty. Grimy. No wonder New York designers use those putrid colors from the bottom of the PMS ink swatch books with all that dingy gray and black in them. California color has – well, what can I say? – more *lime.*" Michael dumps on recycled paper, noting that his designs are timeless and should only be printed on permanent paper made from the finest freshly slaughtered giant redwoods. He claims not to be dismayed by the recent Los Angeles earthquake, or by California's rocky economy. "My business is international; jolts to the local economy mean nothing to an international force in design," he notes with refreshing candor. One can't help thinking: What flair! What attitude! What nerve! What an asshole!

"I Am Not a Dingbat!"
By Hermann Zapt
ABZ Verlag 176 pages,
7" by 10"
345 illustrations; $29.95

"I Am Not A Dingbat!"
By Hermann Zapt

"I Am Not a Dingbat!" by Hermann Zapt

A recent survey by *PC Panorama* magazine revealed that 92 percent of desktop publishers naively think that a Zapt is a dingbat. This widespread belief emerged because the type menu on personal computers calls those little ornaments and symbols Zapt dingbats; however, it doesn't mention that the designer of all those little symbols is Hermann Zapt, the world's preeminent typeface designer. Appalled by this mass display of ignorance, ABZ Verlag commissioned the only too willing Zapt to prepare this book to show his work to the typographically illiterate.

Readers learn that Zapt's over 200 typefaces include Zapt Palatable, Zapt Optometry, Zapt Mellow, Zapt Titian, and his latest, Zapt Interplanetary. When the first laser printers were produced, an international committee of experts selected his calligraphic face Zapt Swoosh for inscriptional purposes.

MEGGS

Real-Life Graphic Design Handbook
By the art department of *Very Popular Mechanix* magazine

Very Popular Mechanix Press
167 pages; 5" by 9"
129 illustrations; $14.95

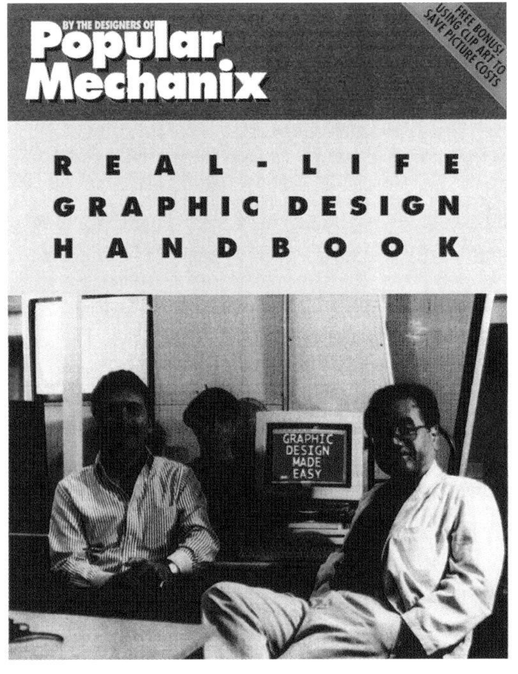

Zapt has the distinction of being the most ripped-off visual designer of the century. A foldout chart in back of the book diagrams the pirating of Zapt's designs, identifying the type machinery manufacturers and large software firms that have copied his work. Always energetic in his own behalf, Zapt has traveled to many countries in order to pressure government officials to punish type pirates. His efforts have paid off: A 32-page supplement describes in detail the punishments that have been instituted, ranging from removal of television privileges (Lower Saxony) to branding the buttocks of accused pirates with a large *P* (Libya), a letter especially designed for this purpose by Zapt himself.

Real-Life Graphic Design Handbook
By the art department of *Very Popular Mechanix* magazine.

The best-selling manual *Do-It-Yourself Desktop Publishing,* written by the art department of Very Popular Mechanix – the magazine that teaches readers how to do their own plumbing, wiring, and wallpapering – showed millions of folks how to use personal computers and page-layout software to become desktop publishers producing newsletters and brochures.

Now, this invaluable sequel teaches desktop publishers, students, and even graduates of fancy design schools everything they need to know to look, talk, act, and design like a real-life designer. The authors call on 60 years of professional experience to explain how being a real designer is mostly a matter of attitude.

The lifestyles chapter gives valuable tips on how to dress like a designer (e.g., wear black, gray, or beige only), and illustrates favored hairstyles. The chapter on designer jargon lists essential, easy-to-use terms like "syntax," "semiotic," and "product differentiation." Practical issues, such as avoiding overtime work, asking for a raise, and blaming the printer, are fully discussed.

The chapter on client management explains how to win over skeptical clients. By telling insurance-company execs, "I'm not an artist, I'm an insurance salesman," you'll so disarm them, they won't see until it's too late that you're a screwball artist doing wild stuff.

There is even a chapter on design, offering such secrets as compressing type so that you can squeeze 10 percent more white space onto a page. To leap from obscure desktop publisher to renowned real-life designer, you need this book! Ready? Set? Jump!

CACA 100
Chicago Arts and Crafts Alliance

Cockamamie Press
100 pages, 10" by 10"
100 illustrations; $100

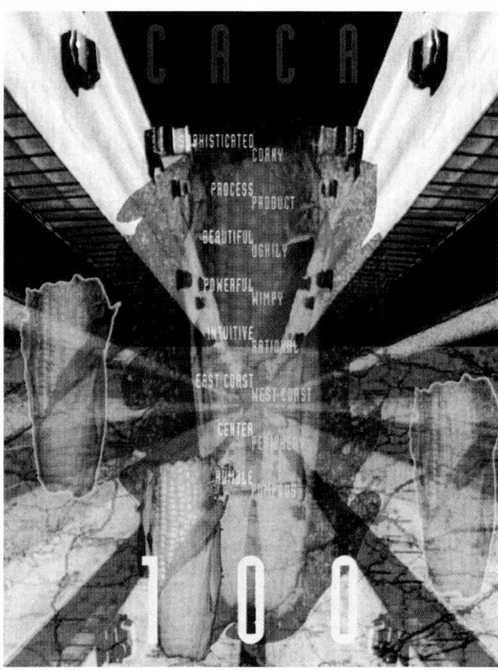

(continued on page 218)

Posters, Ann Arbor Film Festival. From left to right: offset, 18 x 22.25 inches; offset, 18 x 23 inches; offset, 18 x 23 inches; silkscreen, 20 x 26 inches; offset, 14.5 x 22 inches; offset, 17.25 x 22.5 inches. (late 1970s to early 1980s)

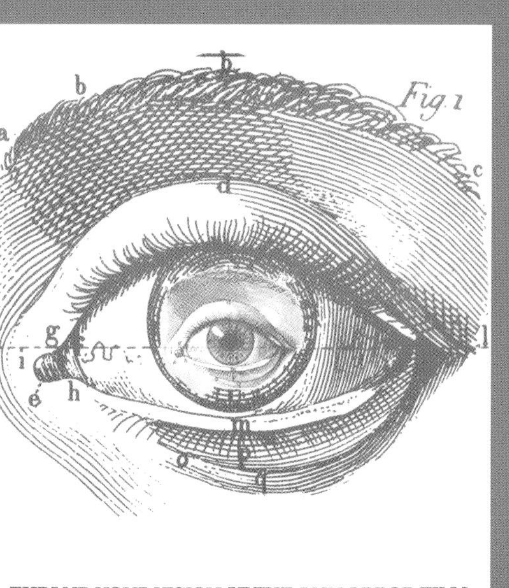

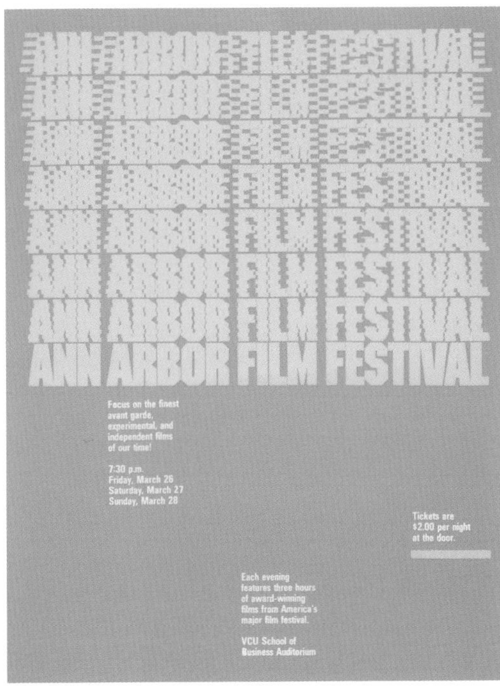
ANN ARBOR FILM FESTIVAL
ANN ARBOR FILM FESTIVAL
ANN ARBOR FILM FESTIVAL
Focus on the finest
avant garde,
experimental, and
independent films
of our time!
7:30 p.m.
Friday, March 26
Saturday, March 27
Sunday, March 28
Tickets are
$2.00 per night
at the door.
Each evening
features three hours
of award-winning
films from America's
major film festival.
VCU School of
Business Auditorium

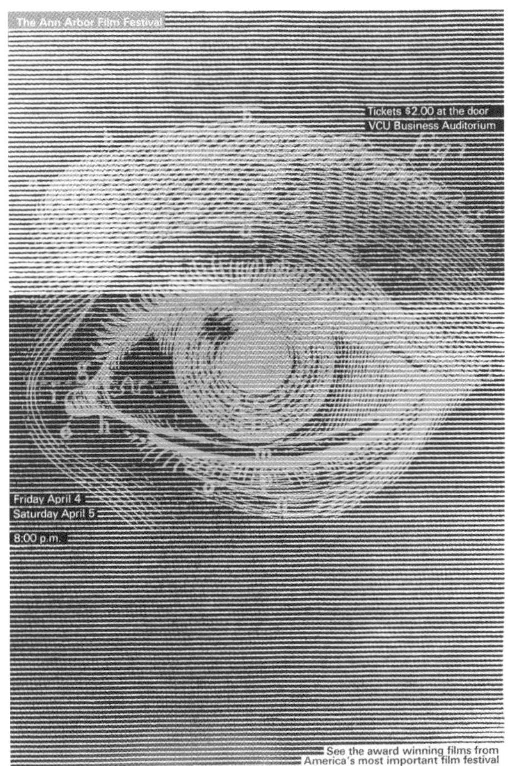
The Ann Arbor Film Festival
Tickets $2.00 at the door
VCU Business Auditorium
Friday April 4
Saturday April 5
8:00 p.m.
See the award winning films from
America's most important film festival

ANN ARBOR
FILM FESTIVAL
Friday March 28
Saturday March 29
VCU Business Auditorium
7:30 p.m.
Each evening features a
different program of over four
hours of the best animated,
documentary, experimental, and
underground films of 1979.
Tickets are $2.00 per
evening. On sale in Pollak
Room 220 or at the door.

CACA 100 Chicago Arts and Crafts Alliance

In the beginning, GAGA (Graphic Arts Group of America) was the only graphic design organization in the U.S., with chapters in New York and Chicago. However, the two chapters never got along and in 1926 went their separate ways. The immediate cause of the split is in dispute. The New York contingent alleges that the Chicago members got roaring drunk at a joint conference held on a cruise ship and were kicked out of the club en masse. The Chicagoans deny this, claiming that they left on their own, having grown weary of sending their annual dues to the snooty New Yorkers. The Chicago renegades formed their own group, CACA (Chicago Axis and Crafts Alliance), which became as much a national organization as GAGA.

Each year, CACA mounts the country club of all design exhibitions, the CACA 100. From over 50,000 entries, only 100 are selected. Now, that's exclusive!

The competition is fierce, with only two-hundredths of one percent of the entries accepted. The 100 pieces in this book survived by winning approval from all 100 judges. Some say to get the nod from 100 nit-picky judges, a design must be perfect. Others say it must be perfectly bland.

So what if it costs a buck each to see what won? We're talking class here, we're talking elite. One hundred winners! Fifty thousand losers! It's a jungle out there in graphic design competition land.

The Pit Bull in American Mass Communications
By Tibor Killum

Bottomline Publishing
165 pages, 8" by 10"
124 illustrations; $29.95

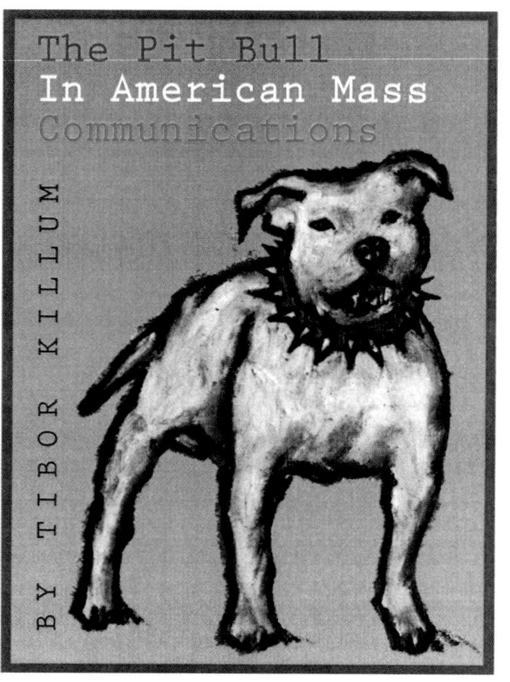

The Pit Bull in American Mass Communications by Tibor Killum

You've met them on your way up; you'll pass them again on your way down. They're the pit bulls running amok in the American corporate world. A pit bull only looks out for number one and will wreck your career to advance its own.

A pit bull undermines you by snitching to the boss; you'll never know what hit you as you head for the unemployment office.
You can't tell these cunning curs by their appearance alone; they're usually smartly dressed in the latest fashions. That young woman who is overly polite and helpful, or that young man willing to work long hours of overtime without pay or complaint: Behind their friendly facades may lurk seething pit bulls ready to attack the minute your back is turned.

Everyone employed in design, publishing, and (especially) advertising desperately needs this guidebook to learn how to recognize and counterattack these manicured demons.

The author, Tibor Killum, is a veteran of countless public relations and design wars. He shows how to recognize the warning signs identifying a pit bull before it strikes. Helpful strategies explain how to get it before it gets you. Killum argues that becoming a foaming-at-the-mouth pit bull yourself is the only sure survival technique in today's mass communications arena.

Note: All covers in the preceeding article were written, produced, and designed by Philip Meggs.

Methods and Philosophies in Design History Research Lecture presented at the Universidad de las Américas Puebla, Cholula, Puebla, Mexico (February 28, 1994)

Some years ago an advertising circular for the then-new design magazine *HOW* arrived in my mailbox; I longed for a new design magazine entitled *WHY.* As we pursue our busy daily schedules as designers, educators, and students, we rarely have time to pause and ask, WHY? Unlike the French post-Impressionist Paul Gauguin, we seldom confront the questions in the title of his 1897 painting, "Where do we come from? What are we? Where are we going?" Like Gauguin, I know some tough questions; it's the answers that elude me. As the social anthropologist Bengt Danielsson noted in his biography of Gauguin, "All who persist, as do rational Westerners, in trying to understand and analyze everything, including the problems of life and death, inevitably grow unhappy, while animals, children, and 'savages' [I need not dwell on the cultural bias of Danielsson's term for persons from other societies; he would probably be embarrassed by it today]... are happy for the very reason that it never enters their heads to reflect on metaphysical problems to which there are no solutions." (Quoted by Jay Jacobs, "Anatomy of a Masterpiece: 'Where do we come from? What are we? Where are we going?'" *Horizon,* Summer 1969, p. 65.)

History is in large measure a myth, because the historian looks back over the great sprawling network of human struggle and attempts to construct a web of meaning. Oversimplification, ignorance of causes and their effects, and the lack of an objective vantage point are grave risks. When we attempt to record the accomplishments of the past, we do so from the vantage point of our own time. History becomes a reflection of the needs, sensibilities, and attitudes of the chronicler's time as surely as it represents the accomplishments of bygone eras. As much as one might strive for objectivity, the limitations of individual knowledge and insights ultimately intrude.

The evolution of graphic design history over the past quarter-century has generated a series of viewpoints and philosophies that don't replace the earlier views or render them obsolete; rather, they have added new levels of complexity and meaning. The efforts of some commentators to discredit other viewpoints are unfortunate, for they seek to deny an emerging richness and pluralism that strengthens the study of graphic design history.

Graphic-design history has not yet emerged as a full-fledged discipline with appropriate educational preparation and certification: It remains anarchic and incohesive. Issues I wish to discuss today are:

1. The art history dilemma
2. Graphic designs as collectibles
3. The unified design history theory
4. The problem of style
5. The cult of individualism
6. Pedagogic imperatives
7. From feminism to Eurocentrism and multiculturalism: politically correct graphic design history
8. Whose design history?
9. Design as Ideology

The Art History Dilemma

In the beginning – of this rapidly fading century, anyway – was Art History, with a capital A. The concept of art for art's sake, a beautiful object that exists solely for its aesthetic value, did not develop until the nineteenth century. Before the Industrial Revolution, the beauty of the forms and images that people made were linked to their function in human society.

Twentieth-century art history has been largely under the spell of art historian Bernard Berenson, an American living in Italy who set out to become the most important connoisseur and authority of Italian Renaissance painting during his day.

Berenson, endowed with a phenomenal memory and keen reasoning ability, put great faith in the personal response to the work under scrutiny. Berenson believed art must be life-enhancing. "In order to be life-enhancing," he wrote, "an object must appeal to the whole of one's being, to one's senses, nerves, muscles, viscera, and to one's feeling for direction, for support and weight, for balance, for stresses and counter-stresses, and for the minimum of space required for one's indispensable bodily autonomy – an autonomy so precious that to yield an iota of it is to be a lover, to be compelled to surrender even an inch is to be a de-individualized prisoner." (Berenson, Bernard. *Aesthetics and History.* New York: Doubleday, 1954, p. 67–68.)

Berenson certainly had a late-Victorian flair for the dramatic. His lofty ideal for aesthetic experience sounds like a combination of orgasm and winning an Olympic gold medal. It transcends everyday experience; yet graphic design by definition is rooted in the ordinary human discourse of information, persuasion, and entertainment.

The traditional research methods of art historians do not fully take into account the complexities of graphic design. A focus upon individual artists, organized into schools or movements, with their masterpieces and unique contributions identified, cannot adequately address graphic design history. Often new developments are shaped by technology, such as the invention of lithography or phototypesetting, or evolve over time as a public dialog by graphic designers eclectically influenced by one another's work.

Graphic design involves a premeditated three-part human relationship between the designer; the client with a communications need; and the intended audience. Add in photographers, illustrators, and printers, and the situation becomes even more complex. These relationships, along with the limitations and capabilities of production, create a context vastly different from the fine arts.

My latest reminder of the gulf existing between the traditional art historian and graphic design occurred last month when an art historian at the university where I teach – Dennis Halloran – and I were both placing slides in adjacent display cases so that our students could review the images shown in his art history class and my design course. Professor Halloran sniffed, "I certainly hope that material you're putting on display won't get mixed in and corrupt my slides."

Yet, the model of the Berensonian connoisseur – with a genuine and informed response to a work with the whole of his or her physical and mental being – cannot be totally abandoned. The aesthetic dimension of graphic design must not be abandoned to the forces of marketing or functionalism. Nikolaus Pevsner believed that "design for the masses must be functional, in the sense that they must be acceptable to all and that their well-functioning is the primary necessity. A chair can be uncomfortable and a work of art, but only the occasional connoisseur can be expected to prefer its aesthetic to its utilitarian qualities." (Pevsner, Nikolaus. *The Sources of Modern Architecture and Design.* New York: Thames and Hudson, 1968, p. 9.)

But utility and aesthetics are not mutually exclusive. In 1935, Jan Tschichold wrote, "Plain utilitarianism and modern design have much in common but remain two different things. Fitness of purpose and usefulness are prerequisites for good work but the real value of a work lies in its spiritual content. The new movement aims to produce a new beauty which 'is more closely bound up with its materials than earlier methods, but whose horizons lie far beyond.' This feeling for materials and proportion can transform the merely functional into a work of art." (Tschichold, Jan. trans., Ruari McLean. *Asymmetric Typography.* New York: Reinhold and Toronto: Cooper and Beatty, p. 72.) The challenge for graphic design and the study of its history must remain a dual one, committed to both the aesthetic and functional dimensions of design.

The value of the scholar/connoisseur is best exemplified in the work of early-20th-century scholars of typography, including Beatrice Warde and Stanley Morison. Beatrice Warde's research into the origins of old style typefaces served not only to correct the mistakes of the past, but to create a renewed appreciation of typographic form and nuance. Their scholarship significantly influenced the evolution of typeface design and the formal vocabulary of the 20th century. The quality of our typographic communications today are greatly improved by their research; this is a paradigm of how design history research can upgrade professional practice and the typographic experience within an entire culture.

Graphic Designs as Collectibles

A wide interest in graphic design artifacts as collectible commodities has emerged, from posters of the avant-garde that sell for thousands of dollars in exclusive galleries, to flea market trafficking in Victorian holiday cards. Is the motivation for this aspect of design history commercial opportunism? Clive Dilnot speaks disparagingly of "junk antiques." Marketing expert Irma Zandl says anthropologists relate the human impulse to collect to ancient activities of gathering, foraging, and hunting. They also note the differences between men and women in collecting and acquiring. Men seek to complete the whole set, while women seek the outstanding specimens. Zandl believes these differences relate to different roles of men and women in the survival of the primeval community. (Conversation with the author, Washington, DC. May 19, 1993.)

Lick'em and Stick'em. Though often superficial in scholarship and lacking any cohesive philosophy, the collectibles movement provides some useful functions. Artifacts and ephemera are preserved that might otherwise be lost, material is documented and catalogued. Information about design is disseminated and a popular audience for design history, however shallow, is created.

The Unified Design History Fallacy

Some seek to approach design history from a unified viewpoint, combining architecture, graphics, fashion, and product design into a unified design history discipline. I believe that this does a great disservice to the cause of graphic design history. A design by definition has a function, and this functional aspect is central to the history of a design discipline. When we consider function, a vast gulf opens between the design disciplines. Shelter; work; communicate: architectural, product, and graphic design exist to serve different needs. While visual attributes might be similar at a given historical moment, such as Renaissance ornament appearing on buildings and book title pages, the real meaning of the cathedral and typographic book lie far apart.

The ephemeral nature of graphic design, combined with its life within the social, economic, and cultural spheres of a society, creates a diversity beyond the range of architecture or industrial design. What architectural or product design equivalences exist to the posters of World War One or World War Two? Or protest posters from the 1960s? Or recent underground or protest graphics addressing pressing social issues of the 1990s? A unified design history excludes artifacts that don't fit a categorical evolution, such as: Victorian to Art Nouveau to Modern to Postmodern. Stylistic evolution denies the dualistic nature of graphic design as graphic form and social message.

Architectural history is so well established that a unified design history inevitably leads to graphic design history becoming an appendage to architecture: This is not an acceptable situation, given graphic design's continuing struggle to gain professional status.

Research methodologies for studying the various design disciplines should vary. Architects produce a relatively small number of buildings and inevitably leave a trail of drawings, models, blueprints and correspondence, providing a rich depository of collateral research materials, while graphic designers produce hundreds of designs and frequently do not retain their process material. Architecture is often studied as artifact and process; graphic design is studied as artifact and for its social and political role.

Of course, a strong relationship exists between various design disciplines and should not be ignored. Graphic design is sufficiently significant to deserve isolated study apart from other disciplines. Its relationship to painting and languaging are at least as significant, if not more significant, than its relationship to architecture and product design.

The Problem of Style

Anyone who sees graphic design as a mere chronicle of *style* misunderstands graphic design. Today the word style is often used to define superficial surface characteristics, dictated by marketing considerations. Its original meaning – distinctive excellence of artistic expression achieved by appropriate forms and their relationships to one another in space – has been corrupted. While the visual attributes of graphic design are critical and should receive appropriate emphasis in the study of design history, we must be equally concerned about designers' underlying philosophic viewpoints, the meaning graphic design holds for its culture and audience, and the signification of forms and their syntactic relationships. In some eras, such as late-19th- and early-20th-century Art Nouveau, a pervasive style becomes an umbrella for the era. In other instances, such as the broad range of work produced in Europe between the two world wars, formalists and propagandists were poles apart. Efforts to create order by organizing graphic design history solely according to visual attributes forces the elimination of important works falling outside the visual parameters.

Graphic design educators have embraced semiotics, the study of signs and sign-using behavior, in an effort to understand a visual communication. In 1938 the behavioral semanticist Charles Morris divided semiotics into three branches: pragmatics, concerned with how signs are used; semantics, concerned with the relations between signs and their meanings; and syntactics, concerned with signs apart from their meanings, including their physical forms and how they are related into a structure. There are problems from a total reliance upon semiotics for design theory. As the *Encyclopaedia Britannica* points out, "Although this three-fold division has been widely adopted by logicians, and more recently by linguists, there is considerable disagreement as to the precise definition of pragmatics in relation to semantics, as also of such key terms as sign, symbol, and signal."

A graphic design isn't just a sign, it is an amalgam of signs, images, and visual elements configured to deliver a complex message that is visual/ verbal/ nonverbal. The ambiguity and disagreements among semioticians has permitted some graphic-design researchers to reshape the meaning of pragmatics, semantics, and syntactics into components of graphic design: form, message, and operation, used here to mean how the graphic design operates upon people and within societies.

Perhaps form, message, and operation are too lucid for scholarly discourse: figuration, impartation, operancy might be more precise and esoteric. With semiotics as a part of the foundation, I believe the time has come for a theory of graphic design, rather than continuing the past practice of piggybacking on other disciplines such as perceptual psychology, semiotics, architecture, and art history.

The Cult of Individualism

There have been calls for a rejection of design history based on the accomplishments of individuals; instead, it is proposed that a collective evolution be substituted. In some periods, a collective vision and imagery evolve which cannot be easily attributable to specific individuals. Design involves a creative process; designs are usually made by an individual or a small collaboration. When we are unable to determine the authorship of historical artifacts such as the director's chair, the designer is not anonymous or collective, but merely unknown to us. George Tscherny has noted that the matter of dates is absolutely critical in graphic design history. Sometimes the time span between an original innovation and the host of imitations is perilously short; making the task of identifying the original from the imitation difficult. An apparently collective outbreak can almost always be traced to a source.

Those who seek to deny the role of seminal individuals – and call for a collective view of design history – produce an equally biased vision. There are pivotal individuals who shaped the direction of graphic design in their times by inventing new typographic and symbolic forms, innovative ways to structure information in graphic space, pioneering imagery, and original methodologies for signifying messages. It would be foolhardy to deny the unique contributions to our graphic heritage by such individuals as John Baskerville or El Lissitzky. During the 1960s, Jan Tschichold wrote of El Lissitzky: "His indirect influence was widespread and enduring.... A generation that has never heard of him... stands upon his shoulders."

Careful analysis of dates of similar works often proves that seemingly collective directions do in fact have an identifiable point of origin; however, when a collective evolution such as popular vernacular Victorian graphics does occur, many works typify the essence of the direction and time period, many artisans contribute to the collective evolution.

Concurrent analysis from two historical points of view – synchrony and diachrony – can help steer an exploration of graphic design around many pitfalls. Synchrony is simultaneous occurrence; while diachrony is a study of phenomena as they occur and change over time. A. M. Cassandre's first poster serves as an example. One can examine its synchronic relationship to other graphic designs of its time, then examine it in relationship to the graphic designs preceding and following it. This poster appears to be unlike other graphic designs of its immediate time and its antecedents; but it significantly influenced work by Cassandre and others in the months and years following its publication. Because the concepts embodied in this poster drew inspiration from advanced art, an understanding of Cubism and Futurism is needed to fully comprehend this poster. This poster gains significance in the historical evolution of post World War One French advertising art due to its profound influence.

Due to the rampart plagiarism and eclecticism in mass communication, synchrony and diachrony are critical to the design historian's efforts to separate an innovator from his or her army of imitators. Sometimes short time spans exist between the creative act and the imitation, making this separation very difficult and prone to error.

A real dilemma surrounds issues of influence and plagiarism, for the evolution of graphic design has often been a continuum, evolving over time. The evolution of 17th-century European typography and design, from Old Style to Transitional to Modern, is but one example of a dialog transcending decades and national boundaries. A building process enabled designers to achieve a gradual transition from Renaissance design to the modern epoch.

Pedagogic Imperatives

Design educators have maintained a focus upon students and to a lesser degree professional designers, while ignoring the need to educate the larger society – the general public, the business community, governmental decision makers – to the value of graphic design.

Clive Dilnot strikes to the heart of this problem when he asks, "When historically does society begin to recognize consciously that things are designed rather than that they simply are?" ("The State of Design History, Part I." *Design Issues,* Vol. 1 No. 1. Spring, 1984.) The design history movement should expand its mission, developing strategies for educating the public and clients. This would serve the needs not only of the design profession, but of the society-at-large.

Feminism, Eurocentrism, and Multiculturalism: Politically Correct Graphic Design History

Great waves of controversy about political correctness have swept through society in the United States during the last few years. Universities and academics have been at the center of this maelstrom, with many universities adopting codes of behavior and speech, some of which have been struck down by the courts for violating the constitutional right of free speech.

It is not surprising that graphic design and its history have become embroiled in the political correctness controversies. Unlike fine art, which is often birthed from an internal necessity on the part of the artist, a graphic design comes into being as a direct result of a social, cultural, or economic need. It is loaded with the attitudes, biases, and values of the designer and/or her client.

The feminist branch of the design history movement seeks an interpretation of past attitudes toward women and an understanding of women's experiences. The line of demarcation between design history and social/political history is a fuzzy one, prone to leakage. This is how it should be, because graphic design almost always has a co-presence of perceptual form and societal message on the same surface, creates a duality of meaning and interpretation. Those who reject the feminist approach due to its narrow focus upon one aspect of the design fail to realize that this topical research is one of the few efforts to address the content and social influence of graphic design. Hopefully, the feminist wing of the design history movement will develop theory and methodology that can be applied to a range of social and political issues.

The feminist design history movement should aspire to the fate of the Easter Seal Society, which struggled for years in the battle against the dread disease, polio. When the Easter Seal Society finally triumphed and effective vaccination virtually ended polio, it lost its reason for existence. But, it turned its expertise toward new problems, notably birth defects. Although I have expressed this optimistic view, recent events such as media hysteria surrounding the Bobbitt trials convinces me that a vaccination against sexism, etc., is probably a long way off.

Eurocentrism is defined as the tendency to focus upon European culture while excluding other cultural traditions. Multiculturalism means an expanding understanding of the rich diversity and values inherent in many cultures. I believe the design history movement should embrace multiculturalism as one of the most important philosophic issues today. It can bring the human community toward greater unity and understanding. Advanced communications and transportation technology are shrinking spaceship earth into Marshall McLuhan's "global village" at an ever-increasing pace. We are evolving a pluralistic, international culture, and the need for cross-cultural understanding has never been greater.

During the mid-1970s, when I was researching and writing the first edition of my graphic design history text, the publisher placed a contractual limit of 300 pages and 600 images. I reduced my material based on their evolutionary linkage to contemporary design practice in the United States. The regrettable result was an overemphasis upon European traditions, while vital topics such as Persian manuscripts and the Korean alphabet were not included. Perhaps my criteria were appropriate based on the vantage

(continued on page 226)

1

2

1
Brochure cover, Security Federal Savings. Offset, 7 x 3.5 inches. (1986)

2
Spread from *SWAP*, results of a workshop on book art, Virginia Commonwealth University. Offset, 10.5 x 5.5 inches. (mid-1980s)

3
Spreads from *Medium and Message*, Texas Christian University, Fort Worth, Texas. Offset, 9 x 12 inches. (1989)

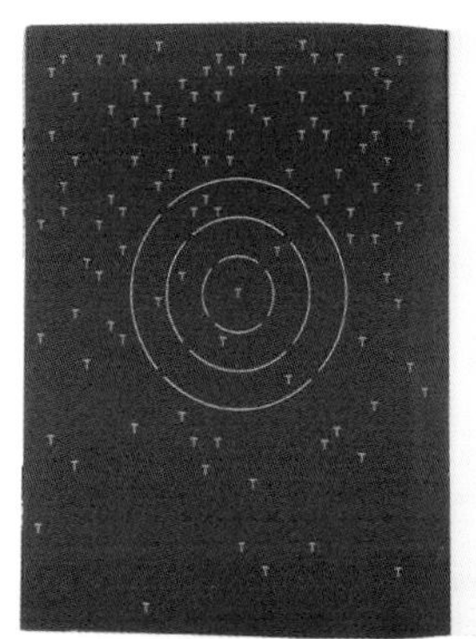

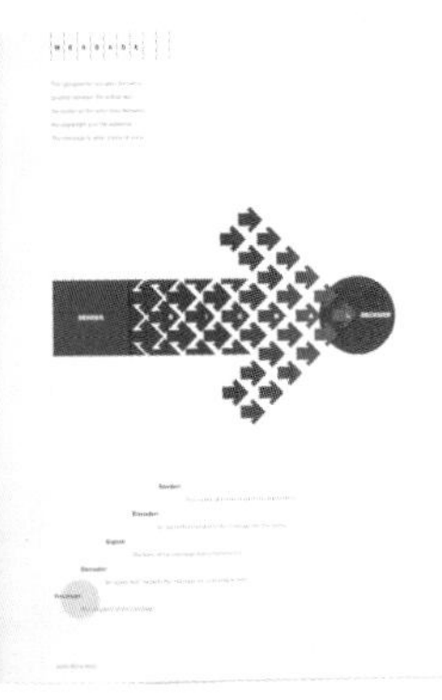

4

5

6

4
Brochure, "Italy," International Studies Program, Virginia Commonwealth University. Offset, open: 19.37 x 8.75 inches. (1990)

5
Poster, "Make Art Happen," School of the Arts, Virginia Commonwealth University. Offset, 23 x 35 inches. (1995)

6
Cover sketches for *A History of Graphic Design,* Third Edition. Digital output, 8.5 x 11 inches. (1998)

points of the 1970s, but I fairly cringe at some of the oversights and biases not clear to us at that time. I hope to rectify some of these problems in the next edition.

In the reaction against Eurocentrism, two cautionary notes are in order. Expanding our research and teaching to embrace and include multiple cultures should not be accompanied by a denunciation and rejection of the European culture heritage. Significant contributions of European culture should not be slighted or ignored in a quest for balance, for the finest impulses of multiculturalism are inclusionary rather than exclusionary. Zealots – whether feminists, multiculturalists, animal rights activists, modernist (or Postmodernist) designers, etc., – can become fascists if they lose their sense of balance and proportion in a drive to correct inequities or right past wrongs.

Whose or Who's Design History?

Diverse philosophies, attitudes, and biases of various components of the design history movement bring us to one of the most perplexing dilemmas of all: How shall we define the parameters of graphic designs we admit into our history? The range of graphic-design artifacts spans postage stamps, to comic books, to art posters by Picasso and Matisse. Each of these subcategories have their own history, traditions, and museums, such as the Postal Museum in Washington and a Museum of Comic Art in New York state. The astounding range of graphic design expression makes this fragmentation unavoidable.

The graphic design history movement has focused upon significant designers and their works, rather than the audience, or the overall cultural impact of design activities. This design-history approach has been closely bound to the training of young designers, who desperately need a system of values, philosophic underpinnings, and a sense of professional worth. Those who seek to discredit this approach to design history fail to recognize the continuing predicaments of graphic design.

Design as Ideology

Every designer is an ideologist, even in situations where he or she does not even realize it. The history of graphic design is filled with symbolic cues about the attitudes and beliefs of client, designer, and audience. This ideological aspect becomes the potent link between design history and social history. The corporate designer embraces a philosophy of capitalism; the advertising designer advocates consumption; the social activist designer protests and demands action. The designer who does not see himself or herself as an ideologue is a sleepwalker oblivious to his or her social role.

Just as we may never know with full certainty whether or not the toxic herbicide commonly known as Agent Orange – unleashed into the environment during the Vietnam War in such massive quantities that it now resides in every living creature on the planet, each of us in this room is a walking depository of Agent Orange – is the direct cause of the cancers and chronic skin ailments plaguing Vietnam War veterans and their offspring, we also may never be able to determine the culpability of Beavis and Butthead in the fire set by a six-year-old viewer that killed his baby sister, or the degree to which Joe Camel encourages teenagers to use lethal tobacco products. The possible link between graphical images and audience behavior should motivate us toward a continual examination of the ideology of graphic communications.

A bias-free communication is virtually impossible. Even benign designs, or movements that sought neutral, objective visual communications, are laden with potent ideologies.

"When one says sentimentality," Berenson observed, "one wants to denounce a sentiment in which one is no longer participating.... When we say for example that Millet is sentimental it simply means that we are reacting against a sentiment that is no longer fashionable, and because of that reaction we forget to appreciate the value of Millet's paintings: solid noble painting which rank with the best of the nineteenth century." (Morra, Umberto. T. and Hammond, Florence. *Conversations with Berenson.* Boston: Houghton Mifflin, 1965, p. 259.) In the study of graphic-design history, the sentiment and attitudes embedded in the artifact can be interpreted in the terms of its time or of our time. We run the risk of revisionist history where we warp and bend the work of an earlier time to suit the values and biases of today.

The final of Gauguin's three questions is, Where are we going? Certainly, technology is a driving force continually reshaping how visual communications are delivered to the audience, who creates them, and what they mean for creators and consumers of visual messages and images. The current circumstance of the human community and planet Earth appears to be entering a crisis phase. Quite possibly we have the power to confront and even solve interlocking problems such as exploding population growth, resource depletion, and environmental degradation; the question is, do we have the *will*? Are our political and economic institutions sufficiently viable to enable us to confront these dilemmas? For the graphic design profession the pivotal question is, are our communications methods capable of delivering the right messages? Can we provide the public and the political decision makers the information needed to respond to looming crises? For the practice of design in the twenty-first century, I advocate a philosophy of planetary humanism. *Planetary,* because we are imperiling the fragile ecosystems – that frail envelope of air, those shallow bodies of water, and that precious thin layer of topsoil – upon which all life on this planet is dependent. *Humanism,* because the graphic design community must awaken from the award-oriented, materialistic attitudes of the 1980s where graphics was treated as a beautiful surface, and address the needs of the people who receive and use the visual messages we create.

Perhaps one could argue that this challenge is beyond the scope of graphic design, but we must define graphic designers, not as decorators, stylists, or form arrangers, but as activists making powerful messages capable of touching people's lives.

In what direction should the design history non-movement go? I've always believed that history was in the understanding business. Graphic design has a pervasive impact upon people's lives. We should reject the narrow definition of scholarship as a closed and exclusive club of esoteric scholars talking to themselves. If we understand how and why our forms, concepts, and imaging techniques emerged and what graphic artifacts meant to the people of their time, we are in a better position to confront the looming challenges of the 21st century. A duality of approaches, addressing both the problem of form and the content of graphic artifacts, can help create the awareness needed to help renew both human and aesthetic values in mass communications. The resulting breath of understanding can help visual-communications professionals, students, and audiences to define their discipline, their work, and their potential for contributing positively to the evolution of the emerging international culture and society.

Back Talk: Philip B. Meggs, Design Historian

From *Print* Vol. 52, No. 6 (Nov/Dec 1998)

(Interview with Steven Heller)

Philip B. Meggs began his design career in 1958 hand-setting metal type. Following his studies at the University of South Carolina and Virginia Commonwealth University, he became senior designer at Reynolds Metals and art director of A.H. Robins Pharmaceuticals. In 1968 he joined Virginia Commonwealth University's Communication Arts and Design Department, where he is currently School of the Arts Research Professor. Meggs is author or coauthor of a dozen books, including his monumental A History of Graphic Design, *which was first published in 1983 and has become the standard text in the field. The third edition of the book was published this fall by John Wiley & Sons.*

Heller: Prior to 20 years ago, there was apparently no codified graphic design history. Based on your own research, is that assumption true?

Meggs: The belief that design history and criticism are new areas of inquiry is not correct; design criticism and history have been around since the early 1500s. Each era documents what is important and/or controversial. People are repelled by the shock of the new; much of my design history is simply recording what appalled the establishment, from Baskerville to the Bauhaus.

Heller: As author of the first (and only) design history textbook, what were your guidelines or standards for what was historically important?

Meggs: My goal, as a design educator teaching design history beginning in the early 1970s, was to construct the legacy of contemporary designers working in the U.S. I believed this could help designers understand their work, comprehend how and where the semantic and syntactic vocabulary of graphic design developed, and aid our field in its struggle for professional status. Design education is advanced when young designers learn what is possible by understanding the philosophy and concepts that shaped graphic design.

Heller: Your book is not THE history of graphic design. What other ways of recording history are there?

Meggs: I insisted that this book be called *A History of Graphic Design* to acknowledge that it was not the Encyclopedia of Graphic Design, but a concise overview for contemporary designers and design students.

The contract called for a 300-page book with 600 illustrations. I delivered a 1,000-page manuscript plus over 1,000 illustrations with captions only after deleting whole countries and hundreds of illustrations. At that time, my decisions were based on the direct lineal relationship between our contemporary spot in time and space and the works that influenced it. Greek and Roman alphabets were included, but my research on Indian Sanskrit was dropped, because it did not have this relationship. Inclusions and exclusions were determined by a "roots" assessment.

The intent of *A History of Graphic Design* is to identify and document innovation in semantic and syntactic aspects of visual communications. Designs from each period discussed were assessed in an attempt to distinguish works and their creators that influenced the ongoing evolution of the discipline. This information provides a conceptual overview useful for further study and practice.

Heller: Why hasn't graphic design history been afforded as serious attention as it has in other arts?

Meggs: Academics and fine artists have been marginalizing graphic design for a long time. In the past, this related to social class. Nineteenth-century working-class teenagers with art talent went into the industrial arts, while the well-to-do trained in Europe to become portrait painters to the wealthy.

Heller: Is history objective or subjective? And how do you address this issue in your own work?

Meggs: History can be objective or subjective. Much of my work has been written from the vantage point of an educator trying to determine what has significance for the reader/viewer, who is typically a designer or design student. After reading a number of period accounts about World War I posters and studying hundreds of original posters in the Library of Congress poster collection, my question was, "Which selection of images will best convey the range of communicative and formal concepts used by World War I poster designers?"

Anyone who tries to write history should be allowed a margin of subjectivity to explore his or her passions, but not to the point of distorting the record. I don't much like to look at William Morris's work, but to leave him out would have been untenable.

In the third edition I had to grapple with the arrival of Web site design. I did [an Internet] search for graphic design sites and the search engine identified over a million sites. The new edition has three Web sites.... Are these designers canonized over the designers of the other five billion Web pages out there? No, they were selected based on the points about Web site design I wished to make.

Heller: Is criticism a part of this process? As a historian, do you make value judgments about the quality or efficacy of work that ultimately affects the writing of history?

Meggs: Critical evaluation is the root source of any historical account. One searches for significance, and value judgments are often made from the station point of the writer, who is stuck in time and place with a fixed vantage point. If you research deeply, though, you can find out what people from earlier eras valued, and the motivating force behind their work.

Heller: The reception to the first edition was generally positive. How do you feel about that initial work in retrospect?

Meggs: The dialogue created by the first edition educated me about certain omissions and helped me fine-tune my methodology. The world has changed dramatically in the intervening two decades. America is becoming the first truly multicultural nation, and technology has reinvented graphic design once again. My challenge on the third edition was how to better reflect multiculturalism while retaining the documentation of our European and North American design traditions. The chapter on "The Alphabet" becomes "Alphabets" with non-Greco-Roman alphabets added; "Medieval Manuscripts" is changed to "Manuscript Books" with an Islamic section; "Art Nouveau" becomes "Ukiyo-e and Art Nouveau" because Japanese prints are more fully covered. Glaring omissions from the second edition were rectified, such as postwar Dutch design.

Also, I had to deal with a technological revolution occurring by the month. The second edition was produced just before PageMaker or QuarkXPress were advanced enough for a project of this scope. It was one of the very last typeset and pasted-up books. For the third edition, the publisher allowed me color reproductions throughout, so I had to acquire 500 color images – in 18 months.

Graphic design history is very complex, and it is made even more difficult by the large number of gifted designers and sheer volume of work. This makes the selection process very tough.

Heller: Can you address in one book the myriad forms of historical perspective? For example, can you (and would you) inject Marxist, feminist, and postmodernist viewpoints into your narrative?

Meggs: Social, political, and economic history are imbedded in the history of graphic design as content. We need to study design as part of social history, but we also need to study it as an independent force in society.

Let me take your specific examples one at a time. Marxism. Viewpoints from classical Marxism – that people's defining attribute is their creativity, especially in the ability to expand labor to meet needs; and that homo sapiens are "social-species" beings who should direct their labor toward the needs of their community as a whole are significant in the history of ideas. While working on the second edition of *A History of Graphic Design,* I struggled in an effort to inject philosophic ideas from Marxism and capitalism, structuralism and deconstructivist criticism, and so forth, into the book. This became unwieldy, and I was unable to successfully weld together the two opposing approaches, especially in view of the limited number of words available in each chapter. We do need a body of literature relating graphic design to major philosophic concepts, but this is too complex to imbed in an introductory historical overview.

Feminism. Historically, there were very few women designers, but since the 1960s social revolution, large numbers of women have entered the profession with a predictable result. Many, such as April Greiman, Zuzana Licko, Paula Scher, and Carol Twombly, have made significant creative contributions as designers and are finding their way into the history books. Although there is a dearth of identifiable female designers before the 1960s, I believe there were quite a number who weren't identified. Anonymity has been a serious problem for the study of graphic design history, whether male or female.

Postmodernism. This term is so overused, and every discipline – architecture, art history, feminism, literary criticism, even theology – seems to have its own definition. The third edition has a chapter titled "Postmodern Design" that combines the major thrusts in graphic design that have been branded as postmodern.

Heller: How should design history be taught in the classroom? Is it a collection of persons, places, movements, and dates? Or is there a more vital lesson to be taught?

Meggs: I've always believed the purpose of teaching design history is to strengthen studio education and professional practice. It should be taught through critical evaluation: how the work functioned in its culture; its syntactic and semantic attributes; the impact of technology on design; the relationship to religion, politics, business, and industry – all this needs to be articulated.

Heller: Do you feel that the field as a whole has acquired more historical knowledge since you began? Or is history really a marginal area of study in a field that is changing so quickly – and where doing work and getting jobs is the primary concern?

Meggs: Knowing design history can help designers get beyond style and surface and understand their work on a deeper level. It can provide reference points in the rapid flux of contemporary culture. Since 1970, the graphic design community overall has become smarter, better educated, and more capable. This is partly due to the design history movement, stronger education programs, and the development of graduate education.

Heller: Finally, as a historian of the design field, do you feel that the field has changed, in terms of how this will affect the next revision of your book?

Meggs: Technology, the global economy, and the information age have conspired to explode graphic design into a series of interrelated but quite diverse areas of activity – print design, image and identity, environmental design, kinetic and broadcast graphics, Web site design, book art, electronic games, advertising, and information graphics.

Things are changing so fast in the field that only fools predict the future. When I started the third edition of my book, the World Wide Web and Internet were not yet significant factors, then all of a sudden they were the major events of the decade. I was forced to ponder, "How do you write history that is just breaking?"

Landmarks of Book Design, Tenth of a Series: *Before Rosebud Was a Sled*

From *Print* Vol. 53, No. 3 (May/June 1999)

The subject of the book is defunct and the printing method is antiquated, but book designer Clifford A. Harvey's passion is timeless.

Editor's Note: Philip Meggs launched his series "Landmarks of book Design" in the January/February 1990 issue with Herbert Bayer's epic volume *World Geo-Graphic Atlas.* In subsequent issues, he ranged through the centuries with such visual classics as El Lissitzky's *For the Voice* (1923), *Mira Calligraphiae Monumenta* (16th century), and William Pickering's *The Elements of Euclid* (1847). Two years ago, having curtailed his writing schedule in order to complete the third edition of his *A History of Graphic Design,* Meggs put "Landmarks" on hold. We welcome his resumption of the series in this issue.

Events leading to the publication of the 1998 private-press book *Before Rosebud Was a Sled* began during the 1870s. In the small town of Wellsburg, on the sliver of West Virginia jutting up between Ohio and Pennsylvania along the Ohio River, entrepreneur Samuel George, Sr. opened a paper mill to produce paper for flour sacks. The mill prospered and soon began manufacturing the sacks, printing customers' labels on them by means of hand-engraved woodblocks. S. George Company's paper contained Manila hemp rope fibers, making it sturdier than ordinary bags created from wood-pulp paper. S. George sacks stood up well under the pressure of automatic filling machines, shipping, and handling. Their insides were printed a deep purple, which made the flour appear even whiter. In addition to flour sacks, the company made sacks for cornmeal, animal feed, and industrial products.

For decades, individual families purchased white milled flour in 25-pound sacks, and the company thrived by producing sacks for such large customers as Pillsbury and for countless smaller mills. More than 2,000 woodblocks used to print sacks and labels by letterpress were stored upright in vertical racks to minimize warping. Most of the blocks were designed and engraved between 1895 and 1910. The artists, engravers, dates, and locales for most of the blocks are unknown. While stereotypes and metal engravings were mostly used during S. George Company's last few decades in business, some of the woodblocks were still in use as recently as the 1960s.

S. George Company closed its doors in 1977 after more than a century of operation. During the liquidation process, business partners Bob Graham and Pat Lee purchased nine tons of printing materials including the 2,000 woodblocks, 120 drawers of wood type, and hundreds of metal engravings. Fifteen trips were required to transfer this hoard from Wellsburg to a storage facility near Pittsburgh. The partners planned to resell the materials as collectibles, or find some other commercial use.

Clifford A. Harvey learned of the GramLee Collection, and offered to proof the blocks. In addition to heading the graphic design program at West Virginia University in Morgantown, Harvey is proprietor of the Permutation Press, established in 1977 as a means to experiment with design and printing and to produce fine limited-edition works. The S. George blocks proved compatible with Harvey's iron 12-by-18-inch 1907 Albion letterpress, and his proofs revealed an extraordinary level of design and engraving.

Many of the blocks are three- and four-color sets consisting of a key block that registered carefully over colors printed beneath it. During the 1980s, Harvey printed a series of limited-edition prints of these multicolor labels. Often, the original color combinations weren't known, although many labels had the key block printed in black ink over bright primary colors. Rather than attempt to mimic likely color combinations, Harvey gave the blocks a second life as fine-art prints by exploring the esthetics of color through innovative color combinations.

When Harvey established the Permutation Press, one of his goals had been to publish and print a major private-press book. In 1992, he began work on *Before Rosebud Was a Sled,* a book about 19th-century American wood engraving, illustrated with the GramLee Collection woodblocks. (The title was inspired by the label of a flour brand and references the name of the childhood sled from *Citizen Kane.*) Handprinting of pages on a Vandercook SP20 flatbed proof press commenced in 1993 and occupied Harvey through 1997, when the binding process began.

Rosebud's cover is hand-bound in Dutch bookbinding cloth using a flexible-back binding technique that permits the book to be perfectly flat when open. Each copy has an original 1930s, one-of-a-kind printed proof of an original S. George flour sack label archivally mounted to the cover. After adhering each proof to rice paper with PVA glue that permeated the old proof paper, Harvey dry-mounted it to the cloth binding with a new type of dry-mount tissue. *Rosebud's* 80 pages measure 15 inches high by 9 inches wide, a size inspired by S. George's storage racks. The book's end papers are a deep purple Ingres sheet, echoing the color found inside the S. George flour sacks.

For the title page, Harvey chose a cut evoking the spirit and character of 19th-century America. The color blocks for this key block did not survive, so Harvey created polymer letterpress plates for the red and brown inks. One of the American flags shown has 36 stars, while the other has 41. Nevada became the 36th state in 1864; 25 years later, Montana entered the Union as the 41st state. Does this suggest an 1889 date for the block, or is the inconsistent number of stars a drawing error?

The preface spread demonstrates Harvey's grid system. Running text presenting historical information is in 10-point Stymie Light Monotype set by Hill and Dale Typefoundry in Terra Alta, West Virginia. Two 17-pica-wide columns hang from a flow line located 6½ inches from the top of the page. *Rosebud* is self-referential: Harvey's personal comments about the blocks and printing production of the book appear in 8-point Stymie Light Italic, in 10-pica-wide columns placed across the top of the pages, about an inch from the top. These sidebars, or captions, were set on Harvey's Macintosh computer and printed from polymer plates because Hill and Dale was unable to acquire Stymie Italic Monotype matrices. Harvey considers the Amber image opposite the preface to be one of the finest blocks in the collection. This informational graphic showing the marketing process – from harvesting the product (wheat) to filling sacks with it in the mill to transporting it by rail – is unusual for the time.

The preface is followed by a dynamic spread printed in nine colors. Harvey is particularly fond of the sulky block, reminiscent of the famous Currier and Ives racing prints. Using a lively range of muted colors, he repeated the image six times to create a race trotting into the gutter and out again.

Rosebud the flour brand is one of four actual-size prints of multicolor labels in the book. These are placed in center spreads of the eight-page signatures. The special binding technique allows these to lie perfectly flat when the book is open. The Rosebud label demonstrates the 19th-century label designers' ability to create a complex integration of illustration, lettering, and ornamentation.

The four full-spread barrel labels are printed from the original woodblocks; the tan impression for the Rosebud label is the exception. This severely damaged block had broken into several pieces. Harvey made rubbings from the various segments, then used the rubbings to reconstruct the artwork. A film negative was shot and a metal letterpress plate created. Rosebud and Diadem, another brand from the F. W. Stock & Sons flour mill, were the names of two of the mill's draft horses. Because a circular design has no top or bottom or other reference for assembling the pieces, Harvey was unable to get the new tan block to register perfectly with the red, green, and black blocks. This emblematic "Fresh Ground Corn Meal" image is an icon for the product; I recall seeing such a

(continued on page 234)

Philip Meggs: Environmental Design

Phil designed colorful wall graphics to create public awareness of a historic site owned by The Council for America's First Freedom. At this location in 1786, Thomas Jefferson's Statute for Religious Freedom was approved by the Virginia General Assembly. This was the first time religious freedom was guaranteed to a people by law. Meggs is shown inspecting the site.

We the General Assembly of Virginia do enact that no man shall
be compelled to frequent or support any religious worship,
place, or ministry whatsoever, nor shall be enforced, restrained,
molested, or burdened in his body or goods, nor shall otherwise
suffer on account of his religious opinions or belief; but that all
men shall be free to profess, and by argument to maintain, their
opinions in matters of religion, and
wise diminish, enlarge, or affect their
1786
Thomas Jefferson

6:Jefferson's Virginia

On this site:
bly met at the old capitol.
1786:Jefferson's Virginia
tute for Religious
Freedom was adopted.
VAPARK

design on meal sacks in grocery stores and marveling at the survival of Victorian graphics late into the 20th century. Unlike custom blocks designed and engraved for specific mills, such as F. W. Stock's Rosebud, many of the label blocks are stock cuts that could be combined with handset wood or metal type bearing the name of any mill ordering a press run of sacks. Nineteenth-century wood engravers cut a vast inventory of stock images, and type manufacturers got into the act with cast illustrations and ornaments. This is a forerunner of contemporary clip art and CD-ROM disks containing hundreds of royalty-free images. Then as now, the level of stock artwork ranged from crude unschooled efforts to finely executed specimens.

Many of Harvey's spread designs possess an unusual subtlety of color and composition. The Circle Wheat block demonstrates the white-line style of engraving, with white lines carved into a solid background. This design shows the strong graphic qualities achieved by the engravers. The circular border is composed of four printed lines separated by white paper. The outer scalloped curves and triangular points combine to convey a lively optical feeling. Label graphics were very different from magazine engraving of the time. Magazine cuts had descriptive tonal modeling and heightened realism, while label graphics often used simplified forms, strong silhouettes, and elemental shapes. The sheaf block printed on the right-hand page is somewhat enigmatic. Harvey believes that it might be a fragment of a larger design, but he has not located other components in the GramLee Collection. From a former mill employee, he learned that many old blocks were dumped into the Ohio River during the 1930s in order to free badly needed storage space, resulting in the irretrievable loss of countless blocks. Only a few have identifying marks, like the circular stamp on a rectangle printed at the bottom of the right-hand page; these blocks were made between 1889 and 1891 at Hamilton Manufacturing Company, whose facilities were located in Chicago and Two Rivers, Wisconsin.

The Reliance Flour barrel label provided Harvey with an opportunity to show, through reduced-size photo engravings, the progressive overprinting of colors. It is one of numerous examples demonstrating how late-19th-century newspaper photographs were freely appropriated by label designers. The *Reliance* was the U.S. entry in the 1903 America's Cup race. It had over 16,000 feet of sails mounted on a single mast. The sheer weight of these canvas sails broke the mast and kept the *Reliance* out of the race. Undoubtedly, the ill-fated boat's name and image made better graphic branding for flour than its sailing performance would justify.

Another fascinating example of appropriation is a wood engraving of the Empire State Express train No. 999 that set a speed record in 1893 of 102.8 miles per hour. A painting of this train, by A. P. Yates of Syracuse, New York, was reproduced in *Leslie's Weekly,* in 1895. An anonymous wood engraver reversed this copyrighted photograph and used it as a reference for the trademark of Gwinn Brothers Milling Company of Huntington, West Virginia. The engraver was unable to accurately draw the perspective of the cross ties hidden by the people in Yates's painting. This train also appeared on the two-cent 1901 Pan-American Exposition commemorative stamp.

Careful examination of the yellow ocher areas in the farm scene reveals the use of textured scribing tools to apply textured areas. As halftones challenged the dominance of wood engraving, more efficient techniques were explored. The Pride of Dakota cuts suggest the passage of time between blocks. The one on the right seems to be more recent in origin, unlike many blocks that were recut with few changes.

F. W. Stock & Sons' Mikota label is another of the four full-spread blocks printed from the original engravings. As with the Rosebud label, it possesses simplified forms and tight integration of word, image, and decoration. Harvey says that Mucha's posters inspired the soft palette. Many of the blocks have warped, cracked, or uneven areas. Padding and shimmying were required to achieve as even an impression as possible.

Monogram blocks dating from the 19th century are forerunners of contemporary trademarks. Interlocking letters in dimensional space were often highly ornamented and hard to decipher. Although the reading sequence could be quite confusing, the monograms had a strong presence as tangible objects on the page.

The final spread in *Rosebud* presents an expansive hog who was printed on one of the sack proofs surviving from the mid-1930s. The sack contained wheat chop – ground or chopped animal feed made from one or more cereal grains.

Rosebud's back matter consists of an index of illustrations, bibliography, and colophon with production notes.

Harvey printed an edition of 60 books, but only 45 libraries and collectors will be able to acquire a complete book, due to the inevitable spoilage that occurs during fine printing on a handpress. Half the press run was printed on Arches Rives paper; the other half on paper specially handmade for this edition at Twin Rockers Paper Mill in Brookston, Indiana. This paper has strands of rope hemp cast into the sheets to signify the use of rope hemp in S. George papers.

The GramLee Collection of printing artifacts, perhaps the largest single collection of 19th-century handcut woodblocks, is housed at West Virginia University. The university will preserve and protect the materials while making them available for teaching and research activities.

Printing *Rosebud* was a formidable task. Fifty-five separately mixed inks were used, counting all the blacks and grays as one color. Eight-page signatures were printed on 18-by-30-inch press sheets. There were 255 press impressions for 50 copies of the book, requiring a total of 12,750 individual press impressions.

Rosebud speaks to a realm of history often ignored: the vernacular and commercial arts that were an integral part of the lives of ordinary people; and the industrial culture of the 19th century whose remnants are slowly being bulldozed into oblivion. It also speaks to the passion of an author/designer/printer whose vision wrested a limited-edition book from the hand press, a book that transcends its genre to become a timeless work of art. ••

Spreads from *Before Rosebud Was a Sled.*
Design: Clifford A. Harvey
(1997)

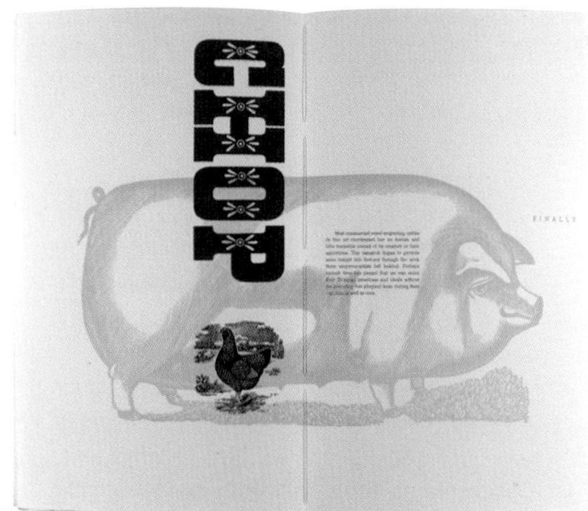

Excerpt from *Fotografiks* (1999)

David Carson, Graphic Designer

It is a bit of a stretch to say David Carson "single-handedly changed the course of graphic design," a claim made by the Chronicle Books marketing department in 1995 when it prepared the flap copy for the initial printing of Carson's first book *The End of Print: The Graphic Design of David Carson.* Carson was embarrassed by this claim, and he became even more chagrined when a book reviewer mistakenly wrote that Carson himself had made this claim "on the cover of his book." The flap copy was rewritten at Carson's request for subsequent printings, as *The End of Print* became one of the best-selling graphic design books in history.

This little controversy prompts the question: why all the fuss about Mr. Carson? Why have his detractors been so quick to damn his work, while a book reviewer seizes upon a publisher's marketing copy to thrash him? Why have noted design spokespersons uttered phrases such as "the degeneration of Western culture" and "the cult of the ugly" in their condemnation of innovative designs of the 1990s.

Many factors account for this circumstance. We are experiencing a watershed shift in human culture as the old order gives way to whatever comes next. One factor in this cataclysmic change is the fracturing of boundaries between creative disciplines; another is the disintegration of graphic design into several pronounced directions. One of these routes might be best described as the rise of the graphic designer-cum-artist. These individuals – whose approach to type and image on a printed (or digital, or kinetic, or three-dimensional) surface involves questioning the traditional syntax of visual communications – have made graphic design more expressive and less formulaic. Traditional methods for organizing information on a surface are defied; new digital typefaces defile norms of letterform design; and images are digitally defaced.

These developments traumatized established graphic design professionals who sensed, not just a challenge to their ownership of the holy grail, but a rejection of their standards and aesthetics. They were blinded by seismic shifts in design thinking. A conspiracy of technology and humanism jolted their boat, and they never even saw it coming.

Perched on the roof of the movement, Carson became a lightning rod for all the voltage hurled at the new design approach. Among designers struggling to redefine graphics in the digital age, Carson's art direction and design of widely available magazines made him the most prolific, most visible, and the most conspicuous designer of his generation.

A scientist once told me that a working definition for research is "when I am doing what I don't know what I'm doing." Carson's approach to design and photography encompasses a similar aspect of open-ended exploration. For the better part of two decades, he has steadily explored new paths, questioned past accomplishments, and experimented with new possibilities. One need only look at his layouts for surfing magazines in the early 1980s to realize that experimentation isn't a passing stage in Carson's career, but a way of life.

Musing on his design work, in 1996 Carson told *Print* magazine: "I didn't try to break rules. I lacked a built-in restrictive understanding of how things are supposed to be done. It's just that I didn't know what the rules were."[4]

Carson majored in sociology and graduated from San Diego State University in 1977. He studied graphic design briefly in 1980, then accepted an internship at Surfer Publications. Carson isn't completely self-taught as is often stated, for apprenticing as a journeyman graphic designer at a magazine publishing firm is no different from the apprenticeships used to educate artists from the medieval era until the second half of the nineteenth century, when more formal schooling for aspiring artists became the norm.

Just before the computer revolution re-formed graphic design, Carson was catapulted to international design prominence as art director/designer of *Beach Culture* (1989–91). This influential publication was followed by *Surfer* (1991–92) and *Ray Gun* (1992–96). Currently he maintains an independent design office in New York, designing a host of projects including (but not limited to) advertisements, music videos, posters, publications, television commercials, and trademarks.

[4]Philip B. Meggs, "Five Top Designers Confess: 'I Never Went to Art School'" *Print* Vol. 50 No. 3, May/June 1996, p. 128.

Phil Meggs and David Carson editing photographs for the book *Fotografiks*. (1999)

Letters to *Print:* Critical Mass

From *Print* Vol. 54, No. 3 (May/June 2000)

Janet Abrams's review of Laurel Harper's *Graphic Radicals/Radical Graphics* and David Carson's *Fotografiks* in the January/February issue brings to mind George Bernard Shaw's observation that critics "see what they look for, not what is actually before them."

In discussing Harper's book, Abrams rejects the introduction as "breathless... like the course outline for Avant-Gardes 101." What does this mean? I read Harper's introduction rather carefully, and it is a thoughtful discussion of controversial design of the last decade. Katherine McCoy's short introduction is debunked as "fleeting (read: rubber-stamp)." McCoy's one-page preface is in fact a concise statement declaring her belief in the risky process of change rather than design based on existing paradigms. Abrams accuses Harper of "relying heavily on other writers' quotations," but there are only a dozen quotes in the 20-page introduction. Hardly excessive.

Abrams asks, "When does the radical become the establishment? In *Graphic Radicals/Radical Graphics,* before your very eyes. The extraordinary thing about *Graphic Radicals* is how tame the work of 40 designers and firms appears in this Yellow Pages format." Abrams misunderstands the process: Radical art doesn't "become the establishment;" it is appropriated by the establishment and neutralized in the process. Cultural familiarity is the only thing that makes graphic forms radical or commonplace. For example, Futura went from being damned as illegible to being used in all newspaper ads for the A&P grocery stores in about two years. This is approximately the same time it took Barry Deck's radical 1990 typeface Stencil Gothic to go from *Emigre* to the fashion magazines.

In her assault on *Fotografiks,* Abrams seems obsessed with David Carson's fame. David Carson is "a certified graphic-design celebrity;" "[we] are supposed to know how famous David Carson is before we start;" "[the text is] laced with reminders of Carson's status;" "a big-name designer who is clearly on the road an awful lot;" "the subtext of this book is still, unavoidably, designer celebrity...."

I think it's wonderful that David Carson and a few other graphic designers have received the public renown they deserve; regrettably, there are far too many other designers who merit public recognition but have not received it. It seems a shame that the few designers who do break out of the profession's status as an anonymous service industry are inevitably subjected to strident attacks by people like Abrams.

Abrams says that *Fotografiks* is "...about Carson's international lecture schedule" and that "all this globetrotting spells *ennui.*" On the contrary, Carson has a genuine passion for travel and loves to take pictures. Abrams, angry about his fame, and suffering *ennui* at the sight of his photographs, is projecting her own feelings onto her subject.

As the author of the brief texts in *Fotografiks,* I regret that Abrams's interpretations of the few captions she singled out for debasement are totally distorted relative to my intent. About a photograph of an old school building, I wrote, "This prosaic picture of an elementary school remains generic, until we are told it was photographed by David when he was eight years old. The anonymous façade is now connected to a person, a life, a time." Abrams then remarks, "From captions like these, we are to deduce that the mere fact that the photographs were taken by Carson means they are of value. I'm not so sure." Here again, her comment reflects her hang-up about Carson's celebrity. I wish she were objective enough to understand my point in this caption, which I state on page 157: "Perhaps there is no more important role for photography than as a preserver of personal and family history." My retired next-door neighbors, Mr. and Mrs. Peterson, recently showed me then-and-now photographs of their high-school friends after a visit to their native Maine. These were just as engaging as Carson's photographs of his schoolhouse and second-grade friends, and the Petersons aren't famous designers.

For a montage of Carson's photographs on pages 150–151, my caption reads, "This visual feast was compiled intuitively. Verbal or conceptual messages are absent: photographic information is put together for the delight (or dismay) of the viewer. It is editorial design without the editorial part, for an intensely visual age." When Abrams asked, "Just what, exactly, is editorial design without the editorial part?" is when I realized that this woman doesn't get it at all. Consider, Ms. Abrams, an editorial spread about New Orleans in a travel magazine. The text talks about New Orleans, and the montage of photographs shows local architecture, food, landmarks, and perhaps a

Letters to *Print:* Departed Icons

From *Print* Vol. 54, No. 4 (July/Aug 2000)

Mardi Gras parade. This content is the editorial part. Now look again at pages 150–151 of Carson's *Fotografiks.* A building façade, a tattered sign, a woman holding a baby, two mannequins smoking, a close-up of a person seen through a glass of ale – it looks like an editorial layout, but it carries no message except its visual presence. It becomes art, Ms. Abrams. Art! Graphic design is becoming an art form, in one of its many post-industrial manifestations. Can't you see this? Or are you too hung up about Carson's fame to see what is before your eyes? ◆

Philip B. Meggs
Richmond, VA

For decades, *Harper's Bazaar* greeted me at the magazine rack in exquisitely bold Didot. Those crisp diagonal *A's* and *Z* with their sharp hairline serifs, bracketed by the curvy *B* and *R,* made a perfect word image. It signified fashion, sophistication, and design. Earlier this year, *Bazaar* completely revamped its format. That stunning logo was replaced by the most generic of contemporary type fads – a large, bold, letterspaced sans serif, just like we see on scores of upstart magazines overcrowding the shelves. An icon is gone.

Print's logo also had remarkable uniqueness. Pushed into the left-hand corner and reproduced much smaller than other magazine logos, it told you it had class. Understatement. It didn't need to shout. Hand-lettered around 1960, this simple five-letter word was timeless. *Print's* covers were always a visual statement unmarred by a list of articles. It was a visual communications magazine that communicated visually! *Print's* new format is very handsome, but *Print* like *Bazaar,* has traded its famous logo for the most generic of contemporary type fads – a large, bold, letterspaced sans serif. Another icon is gone. ◆

Philip B. Meggs
Richmond, VA

Note from Martin Fox, Editor of *Print* magazine, tucked into this issue of *Print* and sent to Phil.

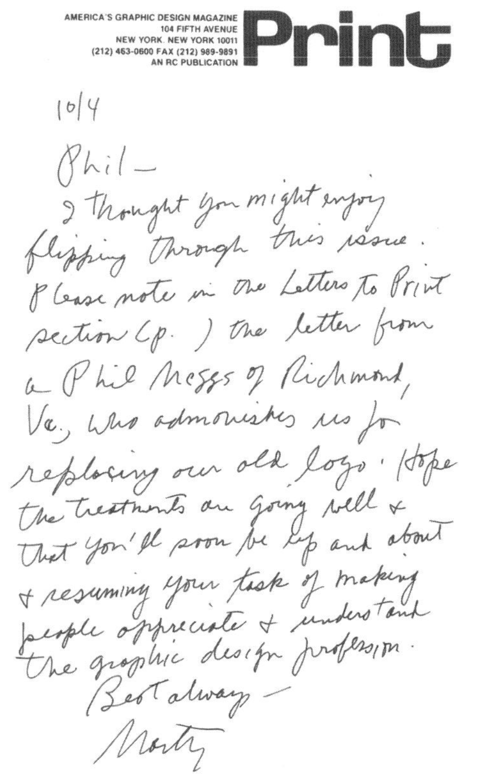

AMERICA'S GRAPHIC DESIGN MAGAZINE
104 FIFTH AVENUE
NEW YORK, NEW YORK 10011
(212) 463-0600 FAX (212) 989-9891
AN RC PUBLICATION

Print

10/4

Phil —

I thought you might enjoy flipping through this issue. Please note in the Letters to Print section (p.) the letter from a Phil Meggs of Richmond, Va., who admonishes us for replacing our old logo. Hope the treatments are going well & that you'll soon be up and about & resuming your task of making people appreciate & understand the graphic design profession.

Best always —

Marty

Foreword to *Revival of the Fittest*, coauthored with Roy McKelvey
(2000)

Over the past two decades, digital technology has changed major aspects of our society. Many of these advances – from computer-regulated automobiles to retail laser scanners – impact our lives in a significant way, but do much of their work behind the scenes. In the realm of visual communications, new technology has completely altered our perceptual experience. Typography, images, and even the very nature of space in graphic and kinetic media have been profoundly reincarnated.

Very few other fields of human endeavor have undergone such rapid and irrevocable change as typography. Two decades ago, our typefaces were produced by a small number of equipment manufacturers and font distributors. Their dominance was challenged and destroyed by the digital revolution. The arrival, damnation, acceptance, and eventual embrace of microprocessors in the 1980s now seems like ancient history. New tools often spawn vast democratizing processes: people who were barely aware of the differences between serif and sans-serif type now discuss their favorite fonts with authority and ease.

Today, individual designers sit at their desktop computers and create all manner of experimental, expressionistic, and downright weird typefaces. Thousands of new fonts have been created by designers exploring every conceivable new direction. Many observers consider this a mixed blessing, as rampant weeds compete with exquisite new flowers in the typographic garden. And many designers disagree vehemently about whether certain new extreme fonts are indeed weeds or flowers.

Much recent typographic dialogue has focused on the new, the different, and the avant-garde. An astounding array of books and periodicals have devoted themselves to documenting and presenting new digital typefaces and examples of their use in graphic design. Less attention has been directed toward a parallel and equally exciting trend. In recent years, as typeface designers hurled unprecedented new typefaces into the cultural milieu, they have also worked intensely to adapt classic typefaces that have stood the test of time to the digital realm. This process is not simply the rote conversion of existing forms from a previous technology to a newer one: a complex set of options exists when one transforms typefaces designed for earlier methodologies into bits of information.

Should a typeface designer slavishly copy the original exemplar, including numerous imperfections and inconsistencies? Or should one draw inspiration from earlier fonts, then exploit the vast potential of digital technology to refine and perfect letters, spacing, and details in the new rendition? Many early type families consisted of only Roman and italic variants, or perhaps two weights and matching italics. To what degree should artistic license be taken to create a myriad of weights, widths, and postures?

Sometimes designers draw inspiration from the look and feel of a classic font to forge a totally new typeface. Fascinating hybrids result when sensitive designers synthesize attributes of one or more typographic directions into completely new fonts. Even such unequivocal distinctions as sans serif and serif have been blurred.

(continued on page 242)

Philip Meggs: Button Jacket

Buttons collected by Phil over a period of 30 years. (1972–2002)

From time to time, he wore this jacket while lecturing to his graphic design history class. Seldom was he seen without a button attached to his clothing. Wearing Phil's jacket is Bizhan Khodabandeh, a former student and advisee.

Jasmine
DAN THE MAN
F.A.T.E. '95
Philip Meggs
I LIKE IKE
KEEP IT CLEAN KEEP IT GREEN
BUSINESS IS GOOD.

Typography is as susceptible to shifting sensibilities and fads as the fashion industry. For those with even a modest experience with type, terms like "gay nineties," "art nouveau," "psychedelic," and "bit-mapped" evoke specific typographic forms related closely to earlier social and cultural eras. These different forms bring richness and historical vitality to typography. While many designers enjoy exploring both period-specific and new digital fonts, they also make wide use of classic typefaces. Digital technology provides unprecedented control over type, and designers are revitalizing classic typefaces in innovative ways. Spatial possibilities such as layering and three-dimensionality; combinations of fonts; extreme scale and size contrasts; and vibrant color applications: these are just some of the ways designers are reinvigorating traditional forms, which would have been unthinkable or prohibitively expensive a decade ago. In the face of all this experimentation, even the most audacious designers are drawn to beautifully crafted traditional type.

This book presents 20 major categories of type, ranging from fonts based on Claude Garamond's work from 500 years ago to contemporary designs like Meta and Frutiger, already acclaimed as classics in their own time. The history and background of each category is discussed. Both historic and recent applications demonstrate these typefaces' potential for use in contemporary practice. Outstanding new versions by leading digital type designers are presented and analyzed. Numerous diagrams and font demonstrations display design properties characterizing closely related faces. A prologue presents several designers' views as to what fundamentally defines a classic typeface. The many forces influencing the evolution of typeface design are discussed in the introduction. This book grew out of our love and fascination with the vitality and diversity of typography today. We hope it will provide information and inspiration for others who share our passion and curiosity about type.

Introduction to *The Allure of Postage Stamps* (2000)

The allure of postage stamps and philately (the term for the collection and study of stamps); the enduring importance of mail service in the daily lives of people everywhere; and the creativity of graphic design are all celebrated by the images in this address book. They were produced by graphic designers in AIGA/SF, the San Francisco Chapter of the American Institute of Graphic Arts, America's largest professional graphic design organization. After an A-to-Z list of philatelic terms had been compiled by Bill Senkus, Sheryn Labate, and Alyson Kuhn, designers at twenty-six Bay Area studios translated them into finished designs. Together, they explore a marvelous range of visual possibilities.

Postal systems operated in ancient cultures, including Babylon, Persia, and Rome. Cyrus, ruler of Persia, stationed horsemen at posts or stations located one day's ride apart. Delivering messages from one station to the next was called "post riding." These Persian post riders made an indelible impression upon the fifth-century B.C. Greek historian Herodotus, who wrote, "And neither snow nor rain nor heat nor gloom of night stays these couriers from the swift completion of their appointed rounds."

Although postal systems have existed for thousands of years, postage stamps are a relatively recent development. In the 1830s, English postage was calculated by a complex system based on the distance and the number of pages in a letter. Reformer Rowland Hill proposed the "penny post," permitting people to mail a half-ounce letter anywhere in the kingdom for a single penny.

Hill's innovations also included the world's first adhesive postage stamps, issued in 1840. Sporting a profile of Queen Victoria printed in black ink with the words "Postage" and "One Penny," these first stamps were denounced by the press. Licking stamps was called a surefire method of spreading the plague and an insult to Her Majesty by "slobbering all over her head." But stamps prevailed over their critics and were soon issued by postal systems around the world.

In a tradition dating to ancient coins, early stamps symbolized autocratic authority through profile portraits of political leaders. These early generic images were joined by commemoratives honoring anniversaries of people or events, and topicals whose illustrations depict flora, fauna, or other attractive subjects. People were fascinated by miniature masterpieces of the engraver's art arriving in the right-hand corner of letters and saved these perforated and gummed receipts of prepaid postage. Collecting stamps developed into a popular pastime, and philately became known as "the hobby of kings."

A rich vocabulary has evolved around postage stamps; for example, the term cinderella is used for stamp-sized graphics that look like stamps but have no value as postage. This brings us to the graphic art presented here: imaginative cinderellas presenting an illustrated alphabet of philatelic terms. Words like bisect, overprint, and se-tenant are expressed with originality and graphic wit. These pages are graced with a fascinating diversity of approaches, offering a fitting tribute to the visual vitality of postage stamps.

"N" is for Numerals
Design: Earl Gee (1997)

"O" is for Over-print
Design: Michael Cronin (1998)

Introduction to the Fiftieth Anniversary Edition of *The Mechanical Bride* by Marshall McLuhan (2000)

[1] *With the exception of this note, the "footnote numbers" in this Introduction refer not to notes, but to the referenced or quoted page in* The Mechanical Bride.

The top-rated television show of 1968–70, *Rowan and Martin's Laugh In,* pushed fast-paced editing to the limits of human comprehension. Each week, one segment featured a joke wall, where cast members opened trap doors in rapid-fire sequence and hurled one-line jokes at the audience. In the midst of one joke blitz, Goldie Hawn, who played the ultimate "dumb blonde," opened a door and giggled, "Marshall McLuhan, what are ya' doin'?"

How did a pensive Toronto college professor escape anonymity and achieve a level of notoriety permitting him to be the subject of a one-liner on a television program watched by millions? McLuhan's fame resulted from his position as oracle of the new electronic information age. As industrial society struggled to understand how it was being transformed by technology; why communications media – especially television – were changing people's thought patterns; and how the media was being used by politicians and corporations to control public opinion, create mass markets, and steer people along paths beneficial to the message makers, McLuhan offered a comprehensible theory about what was happening, and why.

During the turbulent 1960s, McLuhan's book, *Understanding Media: The Extensions of Man,* along with two uncommonly visual sequels, *The Medium Is the Massage: An Inventory of Effects* and *War and Peace in the Global Village* (both with graphic designer Quentin Fiore) proved widely influential for their interpretation of the turbulent changes occurring in society. McLuhan's work led a multitude of interpreters to declare the death of print. Actually, he believed existing media were radically changing in response to television, computers, and other electronic media. The rational world of print spawned by Gutenberg's invention of movable type around 1450, McLuhan thought, would yield to a new world of audiovisual sensation. He warned that new modes of communication were reshaping society. Generations who primarily received information from printed communications were influenced by this medium to sense things one at a time in the logical sequence found in a line of type, while those whose primary communications media are electronic discern multiple communications simultaneously, often through more than one sense. As a result, McLuhan thought, human life was returning to the circumstances of a tribal community, but on a global scale, as new technologies linked the far-flung regions of the planet.

Ironically, far more people knew about McLuhan's ideas than read his books. His genius for turning a phrase and expressing potent ideas as telegraphic probes enabled the media to turn his verbal spears into sound bites, skimming ideas from the surface of complex, multi-layered thinking. His concepts that have become part of the cultural mainstream include "the global village," and "the medium is the message." This conclusion – meaning the nature of a communication media impacts society even more than its content – proved quite controversial.

Behind the public persona, there existed a probing intellect carefully analyzing media and its impact upon citizens. McLuhan began his study of the psychological and social effects of technology and communications media during the 1940s, before electronic media turned *The Gutenberg Galaxy* (as McLuhan titled his 1962 book exploring the condition of typographic man) upside down. A half-century ago, the world was hardly a kinder or simpler place. Humankind confronted the ravages of World War II, the atomic bomb, and the Holocaust. The communications environment was vastly different from today's. Television was just emerging, for by 1950 there were only ten million television-owning American households compared to over a hundred million now. Radio and cinema were in their prime, but print media still provided the primary conduit for information, entertainment, and advertising.

The Mechanical Bride was McLuhan's early effort to assess mass-media culture and the popular arts, analyzing their effect upon people. The techniques of literary and art criticism were deployed onto a new target – the lowly ads, comics, and popular press usually derided and ignored by academicians and analysts of contemporary society. It was published after fifteen years of analyzing and interpreting hundreds of artifacts yanked from the media bombardment. *The Mechanical Bride* is very straightforward. Fifty-nine sections reproduce printed artifacts, including ads, comic strips, movie posters, and covers of magazines and books, accompanied by a short critical essay analyzing each exhibit[1] (as McLuhan calls these artifacts). Each section has a short title and between three and five introductory questions that act as probes, provoking the reader's thinking.

McLuhan's books replaced the traditional linear structure of print media with the fragmentation, flashbacks, and sequences used in film and television. He explodes the tradition of continuity so precious to writers and editors. The organizational techniques are analogous to avant garde films, with disparate information collaged together to make a disjunctive yet interrelated whole. McLuhan explains the need to "use many kinds of positions and views in relationship to the popular imagery of industrial society as a means to getting as clear an over-all sense of the situation as can be done. Using the shifting imagery of our society as a barometer requires range and agility rather than rigid adherence to a single position."[70]

The exhibits in *The Mechanical Bride* can be shuffled without injury to the message, yet a cumulative effect occurs as threads reappear and elaborate upon earlier passages. One need not read his books from start to finish. Each book is a barrage of revolutionary and challenging ideas, alternating between crystal insight and perplexing complexity. Reader participation is required to assemble the parts into a whole.

Evidence of McLuhan's struggle to coalesce his vision is found in four preliminary manuscripts, now housed in the National Archives of Canada. The first is titled *Guide to Chaos,* reflecting McLuhan's perceptions that industrial man now lived in a chaotic society, lacking the rhythmic order of the seasons and harvest found in earlier epochs. The following three are all titled *Typhon in America,* after the Greek mythological monster with one hundred heads. This suggests the complexity and danger of the blitzkrieg of messages aimed at industrial man. The final title, *The Mechanical Bride,* echoes McLuhan's concern about the pervasive commingling of sex and technology in advertising. He feared that "one dream opens into another until reality and fantasy are made interchangeable."[97] Both the title and McLuhan's concerns reflect Marcel Duchamp's large painting on glass, *"The Bride Stripped Bare by her Bachelors, Even."* Like Duchamp, McLuhan was able to observe his society from an outsider's viewpoint and became troubled by unchecked forces shaping people's lives.

The subtitle of *The Mechanical Bride, 'The Folklore of Industrial Man,'* causes one to pause. We think of folklore as the beliefs, customs, and values passed down among a people through media such as tales and songs. It is *of* and *for* the people. McLuhan concluded the folklore of our society is determined, not by education or religion, but by mass media. The exhibits presented in *The Mechanical Bride* were aimed at the people, in hopes of accomplishing a goal: buy this brand of light bulb[17] or wear this color of stocking[81] this season. Advertising agencies and Hollywood are "constantly striving to enter and control the unconscious minds of a vast public... in order to exploit them for profit."[97] An anonymous narrator speaks to an anonymous audience. There are no links between the two, except for the mass-media message. The narrator has an agenda, but the recipient is usually a passive observer being shaped and molded like Silly Putty.™ Perhaps much traditional folklore has been like this as well, fabricated by tribal chieftains, medicine men, nobility, and religious leaders to control the populace.

In the Preface to his earliest hand-written manuscript, McLuhan says the exhibits possess an "invisibility. They are intended to be absorbed through the pores or be gulped in a kind of mental breathing. Taken out of its usual setting and isolated for clinical observation, an ad or comic comes to life at the conscious level. Of course, it was never intended to exist there. Yet at the level of rationality these things are suddenly seen to have a rationale of their own." The significance of *The Mechanical Bride* stems from McLuhan's realization that ads, comics, and movies are not what they seem. This book is a valiant effort to define what the media and its effects really are.

McLuhan was obsessed with the relationship between advertising and the human condition. When discussing books touted as an aid when climbing the corporate ladder, he observes how "the more equality there is in the race for inequality, the more intense the race and the less the inequality which results from the consequent rewards. That means less and less distinction for more and more men of distinction."[37] Warning how "business and political life will take on mainly the character of diversion and entertainment for the passive public,"[40] he anticipated mass-media hysteria over political sex scandals and product failures.

Popular magazines analyzed in *The Mechanical Bride* bear the full force of McLuhan's analysis. *Time* then claimed to be "organized on a principle of COMPLETE ORGANIZATION" and extolled its virtue of covering the news "as if by one man for one man." McLuhan asks whether this suggested a "highly colored and selective approach" with a "strong tinge of the totalitarian in the formula?" [10] (After decades of anonymous journalism with the complete magazine edited into a conforming editorial style, today *Time* magazine features individual writers with prominent photographs and bylines.) *The Reader's Digest* is dubbed "Pollyanna Digest" and accused of packaging the "heap of goodness, beauty, and power in everybody and everything" [148] and rushing it to market. *The New Yorker* is indicted because "snobbery based on economic privilege constitutes the mainstay of its technique and appeal." [9] When *The New Yorker* attacked *The Reader's Digest,* McLuhan sees it as "a wrestling match between two men, each of whom was locked in a separate trunk." [148]

Often, an exhibit is a catalyst prompting a discourse about some aspect of society. An advertisement [127] for a one-volume condensation of twenty-five high school subjects, *High School Subjects Self Taught,* prompted McLuhan to discuss the role of the teacher in America and the relationship between parents and teachers.

McLuhan urges an expanded definition of literacy. Understanding the media that provides our information, and being able to critically evaluate how its form and content changes our lives, is as important as the traditional curriculum. Many now see media literacy as an important part of education, but when *The Mechanical Bride* was first published, people were befuddled by McLuhan's approach. He realized how people's mental habits blinded them to truths hidden behind the facade of surface meaning. The media barrage is a form of unofficial education, and McLuhan thought the only practical way to bring it under control was "uninhibited inspection of popular and commercial culture." [45]

McLuhan searches for semiotics beneath semiotics – levels of meaning beyond the messenger's intent or the recipient's awareness. One can better cope with automobile marketing if one understands the presentation of the vehicle as both womb and phallic symbol, because ads simultaneously sell curvaceous streamlining and comfort along with aggressive power. [84] The monotheistic Gothic Crucifix yields to the industrial age's cluster symbols, such as the Coca-Cola™ girl, [118] who combines sweet innocence with assembly-line showgirl beauty, and the drum majorette, who blends youthful innocence, sexuality, and militarism. [122] We are made aware of pervasive cluster images combining sex, technology, and death. [10] Superman,™ the "comic strip brother of the medieval angels," [103] is revealed for his "strong-armed totalitarian methods" and "immature and barbaric mind." [102]

Unlike many philosophers and theologians actively seeking truth, McLuhan understands the fallacy of a fixed and static viewpoint. The vantage point must shift and evolve as one thinks about new problems and seeks new truths. Quantum mechanics, relativity, and Cubism are cited as manifestations of this seismic shift in technology and the social climate.

McLuhan's facility for throwing out ideas by the bushel provides much insight. It also gives careful readers, who analyze McLuhan's probes as carefully as he scrutinizes his exhibits, many points on which to disagree. McLuhan endorsed these challenges, believing his works were dialogues rather than dogma.

The tenuousness of democracy is exposed, for McLuhan characterizes newspapers as appealing to the Jeffersonian enmity toward federal centralization and corporations, while being vast bureaucratic corporations themselves. [5] Popular ventriloquist Edgar Bergen is seen metaphorically as the massive and powerful organization controlling his dummy, Charlie McCarthy, who signifies everyman – outspoken and fiercely independent but ultimately powerless without the control of the benevolent Bergen. [16] The appeal of western movies is attributed to their ability to give "people overwhelmed by industrial scale" a glimpse of "the primordial image of the lonely entrepreneur" to "a commercial society far advanced along the road of monopolistic bureaucracy." [156] The conduit of control becomes concentrated in movies, the press, and radio. [22] McLuhan fears most citizens "will inevitably sink into a serfdom for which they have already been very well conditioned." [92]

McLuhan is the ultimate phrase turner; wordplay runs throughout his writings. James Joyce is frequently quoted; clearly, McLuhan revered Joyce and learned much from Joyce's creative and expressive manipulations of the English language. McLuhan's metaphors are often astounding, as when he tells us that, after a modern painting or prose doesn't deliver a conventional message, audiences "kick the cigarette machine because it doesn't deliver peanuts."[106] Readers who are alert to McLuhan's subtle word-play will avoid the mistakes of Marvin Kitman, who mistook a paraphrase for a quotation when he reviewed *The Medium is the Massage* in the March 26, 1967, *New York Times.* Kitman wrote, "An alert continuity acceptance department (the editor at Bantam) never should have allowed the misquotation from Shakespeare: 'All the world's a sage.' The correct word is 'stage.'" McLuhan soared right over his reviewer's head.

McLuhan understands the vast potential of communications media to provide collective experiences. Unintentional byproducts of its techniques include reforming the world as one city.[10] "This planet is a single city"[3] spawned the "global village." The seeds of many later ideas formed by McLuhan and others pepper the text. Calling the information conduits of 1950 "the superhighways of thought and feeling stretched across the contemporary...."[22] anticipates today's information superhighway.

The exhibits evaluated in *The Mechanical Bride* are now over fifty years old. For us they are compelling cultural artifacts – wordy, romantic, and pictorial. For mid-century readers, they were part of the environment, surrounding and engulfing their daily life. Readers today will marvel at how McLuhan's exhibits and text make us aware of accelerated change over a short half-century. Imagine the disdain today if a club called the Seniors League were composed of women "frankly over forty."[13] What could be more silly to contemporary mores than McLuhan's quotation from showman Ken Murry, who said, "Over-bustiness is on the way out as a feminine ideal," being killed by television because – unlike movies and the stage – "TV, remember, goes right into the living room where parents, kids, and the old folks all watch it together."[75] Curiously, this is the only mention of television in *The Mechanical Bride.* In a few short years, television overwhelmed Murry's viewpoint and became a focus of McLuhan's investigations during the three decades after publication of *The Mechanical Bride.*

Morally outraged, McLuhan's view of industrial man was rather grim. McLuhan saw a puppet controlled by forces of commerce and advertising that don't merely pull the strings that make him dance, but burrow deeply into his consciousness to shape his view of the world.

Given the phenomenal changes in technology, media, and society in the fifty years since *The Mechanical Bride* was first published, one must ask if this book is still relevant to life in the twenty-first century. The answer is an unqualified yes. The stones McLuhan turned over fifty years ago have grown bigger and heavier; the chaotic mass-media jungle he analyzed has expanded into an information superhighway. But the road map he sketched for understanding and navigating the chaos and manipulation of the mass media still points in the right direction. As an alarmed reviewer, James Scott, observed in *The Telegram* on October 27, 1951, "Maybe Mr. McLuhan has the answer. At any rate, he points to a situation which the still-thinking member of society cannot any longer ignore.... I particularly recommend *[The Mechanical Bride]* to the attention of every teacher, every parent, every man and woman in any way connected with education. Before we lose another generation, let's get busy...."

The Mechanical Bride can help people recognize and understand the forces shaping their lives. The importance of understanding the assault of media is crystallized by McLuhan's observation, "the price of total resistance, like that of total surrender, is still too high."[144]

Upon completion of *A History of Graphic Design,* first edition, Phil posed for a photograph to be used on the back flap of the book. (1982)

Epilogue

From *A History of Graphic Design,*
First Edition (1983)

At the time of this writing, human affairs are undergoing a new revolution comparable to the industrial revolution that launched the machine age. Electronic circuitry, microprocessors, and computer-generated imagery threaten to radically alter our culture's images, communications processes, and the very nature of work itself. Graphic design, like many other spheres of human activity, is undergoing profound changes. The graphic design community is responding to this new age of electronic circuitry by an involvement in mediagraphics, systems design, and computer graphics. The tools — as has happened so often in the past — are changing with the relentless advance of technology, but the essence of graphic design remains unchanged. That essence is an ability to translate ideas and concepts into visual form and to bring order to information.

The need for clear and imaginative visual communications to relate people to their cultural, economic, and social lives has never been greater. Graphic designers have a responsibility to adapt new technology and to express the zeitgeist of their times by inventing new forms and new ways of expressing ideas. The poster and the book, vital communications tools of the industrial revolution, will survive the new age of electronic technology as major art forms; the written word remains.

May 30, 1942
Born: Philip Baxter Meggs
Identical twin to William Joel Meggs
Newberry County Hospital, Newberry, SC
Mother: Sarah Elizabeth Pruitt Meggs
Father: Wallace Nat Meggs

Moved to Florence, SC at four months old

February 18, 1947
Sister born: Elizabeth Pruitt Meggs (Beth)

1948–1954
Attended Harlee Elementary School, Florence, SC

June 7, 1950
Brother born: Wallace Nathaniel Meggs, Jr. (Wally)

1954–1957
Attended Poynor Junior High School, Florence, SC

1957–1960
Attended and graduated from McClenaghan High School, Florence, SC

1960–1961
Attended University of South Carolina, Extension Center, Francis Marion campus, Florence, SC

March, 1962
Awarded diploma for completion of Famous Artists Schools' three-year correspondence course

1961–1964
Attended and graduated with a Bachelor of Fine Arts degree, Richmond Professional Institute, Richmond, Virginia

1962–1964
Lived at 1 North Harvie Street, Richmond, Virginia with Alston Purvis, Emmet Gowin, and Kuhn Caldwell. These four had a profound influence on each others' lives.

1964–1965
Graphic designer, Philip Morris Research Center, Richmond, Virginia

August 15, 1964
Married Sara Elizabeth Phillips (Libby), Greenville, SC

1964–1989
Partner, Meggs & Meggs

1965–1966
Senior graphic designer, Reynolds Metals Company, Department of Styling and Design, Richmond, Virginia

1966–1968
Art Director, A.H. Robins Company, Inc., Richmond, Virginia

1968
Began teaching in the Communication Arts and Design Department, Virginia Commonwealth University

1968–1971
Attended and graduated with a Master of Fine Arts degree in painting, Virginia Commonwealth University, Richmond, Virginia

1974–1987
Department Chair, Communication Arts and Design Department, School of the Arts, Virginia Commonwealth University

August 19, 1975
First child born: Andrew Philip Meggs, St. Mary's Hospital, Richmond, Virginia

October 2, 1977
Second child born: Elizabeth Wilson Meggs, St. Mary's Hospital, Richmond, Virginia

1977–1999
Visiting Graduate Faculty, Syracuse University

1983
Published *A History of Graphic Design*

1983
Award for Excellence in Publishing, Association of American Publishers, for *A History of Graphic Design*

1989
Outstanding Alumni Award, Virginia Commonwealth University, School of the Arts

Cecil and Ida Green Honors Professor, Texas Christian University, Fort Worth, Texas

1989–2002
Contributing Editor, *Print* magazine

1993–2002
Member of the United States Postal Service's Citizens' Stamp Advisory Committee

1994, 1995
Who's Who Among America's Teachers

1995
Who's Who in American Art, Seventeenth Edition

1995, 1997, 1999
Visiting Faculty, National College of Art and Design, Dublin, Ireland

1996
Virginia Commonwealth University, School of the Arts Outstanding Faculty Award for Overall Excellence in Teaching, Research, and Service

1997
Seminars, Universidad de Palermo, Buenos Aires

May 21, 1999
Honorary Doctor of Fine Arts Degree, Massachusetts College of Art, Boston, Massachusetts

1999–2002
Co-curated "US Design 1975–2000," Denver Museum of Art, Denver, Colorado

2000
On September 8, Phil was diagnosed with acute myelogenous leukemia, a particularly vicious and fast-moving killer. Hospitalized from that date until April 14, 2001, he was at death's door three times. He was unconscious for one month at the Medical College of Virginia's medical respiratory intensive care unit, and connected to every available life-support system. Following a miraculous recovery and undergoing intensive physical therapy, Phil spent the next year and a half happily and productively involved in his teaching and research.

November 14, 2002
Induction into the New York Art Directors Hall of Fame, Special Educator's Award

November 24, 2002
Died in Richmond, Virginia, of complications resulting from leukemia

July 27, 2003
Phil Meggs was posthumously awarded the Postmaster General's Medal of Freedom

2004
Phil Meggs was posthumously awarded the American Institute of Graphic Arts Design Leadership Award. The award states: "The AIGA board of directors, on behalf of the entire design profession, awards its greatest honor, the 2004 Design Leadership Award, to Philip B. Meggs, for the definitive history of graphic design and dedication as a design educator."

The Complete Published Writings

Books

Typographic Design: Form and Communication. Third Edition. With Rob Carter. New York: John Wiley & Sons, 2002.

A History of Graphic Design, Third Edition. Spanish Edition. Mexico City: McGraw-Hill Interamericana Editores, S.A. de C.V., 2000.

A History of the Communications Arts and Design Department at Virginia Commonwealth University 1927-2000. Richmond: Virginia Commonwealth University, 2000.

Texts on Type: Critical Writings on Typography. Steven Heller and Philip B. Meggs, editors. New York: Allworth Press, 2001.

Revival of the Fittest: Digital Versions of Classic Typefaces. Philip B. Meggs and Roy McKelvey, editors. New York: RC Publications, 2000.

Fotografiks. Text by Philip B. Meggs; photographs and design by David Carson. London: Calmann & King, and San Francisco: Gingko Press

A History of Graphic Design. Third Edition. New York: John Wiley & Sons, 1998.

A History of Graphic Design. Japanese Edition. Tokyo: Tankosha Publishing Co., 1997.

A History of Graphic Design. Audio Edition. Princeton: Recording for the Blind and Dyslexic, 1995.

Typographic Design: The Great Typefaces. With Rob Carter. New York: Van Nostrand Reinhold, 1993.

Tomás Gonda: A Life in Design. Richmond: Anderson Gallery, 1994.

Typographic Design: Form and Communication. Second Edition. With Rob Carter. New York: John Wiley & Sons, 1993.

Historia del Diseño Gráfico. Spanish Edition, translated by Martha I. Izaguirre, Carlos S. Iriondo, and Vera S. Elvia. Buenos Aires: Editorial Trillas, 1993.

A History of Graphic Design. Second Edition. New York: Van Nostrand Reinhold, 1992.

Type & Image: The Language of Graphic Design. New York: Van Nostrand Reinhold, 1989.

Typographic Design: Form and Communication. With Rob Carter and Ben Day. New York: Van Nostrand Reinhold, 1985.

A History of Graphic Design. New York: Van Nostrand Reinhold, 1983

Encyclopedia Entries

"Graphic Design." *Encyclopaedia Britannica,* 2001.

"The U.S. National Park Service Unigrid." *Contemporary Masterworks.* London: St. James Press, 1992.

"Typography." *Encyclopedia of Communications,* Oxford and Philadelphia: Oxford University Press and Annenberg School of Communications, 1989.

"Graphic Arts." *Compton's Encyclopedia.* Chicago: Encyclopaedia Britannica, 1986.

Contemporary Designers. Morgan, Ann Lee, editor. London and Chicago: St. James Press, 1985. (Ten essays)

Articles and Chapters

"Introduction." *The Mechanical Bride* Fiftieth Anniversary Edition by Marshall McLuhan. Corte Madera, CA: Gingko Press, 2002.

"An Era of Innovation and Diversity in Graphic Design: 1975–2000." *U.S. Design: 1975–2000.* Munich: Prestel Verlag, 2001.

"The Obscene Typography Machine." *Texts on Type.* New York: Allworth Press, 2001.

"I Am Type! Revisited." *Texts on Type.* New York: Allworth Press, 2001.

"Two Magazines of the Turbulent 60s: A 90s Perspective." *Graphic Design History.* New York: Allworth Press, 2001.

"Peter Behrens: Design's Man of the Century?" *Graphic Design History.* New York: Allworth Press, 2001.

"An Eminent Pre-modernist: The Curious Case of T. M. Cleland." *Graphic Design History.* New York: Allworth Press, 2001.

"For the Voice." *Graphic Design History.* New York: Allworth Press, 2001.

"The Bald Soprano" *Graphic Design History.* New York: Allworth Press, 2001.

"The Rise and Fall of Design at a Great Corporation." *Graphic Design History.* New York: Allworth Press, 2001.

"Introduction." *The Allure of Postage Stamps.* Chronicle Books, 2000.

"The Digital Revolution." *Idea* 280. Vol. 48, No. 280, 2000.

"Introduction." *Revival of the Fittest: Digital Versions of Classic Typefaces.* New York: RC Publications, 2000.

"Caslon." *Revival of the Fittest: Digital Versions of Classic Typefaces.* New York: RC Publications, 2000.

'Letters to *Print:* Departed Icons." *Print* Vol. 54, No. 4, July/Aug 2000.

'Letters to *Print:* Critical Mass.' *Print* Vol. 54, No. 3, May/June 2000.

"Landmarks of Book Design, Tenth of a Series: Before Rosebud Was a Sled." *Print* Vol. 53, No. 3, May/June 1999.

"The Glass Box." *Print* 53, No. 6, Nov/Dec 1999.

"Dead History." *Emigre.* No. 51, Summer 1999.

"Books in Print: *Graphic Design Sources,"* by Kenneth J. Hiebert, and "*Working with Computer Type 4: Experimental Typography"* by Rob Carter. *Print* Vol. 52, No. 4, July/Aug 1998.

"Back Talk: Philip B. Meggs, Design Historian." Interview by Steven Heller. *Print* Vol. 52, No. 6, Nov/Dec 1998.

"Hitting on Bill." *Print* Vol. 52, No. 4, July/Aug 1998.

"Foreword." *Trademarks of the 60s and 70s* by Tyler Blik, Chronicle Books, 1998.

"Foreword." *6 Chapters in Design,* Chronicle Books, 1997.

"Landmarks of Book Design, Ninth of a Series: *Piet Zwart's NKF Catalogue." Print* Vol. 50, No. 2, Mar/Apr 1996.

"Five Top Designers Confess: 'I Never Went to Art School!'" *Print* Vol. 50, No. 3, May/June 1996.

"John Massey: AIGA Medalist." *Graphic Design USA.* New York: American Institute of Graphic Arts, 1996.

"Introduction." *Graphic Design Solutions.* by Robin Landa. New York: Delmar Publishing, 1996.

"Experimentation and Professional Practice." *ZED,* Virginia Commonwealth University, 1996.

"Foreword." *A History of Graphic Design.* Reprinted in *Design Issues,* Vol. 11 No. 1, Spring 1995.

"Be Eccentric: It's the Only Way to Conform." *AIGA Journal of Graphic Design,* Vol. 12, No. 4 1995.

"Education Section Introduction." *Print* Vol. 49, No. 6, Nov/Dec 1995.

"They Knew What They Needed: Pros Teaching Pros." *Print* Vol. 49, No. 6, Nov/Dec 1995.

"Type in Print: Monotype Bullmer." *Print* Vol. 49, No. 3, May/June 1995.

"Type in Print: Dead History." *Print* Vol. 49, No. 3, May/June 1995.

"Edgy Baltimore." *Print* Vol. 49, No. 3, May/June 1995.

"An Eminent Pre-Modernist: The Curious Case of T. M. Cleland." *Print* Vol. 49, No. 2, Mar/Apr 1995.

"The Politics of Style." *Print* Vol. 49, No. 2, Mar/Apr 1995.

"Introduction." *Print's Best Typography 2.* New York: RC Publications, 1995.

"Chapter Three: Turn-of-the-Century Posters: Art + Technology + Graphic Design." *Designed to Sell: Turn-of-the-Century American Posters.* Richmond: Virginia Museum of Fine Arts, 1994.

"Chapter Four: Technical Notes." *"Designed to Sell: Turn-of-the-Century American Posters."* Richmond: Virginia Museum of Fine Arts, 1994.

"Notes on the Influence of Dutch Graphic Design." *Dutch Graphic Design: 1918–1945.* Massachusetts College of Art, 1994.

"Art and World War II." *The Portfolio.* Vol. 11, No. 3, Fall 1994.

"The Obscene Typography Machine." *Looking Closer: Critical Writings on Graphic Design.* New York: Allworth Press, 1994.

"Type in Print: Big Caslon CC." *Print* Vol. 48, No. 4, Nov/Dec 1994.

"Required Reading for the Millennium." *Print* Vol. 48, No. 4, Nov/Dec 1994.

"Landmarks of Book Design, Eighth of a Series: *The Bald Soprano." Print* Vol. 48, No. 1, Jan/Feb 1994.

"Exhibiting the Holocaust." *Print* Vol. 48, No. 3, May/June 1994.

"Type in Print: Silica." *Print* Vol. 48, No. 2, Mar/Apr 1994.

"Two Magazines of the Turbulent 60s: A 90s Perspective." *Print* Vol. 48, No. 2, Mar/Apr 1994.

"Has Graphic Design Got a Future?" *Print* Vol. 48, No. 2, Mar/Apr 1994.

"Landmarks of Book Design, Seventh of a Series: *American Typefounders Specimen Book and Catalogue, 1923." Print* Vol. 48, No. 1, Jan/Feb 1994.

"Tribute to an Unrepentant Modernist." *Print* Vol. 48, No. 1, Jan/Feb 1994.

"Outside Milan: The Other 999 Points of Light." *Print* Vol. 47, No. 6, Nov/Dec 1993.

"Books in Print: *Design Form and Chaos."* by Paul Rand. *Print* Vol. 47, No. 3, July/Aug 1993.

"Books in Print: *The Elements of Typographic Style."* by Robert Bringhurst. *Print* Vol. 47, No. 3, July/Aug 1993.

"Books in Print: *Stop Stealing Sheep and Find Out How Type Works."* by Erik Spiekermann and E. M. Ginger. *Print* Vol. 47, No. 3, July/Aug 1993.

"Performing Art." *Print* Vol. 47, No. 3, May/June 1993.

"Books in Print: *Twentieth Century Type."* by Lewis Blackwell. *Print* Vol. 47, No. 3, May/June 1993.

"Rare Show." *Print* Vol. 47, No. 2, Mar/Apr 1993.

"Landmarks in Book Design, Sixth of a Series: *Mira Calligraphiae Monumenta." Print* Vol. 47, No. 1, Jan/Feb 1993.

"Books in Print: *Dutch Graphic Design: 1918–1945."* by Alston Purvis. *Print* Vol. 47, No. 1, Jan/Feb 1993.

"Books in Print: *Angry Graphics: Protest Posters of the Reagan-Bush Era"* by Karrie Jacobs and Steven Heller. *Print* 47, No. 1, Jan/Feb 1993.

"Books in Print: *The Designer's Guide to Creating Corporate I.D. Systems for Companies of All Types and Sizes."* by Rose DeNeve. *Print* Vol. 47, No. 1, Jan/Feb 1993.

"The Crash of the NASA Logo: It Could Have Been Worse." *AIGA Journal of Graphic Design.* Vol. 10, No. 4, 1992.

"A Cold Eye: The New Illegibility." *Print* Vol. 47, No. 1, Sept/Oct 1992.

"Landmarks of Book Design, Fifth of a Series: *The End of the World as Filmed by the Angel of Notre Dame." Print* Vol. 46, No. 5, Sept/Oct 1992.

"The Rise and Fall of Design at a Great Corporation." *Print* Vol. 46, No. 3, May/June 1992.

"Hitch Your Wagon to a Star." *AIGA Journal of Graphic Design,* Vol. 9, No. 4 1992.

"Landmarks of Book Design, Fourth of a Series: *The Elements of Euclid." Print* Vol. 46, No. 1, Jan/Feb 1992.

"Books in Print: *Graphic Design Processes: Universal to Unique."* by Kenneth J. Hiebert. *Print* Vol. 46, No. 2, Mar/Apr 1992.

"Books in Print: *Visual Literacy: A Conceptual Approach to Graphic Design Problem Solving."* by Judith Wilde and Richard Wilde. *Print* Vol. 46, No. 2, Mar/Apr 1992.

"Books in Print: *Ulm Design: The Mortality of Objects."* by Herbert Lindinger. *Print* Vol. 46, No. 2, Mar/Apr 1992.

"Books in Print: *The New Cranbrook Design Discourse."* by Hugh Aldersey-Williams, et. al. *Print* Vol. 46, No. 2, Mar/Apr 1992.

"Introduction." *Print's Best Typography 1.* New York: RC Publications, 1992.

"Books in Print: *On Stone: The Art and Use of Typography on the Personal Computer.*" by Sumner Stone. *Print* Vol. 45, No. 6, Nov/Dec 1991.

"Books in Print: *Modern Encyclopedia of Typefaces*" by Lawrence W. Wallis. *Print* Vol. 45, No. 6, Nov/Dec 1991.

"Wild Plakken: A Radical Bent." *Print* Vol. 45, No. 6, Nov/Dec 1991.

"Blaeu's *Atlas Major*: A Landmark of the Dutch Book." *Print* Vol. 45, No. 6, Nov/Dec 1991.

"Post War Post Mortem: Made for Television." *Print* Vol. 45, No. 6, Nov/Dec 1992.

"A Cold Eye: Tibor the Pit Bull." *Print* Vol. 45, No. 3, May/June 1991.

"The Death of *Eros*." *Print* Vol. 45, No. 3, May/June 1991.

"Landmarks of Book Design, Third of a Series: *The Knave of Hearts.*" *Print* Vol. 45, No. 3, May/June 1991

"Peter Behrens: Design's Man of the Century?" *Print* Vol. 45, No. 2, Mar/Apr 1991.

"A Cold Eye: Holding Education Accountable." *Print* Vol. 45, No. 2, Mar/Apr 1991.

"CBS Records." *Graphis* 271, Jan/Feb, 1991.

"Design USA: To Russia with Love." *Print* 44, No. 2, Mar/Apr 1991.

"Is a Design History Canon Really Dangerous?" *AIGA Journal of Graphic Design,* Vol. 9, No. 3, 1991.

"The Designer, Paper, and the Environment." *Communication Arts,* Vol. 32, No. 4, 1990.

"Notes on a Grand Master." *Print* Vol. 44, No. 5, Sept/Oct 1990.

"Landmarks of Book Design, Second of a Series: *For the Voice.*" *Print* Vol. 44, No. 5, Sept/Oct 1990.

"Women's Place: Two at the Top." *Print* Vol. 44, No. 6, Nov/Dec 1990.

"A Cold Eye: The Last Word on the Walker Show." *Print* Vol. 44, No. 6, Nov/Dec 1990.

"Books in Print: *Basic Typography: Handbook for Technique and Design.*" by Reudi Ruegg. *Print* Vol. 44, No. 4, Jul/Aug 1990.

"Books in Print: *Signs and Symbols.*" by Adrian Frutiger. *Print* Vol. 44, No. 4, Jul/Aug 1990.

"Books in Print: *Typographie.*" by Otl Aicher. *Print* Vol. 44, No. 4, Jul/Aug 1990.

"Landmarks of Book Design, First of a Series: *World Geographic Atlas.*" *Print* Vol. 44, No. 1, Jan/Feb 1990.

"Is the Sleepwalking Giant Waking Up?" *Print* Vol. 44, No. 1, Jan/Feb 1990.

"The Vitality of Risk." *AIGA Journal of Graphic Design,* Vol. 8, No. 4, 1990.

"The Design Education Quandary." *AIGA Journal of Graphic Design,* Vol. 8, No. 3, 1990.

"Mondrian As a Marketing Tool." *AIGA Journal of Graphic Design,* Vol. 8, No. 2, 1990.

"Saul Bass on Corporate Identity." *AIGA Journal of Graphic Design,* Vol. 8, No. 1, 1990.

"Deconstructing Typography." *Step-By-Step Graphics,* Vol. 6, No. 2, 1990.

"Where Have All the Icons Gone?" *Great American Icons: Strathmore Americana.* Strathmore Paper Company, 1990.

"Test Your Typographic IQ." *AIGA Journal of Graphic Design,* Vol. 6, No. 4, 1989.

"Louis Prang: The Man Who Brought Out the Artist in Children." *AIGA Journal of Graphic Design,* Vol. 7, No. 1, 1989.

"A Pantheon of Design Eccentricity." *AIGA Journal of Graphic Design,* Vol. 7, No. 2, 1989.

"Farewell to the Opulent Eighties." *AIGA Journal of Graphic Design,* Vol. 7, No. 3, 1989.

"Sounding the Retreat: Federal Design Today." *Print* Vol. 43, No. 5, Sept/Oct 1989.

"The Obscene Typography Machine." *Print* Vol. 43, No. 5, Sept/Oct 1989.

"The 1940s: Rise of the Modernists." *Print* Vol. 43, No. 6, Nov/Dec 1989.

"Books in Print: *Bradbury Thompson: The Art of Graphic Design.*" *Print* Vol. 43, No. 4, May/June 1989.

"Books in Print: *Typographic Communications Today.*" by Edward M. Gottshall. *Print* Vol. 43, No. 5, Sept/Oct 1989.

"The Women Who Saved New York." *Print* Vol. 43, No. 1, Jan/Feb 1989.

"A Cold Eye: The Logo-ette Fetish." *Print* 43, No. 6, Nov/Dec 1989.

"Test Your Typographic IQ." *AIGA Journal of Graphic Design,* Vol. 6, No. 4 1989.

"Celebrating the Feminization of Design." *AIGA Journal of Graphic Design,* Vol. 6, No. 3, 1989.

"Foreword." *American Typography Today.* by Rob Carter. New York: Van Nostrand Reinhold, 1989.

"End of the Design Superstar?" *Print* Vol. 42, No. 3, May/June 1988.

"*Time* vs. *Newsweek:* Coping and Competing in the World of CNN." *Print* Vol. 42, No. 5, Sept/Oct 1988.

"Government Style: Design Consciousness and the Feds." *AIGA Journal of Graphic Design,* Vol. 6, No. 1, 1988.

"Perils of Disinformation." *AIGA Journal of Graphic Design,* Vol. 6, No. 2, 1988.

"Design Papers: Theory, Rhetoric, and Revolution." *AIGA Journal of Graphic Design,* Vol. 6, No. 3, 1988.

"ITC Bashing." *Print* Vol. 42, No. 6, Nov/Dec 1988.

"The Federal Design Improvement Program." *AIGA Journal of Graphic Design,* Vol. 6, No. 1, 1988.

"The Emporer's Dour Critics." *Print* Vol. 42, No. 1, Jan/Feb 1988.

"Polemic Design: When Message Reigns Supreme." *AIGA Journal of Graphic Design,* Vol. 5, No. 4, 1987.

"Esprit Graphic Design." *AIGA Journal of Graphic Design,* Vol. 5, No. 3, 1987.

"Design at Esprit." *Graphic Design USA: 8.* New York: Watson-Guptill, 1987.

"What is American About American Graphic Design?" *AIGA Journal of Graphic Design,* Vol. 5, No. 3, 1987.

"Frank Heller." *School of the Arts Journal.* School of the Arts, Virginia Commonwealth University, Spring 1987.

"Remembering Mallory Callan." *School of the Arts Journal.* School of the Arts, Virginia Commonwealth University, Spring 1987.

"An Oracle of the 21st Century Book." *AIGA Journal of Graphic Design,* Vol. 5, No. 2, 1987.

"High Style, Low Style, Vile Style." *AIGA Journal of Graphic Design,* Vol. 5, No. 1, 1987.

"The AIGA Leadership Award 1985: WBGH Education Foundation." *Graphic Design USA: 7.* New York: Watson-Guptill, 1986.

"*The Atlantic Monthly*: A New Vision for a Vintage Periodical." Graphis, Jan/Feb 1986.

"Introduction." *30-Year Retrospective of Annual Reports: 1956–1986.* Exhibition Catalog. Dayton: Mead, 1986.

"Toulouse-Lautrec: Superb But Not Alone." *AIGA Journal of Graphic Design,* Vol. 4, No. 2, 1986.

"Design Education: Pedagogy vs. the Real World." *AIGA Journal of Graphic Design,* Vol. 4, No. 1, 1986.

"The Swiss Influence: The Old New Wave." *AIGA Journal of Graphic Design,* Vol. 4, No. 1, 1986.

"When Norman Rockwell Painted Herb Lubalin." *AIGA Journal of Graphic Design,* Vol. 4, No. 3, 1986.

"Graphic Design History: Discipline or Anarchy?" *AIGA Journal of Graphic Design,* Vol. 3, No. 4, 1985.

"The Demilitarization of Graphic Design." *AIGA Journal of Graphic Design,* Vol. 3, No. 3, 1985.

"Preface." *Graphis Annual 1984-85.* Zurich: Graphis Press, 1985.

"Herbert Bayer." *Design Issues,* Vol. II, No. 2, Fall 1985

"George Tscherny." *Graphis* 230, Mar/Apr 1984.

"Book Reviews:" *Art and Graphics* and *Top Graphic Design. Design Book Review.* Fall 1984.

"From Proclamation to Art Form." *Research in Action.* Vol. 6, No. 2, 1982.

"Novum Education: Virginia Commonwealth University, Richmond." *Novum Gebrauchs-graphik,* Nov 11, 1976.

Rob Carter is a professor of typography and graphic design at Virginia Commonwealth University, and has served as a visiting professor at the Gerrit Rietveld Academy in Amsterdam. For his work he has received numerous awards from organizations such as the American Institute of Graphic Arts, New York Type Directors Club, New York Art Directors Club, Society of Typographic Arts, *Creativity,* and *Print* regional annual. He is the author of *American Typography Today,* the five-volume *Working with Type* series, and *Digital Color and Type.* He is also the co-author with Philip B. Meggs of *Typographic Design: Form and Communication* (four editions) and *Typographic Specimens: The Great Typefaces.*

Steven Heller is co-chair of the MFA Designer as Author program and co-founder of the MFA in Design Criticism at the School of Visual Arts in New York. He is the editor of the *AIGA VOICE:* Online Journal of Design and author, editor, or coauthor of over one hundred books on design and popular culture, including *Stylepedia: A Guide to Graphic Design Mannerisms, Quirks, and Conceits* (Chronicle Books); *Becoming a Graphic Designer* (John Wiley & Sons); and *Becoming a Digital Designer* (John Wiley & Sons).

Roy McKelvey has an MS in visual interface design from Carnegie Mellon University and is currently Director of the MFA program at Virginia Commonwealth University. He is author and designer of *Hypergraphics,* a book on designing for the Web (Rotovision), and was a co-editor, co–art director, and contributor to *Revival of the Fittest: Classic Versions of Digital Typefaces* (RC Publications, a subsidiary of *Print* Magazine). In 1999, Roy and VCU colleague Steven Hoskins founded the online journal *Loop: AIGA Journal of Interaction Design Education,* serving as coeditors of the publication until 2004. His research interests include interaction design, usability, and issues related to designing for the Web.

Dr. William Meggs, professor and chief of the Division of Toxicology at the Brody School of Medicine in Greenville, NC, is a physician practicing medical toxicology and emergency medicine. He is also active in medical research. His education includes an MD from the University of Miami, a PhD in theoretical physics from Syracuse University, an internal medicine residency at Rochester Institute ofTechnology, a fellowship in allergy and immunology at the National Institute of Health, and a fellowship in medical toxicology at New York University. He is board certified in medical toxicology, allergy and immunology, emergency medicine, and internal medicine. His book, *The Inflammation Cure,* was favorably reviewed by the *New York Times* and the *Library Review.* He served on the National Academy of Science's subcommittee on immunotoxicology that co-authored *Biomarkers of Immunotoxicology.* Dr. Meggs has over one hundred publications in medical and physics literature. He has lectured from Rome to Tokyo and in virtually every major American city. His biological homing theory of life has received international recognition.

Elizabeth Meggs was born in a yellow house with blue shutters in 1977 in Richmond, Virginia, the same year *Star Wars* was released and Elvis Presley died. A Brooklyn-based artist, she graduated summa cum laude with a BFA from Virginia Commonwealth University, and at press time was pursuing a painting MFA at Pratt Institute. Elizabeth has been employed in a variety of positions, from editor/writer at the Los Angeles *Daily News' Today* magazine to designer in the art department at Hearst's *Victoria* magazine; from evening receptionist at Deustche Bank's lower Manhattan building when it was destroyed during the September 11th terrorist attacks, to teaching in the Communication Arts Department at Virginia Commonwealth University. On January 8, 2004, she was inducted into the Visual Lunacy Society.

Libby Phillips Meggs was married to Phil Meggs for thirty-eight years, and is the mother of their two children, Andrew and Elizabeth. She also enjoys a professional life that includes working as an advertising art director, graphic designer, writer, and illustrator. Born in Greenville, SC, she earned a BFA from Richmond Professional Institute in 1965. Highlights from her career include art directing Norman Rockwell and authoring and illustrating the award-winning children's book *Go Home! The True Story of James the Cat.* More books are in the works.

Alston Purvis is an associate professor at the Boston University College of Fine Arts, where he serves as chairman of the Department of Graphic Design. He is a graduate of Virginia Commonwealth University and Yale University and is active as a graphic designer, writer, and fine artist. From 1971 until 1981 he was a faculty member at the Koninklijke Academie van Beeldende Kunsten (Royal Academy of Fine Arts) at The Hague, Netherlands, where he taught graphic design and drawing. He has authored numerous publications, including the books *Dutch Graphic Design, 1918–1945* (1992); *H.N. Werkman* (2004); *The Vendetta,* a biography of his father, the late Melvin Purvis; and *Dutch Graphic Design, A Century of Innovation* (2006). He also coauthored *Wendingen 1918–1932* (2001), *A Century of Posters* (2002), *Graphic Design 20th Century* (2003), *Creative Type* (2005), and *Jan Tschichold: Posters of the Avant Garde* (2007). He is editor and reviser of the 4th edition of *Meggs' History of Graphic Design,* published in 2005, and is now conducting research for the 5th edition.

Since 1982 **R. Roger Remington** has been seriously engaged in the research, interpretation, and preservation of the history of graphic design. He has written four books: *Nine Pioneers in American Graphic Design; Lester Beall: Trailblazer of American Graphic Design; American Modernism: Graphic Design 1920–1960;* and his new book, *Design and Science: The Life and Work of Will Burtin,* which will be published in 2007. At RIT he has developed a unique scholarly resource, the Graphic Design Archive, which involves preserving and interpreting the original source materials of twenty-six Modernist design pioneers. In 2006 he was named the Massimo and Lella Vignelli distinguished professor of design.

Sandra Wheeler is associate professor of graphic design at Virginia Commonwealth University, where she teaches in the department's MFA and undergraduate programs. She is also active as a graphic designer and fine artist. From 1993–99 she was senior designer in Cambridge, MA, developing and designing interpretive exhibitions for numerous institutions, including New Mexico's Office of Cultural Affairs; the Smithsonian, SITES; the U.S. National Park Service; and the Strong Museum. In Boston, she taught at Northeastern University and the Massachusetts College of Art. She coauthored and codesigned *Working With Type 5: Exhibitions.* Her work has been recognized by organizations such as the American Association of Museums and *Print*'s regional design annual.

Biography of Philip Meggs

By Phil Meggs on the occasion of his induction into the New York Art Directors Hall of Fame (2001)

Philip B. Meggs began his graphic arts career at age sixteen, setting handset metal type in the afternoons after high school in his hometown of Florence, South Carolina. A great love for the types and the letter forms they printed developed. An avid reader who pored over the words and illustrations in books and magazines, he spent many hours drawing and painting. As the time to choose a career approached, he decided to go into graphic design.

In the early 1960s there was no place to study illustration and layout in his state, but a guidance counselor told him the Richmond Professional Institute (which later merged with the Medical College of Virginia to form Virginia Commonwealth University) was one of the finer art schools in the country. A train trip to Richmond convinced Meggs that the students were doing exciting work there. After a year at what is now Francis Marion University, Meggs transferred to RPI. His teachers included abstract expressionist painters and European modern designers educated at Moholy-Nagy's Institute of Design in Chicago. Meggs says, "This dualism forced my classmates and me to deal with conflicting aesthetics and find our own paths."

After college Meggs worked as senior designer at Reynolds Aluminum, then at age twenty-four became art director of A.H. Robins Pharmaceuticals, one of the ten largest pharmaceutical companies in America. These jobs gave him the opportunity to design an amazing range of projects – posters, booklets, packages, a quarterly magazine, exhibitions, annual reports, and even advertising campaigns, because Robins followed the European model of having some pharmaceutical product advertising designed by in-house staff. This diversity provided useful experience when he moved into teaching.

In 1968 Meggs' former teacher John Hilton, the Chairman of the Communication Arts and Design Department at Virginia Commonwealth University, invited Meggs to lunch and persuaded him to try his hand at teaching.

Meggs recalls, "Although Hilton overstated the advantages and understated the dilemmas of teaching, I found it to be a magical yet challenging experience. Teaching a creative endeavor is a difficult balancing act – imparting information, coaching and critiquing without destroying the student's confidence, and trying not to impose your vision onto the student's work." During over thirty years at VCU, Meggs has watched VCU's art school grow into one of the largest in the country, ranked in the top twenty by *U.S. News and World Report.* He also serves as visiting faculty at Syracuse University and the National College of Art and Design, Dublin.

From 1974 until 1987, Meggs chaired the VCU Department of Communication Arts and Design. During that time, the enrollment doubled, and the graphic design program was augmented with majors in illustration, photography, and media. Courses in the history of visual communications, along with design and communications theory, were added to the curriculum. Competency-based instruction was introduced in typography, print production, layout techniques, and later, computer graphics courses. Beginning in the 1970s, the program has been widely respected in the industry as one whose graduates are well prepared for the profession. A master of fine arts in design program was launched in 1978 and emerged as a major producer of design innovators and educators.

During Meggs' first semester of teaching, a search for information about design history, theory, and creative methodology convinced him that design educators desperately needed educational materials that did not exist. He began to compile information for use in his classes; this activity led to an active involvement in writing. In 1974 he began teaching a course in the history of visual communications and started work on his first book, *A History of Graphic Design.* The first edition of this five-hundred-page book, with over 1,200 illustrations, was published in 1983. It received an award for excellence in publishing from the Association of American Publishers. Now in its third edition, *A History of Graphic Design* has been translated into Chinese, Hebrew, Japanese, Korean, and Spanish. A *Communication Arts* reviewer wrote, "I expect it to become a foundation and keystone of serious study…it is a fortress work." The *New York Times* hailed it as "A significant attempt at a comprehensive history of graphic design…it will be an eye-opener not only for general readers, but for designers who have been unaware of their legacy."

Typographic Design: Form and Communication, written and designed with his colleagues Rob Carter and Ben Day, was selected for the 1985 AIGA book show as one of the best designed books of the year. First published in 1989, *Type & Image: The Language of Graphic Design,* presents Meggs' approach to graphic design.

Meggs has written a dozen books and over 150 articles and papers on design and typography. His articles have appeared in many leading design and communications publications, including *Communication Arts, Graphis,* and *Print.*

Meggs' graphic designs have been exhibited widely, including the New York Art Director's Club, *Graphis Annual, Graphis Posters, Communication Arts Design Annual,* and *Print* magazine's *Regional Design Annual.* In 1995, Virginia Commonwealth University awarded Meggs its annual faculty Award for Excellence in Teaching, Research, and Service. Massachusetts College of Art bestowed an Honorary Doctor of Fine Arts degree in 1999, and he was inducted into the New York Art Directors Hall of Fame in 2001.

Since 1993 he has been a member of the U. S. Postal Service's Citizens Stamp Advisory Committee, which recommends subjects and designs for United States postage stamps. Currently, he chairs the subject subcommittee, which is charged with recommending the subjects for all United States postage stamps.

Meggs married his college girlfriend, Libby Phillips Meggs. They have been married for thirty-seven years and have two children. An art director and illustrator, Libby Phillips Meggs wrote and illustrated a children's book, *Go Home! The True Story of James the Cat,* that won the First Annual ASPCA Henry Bergh Children's Book Award for Excellence in Humane Literature In 2001.

Although he is best known for his books, Meggs says, "Of all the things I've been involved in, I am most proud of my children and my students."

Acknowledgments

This book is the result of the committed effort and generosity of many individuals. The editors extend heartfelt thanks to the contributing essayists whose words provide a gateway into the life of Phil Meggs. Three years ago, during the preliminary stages of this project, Mindy Carter-Bruns shared precious time and a selective eye. We are also indebted to Susan Westwood for her time and expertise in editing many components of the text. The book would not have been realized without the support of Jerry Bates and his staff at the VCUArts Graphics Lab. Jerry shared a long and productive relationship with Phil. Marc O'Brien dedicated countless hours skillfully and patiently photographing, scanning, and preparing images for printing. Staff members Sage Brown, Matt Charboneau, Ravi Jindal, Bizhan Khodabandeh, Veronica Ledford, Will Pinholster, and Cody Whitby provided invaluable assistance. Generous financial and logistical support was provided by VCUArts, Virginia Commonwealth University. We are grateful to Richard Toscan, dean, School of the Arts, for his generous sponsorship and commitment. Matt Woolman, chair of the Department of Graphic Design, offered unwavering encouragement and financial support. We extend our thanks to Beth Shumaker and Peter van Tolingen for their help and advice. We wish to especially thank the editorial and production teams at John Wiley & Sons: Margaret Cummins, Senior Editor; David Sassian, Senior Production Editor; Lauren Poplawski, Editorial Assistant; Tom Hyland, Manufacturing Manager; Amanda Miller, Vice President and Publisher; and Diana Cisek, Production Director.

Colophon

Graphic Design
Rob Carter and Sandra Wheeler

Digital Photography and Scanning
Marc O'Brien

Printing
RR Donnelley
Crawfordsville, Indiana

Binding
RR Donnelley/Reynosa Division
Reynosa, Mexico.

Paper
Scheufelen PhoeniXmotion
Xenon #90 text

Typography
This book is typeset in Akzidenz-Grotesk. In *Typographic Specimens: The Great Typefaces* (1993), Phil Meggs wrote:

Akzidenz-Grotesk, distributed under the name Standard in England and the United States, was first issued in 1898 by the Berthold type foundry of Berlin. The original type family consisted of ten fonts whose design was carefully coordinated. Berthold issued the family in light, regular, medium, and bold stroke weights, plus three extended and three condensed versions. There were no italic fonts in the original family. As additional variations were cast and released, Akzidenz-Grotesk was an early example of a type family promoted to printers and designers as a complete range. The Bauer type foundry, one of Berthold's leading German competitors, countered in 1906 with the similar Venus type family in light, medium, and bold weights, plus three condensed and two extended versions. During the first decade of the century, American advertising designers used Standard and Venus with great frequency. Competitive sans-serif display fonts, such as Franklin Gothic and News Gothic from American Type Founders, were developed.

Akzidenz-Grotesk has little discernable variation in stroke weight. The top of the *A* is flat, and the *G* has a spur. The *a* and *t* have a curved serif at the foot. The x-height is larger than most typefaces from the turn of the century, and ascenders and descenders are rather short.

Akzidenz-Grotesk fell from favor as designers embraced geometric sans-serif fonts such as Futura during the 1930s and 1940s; it became widely used again during the 1950s under the influence of the Swiss design movement that advocated asymmetrical organization of Akzidenz-Grotesk on grid systems. It inspired important new sans serifs, including Univers and Helvetica.

Note: All photographs of Phil Meggs were taken by Libby Meggs, unless otherwise noted.